AFTER THE PROPAGANDA STATE

After the Propaganda State

MEDIA, POLITICS, AND "THOUGHT WORK"
IN REFORMED CHINA

Daniel C. Lynch

STANFORD UNIVERSITY PRESS
STANFORD, CALIFORNIA

Stanford University Press
Stanford, California

© 1999 by the Board of Trustees of the
Leland Stanford Junior University

Printed in the United States of America

CIP data appear at the end of the book

Portions of Chapter 6 first appeared in
Daniel C. Lynch, "Dilemmas of 'Thought
Work' in Fin-de-siècle China," *China
Quarterly* 157 (Mar. 1999). Reprinted with
permission of the School of Oriental and
African Studies, University of London.

For Miao

ACKNOWLEDGMENTS

This book began as a Ph.D. dissertation in the Department of Political Science at the University of Michigan, so it is not surprising that I continue to owe my greatest intellectual debts to scholars either currently or formerly resident in Ann Arbor. Most important are the members of my dissertation committee, because no candidate—regardless of his or her enthusiasm about the project—could write a good dissertation without the careful attention and sustained encouragement of a dedicated committee. In my own case, Kenneth Lieberthal and Michel Oksenberg began sharing their attention and encouragement as early as the fall of 1990, long before research actually began. From 1992 to 1996 in particular, Professor Lieberthal was exceptionally generous with his time and advice, easily exceeding the normal expectations of a dissertation committee chair. Professor Oksenberg's advice came in concentrated, powerful bursts about every three months, and each burst prompted a serious rethinking of key issues. Robert Pahre, whom I met in 1993, displayed an extraordinary talent for offering sound—even penetrating—criticism without losing a humorous perspective on things. And Vincent Price's advice prompted a thorough reconsideration of the context of the manuscript in the larger body of social science theoretical literature, particularly the literature on communication. To all four of these individuals I extend my deep appreciation and gratitude.

Others deserving thanks for their suggestions, comments, and encouragement over the past few years include Jonathan Aronson, John Campbell, Joseph Chan, Yasheng Huang, Jean Hung, Paul Huth, C. C. Lee, Abraham Lowenthal, Daniel Okimoto, Stanley Rosen, and Mingming Shen. I have also profited from numerous discussions with my Michigan *tongxue* both at home and abroad, especially Bruce Dickson,

Elizabeth Economy, Helen Haley, Leslyn Hall, Elizabeth Henderson, Marc Lambert, Pierre Landry, Andrew Mertha, Bettina Schroeder, and Kaja Sehrt.

The Social Science Research Council / MacArthur Foundation Program on International Peace and Security and the University of Michigan Center for Chinese Studies provided the funds necessary to gather data and write the dissertation. The University of Southern California's Center for International Studies and the Pacific Council on International Policy funded the difficult task of transforming the dissertation into a book, while at the same time providing a wonderfully stimulating environment of discussions and seminars in which to work. To these institutions I owe an enormous debt of gratitude. Other institutions deserving thanks include the Asia/Pacific Research Center at Stanford University, the Universities Service Centre at the Chinese University of Hong Kong, the Research Center on Contemporary China at Beijing University, and the Inter-University Program for Chinese Language Studies (now the International Chinese Language Program) in Taipei. Each of these institutions graciously hosted me during various phases of the research, and their personnel made the work significantly more pleasurable and productive than it would have been otherwise.

Three anonymous reviewers suggested crucial changes in the manuscript; I am also very grateful to them. The third reviewer even suggested the title, which is adapted from Peter Kenez's fine study of the interaction of propaganda and politics in the early years of the Soviet Union, *The Birth of the Propaganda State*.

Of course, there would have been no book of this or any title without the hard work of the editors at Stanford University Press, notably Muriel Bell, Nathan MacBrien, Jason Bovberg, and Andrew Lewis, who challenged me to improve the manuscript without ever letting me feel disheartened. I learned a great deal from all of them.

And finally, I want to express my appreciation to all of the anonymous individuals I interviewed during the course of my research in China and Hong Kong. These people were unfailingly generous with their time and information, and they received nothing in return but the promise that they were "advancing the scholarly world's understanding of China." I hope that was sufficient.

D.C.L.

CONTENTS

FIGURES AND TABLES

Figures

Tables

The following abbreviations are used throughout the text. For abbreviations used in the Bibliography, see p. 283.

CAS	Chinese Academy of Sciences
CBS	Columbia Broadcasting System
CERNET	China Education and Research Network
CNN	Cable News Network
CPD	Central Propaganda Department
FBIS	Foreign Broadcast Information Service
GBRFT	General Bureau of Radio, Film, and Television
MEI	Ministry of Electronics Industry
MII	Ministry of Information Industries
MOC	Ministry of Culture
MPS	Ministry of Public Security
MPT	Ministry of Posts and Telecommunications
MRFT	Ministry of Radio, Film, and Television
MSS	Ministry of State Security
PLA	People's Liberation Army
PRC	People's Republic of China
RFA	Radio Free Asia
SAIC	State Administration of Industry and Commerce
SPPA	State Press and Publications Administration
STAR	Satellite Television Asia Region
TVBI	Television Broadcasts International
VSAT	Very Small Aperture Terminal

AFTER THE PROPAGANDA STATE

CHAPTER ONE

"Thought Work" in the Praetorian Public Sphere

> Don't think that a little spiritual pollution doesn't matter much, that it's nothing to be alarmed at. Some of its ill effects may not be immediately apparent. But unless we take it seriously and adopt firm measures right now to prevent its spread, many people will fall prey to it and be led astray, with grave consequences. In the long run, this question will determine what kind of people will succeed us to carry on the cause and what the future of the Party and state will be.
>
> —*Deng Xiaoping,* OCTOBER 12, 1983

Eleven years after Deng Xiaoping issued this injunction to the Twelfth Central Committee of the Chinese Communist Party,[1] a developmental psychologist in Beijing told a visiting foreign academic that in recent years he had noticed a significant change in the way Chinese children play. With increasing frequency, Chinese children play "cops and robbers" games, and when the "robbers" are arrested they demand to be "read their rights." In the psychologist's estimation, this phenomenon has only one explanation: "The children are watching too much American television," now easy to do given that huge volumes of foreign media products surge through Chinese society virtually unchecked, despite strenuous government efforts to staunch the flow.[2]

Beijing's difficulties in managing the information revolution have become common knowledge to informed publics everywhere, but few scholars have sought to explain why the Chinese government is losing control and what the implications are. If advanced technologies themselves make it impossible for authoritarian states to control communications flows, and if the inevitable result is worldwide democratization, then there is no need for students of liberalization to examine the matter further. Yet close scrutiny of the Chinese case suggests that far more than technology is involved in eviscerating the state's control over communications flows; and the results are far more subtle than the automatic creation of the liberal "public sphere" and "civil society" necessary to effect a transition from authoritarian rule. What actually is undermining Beijing's control is technological advance combined with administrative fragmentation and property-rights reform. The result is "public-sphere praetorianism," a condition in which neither the state nor any other organized political force can impose order and purpose upon the initiation and circulation of society's communications messages—the building blocks of the "symbolic environment" from which people derive their worldviews, values, and action strategies.

The term "thought work" (*sixiang gongzuo*) refers precisely to this struggle to control communications flows and thus "structuration"of the symbolic environment.[3] It is easy to understand why the Chinese government—indeed, any government—would want carefully to manage thought work and not let it fall into the hands of foreigners or autonomous groups in society. In the words of Douglass North, "The costs of maintenance of an existing [political] order are inversely related to the perceived legitimacy of the existing system."[4] Legitimacy is rooted in ideational culture, which is constituted by communication and is identical to the symbolic environment. If a state can control society's communications processes, it can structure the symbolic environment in such a way that citizens will be more likely to accept that state's political order as legitimate. There will be fewer challenges to the state's rule and citizens might even be encouraged to identify affirmatively and enthusiastically with state goals. Conversely, states that are perceived as illegitimate must increasingly rely on physical coercion and the satisfaction of material wants to maintain control.[5]

Of course, successfully controlling communications flows does not guarantee that a state will be considered legitimate. The classic Gramscian formulation—that hegemonic classes, partly by manipulating the state to dominate structuration of the symbolic environment, can easily induce the subjugated to accept their situation as just—is flawed.[6] Equally flawed are the claims of extreme hermeneuticists that individuals in society are passively "enacted" by culture and that human agency plays no significant role in social processes.[7] If that were the case, states could in principle seize control over communications flows and easily direct society toward desired ends. A more satisfying formulation is that of James Scott, who argues that repressed groups will frequently pierce the veil of official obfuscation and recognize their situation as unjust—even when power relationships and material deprivation prevent them from taking effective steps to resolve their predicament.[8]

Similarly, as Geertz has argued, cultural patterns "provide a template or blueprint for the organization of social and psychological processes," but do not determine exactly how people will act.[9]

These caveats notwithstanding, controlling the provision of such templates can be strategically advantageous, and that is the chief reason states worldwide have since the nineteenth century sought to increase control over communications flows at the expense of foreigners and other groups in society. In particular, they have sought to use communications to inculcate nationalism.[10] A variety of states have, in short, engaged in thought work, even though that Orwellian term is used only in China. Of course, states vary in the degree to which they try to control communications flows. Some are relatively passive participants in the marketplace of ideas. What Peter Kenez calls "propaganda states," however, overwhelm their citizens—in the media, in the workplace, and even in the home—with official information and interpretations of reality. Initiating political challenges to these states becomes virtually unthinkable—which is precisely the goal.[11]

The seminal propaganda state was Stalin's Soviet Union, and it was from the Soviet Union that China imported its model in the 1950s. The Chinese propaganda state remained in place throughout the Maoist period (1949–76) and into the 1980s. In fact, it persists in name to this day. The problem is that its effectiveness has crumbled dramatically; as a result, China's leaders can no longer rely on thought work to manage a rapidly changing society.

The purpose of this book is to explain why thought work is escaping the Chinese state's control and to assess the implications for China's future.[12] The book is not concerned with analyzing the content of the numerous new communications messages now swirling through Chinese society as a result of the propaganda state's breakdown; such content analysis is best left to other writers.[13] This book focuses on *processes* and *institutions,* on how two decades of "reform and opening" have thoroughly transformed the setting—administrative, economic, and technological—in which Chinese people construct their symbolic environment. New, empowering capabilities and radically changed incentives allow the Chinese people to initiate and circulate messages that often differ widely from what the central party-state defines as desirable.[14]

After the Propaganda State: A Liberal Public Sphere?

The model logically "opposite" the propaganda state is the liberal model, in which individuals and groups in an autonomous civil society freely create and circulate messages in a well-structured and institutionalized public sphere.[15] The state's role is simply to make certain the rules of the game are enforced, meaning primarily rules against libel, slander, sedition, and treason. Occasionally, liberal states circulate "public service messages," but they do not forcefully direct the public sphere in the way propaganda states do. In liberal systems, the public sphere is in principle "owned" by all members of the polity, who concede to the state only those powers necessary to keep the public sphere functioning and fair. Almost by definition, liberal systems are found exclusively in democracies, whereas propaganda-state systems are found exclusively in modern authoritarian and quasi-totalitarian countries. Indeed, the type of communications system is virtually conterminous with the type of regime.

This book demonstrates that when propaganda states crumble, they do not automatically evolve into liberal democracies. This may seem self-evident, but the notion of linear movement is an insidious, unanalyzed assumption behind the vast bulk of development-communication literature,[16] as well as behind the "common knowledge" conveyed in newspapers. Political scientists studying transitions from authoritarian rule rarely bother to address the role of communication in these processes, other than as passive barometers of liberalization. The same is true of international-relations scholars interested in globalization, transnational relations, and the "democratic peace."

This book argues that although the Chinese state has lost a significant degree of control over thought work, the new marketplace of ideas has not yet earned the appellation "liberal public sphere," a term that implies order, predictability, and vigorous political debate. Tawdry entertainment is much more likely to appear in the Chinese media these days than serious political debate—though underground political journals (including at least one that is Internet-based) do circulate. The power to initiate communications messages has become shattered into a complex mosaic, with all manner of individuals and groups circulating an enormous variety of messages in a confusing and patternless cacophony. The central party-state still dominates the initiation and circulation of sensitive political information, but its control over every other kind of communication has eroded significantly.

This development is undoubtedly empowering to the Chinese people in the Gramscian sense that it allows them to resist state attempts to impose hegemony. Individuals in Chinese society no longer need actively accept the state's definition of reality, even if in constructing their own definitions they find that certain political questions remain off limits. It would be inaccurate, however, to identify the chaos of contemporary Chinese thought work as "liberal." It is instead "praetorian," to borrow Samuel Huntington's term for uninstitutionalized and chaotic patterns of political participation.

In Huntingtonian praetorianism, rapid economic development politically activates a broad range of social groups, the members of which face strong incentives to participate in politics precisely because of their new stake in the economy. But because economic growth and the accompanying social transformation frequently occur faster than political change, the participation of newly activated social groups cannot be channeled effectively or structured in a way that would maximize the collective good. Hence, the groups compete nakedly in politics by using the form of participation in which they have a comparative advantage: Business people pay bribes, workers strike, and military officers stage coups. Because violence trumps money and numbers, the equilibrium outcome is the coup d'état, but the coup is a highly unstable equilibrium, and unless military leaders themselves develop effective political institutions, praetorianism will persist and politics will remain uninstitutionalized.[17]

In China, public-sphere praetorianism—the cacophonous and unstructured circulation of communications messages—is manifested in three specific processes: commercialization, globalization, and pluralization. Taken together, these overlapping processes constitute this study's dependent variable, the breakdown of state control over thought work.

Commercialization refers to the increasing tendency of mass media to create products that appeal to the assumed tastes of target audiences in society, as opposed to the tastes of the central party-state's propaganda cadres. The result is a saturation of the media with so-called "spiritually polluting," "vulgar," "pornographic," and "feudal superstitious" communications that undermine the state's efforts to build a "socialist spiritual civilization." Of course, not all of the media products circulating through Chinese society are "polluting" the symbolic environment in this way, not all audience members want to consume such products, and not all products that appeal to audience tastes contravene the state's thought-work goals. But there is a raging torrent of such products and a significant number of them do evidently undermine official thought-work goals. As a result, these products have become targets of vigorous criticism and political campaigns since the mid-1980s.

Globalization, integrally related to commercialization, refers to the steady increase in the proportion of communications messages circulating in China that originate abroad. Most such messages take the form of films and teleplays produced in Hong Kong and the United States, but broadcast satellites now transmit them from Japan, Russia, and many other Asian and European countries. Shortwave radio carries news, discussion, and the arts from every corner of the globe. And the rapidly advancing *telecommunications* network now links Chinese individuals and organizations—via telephone, fax, and the Internet—with potential interlocutors in nearly 200 foreign countries and regions.[18]

Pluralization, which partly (but not exclusively) results from commercialization and globalization, indicates the growing diversity of sources of communications messages in China. It is a development that implies the "drowning out" of messages the central party-state seeks to impart, as well as increases in the number of points at which the Center must exert power or authority to interdict undesirable communications flows.[19] The number of newspaper and magazine publishers, television stations, and individuals with access to telephones, fax machines, and modems in China is increasing at a rapid rate, reducing the state's overall relevance in the construction of the symbolic environment. This situation is sharply different from that which prevailed under Mao, when control over communications flows was highly centralized. Now, millions of individuals and organizations contribute to the construction of the symbolic environment, and the central party-state wages a constant struggle to maintain its pertinence.[20]

Pathways to Praetorianism: The Causal Variables

Were it not for reform and opening, the Chinese state would probably have retained the level of control over thought work it demonstrated in the late 1970s. But reform and opening were necessary to develop the economy and restore legitimacy to the political system. Loss of control over thought work was a major, unanticipated consequence. Three developments in the post-Mao period—administrative fragmentation, property-rights reform, and technological advance—have led to this breakdown, and together they constitute this study's causal variables.

Administrative fragmentation is a secondary consequence of an intentional deconcentration of Chinese authority begun in the early 1980s. The regulatory system is fundamentally top-down, and territorial-level governments currently enjoy primary regulatory authority over the activities of media and telecommunications units within their regions (see Figure 1). At the same time, management of many media products and communications processes is fragmented horizontally—that is, at each level of the administrative hierarchy—partly as a result of trends begun in the pre-reform period, and partly as a result of the state's inability to keep pace with the development and dissemination of new technologies (videotape and the compact disc have proved particularly vexing).

Property-rights reform refers to changes in the material-incentive structures facing *mass*-media units in particular, changes that prompt them to create and circulate spiritually polluting and bourgeois-liberal messages in a way that undermines the Center's thought-work goals. Most media units (and telecommunications units) are now formally "responsible for profits and losses"—a reform that gives unit managers and workers

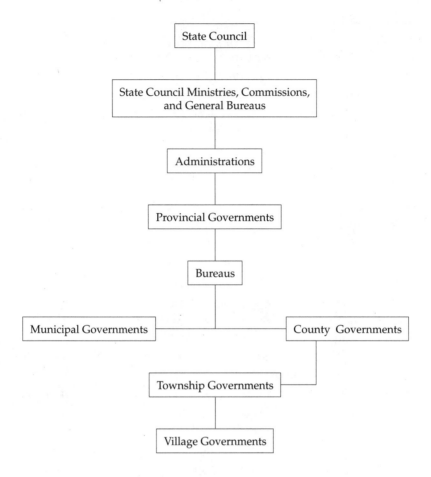

FIGURE 1. Structure of the Chinese Government

strong incentives to increase advertising income by catering to audience demands. At the same time, rapid economic growth in general has finally enabled vast numbers of Chinese citizens to purchase the many consumer products that advertisers seek to sell, as well as the television sets and other technologies that expose them to the advertising. This, too, would have been impossible in the absence of property-rights reform.

Technological advance refers to the rapid dissemination throughout

Chinese society of all manner of communications technologies that, by their very nature, increase the state's difficulties in managing communications flows. The most influential of these technologies are small satellite receiving dishes, automated telecommunications switching equipment, optical-fiber transmission systems, fax machines, modems, and computers. Although in principle these technologies might be managed effectively, in practice they are not, because the cost of such maintenance is extremely high and the Chinese bureaucracy lacks the necessary information and expertise.

None of these causal variables can alone explain the breakdown of China's propaganda state. Rather, they are interrelated. Administrative fragmentation, for example, may sound identical to "loss of central-state control," but before the reform era the Center could control thought work even without holding tight rein over administration by making use of Mao's awe-inspiring prestige. Today, the state *requires* tight administrative control not only because charisma has been poorly routinized in orderly bureaucratic procedures but also because property-rights reform and technological advance allow individuals in society and abroad easily to circulate messages inconsistent with Beijing's thought-work goals. Administrative fragmentation explains only part of the problem. Similarly, property-rights reform cannot by itself explain commercialization. The three variables thus interact, and in combination they produce the processes of commercialization, globalization, and pluralization, which together constitute the central party-state's loss of control over thought work.

The Political Consequences of "Apolitical" Communications

If China's central party-state still dominates the circulation of sensitive political information, and if the praetorian public sphere is awash not in serious political discussion but in meretricious entertainment, then why should people concerned about Chinese politics read this book?

First, Beijing's domination of the circulation of political information is itself eroding as part of the overall crumbling of the propaganda state. The Center cannot prevent the broadcasts of the Voice of America (VOA), Radio Free Asia (RFA), and the British Broadcasting Corporation (BBC) from entering the country's communications networks, whether via shortwave radio or, since 1994, satellite television. Nor can it easily block incoming Internet transmissions or prevent the clandestine circulation of critical books, magazines, and videotapes. It can raise the costs and increase the difficulties, but it cannot staunch the flow. There is also no reasonable way to stop the citizenry from using the telecommunications system to circulate politicized messages out of public view, even if most people use their telephones and fax machines to send only mundane or technical messages. Given the rapid rise of electronic mail and the Internet, the Center's difficulties in this regard seem certain to increase.

Second, lost control over communications flows could combine with an economic recession—possibly produced by state-owned enterprise reform—to generate a genuine political crisis. As suggested above, the three pillars of state control over society are thought work, physical coercion, and material reward. Although the Chinese state has lost a great deal of control over thought work, it certainly retains control over the People's Armed Police (PAP) and the People's Liberation Army (PLA). The sustained, rapid growth of the economy has resulted in plenty of material rewards to go around for most people, inequality notwithstanding. But if the economy were suddenly to slow down, and millions of workers to lose their jobs, the pressure on coercion would correspondingly increase, and it is uncertain whether the PAP and PLA would repeat their 1989 performance in Tiananmen Square, if that proved necessary.

Third, the general absence of open political discussion in the era of economic reform is itself an inherently political fact. Contrary to what many writers on post-Tiananmen China have argued, the country is not developing either a classically liberal public sphere or the attendant autonomous civil society that would suggest an imminent transition to democracy.[21] This book suggests that unless public-sphere praetorianism is reversed, no such transition is likely—at least, not by the mechanisms that those who have "discovered" a Chinese civil society suggest.

Fourth, the state is evidently incapable of building its desired socialist spiritual civilization,[22] a fact also inherently political. The state is even incapable of holding the line defensively against spiritual pollution (excessive sex, violence, and superstition in the symbolic environment) and bourgeois liberalization (assertions of the superiority of capitalism over socialism, of democracy over the "people's democratic dictatorship," and of foreign countries over China). When both the state and civil society are hamstrung, the situation only appears apolitical on the surface. The fact that neither the state nor society seems capable of reversing public-sphere praetorianism suggests that China will be politically adrift and rudderless for some time to come.

Finally, even apparently apolitical communications can be loaded with subtle political implications whose consequences are only visible in the long run—a possibility suggested by the Beijing psychologist's analysis of children at play. As argued by Gramsci, "Popular literature [adventure stories, detective novels, and the like] is the dominant fact. It diffuses ideological models and systems of attitudes that bear on the lived relationships of men and women to their world."[23] Certainly many of China's leaders have come to embrace this perspective. For example, in the March 1996 issue of *Qiushi*—the party's authoritative ideological journal—one theorist argued against more lax and liberal comrades that the arts can be equally as important as news in the formation of people's political attitudes, even if the arts typically are less centrally concerned with politics:

> When ideology is mentioned, some people always fix their eyes on the core, naively thinking that nothing serious will come of it so long as the core is not touched upon. We cannot but say that this is an ossified point of view. Content and form, and contents and levels can infiltrate and transform one into the other. . . . In this regard, certain Western political bigwigs are much wiser than some of our comrades. They said: As long as the youth of the country to be overturned have learned our language and dances and have a weakness for our movies and television programs, they will, sooner or later, accept our concepts of value. Unfortunately, this remark has been proved by what happened in the Soviet Union and Eastern Europe.[24]

The Chinese leadership has, to be sure, significantly reduced in scope the definition of what, under reform, counts as political,[25] but it continues to regard messages that in other societies would be considered innocuous as holding the potential to undermine Communist Party rule—if not today, then tomorrow. In fact, as elaborated in Chapter 6, the central party-state appears actually to have increased in scope the definition of the political since the trauma of 1989, and as of this writing is engaged in a desperate, omnidirectional campaign to eliminate rotten thought work and build a socialist spiritual civilization.

Alternative Explanations of Public-Sphere Praetorianism

Not everyone would accept the assertion that a combination of administrative fragmentation, property-rights reform, and technological advance has produced a significant decline in state control over thought work in China—even granting that no claim has been made that thought work is completely out of control. Objections to the theory are serious and worth careful consideration.[26]

The first set of objections disputes the very existence of the dependent variable. The Center has not "lost" any control over thought work, according to these objections. Instead, it has willingly relinquished control over thought work in the pursuit of other interests ranked higher in its "preference schedule." In particular, the Center has—since the late 1970s—put a premium on economic growth and has been willing to tolerate the circulation of otherwise undesirable communications messages in pursuit of this primary goal. Market-driven economic growth requires advertising, which requires meretricious entertainment, which implies a need to tolerate spiritual pollution. But should the rankings of the Center's preference schedule change, it could easily resume control over thought work and crush heterodoxy into the ground. An important variation on this argument stresses the Center's positive interest in seeing the Chinese people acquire values from abroad that contribute positively to economic growth. For example, when people embrace the notion that conspicuous consumption is good, and that they can conspicuously consume by working hard and competing, China as a whole is made wealthy and strong.

In extreme forms, the "omnipotent state" argument is obviously absurd, because it implies that all phenomena present in Chinese society must be the product of the state's rational choice, and that the state can easily eliminate any phenomenon that it finds to be "truly" objection-able. Clearly, such a view is tautological, because it rules out the possi-bility that the state could fail at anything. Even corruption would be re-defined as tolerable: It is rampant; state leaders say they dislike it; but the mere fact that it remains rampant "proves" that state leaders do not "really" dislike it.

But moderate versions of the rational-state argument are reasonable and not inconsistent with the findings of this study. It seems unques-tionable that reformist leaders did consciously decide in the late 1970s to sacrifice a measure of control over thought work and to tolerate a greater degree of heterodoxy in public communications, partly for the purpose of achieving faster economic growth. Advertising would stim-ulate the economy, audiences had to be attracted to advertising by the provision of popular media products, and so on. Allowing foreign and Hong Kong films and television programs into the country would have the added benefit of providing the population with models of entrepre-neurial behavior and hard work.

But, as elaborated in Chapter 6, China's leaders are deeply concerned with inculcating values other than "good businessmanship." Most no-tably, they seek to build a socialist spiritual civilization in which indi-viduals behave altruistically and support the production of such public goods as a clean environment, social order, and refined art. The leaders have never officially replaced Marxism-Leninism-Mao Zedong Thought with a pure economist ideology, even if behaviorally they do emphasize material civilization over spiritual civilization. As explained by Guang-dong Provincial Party Secretary Xie Fei, "Some people once thought: After economic construction became the focus of our work, propaganda and ideological work were no longer very important. . . . Even to this day, this idea is still in the belief system of very many people. But the objective facts have proved otherwise. Why? The reason is very simple. It is because the economic construction we are practicing is no ordinary economic construction, but is socialist modernization."[27]

Similarly, the resolution of the Sixth Plenum of the Fourteenth Cen-tral Committee (October 1996) declared straightforwardly, "We are at present building and developing socialism with Chinese characteristics, with the ultimate goal of realizing communism, and we should conscientiously promote socialist and communist ideology and ethics in the whole society."[28]

The problem is that China's leaders failed to anticipate the terms of the trade-off between controlling thought work and implementing economic reform. They did not realize that the degree of control they would have to sacrifice over thought work would be so high. They did not foresee that the effects of encouraging the media to become more appealing could not easily be limited to economy-stimulating "commodity fetishism." Opening up society's communications channels allowed for the proliferation of all manner of heterodox messages. The Chinese people can now far too easily derive alternative conceptions of what their society might be like—especially from foreign and Hong Kong media products—and exchange their views along the sinews of a fast-developing telecommunications network. In the process, they are generating an autonomous (from the state), cynical, and frequently critical "societal public opinion."[29]

Thus, the leadership has frequently found it necessary to crack down on the freer flow of information when it is associated with threatening political movements—most visibly in 1979–80, 1983–84, 1986–87, and 1989–92. Indeed, the political crisis of 1989 induced a qualitative change in the leaders' understanding of the trade-off between economic reform and communications control, and prompted a much more thoroughgoing attempt to root spiritual pollution and bourgeois liberalization out of the thought-work market: the omnidirectional crackdown launched in the summer of 1993. But both the omnidirectional crackdown and the earlier, episodic campaigns have enjoyed only temporary, limited success. The only reasonable conclusion is that the central leadership is seriously concerned about the state of thought work but does not wield sufficient power either to remove undesirable messages from the thought-work market or to ensure that desirable messages are widely received.

One common rejoinder to this assertion is that even the efforts to crack down are not serious, and so do not demonstrate "real" high-level concern. So-called "crackdowns" can be dismissed as either empty rituals or devious stratagems used by reformist political coalitions to appease more conservative factions. While again there is a grain of truth to this assertion—certainly there are a variety of opinions about how much control over thought work may be sacrificed in pursuit of economic development—the evidence presented in Chapter 6 suggests strongly that the frustration and concern among central leaders are deep and widely shared.

Even reformers view heterodoxy as a serious problem because it threatens the "people's democratic dictatorship," without which they would be unable to implement their policies effectively and bring China both prosperity and order. Reformers can point to Eastern Europe and the former Soviet Union as examples of what might happen should the central party-state completely lose control. To prevent such an outcome, reformers and conservatives alike seek earnestly to recover control and to combat vigorously at least the more serious manifestations of spiritual pollution and bourgeois liberalization. Of course, some radical reformers do not concern themselves with these matters, and worry that campaigns against heterodoxy could endanger economic reform. But among Chinese leaders, those genuinely believing in a complete liberalization of thought work are "as rare as phoenix feathers and unicorn horns."

Yet another criticism argues that "less control is actually more," that in sacrificing control over forms of thought work that are less directly political, the Center can more effectively focus attention on the messages it really wants to impart. While this argument sounds plausible, the evidence presented in Chapter 5 on pluralization makes clear that less control is actually less, and that even the central political news no longer reaches large sections of the population. Of course, it is probable that the central political news does continue effectively to reach that section of the population that "really matters": the party-state cadres. Certainly the cadres seem fully capable of acquiring the information they need to function effectively in their working environments. But cadres tend also to be the most corrupt elements in society, with the greatest access to so-called "vulgar," feudal superstitious, foreign, and other proscribed communications. Moreover, the central party-state remains convinced that to build a good society—a socialist spiritual civilization—it is necessary to reach not only the cadres, but everyone in that society. This becomes extremely difficult as central control over communications flows erodes.

Implications

What, then, are the larger conclusions to be drawn from this study? What implications do the findings have for understanding China, the state-society relationship in other countries, and the nature of world politics? Although these issues are addressed in more detail in Chapter 7, it is important to raise them here so that they can inform the reading of Chapters 2 through 6.

First, it should be recognized that the Chinese state is not alone in its concern to manage structuration of the symbolic environment. All states share this concern—albeit to varying degrees. It is implicit in the very definition of the "modern state." The problem is that the rise and diffusion of the modern state over the past two centuries has coincided with a steady increase in the efficiency and effectiveness of communications technologies. Individuals and groups in society, whose worldviews, values, and action strategies state leaders would like to shape, are now empowered with ever-increasing volumes of alternative information and conceptions of reality. The long-term historical trend toward state-building thus clashes with the strengthening of society and the generation of cross-border networks facilitated first by the printing press and eventually by the telephone, the radio, the television, the fax machine, and now the Internet.

The struggle for power over thought work, by whatever name, is thus a central component of the contest between all states and societies to direct the course of their countries' political evolution. But some states do evince more concern than others. For these propaganda states, the implications of this study are quite disturbing, because they suggest that states shifting from a centrally planned economy to a market economy, and integrating into the world system at current levels of communications technology development, are likely to lose a significant degree of control over thought work—and as a result, the ability to shape their citizens' worldviews, values, and action strategies. This will make it much more difficult for these states to achieve their goals in other issue areas and could contribute to the generation of legitimacy crises that threaten fundamental changes in the political order.

In the case of China, the result is that state leaders feel threatened and respond ineffectively with a desperate series of policies designed to restore lost control. They cannot articulate nor foresee the ultimate consequences of present trends, but they do sense acutely that their power is waning and that the consequences can in no way be good for them. They view power from a zero-sum perspective and believe that if they are losing it, some other organized force must be gaining it—and this force is likely to be hostile. Thus, they begin lashing out at phantom enemies at home and abroad. Foreign forces, particularly the United States, are accused of pursuing a "peaceful evolution" of Chinese society into capitalism and of actively establishing alliances with the forces of bourgeois liberalization at home. The popularity of American television and films, combined with the patently political content of the VOA, RFA, and BBC, suggest an intentional, willful subversion.

The result is actually increased tensions between states precisely at a time when some adherents to the transnational or liberal school of international relations would predict tension reduction.[30] Because integration into the global order apparently cannot be divorced from declining state control over thought work, integration becomes a rocky and even dangerous process, one that could actually contribute to (though certainly not individually cause) the outbreak of military conflict—for example, in the Taiwan Strait.[31] In the long run, thought-work commercialization, globalization, and pluralization might lead to enhanced international harmony, in line with the predictions of many transnationalists and liberals. The problem will be getting through the current period of integration unscathed.

CHAPTER TWO

Thought-Work Institutions Under Reform

To understand fully how administrative fragmentation, property-rights reform, and technological advance have combined to erode the Chinese state's control over thought work, it is essential to recognize that communications control was central to the Maoist sociopolitical system. In fact, even the imperial Chinese state made use of a premodern and rudimentary form of thought work, underscoring the deep roots of the statist impulse. Following earlier examples, the Qing Dynasty (1644–1911) promulgated the Confucian *Six Maxims* in 1652 and required that they be read aloud "in plain and simple language on the first and fifteenth of every month" in every village. The *Six Maxims* were expanded and formalized in 1670 in the Kangxi Emperor's famous *Sacred Edict*, which called upon the Chinese people inter alia to "extirpate strange principles, in order to exalt the correct doctrine." The text also "warned against sheltering deserters" and reminded citizens to "fully remit [their] taxes."[1] Of course, the Qing state enjoyed only mixed success in inculcating these principles, given the limitations of premodern technology. But the notion that the state had a right and responsibility to manage the way its citizens think was firmly established in China when the Communist Party was founded in 1921.

Also during the Qing Dynasty, however, China showed signs of developing a liberal public sphere independent of state control. The historian William Rowe has argued that

> like Western Europe, China after the sixteenth century witnessed a qualitative intensification in the volume of long-distance trade; the rise of larger-scale commercial firms, financial institutions, and organized merchant networks; a continuing process of regional urbanization and development

of a more distinctive urban culture (based, in large part, on the institution of the teahouse, China's equivalent of the pub or coffeehouse); and a major expansion of the printing industry, popular literacy, and the circulation of popular literature, much of which contained a heavy dose of social criticism.[2]

As the Qing state unraveled at the end of the nineteenth century, foreign imperialistic onslaughts, combined with the introduction of newspapers and other new forms of mass communication, spawned an unprecedented flowering of public discussion about China's social, economic, and geopolitical problems. Leo Lee and Andrew Nathan trace the beginnings of this "great awakening" to around 1895,[3] but its roots may go back to the teahouses and popular literature of previous centuries. In any case, it is clear that in the decades after 1895 tens and eventually hundreds of thousands of people became mobilized into politics as a direct result of media-produced changes in consciousness about China's pressing problems. This decidedly praetorian political activity included boycotts, demonstrations, strikes, and eventually military uprisings.[4]

Recognizing the link between praetorian politics and uncontrolled communications flows, the Qing state tried desperately to restrict the burgeoning new media. Most imported books and journals were banned in 1906 thanks to the introduction of a new publications law, and domestic publishers were required to submit to censorship and licensing. A 1908 press law reinforced these measures, but they were never effectively enforced.[5] With the collapse of the dynasty in 1911, China entered a period of full-blown public-sphere praetorianism, during which the radical New Culture Movement and May Fourth Movement flourished for two decades.

Out of the maelstrom of warlord politics, the Kuomintang (KMT) in 1928 finally secured power over a large enough area of China to declare itself an effective national government and set about the task of putting a lid on public-sphere praetorianism. Uncontrolled thought work had allowed for the birth and expansion of the Communist Party after 1921; now uncontrolled thought work combined with lingering warlordism and the Communist armed rebellion to undermine the KMT's legitimacy as it struggled to contend with a predatory Japan. In this mortally dangerous situation, the control of communications flows was perceived as crucial. Hence, the KMT promulgated a publications law in 1930, stiffened the requirements in 1931, established a Censorship Commission in 1934, and strengthened the publications law even further in 1937. Qing efforts to control thought work had been defensive and reactive, but the KMT laws were far more modern and proactive. They prohibited all works that violated Sun Yat-sen's "Three People's Principles," censored "erroneous" and "reactionary" utterances, and promoted cultural revitalization through the New Life Movement.[6] In fact, the KMT consciously borrowed from fascist and Leninist models to try to contain and channel China's sociopolitical mobilization. The KMT might well have established a propaganda state had it not been dealt a death blow by the 1937 Japanese invasion.

Meanwhile, Marxist-Leninist views on the invasive role of the party-state in thought work had struck a particular chord with Mao Zedong, who studied the Confucian classics as a child. As Maurice Meisner has explained,

> for Mao, the essential factor in determining the course of history was conscious human activity and the most important ingredients for revolution were how men thought and their willingness to engage in revolutionary action. . . . [This view] implied a special concern for developing and maintaining a "correct ideological consciousness," the ultimately decisive factor in determining success or failure. Correct thought, in the Maoist view, is the first and essential prerequisite for effective revolutionary action, and it is this assumption that lies behind the enormous stress on the distinctively Maoist techniques of "thought reform" and "ideological remolding" developed and refined in the Yenan [Yan'an] era.[7]

Originally, Mao used thought work to "rectify" Communist Party cadres whom he considered to be vacillating in their loyalty or straying from ideological orthodoxy. In the Yan'an period (1935–45) the Communist Party was already a large organization requiring sophisticated cybernetic techniques to manage. Rectification of thought was particularly useful in this context: If party cadres could be "cultivated" by undergoing rigorous and public self-examination in small-group study sessions, then when they fanned out across China to govern, there would be less need to monitor their decision-making. In wartime con-

ditions, this was essential for a large country with an extremely rudimentary transportation and communications infrastructure.

But thought work was more than simply a tool for correcting cadre
deviance. It was designed also to effect a "fundamental transformation"
in the way cadres viewed the world.[8] If cadres could be "cultivated,"
they would make their own decisions, and yet—precisely because they
had undergone the mental transformation—they would still be enacting Mao's will. Once mentally transformed, cadres no longer needed
Mao's direct guidance to analyze and act in the ways that Mao and his
trusted lieutenants conceived to be in China's best interest.

Once the People's Republic was established in 1949, thought work
was used to manage not only the cadre corps but society as a whole.
This was the birth of the genuinely effective, modern Chinese propaganda state. In April 1950 the Communist Party's Propaganda Department began attacking the problem of public-sphere praetorianism by
forcefully consolidating and centralizing China's numerous newspapers.[9] Since newspapers reached only a small portion of the country's
largely illiterate population, the party also established a nationwide radio loudspeaker network in the mid-1950s. In 1964 one analyst concluded that "the Communists have succeeded in bringing more people
into direct and close contact with the central government than ever before in Chinese history."[10]

Not only were people forced exclusively to consume the party-state's
media messages, but local cadres established study groups on the
Yan'an model to make certain the citizenry understood and embraced
the Center's messages. Participation in small thought-work groups became an inescapable and distressing ritual for millions of urban residents and peasants. In the cities, groups consisted typically of eight to
fifteen members, with the leader often the only literate person among
them. Group members usually met three times a week during "normal"
periods and daily during campaigns. The central party-state provided
"study" material for the groups. As explained by Martin King Whyte,
"The ideal is that all members of the group should state their understanding of the message in their own words and give their reaction to it,
so that higher authorities can be sure the message is getting across."[11]

In contemporary social-science terminology, the state was trying to control the entire multistep flow of communications, from opinion leaders to relatively passive opinion followers at the "rice roots."[12] Because of the profusion of mass-media channels since 1978, the state no longer can control the "texts" that people "study," while the development of the telecommunications system has allowed people to discuss and analyze whatever texts they want in a much broader and more diversified context. Under Mao, however, the state exerted enormous control over the multistep flow. Understanding the message properly was of extreme importance, because the state also monopolized economic opportunity and wielded a terrifying power over those who "misunderstood."[13]

Other salient aspects of the Maoist propaganda state that can be contrasted with the present-day situation include the following five elements:

Decentralization and mobilized participation. Unlike the highly centralized Soviet propaganda state, China's was never run by a heavy-handed corps of professionals. A rarefied propaganda bureaucracy was established in 1951, but after 1953 the bulk of its responsibilities was transferred to local activists and ad hoc agitators.[14] The propaganda bureaucracy was never disbanded, but in operational practice it became notably decentralized.[15] A pattern of oscillation then set in. During revolutionary campaigns, the professional propagandists would stay on the sidelines in deference to lower-level cadres and "the masses," but during retrenchment they would resume their close management of thought work. For example, lower-level cadres mobilized the masses both to criticize dissident intellectuals during the Anti-Rightist Campaign in the second half of 1957 and to achieve murky Maoist utopian goals (including the writing of proletarian poetry) during the Great Leap Forward the following year. After the failures of the Great Leap became apparent in the fall of 1958, however, the party resuscitated a propaganda policy emphasizing reliance on professional writers and artists. After the Great Leap, writes Alan Liu, "instead of Mao's emphasis on quick transformation of the people's 'revolutionary spirit,' slow cultivation and education were preferred."[16] This phase would continue until 1966, when the Cultural Revolution, the greatest mobilizational period in Chinese history, began.

Although thought work was usually decentralized in form, there were ironclad (if paradoxically uncertain) expectations about what sorts of opinions lower-level cadres should inculcate, and what sort the people could express. As the theoretical journal *Hongqi* (Red flag) editorialized in November 1960:

> Our nation is a huge nation of 700 million people. If the entire nation possesses a uniform ideology, and if the nation is unified by the thought of Mao Tse-tung, then it will enjoy unified actions. If a nation of 700 million people does not possess a uniform ideology, then it will be generally scattered sand. The ideologies of the entire populace can only be unified with the power of the thought of Mao Tse-tung.[17]

The problem, of course, was that Mao's thought could be difficult to decipher and was subject to sudden change. For example, from mid-1956 to the spring of 1957, Mao repeatedly urged intellectuals and others with sociopolitical grievances to stand up and speak out, to let "100 flowers bloom, 100 schools of thought contend." After initial hesitation, the intellectuals finally took up the challenge. Clearly, they shocked Mao with their hostility. In response, *Renmin Ribao* (People's daily) on June 19, 1957, published a revised version of Mao's famous (originally secret) February 27, 1957, speech, "On the Correct Handling of Contradictions Among the People." The new version included six vague criteria "for distinguishing fragrant flowers from poisonous weeds":

1. Words and actions should help to unite, and not divide, the people of our various nationalities.
2. They should be beneficial, and not harmful, to socialist transformation and socialist construction.
3. They should help to consolidate, and not undermine or weaken, the people's democratic dictatorship.
4. They should help to consolidate, and not undermine or weaken, democratic centralism.
5. They should help to strengthen, and not discard or weaken, the leadership of the Communist Party.
6. They should be beneficial, and not harmful, to international socialist unity and the unity of the peace-loving people of the world.[18]

Thousands of intellectuals were imprisoned or sent to labor camps during the second half of 1957 because they failed to anticipate Mao's limitations on free expression—which, even still, were subject to varieties of interpretation. These intellectuals either died in prison or lingered in horrific conditions for the next twenty years.

The paradox of societal totalitarianism. Mobilizational participation and Mao's famous "mass line" suggest that society played a paradoxically important role in thought-work management vis-à-vis the state, at least during campaigns. But the paradox is illusory. Members of society did participate in campaigns eagerly—often becoming excited enough to kill—but they were not permitted to generate or express independent thoughts and opinions. Society itself, in effect, enacted state totalitarianism. In the summer of 1943 the Politburo passed a resolution on leadership that formalized Mao's concept of the mass line. The party should receive, coordinate, systematize, and interpret the views of the masses and would then be responsible for "taking the resulting ideas back to the masses, explaining and popularizing them until the masses embrace the ideas as their own, stand up for them, and translate them into action."[19] Although there may have been a degree of sincerity about the mass line during the Yan'an era, by the 1960s it had degenerated into a cloak for state domination. In the societal totalitarianism of the Cultural Revolution, that deception attained fearsome heights.

Communication compression. A sharp reduction in the number of communication symbols available to the population for public use, particularly during the Cultural Revolution, had an effect similar to that of societal totalitarianism. This "communication compression" intensified with the appearance of Mao's wife Jiang Qing on the political stage in 1962. In the early 1960s members of the political establishment displeased with Mao's rule had begun staging historical plays and operas to criticize the Chairman allegorically. One rejoinder to these challenges, conjured up by Jiang and Mao's other allies, was to reduce or "compress" the number of plays and operas that could be staged publicly. The purpose was to limit the range of symbols available to Mao's opponents. Jiang spent four years, from 1962 to 1966, developing a series of sanitized plays and operas, and then after the Cultural Revolution began restricting the media to publishing or broadcasting only eight plays, eight songs, and three film clips for "a rather long period of time."[20] At the same time, under the slogan "unify our line of action," local radio stations were forced to turn their broadcasts over entirely to retransmissions of central programs, which consisted almost exclusively of announcers reading central newspaper and Xinhua News Agency paeans to Mao.[21]

If the eight plays, eight songs, three film clips, and regurgitated newspaper hagiography failed to satisfy the media audience, there was one other source the people could turn to for edification and/or entertainment in the era of communication compression: the works of Mao Zedong himself.[22] Between January 1, 1966, and November 30, 1968, Chinese publishers issued 150 million sets of *The Selected Works of Mao Zedong* and 140 million copies of *The Selected Readings of Mao Zedong*. An astonishing 740 million copies of the famous, red-covered *Quotations of Mao Tse-tung* were published, or about one copy for every man, woman, and child in China, half of whom were illiterate. (In contrast, during the "revisionist" regime of Liu Shaoqi in 1962 it was claimed that Mao's works had constituted only 0.57 percent of all books published.)[23] Cognizant of the illiteracy problem, toward the end of 1966 the People's Liberation Army (PLA) began sending out mobile propaganda teams to supervise Mao Zedong Thought Study Classes. The goal was to have a study class "within every institution," urban or rural, in all of China. By 1970 much progress had been made toward this goal.[24] In the cities, people carried around copies of Mao's *Quotations* like talismans; in the countryside, Mao's portrait was placed in altars formerly reserved for icons of ancestors.

The proactive provision of social models. After Defense Minister Lin Biao secured control over the PLA and formed his alliance with Jiang Qing in the early 1960s, the state began increasingly to supply the populace with "models" to emulate. This practice is common in propaganda states, most notably in the Soviet Union and Nazi Germany. In the 1960s the Chinese state supplied models for industry, agriculture, and even intellectual work. By far the most famous model was the soldier Lei Feng, a kind of superheroic Boy Scout whose goal was to establish himself as "the perfect screw" in China's giant communist machine. Lei is said to have died sacrificing himself in this glorious pursuit, but fortunately his diary was discovered post mortem, making it possible to present his worldviews, values, and action strategies to all Chinese, particularly to the young, for emulation.[25] In February 1964 the "Learn from Lei Feng" campaign was expanded into a "Learn from the PLA" campaign. After the Cultural Revolution got under way, however, the only suitable model for nationwide emulation was Mao himself. "Thus, the Chinese people [were] told not only to internalize Mao's thoughts, but also to use them as guides in all kinds of action." They should take his thought "as the criterion for their words and deeds, whether in the collective or at home."[26]

Absence of horizontal communications. The flow of messages in the Maoist propaganda state was decidedly top-down and vertical. Emphasis was placed on constructing a mass-media and telecommunications system that could relay orders hierarchically from Beijing to the communes, and from the state to society. The main tools were *Renmin Ribao*, its "little brother" party papers in the provincial capitals, the Xinhua News Agency, and the Central People's Radio Network (CPRN).[27] The system was highly centralized, particularly (as indicated above) after the beginning of the Cultural Revolution.

Emphasis on creating a top-down mass-media system was paralleled by a de-emphasis on building a society-wide telecommunications network. Simply put, the Maoist leadership did not want Chinese people communicating horizontally by telephone. If there was something happening in Sichuan that the Anhuinese needed to know, they would find out from the mass media or through the relevant bureaucratic hierarchy. These hierarchies themselves, it should be noted, did have need for telecommunications to receive and transmit orders; many built their own systems because the public network was unreliable.[28] Markets played only limited and localized roles in the planned economy. As a result, it was not only considered dangerous for people to communicate cross-regionally, it was also economically unnecessary.

The Deng Thaw and Its Limitations

After 1978 Deng Xiaoping sought to move China away from the rigidly restrictive communication patterns of the Mao Zedong era, but he never abandoned the notion that the party-state should retain ultimate control over thought work. Deng believed that control could best be achieved by relaxing restrictions, and that relaxation in and of itself could ensure that China developed a lively culture and a vibrant economy. But his writings and actions also show belief that China's future would not be bright if forces in society secured control over thought work. The result might be Cultural Revolution chaos or the transmogrification of the communist regime.

In pursuing supreme leadership over the Communist Party, part of Deng's original strategy had been to encourage people wounded by the Cultural Revolution to express their grievances by placing posters on Democracy Wall, located in Beijing's busy Xidan commercial district.[29] But immediately following his political triumph at the Third Plenum of the Eleventh Central Committee (December 1978), Deng launched a crackdown on Democracy Wall and the accompanying samizdat movement. He ordered the dissident Wei Jingsheng arrested for demanding democracy as "the fifth modernization," and he enunciated "four cardinal principles" to specify his determination to maintain "the people's democratic dictatorship" and the propaganda state in power:

> We must . . . struggle unremittingly against currents of thought which throw doubt on the four cardinal principles. . . . [1] Some people are now openly saying that socialism is inferior to capitalism. We must demolish this contention. . . . [2] The development of socialist democracy in no way means that we can dispense with the proletarian dictatorship over forces hostile to socialism. . . . [W]e must recognize that in our socialist society there are still counter-revolutionaries, enemy agents, criminals, and other bad elements of all kinds who undermine socialist public order. . . . [3] Party leadership, of course, is not infallible, and the problem of how the Party can maintain close links with the masses and exercise correct and effective leadership is still one that we must seriously study and try to solve. But this can never be made a pretext for demanding the weakening or liquidation of the Party's leadership. . . . [4] What we consistently take as our guide to action are the basic tenets of Marxism-Leninism and Mao Zedong Thought.[30]

The limits to liberalized thought work inherent in the four cardinal principles are palpable. In 1980 the National People's Congress formally codified the limits by deleting from the state constitution the right of the citizens of the People's Republic of China (PRC) to "speak out freely, air their views fully, hold great debates, and write big-character posters."[31] Deng later explained that "those who worship Western 'democracy' are always insisting on those rights. But having gone through the bitter experience of the ten-year 'cultural revolution,' China cannot restore them."[32] The stratagem of equating the autonomous formation of public opinion with the "societal totalitarianism" of the Cultural Revolution struck many a responsive chord in China and would be used again in June 1989 to justify the Tiananmen massacre.

Indeed, several times during the 1980s Deng's leadership felt control over thought work was slipping and sought to rein it in. Each time the senior leader himself authored ideological rationales and other statements that made clear the party-state's intention to maintain control. For example, in criticizing the writer Bai Hua and his film script *Unrequited Love* in 1981, Deng stated that "some persons are not on the right track ideologically. They make statements contrary to Party principles and are neither honest nor upright. Yet there are other people who admire them and eagerly publish their articles. This is quite wrong."[33]

Two years later, launching the 1983–84 Campaign Against Spiritual Pollution, Deng made clear that limitations would not be restricted to overtly political thought work, but would include all forms of propagandistic public communication:

> As "engineers of the soul," our ideological workers should hold aloft the banner of Marxism and socialism. They should use their articles, literary works, lectures, speeches, and performances to educate people, teaching them to assess the past correctly, to understand the present, and to have unshakeable faith in socialism and in leadership by the Party. . . . But some [ideological workers], flying in the face of the requirements of the times and our people, are polluting people's minds with unwholesome ideas, works, and performances. In essence, spiritual pollution means the spread of *all kinds* of corrupt and decadent ideas of the bourgeoisie and other exploiting classes and the spread of distrust of socialism, communism, and leadership by the Communist Party.[34]

Deng found it necessary to speak out against degenerate thought work yet again in the winter of 1986–87, after antiregime demonstrations broke out nationwide, most notably in Shanghai. This time, the bad currents were referred to not as "spiritual pollution" but as "bourgeois liberalization"—a term that carries a much stronger political connotation—and Party General Secretary Hu Yaobang lost his job, partly for being lax on thought work.[35] "The struggle against bourgeois liberalization," Deng warned, "will last for at least twenty years. . . . Bourgeois liberalization would plunge the country into turmoil once more. Bourgeois liberalization means rejection of the Party's leadership."[36] Yet bourgeois liberalization raged across the Chinese political landscape once again in 1989, this time threatening the regime to its core and prompting a furious, violent crackdown in response.

Why was Deng unable to prevent the spread of spiritual pollution and bourgeois liberalization? Why did the Chinese public sphere gradually slip out of state control and into a condition of praetorianism—albeit not a praetorianism as advanced or politicized as that of the early twentieth century? The answer lies in administrative fragmentation, property-rights reform, and technological advance.

Administrative Fragmentation

Even during the height of the Cultural Revolution, the Chinese propaganda system remained decentralized in form, as it had been since Mao decided in the early 1950s not to emulate the Soviet Union's hyperbureaucratized approach to thought work. But cadres in the provinces, municipalities, communes, and other lower levels of administration understood clearly that they were not free to diverge from the centrally mandated thought-work line, even if they were not always certain exactly what communications that line allowed and disallowed. Only in the 1980s did the state finally implement a genuine deconcentration of decision-making authority over thought work. This, combined with the ideological decompression of the post-Mao period, produced administrative fragmentation. Lower levels in the administrative hierarchy assumed significant regulatory power over media content and telecommunications flows, and authority over certain types of message formation and transmission divided among two or more bureaucracies at the same administrative level.

The logic behind the deconcentration policies of the 1980s was simply this: Because media and telecommunications units and their immediate, territorial-level regulators have access to superior information about the needs of local consumers, allowing territorial authorities to "give play to their inherent capabilities" and manage the local units directly should produce a faster, more efficient development of the information industries. Faster and more efficient development was essential because information would have to flow more freely through society if a "socialist commodity" (eventually "socialist market") economy were to put down roots and to flourish.[37] At the same time, much of the burden of financing a communications expansion could profitably be shifted to lower levels of the hierarchy. The problem was that the Center failed to anticipate the consequences of the trade-off. The Center expected that the information, which would flow more freely under locally financed expansion, could be limited to the technical and the commercial and remain separate from the propagandistic.[38] Only in the aftermath of the 1989 political crisis did shocked leaders understand the magnitude of the problem, which had developed partly as an unintended, secondary consequence of administrative deconcentration.

The phenomenon of horizontal administrative fragmentation emerged primarily because of the rapid diffusion of new communications technologies. Bureaucratic responses to the arrival of videotapes, audiotapes, and compact discs in the 1980s and 1990s have been woefully ineffective. Frequently it is unclear which bureaucracy should manage a particular technology; as a result, none does. Rooting out pornography and other politically unacceptable media products from the so-called "cultural market" has become a serious problem in administrative coordination, requiring great expenditures of time and effort.

Broadcasting. The development of television was considered especially important in the early years of reform both to help the central party-state attain its goals in thought work and to reverse the excessive austerity and communication compression of the Maoist era.[39] The people would have to be provided with pleasant diversions if the legitimacy of the political system were to be restored, just as they would have to be provided with more and better food and consumer goods. At the same time, television in particular would serve as an excellent medium for the advertising industry, revived in 1979 and expected to play a strategically important role in the socialist commodity/market economy. The best way to "decompress" both television and radio would be to allow lower-level authorities greater power to select and create programming, including news programming. In 1979 Zuo Hanye, director of the new Central China Television (CCTV, established May 1, 1978), resurrected a slogan first enunciated by senior propaganda commissar Hu Qiaomu in the early 1950s: Media units should "walk on their own two feet." The intent of this slogan was to encourage radio and television stations at subcentral levels to originate more of their own programming, and in particular to cease the practice of merely rereading central party newspaper and Xinhua News Agency dispatches over the air.[40] The slogan was formally embraced at the All-China Broadcasting Work Conference in October 1980.

Also in 1980, the State Council issued a document declaring explicitly that authority over radio and television stations would rest primarily with equivalent-level territorial administrations, reinstating the situation that had prevailed de jure (though not usually de facto) from 1956 to 1967.[41] Three years later, at the March/April 1983 All-China Radio and Television Work Conference, central broadcasting authorities spelled out in greater detail the form that decentralization should take. A new slogan was adopted for the television industry: "Four levels run television, four levels together cover [the country with television signals]."[42] The "four levels" were center, province, city, and county. But the counties, while "running" television stations, were not expected to originate programming. Rather, they were merely to use local funds enthusiastically and efficiently to build the facilities necessary to retransmit central and provincial programs, which, it was thought, more reliably embodied the goals of thought work. No station at any level would be permitted to air locally produced programs exclusively.[43]

The March/April 1983 conference also called for steadily expanding the proportion of radio and television station personnel recruited locally by the stations themselves, as opposed to personnel assigned by the state.[44] Subsequently, at the July 1983 Central Organizational Work Conference, Beijing decided formally to decentralize personnel management in the broadcasting *xitong* (among others), giving lower levels greater authority to hire and fire.[45] Over the next year, a system that emphasized "only managing the chief leading cadres of the next level down" was implemented. The result was immediate experimentation throughout the country in the hiring of editors, journalists, announcers, and producers directly from society, on the basis of contracts that could be canceled for poor performance. By the mid-1990s, a mixed system prevailed in practice: Equivalent-level radio and television administrative offices, in consultation with officials elsewhere in the region and at the next highest level in the xitong, appointed most major media outlets' higher-ranking personnel. (The media units themselves were responsible for hiring lower-ranking personnel.) The degree of consultation required varied widely from place to place, and hiring without consultation appeared to be easier than firing without consultation. Because all broadcasting outlets were formally state-owned (i.e., they "belonged" to the regulatory bureaucracy at the equivalent level), dismissing employees remained difficult.[46]

The central government itself lacked the resources necessary to fund television's desired rapid development. As Table 1 shows, Beijing suffered from serious budget deficits during the early years of reform and still does. These deficits sharply constrained the Center's ability to finance the communications system's overall development and improvement, considered essential to building both the material and spiritual civilizations. The central leadership therefore adopted the two-pronged strategy of shifting the financial burden to lower levels and dangling the carrots of greater administrative responsibility and advertising revenue.

But it was still not entirely clear precisely who would wield authority as a result of the 1980–83 reforms. In the Chinese bureaucratic system, a provincial governor was equivalent in rank to the Minister of Radio, Film, and Television, a city mayor was equivalent in rank to a provincial director of the Bureau of Radio and Television, and so on all the way down the hierarchy. Granting primary authority over radio and television to the provincial administration did not absolve provincial authorities of the need to "harmonize" their policies with the Ministry of Radio, Film, and Television (MRFT) in Beijing.[47] A lingering im-

TABLE 1

Central Government Budget Deficits, 1978–1996

(*100 million yuan*)[a]

Year	Revenue	Expenditures	Balance	Deficit/ Revenue
1978	1,132.26	1,122.09	10.17	
1979	1,146.38	1,281.79	(135.41)	0.118
1980	1,159.93	1,223.83	(68.90)	0.059
1981	1,175.79	1,138.41	37.81	
1982	1,212.33	1,229.98	(17.65)	0.015
1983	1,366.95	1,409.52	(42.57)	0.031
1984	1,642.86	1,701.02	(58.16)	0.035
1985	2,004.82	2,004.25	0.57	
1986	2,122.01	2,204.91	(82.90)	0.039
1987	2,199.35	2,262.18	(62.83)	0.029
1988	2,357.24	2,491.21	(133.97)	0.057
1989	2,664.90	2,823.78	(158.88)	0.060
1990	2,937.10	3,083.59	(146.49)	0.050
1991	3,149.48	3,386.62	(237.14)	0.075
1992	3,483.37	3,742.20	(258.83)	0.074
1993	4,348.95	4,642.30	(293.35)	0.067
1994	5,218.10	5,792.62	(574.52)	0.110
1995	6,242.20	6,823.72	(581.52)	0.093
1996	7,407.99	7,937.55	(529.56)	0.071

SOURCE: Guojia Tongjiju, ed., *Zhongguo Tongji Nianjian, 1997*, p. 247.
    [a] constant units.

pulse to maintain centralized influence was probably one reason the old Central Broadcasting Bureau was abolished in May 1982 and replaced with a new Ministry of Radio and Television.[48] A ministry is significantly higher in status than a bureau. At a time when formal power was being devolved to the *kuai* (territorial) administrations, it was important to upgrade the status of the *tiao* (vertical) broadcasting bureaucracy, lest the *kuai* begin to exceed their mandate.[49] Nevertheless, the broadcasting xitong would eventually become significantly "looser" and less centralized than other systems such as transportation and banking.[50]

Print. Management of the print media is even less centralized than management of the broadcast media; there is no counterpart even to the relatively weak MRFT, or to its successor, the General Bureau of Radio, Film, and Television (GBRFT). This is a legacy of the Maoist era, when managing print was the sacred responsibility of territorial-level party committees. Only the party's Central Propaganda Department (CPD) effected any organizational centralization, and that department, as explained above, was itself decentralized in the early 1950s. As a result, not only do the central party papers enjoy only so-called professional relations with the provincial party papers—as opposed to leadership or even guidance relations—but the provincial party papers themselves enjoy only professional relations with the municipal and county party papers. There simply is no hierarchy of print periodicals in China.

Throughout the Maoist period and during Deng's first decade in power, the Ministry of Culture (MoC) did have an office responsible for regulating non-party print periodicals. The vast majority of these periodicals, however, had disappeared during the Cultural Revolution.[51] The need for a strong government bureaucracy to oversee the development of the broadcast media (especially television) seemed self-evident in the early 1980s, given the necessity of harmonizing technical standards. But that was the only reason. As explained above, radio and television management was itself decentralized in the early 1980s, concretely affecting investment, personnel, and programming decisions. There was never any perceived technical need to centralize the print media. As a result, when the general decentralization of authority became orthodoxy in the early 1980s, local print-media outlets were able to turn the de jure autonomy they had long enjoyed under Mao into a high degree of de facto autonomy, with very little administrative constraint.

In January 1987, following student demonstrations in Shanghai and other cities, the Center upgraded the MoC bureau (*ju*) responsible for managing non-party papers into a new administration (*shu*)—the State Press and Publications Administration (SPPA). This office was charged with the task of regulating the numerous new non-party newspapers, magazines, and books that had sprung up "like mushrooms after a spring rain" in the first decade of reform. Such print media were thought to have played a key role in the spread of spiritual pollution and bourgeois liberalization in the years preceding the demonstrations. But an administration (*shu*) is lower in rank than a ministry (*bu*). Because the SPPA's jurisdiction would be limited to non-party publications, it was deemed unnecessary and even undesirable to give it the status of a ministry, despite the fact that the broadcast media and telecommunications had been managed by ministries since the early 1980s.[52] The SPPA is, therefore, a weak bureaucracy that only modestly counters the tendency toward administrative fragmentation in print communication. The most important print periodicals remain under the jurisdiction of territorial-level party committees, and—as explained in Chapter 5—the SPPA's provincial-level bureaus are often dominated by the provincial governments.[53]

Telecommunications. Telecommunications is not, and has never been, classified as part of the propaganda xitong, which has primary jurisdiction over thought work. The importance of this point can hardly be exaggerated. Though newspapers, television stations, radio stations, and other mass media are all parts of the propaganda xitong, telecommunications is classified bureaucratically as a subsection of the finance and economics xitong. At the same time, policing telecommunications networks is primarily the responsibility of the public-security apparatus, which is itself part of yet another xitong. The rationale for classifying telecommunications as essentially an instrument of economic management rather than propaganda is simply that, historically, China's telecommunications networks were used only to convey technical orders down and information up bureaucratic hierarchies, not for cross-regional or cross-xitong communication of what would normally be considered propagandistic messages. Telecommunications networks were also considered to be mere carriers of messages—like roads and railways—rather than originators of messages, and therefore relatively passive components of the overall thought-work enterprise. Today, however, the telecommunications networks' expanding capabilities have transformed them into powerful tools for initiating and sending messages of all types, including those of an obviously propagandistic nature.[54]

Not only does the propaganda xitong exercise very little influence over telecommunications, but ironically even the Ministry of Posts and Telecommunications (MPT) itself has little influence over telecommunications development at the provincial level and below. The lingering influence it does have is rapidly declining as a result of intentional administrative deconcentration.[55] This is unusual from a comparative perspective, because as the geographer Ronald Abler points out, "Throughout history, telecommunications industries and services have never diffused; they have always been deliberately expanded by strong centralized authorities."[56]

Chinese authorities designed the MPT in the early 1950s to be a relatively powerful bureaucracy that would plan the nation's telecommunications development in a centralized, authoritative way. But in 1958, during the Great Leap Forward, most of the MPT's key decision-making powers were decentralized to the localities, which afterward became responsible for planning regional telecommunications development. This policy line continued until 1961, when economic retrenchment forced a recentralization. However, in 1971, during the chaos of the Cultural Revolution, the MPT was merged into a new Ministry of Communications, itself dominated by the PLA. The MPT was reinstated in 1973, but authority over telecommunications development was again decentralized to the localities. The MPT's legacy, then, is one of a very weak bureaucracy managing the development of a modern social function that in other societies is managed by very strong bureaucracies (or strong parastatal firms).[57]

The MPT was also constrained financially on the eve of reform. The budget deficits that helped convince the central party-state to transfer responsibility for developing the broadcasting industry to the provincial level and below reinforced the tendency toward decentralization in the MPT system.[58] The state thus formally granted provincial telecommunications bureaus independent accounting status in 1978, along with the rights to retain significant portions of their revenues for reinvestment and to seek other sources of investment.[59] In 1980 this line was taken a step further when the State Council adopted a policy of "developing intra-city telephone service with intra-city telephone revenue." After 1980 all municipal telecommunications revenue (except for taxes) was retained by the local provider.[60] Partly as a result, the overall proportion of telecommunications investment originating from the Center decreased from 60 percent in 1983 to less than 9 percent in 1989.[61]

During the early years of reform, the State Council did take steps to counter this tendency toward administrative fragmentation so that telecommunications development could be coordinated rationally for the grand project of building a socialist commodity (eventually market) economy. In 1984 the Council established the Leading Group for the Revitalization of the Electronics Industry, which began the following year to outline in broad terms the priorities for development of the telecommunications industry. The State Planning Commission, the State Economic Commission, and all the important economy-related ministries were represented on the Leading Group, and all helped to thrash out what was expected to become the blueprint for China's telecommunications development. However, the biggest bureaucratic beneficiary of this process was not the MPT, as might have been expected, but rather the Ministry of Electronics Industry (MEI), which was assigned the key role of designing and producing the technically advanced equipment that would undergird China's telecommunications modernization.[62] Naturally, this incursion into the MPT's equipment-producing responsibilities served only to weaken the bureaucracy further.[63] As a result, Ken Zita concluded in 1987 that the MPT "is more of a middleman, a political clearinghouse between policy formation in the central government, and policy execution with provincial and municipal planners. It has absolute responsibility neither for the strategic development of the industry, nor for the local plans for implementation."[64]

In fact, by the late 1980s the MPT's responsibilities were limited almost exclusively to managing the national trunk network (i.e., the linkages above the provincial level) and international connections. This was no small responsibility, of course. It involved the construction of nationwide optical fiber, microwave, and satellite grids. The MPT took up the task with alacrity, successfully building an impressive and well-functioning network within a very short period of time. Nevertheless, at the provincial level and below, the MPT was largely powerless to affect telecommunications development—except insofar as central intervention was necessary to ensure nationwide intercompatibility of technical standards. These MPT weaknesses only intensified during the

1990s.[65] By 1995, some multinational equipment providers even asserted that the ministry "doesn't have a clue" about the telecommunications development plans of many locales. In general, the richer the lo-
cale, the less likely the MPT has a significant influence over its strategy
of development.[66]

There is yet another legacy of the pre-reform period that contributes
to today's fragmented telecommunications management. In the 1950s
bureaucratic systems began establishing their own private telecommunications networks rather than relying on the MPT's public network to
fulfill their internal telecommunications needs.[67] Most important in this
regard are the networks belonging to the PLA and certain energy and
transportation ministries (railways, coal, petroleum, and water and
power). These bureaucracies have always required relatively advanced
and reliable telecommunications capabilities to coordinate their far-
flung activities, and they could not rely on the rudimentary MPT network. As in most socialist systems, the economic bureaucracies in pre-
reform China faced strong incentives to produce as many of their own
input supplies as possible, since they could not count on the profit motive disciplining other bureaucratic agencies.[68] Telecommunications
was sufficiently important to the military and the energy and transportation ministries to induce them to build their own networks.

Consequently, by 1993, of China's 32 million telecommunications
lines, an amazing 12.74 million (40 percent) belonged to these vertical
bureaucracies, and only the lines of the PLA and the Ministry of Railways had formal interconnection capability with the MPT's 19.26 million public lines.[69] The private networks did not even rely on the MPT
for transprovincial telecommunications, having constructed their own
long-distance trunk networks.[70] Even at the territorial level there was a
tendency under the planned economy to establish private, intrabureau-
cratic networks. These networks form the basis of most of these xitongs'
internal telecommunications today. For example, in Shanghai, as of
1992, there were 92 private networks being used by various branches of
the Shanghai government, and an additional 125 networks being used
by field offices of the national ministries.[71]

But this picture of MPT weakness should be modified by three crucial considerations. First, and most important, the MPT presides over a

nationwide, intra-xitong revenue-redistribution system that requires richer provinces to transfer portions of their telecommunications revenue to poorer provinces.[72] For example, Guangdong is required to give a certain portion of its provincial telecommunications revenue to the MPT in Beijing, which uses the money to help fund the development of telecommunications in Xinjiang, Gansu, and other poor provinces. This redistribution system is completely separate from the national taxation system. It is a purely intra-xitong system managed by the MPT.

Second, the MPT does hold veto power over extremely large telecommunications investments that the provinces and localities propose to make. The precise cut-off point at which MPT approval must be secured is not a figure the authorities are willing to divulge. Apparently, it varies by province and locality. In general, though, the figure "does get a bit higher each year" (even adjusting for inflation), implying a progressive decline in central authority over local telecommunications investments.[73] Certainly the MPT continues to exercise a residual power to reject investments that would result in local or provincial systems technically incompatible with the national network. The MPT also has the vague, macroregulatory authority to ensure that components of the China-wide public network support the advance of the nation's overall telecommunications grid. The grand strategy, however, is developed at the State Council level, and the MPT acts merely as a weak agent to oversee its implementation.

Third, the MPT does wield some residual authority as the center of the xitong, a distinction that generates a modicum of lingering loyalty—not a completely unimportant consideration now that the MPT's China Telecom must compete with the alternative telecommunications providers Liantong and Jitong. The MPT has been able to use its position as the center of the xitong to discourage some local-level telecommunications authorities from allowing the alternative providers access to the public network. The position also sometimes discourages the locales from cooperating with multinational equipment providers that have struck deals with Liantong and Jitong. Richer locales feel completely free to ignore this advice. In general the provincial and local telecommunications authorities want to do whatever it takes to develop the industry within their regions, even at the expense of contributing to the ongoing weakening of the xitong. If the local telecommunications equipment factory happens to be in the MEI xitong, for example, the local telecommunications provider will purchase its products, not the products of an MPT factory located somewhere else.[74]

On March 31, 1998, the State Council reorganized the MPT and MEI into bureaus under the new Ministry of Information Industries (MII). At the same time, the MRFT was converted into a "general bureau" (*zongju*) directly under the State Council; the new MII assumed some of its technical responsibilities. The precise implications of these reforms for control over telecommunications and the media will take years to assess. Quite possibly, the reforms will prove virtually meaningless—except insofar as they soothe the jealousies and tensions between the MPT and MEI (discussed in Chapter 5). Certainly any attempt to recover powers handed down to the localities in the 1980s would be a colossal bureaucratic challenge. Most localities benefit enormously from their control over the riches of the communications industry, and they would certainly resist encroachments from on high.

The sociopolitical effect of administrative fragmentation is to multiply the number of points at which the Center must exercise power or authority to control the flow of undesirable communications messages. By the mid-1990s, messages could easily be initiated and received throughout the system at numerous points over which the Center did not have direct jurisdiction. The situation at lower levels of administration was particularly vexing to Beijing because that is where its authority was most attenuated. The logic of multiple-level principal-agent models is useful in conceptualizing this problem. The principal (the central party-state) can oversee directly only the activities of the agent one step down in the hierarchy (primarily the provinces). It cannot usually oversee directly the activities of agents even lower in the hierarchy. Thus, although the provinces did hold significantly greater (nominal) authority over propagandistic public communications than in the pre-reform period, the Center, by controlling certain personnel and other decisions, could ensure that the provinces did not step too far out of line. The Center's monitoring capabilities were not perfect; provinces did step out of line, but not nearly as far out of line as the lower-level cities, counties, and (in some places) townships and villages.

Property-Rights Reform

Property-rights reform by the 1990s affected almost all state-owned enterprises, including those in the communications industry. It is defined as the devolution of significant economic (as opposed to legal) property rights to managers and workers and to their immediate, territorial-level supervisors. There has not yet been in China (and there may never be) a full-scale, formal privatization of media and telecommunications firms. That would require the state to grant unofficial organizations and individuals in Chinese society legal ownership of those firms.[75] But managers and workers in the media and telecommunications industries have secured significant economic property rights to firm income along with broad decision-making authority over the utilization of firm assets.

Yoram Barzel defines economic property rights as the "rights, or the powers, to consume, obtain income from, and alienate these assets," de facto, if not necessarily de jure.[76] In the same spirit, Janos Kornai (following others) classifies economic property rights into three types:

1. *Rights to residual income*, in which, "having deducted all the costs associated with utilization of the property from the income obtained with the help of it, the remaining income belongs to the owner. The owner is free to decide how much of the residual income to use for such specific purposes as individual and family consumption, investment, the acquisition of further property, and so on."

2. *Rights of alienation or transferability*, by which the owner may "sell property for money, rent it out, present it as a gift, or bequeath it to others."

3. *Rights of control*, which "concern the utilization of property (management, decision making, and supervision)."[77]

All major media outlets and telecommunications firms in China remain the legal property of the equivalent-level party-state administration. Thus, for example, CCTV "belongs" to the GBRFT, the Xinhua News Agency "belongs" to the State Council, China Telecom "belongs" to the MII, and *Nanfang Ribao* (Southern daily) "belongs" to the Guangdong Provincial Communist Party Committee. No individual or private group in Chinese society owns full property rights—legal or economic—to any major mass-media or telecommunications firm. However, in all societies, "an unconditional property right is extremely rare," because of constraints imposed "by state and legal regulations, or at least by customary law, tradition, and accepted codes of morality."[78] Primarily as a result of being made "responsible for profits and losses" (*zifuyingkui*) in the early 1980s, most Chinese media and telecommunications firms now do have significant rights to residual income while their managers have rights of control.[79]

These rights are not absolute. While it is true that property rights are not absolute in any political system, they are particularly ill-defined and uncertain in China. As elaborated in Chapter 3, taxation is subject to negotiation, and the state continues to restrict (often ineffectively) the kinds of income-raising activities in which media and telecommunications firms may engage. It also continues to restrict (again, ineffectively) the kinds of programs and articles that media units may convey to audiences. There is strong pressure on unit managers to allot significant proportions of unit income toward subsidizing money-losing units elsewhere in the xitong, as well as to provide housing, health care, and other services to workers. Expenditure of remaining income is subject to additional restrictions.[80] But overall, as Walder concludes in reference to state-owned and collective enterprises in general, "Although the reassigned rights are still vague and subject to bargaining, state managers now enjoy significantly expanded rights to appropriate and use shares of profit at their discretion."[81]

This fact has been documented by, among others, Thomas Rawski and Theodore Groves. Surveys of state-owned enterprises reveal a strong correlation between profit and retained earnings, indicating that "financial outcomes are not equalized by 'whipping the fast ox.'"[82] Additionally, Rawski finds that workers benefit directly from increased firm income in the form of financial bonuses. Groves et al. report a similar finding, but they also claim that managers' incomes do not increase when firm income increases. However, the Groves et al. study does not examine the question of whether managers (or workers) secure benefits in the form of improved housing, opportunities for travel, expense accounts, and fancy cars, which seems almost certainly to be the case.[83]

Making media firms responsible for profits and losses presents their managers and employees with strong incentives to cater to audience demand in creating content—a driving force behind thought-work commercialization, globalization, and pluralization. To the extent that media regulators also benefit from the firms' financial successes, reform creates incentives for the regulators to "turn a blind eye" to content that, although inconsistent with the party-state's thought-work goals, appeals to large audiences. The reason is simply that content with high audience appeal can serve as a magnet to attract advertisers, and advertising is now the major source of income for most media units.

This is not to say that media units no longer enjoy subsidies. The poorer media units—most notably radio stations—continue to receive subsidies in the form of direct cash transfers from the bureaucracies that macromanage them. At the same time, all media units throughout the system inevitably benefit from a variety of hidden subsidies in the form of low-interest loans, assumption of legal ownership over property inherited from the pre-reform era, distorted prices, and so on. Of course, they also suffer from the need to subsidize others; for example, they must provide social services to their workers, they sometimes face pressures to keep advertising rates down, and so on. They are not, in short, completely autonomous units, despite the fact that their share of property rights in the income they generate has risen significantly under reform. In this respect, "responsible for profits and losses" is not completely accurate. A better phrase would be "somewhat responsible for profits and losses," because there are always ways to avoid full responsibility for the firm's financial situation. Most media and telecommunications firms in fact seem more responsible for profits than for losses, and no communications firm of any importance has ever (as of this writing) gone bankrupt.

But while Kornai believes that a "soft budget constraint" ultimately will result in managers and workers lacking the incentive to work hard and take the myriad steps necessary to meet customer demand and improve operational efficiency,[84] the situation in China's communications industries is more subtle. Budget constraints can vary in their softness, and almost all Chinese media and telecommunications firms (even those still receiving direct subsidies) are under strong pressure to achieve full responsibility for profits and losses at an early date. In this climate, it is costly to bargain for a subsidy. When the economy is growing rapidly and shifting to a consumer orientation, it is often easier to redesign content and services to appeal to audiences and sell advertising than to seek rents from government bureaucrats.[85] And though media and telecommunications units appear to be more responsible for profits than for losses, losses still hurt because they result in foregone consumption: lower bonuses and fewer fringe benefits.

The strong incentives for mass-media outlets to cater to audience tastes that result from property-rights reform contribute obviously and directly to thought-work commercialization, globalization, and pluralization. Telecommunications units face analogous incentives to supply their customers with more and better equipment and services, which facilitate the rapid diffusion of the new worldviews, values, and action strategies acquired from the transformed mass media. Telecommunications commercialization also empowers individuals and organizations to create and circulate their own thought-work messages. The causal dynamics of these processes are detailed in Chapters 3 through 5.

Technological Advance

Each of the causal variables analyzed in this study can alone be viewed as necessary, but not sufficient, to reduce central control over thought work. Pundits and scholars are wont to attribute massive sociopolitical changes to the power of technology alone, particularly communications technology. In reality, technology never exerts its effects in a social, political, economic, or cultural vacuum. Its effects are always mediated by an array of other factors, the most important ones to this study being administrative fragmentation and property-rights reform. The diffusion of communications technologies in China itself is partly a function of the economic growth produced by property-rights reform and the interregional competition spawned by administrative fragmentation. Collinearity makes specifying the precise contribution of the technological variable difficult. It seems unquestionable, however, that without the mass dissemination of television sets, satellite dishes, fax machines, and now computers and modems, the Chinese central party-state could much more easily maintain its desired degree of control over thought work.

It is ironic in this respect that Beijing itself has promoted rapid tech-nological advance, including the building of a national "information superhighway" connected to the potentially subversive Internet.[86] But the motive is clear: Unless China modernizes technologically, it will be unable to compete either economically or militarily with the outside world—and thus could eventually face mortal security threats from the United States or Japan. China must integrate into the global economy in order to strengthen itself for competition, and integration requires not only economic and administrative reform but also absorption of ad-vanced technologies.[87] A sharp reduction in control over thought work is simply the unavoidable price to be paid, whether anyone in Beijing recognizes the fact or not.

Television. Because its wide channel capacity allows for the trans-mission of images as well as sounds, television is considered by many communications scholars to be the medium with the greatest social im-pact. In China, this impact is likely to be all the more significant as a re-sult of television's extremely rapid diffusion through the society under reform (see Table 2). An audience of 78 million in 1978 had by 1992 grown to 800 million—about 70 percent of the population—and contin-ued to increase steadily thereafter.[88] The proportion of the population in possession of a television set quickly approximated the proportions in countries like Malaysia and Thailand, where the per-capita income was three to five times as high.[89] Indeed, as Table 2 makes clear, by the late 1980s China's urban television viewers had become so wealthy that they started abandoning black-and-white television sets in favor of color sets.

Of course, television's saturation of China is not by itself sufficient to undermine central control over thought work. Indeed, the Center could in principle make excellent use of television technology to reach even more people with more "impactful" propagandistic messages. Only in interaction with administrative fragmentation and property-rights re-form—which stimulate a pluralization in sources of television mes-sages and the commercialization and globalization of their content—does technology contribute to weakened control.

One of the most important new sources of television signals in China

TABLE 2

Television Ownership in China, 1978–1996

(sets per household)

Year	Total	Color		Black and white	
		Urban	Rural	Urban	Rural
1978	0.011	—	—	—	—
1980	0.032	—	—	—	—
1985	0.250	0.172	0.008	0.669	0.109
1990	0.583	0.590	0.005	0.524	0.397
1993	—	0.795	0.109	0.359	0.583
1994	—	0.862	0.135	0.305	0.618
1995	—	0.898	0.169	0.280	0.638
1996	—	0.935	0.229	0.255	0.651

SOURCES: Guojia Tongjiju, ed., *Zhongguo Tongji Nianjian, 1990, 1993, 1996, 1997.*

is broadcast satellites, which for obvious reasons have been particularly instrumental in thought-work globalization. By the early 1990s some 40 satellites illuminated the Asia-Pacific region, providing a total of 700 transponders, of which 150 (21 percent) were used for broadcast transmissions of various kinds, including television.[90] Digital-compression technology, which enhanced the efficiency of spectrum use, also allowed broadcasters to trade bandwidth for power, resulting in a sharp decrease in the necessary diameter size of satellite receiving dishes to about eighteen inches.[91] The technological stage was thus set for a massive growth in direct, cross-border satellite-television broadcasting throughout the Asia-Pacific.

In 1988 the Hong Kong–based Asia Satellite Telecommunications Corporation (Asiasat) became the first privately owned satellite-services provider in the region, at a time when most satellite services were still being supplied by the government-owned international consortium INTELSAT. Asiasat-1, launched in April 1990, was originally expected to be used almost exclusively for telecommunications, but by 1995 70 percent of its transponders were devoted to television. The chief reason for this shift was the fateful decision by one of Asiasat's three co-owners—Li Ka-shing's Hutchison-Whampoa Ltd.—to establish the Satellite Television Asia Region company (better known as STAR-TV) in April 1991.[92]

It is important to understand the legal loophole that allows Asiasat and other broadcasters such as Apstar and PanAmSat to transmit satellite television signals into China and other Asia-Pacific countries. Both the 1971 and 1977 World Administrative Radio Conferences (WARCs), held under the auspices of the International Telecommunications Union (ITU), had taken steps to increase the difficulty of legally broadcasting across borders in the absence of permission from receiving states. All companies supplying "broadcast satellite services" that crossed borders were required first to obtain permission from the receiving states. If they failed to do so, receiving states could take up the issue with the governments that granted the broadcasters their licenses.[93] But companies providing so-called "fixed satellite services" did not need to obtain the permission of states in whose territories their satellite "footprints" happened to fall.

The distinction between fixed and broadcast satellite services would appear to be clear cut, but in fact is virtually meaningless. Satellite companies have successfully argued that they are not actually broadcasting into, say, China, but rather are supplying satellite services to numerous fixed points, such as the central nodes of cable television networks. If receiving states are concerned about the content of these services, they should take it up with the fixed points, not the satellite companies. All of the major satellite companies serving the Asia-Pacific market now have "fixed satellite service" licenses, even if the lion's share of their business comes from broadcasting. As a result, neither Asiasat nor any other satellite company ever had need to secure Beijing's permission before broadcasting to the Chinese people. The companies are completely unconstrained in this regard by the international communications regime.[94]

China launched its own first experimental satellite, the Dongfanghong-1, in 1970, and in 1984 succeeded in using the Dongfanghong-2 to broadcast the 35th National Day ceremonies in Tiananmen Square, seen for the first time "live" in places as far from Beijing as Urumqi and Lhasa.[95] Satellite broadcasting was an important component of the central party-state's strategy to achieve rapid development of the communications industries, as mapped out at the important work conferences of the early 1980s. Broadcasting by satellite would allow China to avoid the problem of setting up numerous microwave transmission stations across a huge territory characterized by great extremes in topography and climate. Development of the satellite industry also appears to have been motivated by a technological nationalism that blinded China's leaders to the potential dangers of a rapid dissemination of satellite receiving dishes, which officially numbered about 6,000 at the end of 1988, 15,000 on the eve of the Tiananmen demonstrations, and 50,000 by the end of 1993.[96]

To date, the most important provider of external television messages to China is STAR-TV, broadcasting by Asiasat. It is not technically difficult for Chinese citizens to receive STAR-TV broadcasts—although, as explained in Chapter 6, it is now somewhat more legally difficult. STAR-TV does not encrypt its signals, and the signals require a satellite dish of only about 2.4 to 8 meters in diameter to receive.[97] In January 1993 dishes of this size cost about 4,000 *yuan* (U.S.$481); by early 1995 the price had fallen to about 2,400 yuan (U.S.$288).[98] Each dish can service several hundred households, so when work units are deciding whether to establish in-house cable networks, cost is a very minor consideration. As a result, as early as February 1992—two months after STAR-TV began regular broadcasting—an estimated 25,000 dishes in China were capable of receiving its signals.[99] But Chinese consumers, apparently stimulated by the excitement generated by STAR-TV, purchased an astonishing 500,000 satellite dishes during 1992, STAR's first full year of existence.[100]

Videotapes, Audiotapes, and Compact Discs. Gathering data on the number of videotapes, audiotapes, and compact discs in China is exceptionally difficult because no single bureaucracy is responsible for managing them. In early 1996 there were 298 authorized audio-video publishing houses (up from 1 in 1978), but countless other units engaged in unauthorized reproduction of works produced originally in China or abroad.[101] The MoC, GBRFT, and SPPA are each responsible for regulating about a third of these publishing houses, a confusing situation contributing to a chaos in the cultural market that will be discussed in later chapters.

In 1996 about 20.2 percent of urban households owned a videocassette recorder, 12.2 percent owned "hi-fi stereo component systems," 26.5 percent owned stereo recorders, and 46.2 percent owned ordinary recorders. In the countryside, ownership of video equipment and advanced audio equipment was negligible, but 31.2 percent of that population did own radio cassette players.[102] Even though these numbers are still relatively low, the impact of videotapes, audiotapes, and compact discs is magnified by the fact that many are rebroadcast (often illegally) by television stations (especially lower-level stations and cable networks) and radio stations, and also reach vast audiences in the approximately 80,000 karaoke bars and "MTVs" throughout the country.[103] Minister of Culture Liu Zhongde reported in May 1996 that more than 100 million people were watching videotapes each year in China's MTVs.[104]

Telecommunications. Extremely rapid growth has characterized the telecommunications industry since its takeoff around 1985. The original driving force came from business and industry, pressured from the early 1980s to establish horizontal linkages with other firms as the old vertical planning system was slowly dismantled and replaced with a socialist commodity/market economy. In the early 1990s demand from private households contributed to continuing rapid growth.[105] Yet another impetus was competition among regions for both foreign and extraregional domestic investment. Multinational firms, in particular, required relatively advanced telecommunications capabilities to integrate their global operations.[106]

Table 3 presents some indicative data. In every major category, the capacity of telecommunications is expanding with an astonishing rapidity, facilitating among other things an extraordinary fifteenfold increase in the annual number of long-distance telephone calls per capita between 1989 and 1996. This rapid growth shows no sign of abating. Indeed, the MPT annually revises upward its projections for various targets of telecommunications development. For example, in 1991 the ministry projected that China would have 48 million exchange lines in place by the year 2000; in 1994 it projected 140 million lines; and in 1996

TABLE 3

Telecommunications Development by Type of Technology and Use, 1970–1996

Year	Telephones per capita	Long distance calls per capita	Mobile cellular subscribers	Paging service subscribers	Fax machines	Faxes sent
1970	0.003	0.10			83	
1978	0.004	0.19			1,484	
1985	0.006	0.36			1,266	139,242
1986	0.007	0.39			1,341	145,119
1987	0.007	0.47			1,413	152,101
1988	0.009	0.58			1,876	176,177
1989	0.010	0.70			2,600	241,457
1990	0.011	1.02			3,826	555,481
1991	0.013	1.49			6,183	968,834
1992	0.016	2.45	176,943	2,220,000	9,410	1,712,182
1993	0.022	4.28	638,268	5,614,000	12,276	2,706,055
1994	0.033	6.32	1,567,780	10,330,000		3,423,700
1995	0.048	8.37	3,629,416	17,392,000		4,423,080
1996	0.058	10.41	6,852,752	25,362,000		5,650,000

SOURCES: Guojia Tongjiju, ed., *Zhongguo Tongji Nianjian, 1988, 1990, 1997.*

it projected 170 million lines. Similarly, the number of telephones per 100 people was expected in 1991 to reach 3 by 2000; in 1994 the figure was raised to 8 per 100; and in 1996 it was increased to 10.5 per 100.[107] Of course, there is significant inequality in the distribution of telecommunications capacity, with the big urban areas enjoying the greatest capacity and the fastest growth. In 1996 China's 360 million urban residents had access to 55 million telephones, a ratio of 1 phone for every 6.5 people. But in the countryside, 864 million Chinese citizens shared a mere 15 million telephones—about 1 phone for every 57.5 people.[108] On average, every urban household is expected to own a telephone shortly after the turn of the century, and rural households are expected to catch up 20 to 25 years later.[109]

Despite this celeritous growth, telecommunications still constitutes a costly bottleneck in the Chinese economy. The country's transformation into a market economy has been unexpectedly fast, and annual growth rates were perennially in the 8 to 12 percent range until 1998, when growth fell as a result of the pan-Asian economic downturn. Yet fixed telephone density is still very low because development started from such a low base. Fortunately for China, this transformation and growth began at precisely the time cellular telephony was taking off worldwide. Hence, China has been able to leap-frog past some of the bottlenecks by developing—primarily, importing—advanced mobile and paging capacity. Table 3 reveals the startlingly rapid growth of this capacity. The figure of 6.9 million cellular subscribers in 1996 was expected to increase to 18 million by 2000.[110] When the Qinghai city of Xining inaugurated services in March 1994, all of China's provincial capitals had at least one mobile cellular service. A nationwide "roaming" capability—the ability to call people on mobile phones in other regions—was achieved with extensive foreign assistance in October 1994.[111] Meanwhile, the ranks of the 25.4 million pager owners in 1996 were expected to increase to an amazing 100 million by 2000—nearly 8 percent of the population.[112] People from all walks of life in China increasingly use pagers as substitutes for personal telephones. A friend or colleague dials the paging service and requests a return call, which the recipient makes a few minutes later from a public phone. This capability is of subtle but crucial importance in making the market economy work but also helps further undermine state control over the flow of information.

Mobile telephony and paging services also exemplify important qualitative improvements in the Chinese telecommunications system. These improvements are laying the groundwork for the establishment of a high-capacity, digital, broadband network that will become the envy of even some more economically advanced countries suffering from high sunk costs in copper-wire networks. Optical-fiber transmission networks have spread rapidly throughout China, as has automated switching technology. A national trunk transmission network consisting entirely of optical fiber was expected to link all provincial capitals and 80 percent of prefectural-level cities—domestically and internationally—by 2000.[113] Already by 1994, some 86 percent of the entire telecommunications network was automated (i.e., required no operator intervention to complete calls), with the figure approaching 100 percent in the big cities.[114] Also by 1994, residents of 876 Chinese cities could make direct-dial, automated calls to 198 countries and regions around the world, as well as to each other.[115] All major cities were expected to be linked into this automated network by 2000.[116] No other country's telecommunications system will have ever developed this rapidly, both in terms of overall capacity and degree of technical sophistication.

The relationships among the three causal variables—administrative, economic, and technological—are complex, but in general they are mutually reinforcing. To be sure, at a certain point further administrative fragmentation could reduce the impact of property-rights reform by introducing unpredictability and greater insecurity over property rights. Similarly, a certain degree of administrative coherence is necessary for advanced communications systems to operate—particularly at the national level. But from the early 1980s through the late 1990s, administrative fragmentation, property-rights reform, and technological advance all covaried positively and all contributed to each form of the breakdown of central state control over thought work: commercialization, globalization, and pluralization. This was a major change from the days of the Maoist propaganda state and held enormous implications for China's future. The precise causal mechanisms by which the state lost control are detailed in the chapters that follow.

CHAPTER THREE

The Commercialization of Thought Work

With increasing frequency, China's mass-media units are targeting the perceived interests of the general public—not state propaganda cadres—in marketing books, periodicals, films, television shows, and radio programs. Termed "commercialization," or even "vulgarization," this shift in orientation is of course not absolute. Very few media units dare to ignore the wishes and concerns of state administrators completely. The level of obedience varies depending on the administrative proximity of the unit to the Center and the security of the unit's audience size as a result of state subscription and retransmission requirements. But almost all Chinese media units have, since the mid-1980s, significantly altered the content of their offerings to the public in an effort to increase audience size and sell more advertising.[1]

The result, conceptually, is a significant transfer of power over thought work from the state to society, a shift from propaganda commissars to the unofficial groups and individuals in the marketplace whose buying power now indirectly shapes, to a substantial degree, the content of the communications messages that mass-media units impart.[2] To be sure, the dynamics of this mechanism are not perfect. The unsophisticated nature of market research means that media-unit managers cannot know with certainty what sorts of messages audiences would like to consume, and firms wishing to advertise cannot be certain about the composition and size of the audiences whose attention media units are trying to sell.[3] But as a result of the potential to improve unit members' material living conditions—made possible by property-rights reform—firms throughout the Chinese economy have become strongly motivated to purchase advertising just as media units have become strongly motivated to sell it. The result is a restructuration of the symbolic environment as media units strive to create programs and articles with high audience appeal.[4] The balance of power over the entire thought-work enterprise has thus shifted significantly away from the central party-state and in the direction of society, filtered through the operations of mass-media units.

At the same time, the decentralized and newly market-oriented telecommunications companies, which, in exchange for profit, eagerly supply society with telephones, fax machines, and the networks to support them, are in fact giving individuals and groups the power to create and circulate their own thought-work messages. Even if only a small proportion of the messages circulating on the Chinese telecommunications system is propagandistic—as opposed to technical or mundane—the absolute volume of society-generated propagandistic messages is probably increasing as telecommunications technology spreads rapidly. This technology also facilitates a wider diffusion of the new worldviews, values, and action strategies acquired by social opinion leaders directly from the market-oriented mass media.

While it is obvious that property-rights reform is the most potent independent variable explaining thought-work commercialization, administrative fragmentation and technological advance remain essential factors. As explained below, administrative fragmentation results in lower-level, macroregulatory media and telecommunications agencies deriving direct pecuniary benefits from the commercial successes of the publishers and broadcasters they supervise. Meanwhile, because of television—China's richest media industry—technological advance is clearly central to fueling thought-work commercialization and to what might be called "societalization" by telecommunications. But even newspapers benefit from technological advance because their editorial offices now house computers and other equipment that allow them to respond to consumers' wishes in news gathering and production easily and quickly.

The Rise of Advertising and Its Effects on Media Content

The immediate roots of thought-work commercialization can be traced to the decision made at the end of the 1970s to allow media units to resume selling advertising. Before the 1980s, the media faced little incentive to cater to audience demand, precisely because they were not permitted to sell advertising. It is true that as early as 1956, Liu Shaoqi, in a "directive" to the Central Broadcasting Bureau's Party Organization, "anticipated" the need for broadcasting enterprises eventually to sell at least enough advertising to fund their daily operating expenses.[5] But details of the Liu directive are murky, and while it was circulating, China's prerevolutionary advertising agencies were all being brought under state ownership. Xuejun Yu reports that in 1956, 108 private ad agencies were combined into the single, monopolistic, state-owned Shanghai Advertising Corporation in Shanghai alone.[6]

A decade later, during the Cultural Revolution, commercial advertising was banned as a tool by which capitalists manipulate public opinion. Billboards were turned over to the likenesses and quotations of Mao Zedong (a good example of "communication compression").[7] The very small role played by markets and competition in the economic life of China during this period implied very little need for advertising anyway. Until 1979, most economic activity was devoted not to the production of consumer goods, whose sales advertising might stimulate, but instead to the production of heavy industrial products. The state-owned industries that utilized these products did not need to be convinced of their good quality. Their only task was to take whatever inputs they were assigned and produce whatever items state planners ordered them to produce. Advertising played virtually no role in the planned economy.

As a result, when Deng Xiaoping secured power at the end of 1978, only 10 or 20 units throughout the country specialized in advertising, including divisions of newspapers and other media outlets. Under reform, however, the number increased rapidly, reaching 43,000 licensed units by the end of 1994 and an untold number of private, unlicensed units, which typically produce ads for smaller private and collective firms to broadcast on subprovincial radio stations, television stations, and cable networks, and/or to publish in smaller-circulation periodicals.[8] Growth in the advertising industry began almost immediately after Deng's political triumph in December 1978, signaling the end of an era in which advertising was defined as a tool of capitalist domination.[9]

The specific decision to allow the media to resume selling advertising was motivated primarily by two considerations. First, as discussed in Chapter 2, the central government suffered from serious and persistent budget deficits that rendered it incapable of funding the large-scale expansion of media channels expected and desired under reform to bring about a "flourishing culture." Second, and more important, even as early as 1979 the reformers anticipated moving in the direction of a market economy—despite the fact that the terminology would not be embraced until 1992.[10] It was fully understood that advertising played a key role in transferring information about available goods and services among potential buyers and sellers. As progressively more enterprises became responsible for profits and losses, managers were forced and enticed to expend more energy locating supplies and convincing consumers to purchase their firms' products. Advertising lay at the heart of these activities. Without advertising, it would have been much more difficult to discover what goods and services were available for the manager to use to increase his or her firm's efficiency. Without advertising, it would also have been substantially more difficult for the manager to craft the sort of image necessary to increase sales.

Increasing sales was an extremely important consideration now that so many competing firms had become responsible for profits and losses and was highly desirable now that the firm—particularly its higher-ranking personnel—exercised much more discretion over how revenues would be spent and could therefore justify spending them on increased personal consumption. As the business activities of successively more enterprises thus became market-oriented, advertising demand mushroomed; and as previously laggard enterprises saw their competitors advertise, they too jumped into the advertising game, fueling the spiraling growth of this industry evident in Table 4.[11]

From the start, the party-state failed—institutionally—to recognize that advertising itself is a form of thought work, quite apart from its indirect effects on other media content. The leadership did not officially embrace perspectives like that of the Marxist theorist Liu Renwei, who wrote in March 1996 that "advertisements participate in the cultural invasion. Kind-hearted people think that advertising is nothing but promotion of merchandise, but in fact the issue is far from being so simple. On the one hand, people blow their own trumpets by means of adver-

TABLE 4

Chinese Advertising Industry Revenue,
1981–1994

Year	Annual advertising revenue (10,000 yuan)[a]	Percent of GDP
1981	11,800.00	0.024%
1982	15,000.00	0.028
1983	23,407.40	0.040
1984	36,527.80	0.052
1985	60,522.50	0.070
1986	84,477.70	0.087
1987	111,200.30	0.098
1988	149,293.90	0.107
1989	199,899.80	0.127
1990	250,172.60	0.144
1991	350,892.60	0.177
1992	678,675.40	0.283
1993	1,342,493.30	0.499
1994	2,003,000.00	0.678

SOURCES: Lu Lin, "1992-nian de Zhongguo Guanggaoye," in *Zhongguo Guanggao*, pp. 4–6; Interview 138.
[a] constant units.

tisements, but on the other hand, [ads] are comprehensive manifestations of a consumption concept, a way of life, and value-orientation of the countries where such merchandise is produced."[12] The State Council decided in 1980 to place advertising not under the jurisdiction of the propaganda and education xitong—where cadres like Liu Renwei could more easily keep an eye on it—but instead under the jurisdiction of the finance and economics xitong, or more concretely, the State Administration of Industry and Commerce (SAIC).[13] Here is an excellent illustration of the effects of administrative fragmentation on thought work. In a joint notice issued in April 1984 by the SAIC and the Ministries of Culture, Education, and Public Health, even cultural, educational, social, and public-health advertisements were placed under the jurisdiction of the Industry and Commerce system. All such ads were required to be "examined" (*shencha*) before publication by the equivalent-level Industry and Commerce government office, and to receive certification that they did not contain pornography, lies, feudal superstition, or counter-revolutionary themes. Thus, Industry and Commerce system offices were charged with regulating one very important aspect of thought work, reducing the potential reach and influence of the propaganda xitong.[14]

As Table 5 makes clear, among major media outlets, newspapers and television stations have made the most money from advertising; radio stations and magazines lag far behind. Newspapers actually collected more aggregate ad revenues than did television stations in the early 1990s, but newspapers are more numerous. Television is the medium that has profited most from advertising's explosive growth.[15] Here the contributions of technological advance to thought-work commercialization become clear, because television is at the center of the commercialization processes. The most profitable television stations are probably CCTV and the provincial stations in the richer coastal regions.[16] Where the economy flourishes, so does advertising, and so, therefore, do the media, ceteris paribus. It is precisely the enormous profits that higher-level television stations (and newspapers) have made from selling ads that have fueled the rapid growth of the media industries since the mid-1980s.

The fact that television and newspapers are benefiting most from the ad boom, however, does not mean that the content of other, less successful media has not become more audience-oriented under reform. Consider the case of radio. Advertising revenues in radio grew very slowly during the first decade of reform, not experiencing sharp increases until the early 1990s (see Table 5). The proportion of all ad revenues earned by radio stations fell by 50 percent between 1983 and 1993. This particular segment of the media industry was simply unable to keep up with television and newspapers in the competition for ad revenues.

The problems facing the Central People's Radio Network (CPRN)—as well as its response—illustrate cogently the commercialization of "ra-

TABLE 5

Advertising Revenue by Type of Medium, 1983–1994

(10,000 yuan)[a]

Year	Television	Newspapers	Radio	Magazines	Total
1983	1,624.37	7,330.34	1,806.93	1,081.12	11,842.76
1984	3,397.00	11,864.72	2,322.99	1,297.54	18,882.25
1985	6,869.58	22,011.35	2,670.71	2,809.28	34,360.92
1986	11,514.37	25,602.77	3,563.95	3,565.23	44,246.32
1987	16,297.26	35,549.21	4,721.22	4,542.91	61,110.60
1988	27,178.90	53,411.58	7,028.62	7,164.87	94,783.97
1989	36,190.20	62,940.10	7,459.90	8,506.40	115,096.60
1990	56,136.80	67,710.50	8,641.60	8,683.00	141,171.90
1991	100,052.10	96,187.60	14,049.20	9,989.30	220,278.20
1992	205,471.00	161,832.40	19,920.00	17,267.00	404,490.40
1993	294,000.00	371,000.00	35,000.00	18,000.00	718,000.00
1994	448,000.00	505,000.00	51,000.00	39,000.00	1,043,000.00

SOURCES: Ma Dawei, "Shilun Wo Guo Dianshi Guanggao de Fazhan," in *Xinwen Yanjiu Ziliao*, p. 20; Interview 138.

[a] excludes ad agency and "other" recipients of ad revenue.

dio thought work." The CPRN, one of the Center's most important thought-work tools, began carrying advertising in the early 1980s, but its business failed to take off until around 1989. By 1995 some 80 percent of the CPRN's operating expenses was covered by advertising revenues, with the difference being made up by a government subsidy channeled through the Ministry of Radio, Film, and Television (MRFT). The goal was to have the station move in the direction of full responsibility for profits and losses, but the CPRN did not expect to attain that goal anytime soon. Although it had permission to broadcast up to six minutes of advertising per hour, the CPRN's seven channels on average could sell only about one minute per hour. While the average world ratio of the price of television ads to radio ads is about six to one, CCTV's ads sold for 288 times the price of the CPRN's ads.[17] The CPRN is not alone in facing difficulties on the road to becoming responsible for profits and losses. All of China's radio stations are wrestling with this same difficulty.

Significantly, their solution has not been to appease the state by re-
fusing to take risks with thought work. Instead, their solution has been
to become even more bold in creating programs that appeal to audience
tastes. The CPRN neatly sums up the goals of radio reform in its motto:
"Get close to reality, get close to life, get close to the masses!"[18] Given
the context of the publicity materials in which this slogan is trumpeted,
the phrase might just as easily be translated: "Become more audience-
and market-oriented!" In most of the more prosperous provincial capitals, in addition to pursuing the commercialization goal by airing call-
in programs, covering social "hot topics" in the news, and playing more
popular music, radio authorities have established "economic stations"
designed exclusively to make money by specializing in the broadcast of
programs with high audience appeal.[19] Much of this money is used to
subsidize the more politically purist "propaganda stations," but the important point is that *the audience is not required to listen to the propaganda
stations.* If the audience goes away, the radio station will follow, not
lead. The result is a transfer of power over thought work to the audience, to society.

The first economic station was the Zhujiang Economic Station,
founded by the Guangdong Provincial Department of Radio and Television in December 1986.[20] By 1988 the Zhujiang Station had been judged
to be one of Guangdong's "10 Greatest Achievements during a Decade
of Reform," after which it became a model for emulation nationwide.
The Zhujiang model emphasized "appealing to audience tastes, supplying the audience with large quantities of information, serving the audience, and being entertaining."[21] It thus represented the first big step toward legitimizing the tendency for radio thought work to become primarily audience- or society-oriented, as opposed to government- or
state-oriented. Zhujiang airs all of its programs live, whereas before,
most items were on tape. Zhujiang carries news but has replaced the
ponderous politicized broadcasts of old with short, lively bits emphasizing commercial and lifestyle information at the top and bottom of
every hour. Not content to rely on the organization and personnel xitong, Zhujiang attracted more than 100 talented broadcasters from
around the country to create its programming. It quickly emerged as the
most popular station in Guangdong and maintains that status today. Its

high income from advertising is used to subsidize the broadcasts of the propaganda channels, to which very few people listen.

"Paid News"

The discussion of the remarkably rapid development of China's advertising industry and its direct and indirect effects on media content has been limited so far to "hard advertising" (*ying guanggao*). This is the kind of advertising with which citizens of industrialized democracies are most familiar. The marketing department of a business enterprise purchases time on a broadcasting station or space in a periodical to assert the superiority of the enterprise's products or to improve the enterprise's image and reputation. This is the only kind of advertising about which the Chinese government publishes statistics. But two other kinds flourish and contribute to the corrosion of state control over thought work: "paid news" (*youchang xinwen*) and "soft advertising" (*ruan guanggao*).[22]

Paid news can be found in all of the mass media, even the highest-level organs of the party and state. As the name implies, paid news denotes the exchange between business enterprises and reporters of money or other considerations for favorable publicity "disguised" (often not very well) as news. The reporters pocket the money and consume the considerations in their private capacity; that is, the money never reaches the station or periodical. (As explained below, this is the key distinction between paid news and soft advertising.) It is true that sometimes the reporters share the considerations with their fellow reporters, but they do not invest any of the money gathered this way into the relatively "public" operations of the media outlet.

In a carefully researched 1993 article, one Hong Kong analyst uncovered three main types of paid news:

1. Township enterprises will hold "news conferences" to promote their products in specially targeted, big-city markets where they lack good connections. The only way to ensure that reporters attend the "news conferences" is to provide them with food and drink and present them with red envelopes containing 200–500 yuan (U.S.$24–$60). This is equivalent to one month's salary for the typical journalist. A favorable story about the products will result in even more money.

2. Established urban enterprises will buy news even when the alternative of buying hard advertising is available and connections in the city are good. Paid news costs less than hard advertising, encouraging both the reporter and the enterprise to enter into an exchange. From the point of view of the enterprise, news is considered more credible than advertising, which in a Chinese context can come across as unendurable boasting. It is always better to have an "objective" third party praise the enterprise than for the enterprise to praise itself.

3. Reporters will go out to "shake down" enterprises, demanding that they advertise in the reporters' media outlets or else face the prospect of slanderous "news" reports. This tactic often results in enterprises purchasing hard advertising, but with the reporters privately enjoying a 5 to 20 percent commission.[23]

By the autumn of 1993 paid news had become so widespread and even socially accepted in China that some lower-level television stations began openly publishing prices. "For instance, a news report on the holding of an enterprise meeting, the ordering of goods, or a product show will cost 500 yuan, while a five-minute feature story will cost 5,000 yuan."[24] And the purchasers of paid news are not restricted to Chinese companies. Many foreign companies are said to buy news, including—according to one source—American companies. Like their foreign and Chinese counterparts, Americans must also include additional private compensation for the sales person even when buying hard advertising, to guard against negative publicity.[25]

By far the most shocking case of paid news was exposed at none other than the flagship *Renmin Ribao* in 1993. While details of this case are murky, given Beijing's reluctance to discuss corruption at the highest-level thought-work organ of the central party-state, the basic facts are clear. In exchange for money, several *Renmin Ribao* reporters wrote favorable stories about the new Great Wall Science and Technology Corporation, which was preparing to float a stock offering. Obviously, the hope was that if a paper as authoritative as *Renmin Ribao* praised Great Wall S&T's prospects, a great number of individuals and organizations would purchase the company's stock, artificially bidding up its price. Unfortunately for the reporters, the scam was uncovered. The result was a furious crackdown on paid news that apparently succeeded in uprooting the problem at *Renmin Ribao*, but nowhere else.[26]

Paid news is not a completely new phenomenon. It was born with the introduction of the 1980s media reforms and has grown steadily more serious as the reforms have taken deeper root. As early as 1985, the State Council issued a "circular on strengthening control over advertisements" that specifically prohibited paid news.[27] By 1993 the SAIC had decided that the best way to squelch paid news was to separate the functions of producing advertising and publishing advertising by forbidding media units to produce ads directly or have any direct contact with ad buyers, thereby strengthening the ad agency system. But media units cleverly circumvented this regulation even before it was implemented by setting up their own ad agencies, leading to an increase in the number of agencies from 16,600 in 1992 to 43,000 in 1994.[28] The party's Central Propaganda Department (CPD) and the State Press and Publications Administration (SPPA) subsequently convened a conference, in August 1993, that produced a "Notice on Improving Professional Ethics in Journalism's Ranks and Forbidding 'Paid News.'" A campaign against paid news commenced, and continues as of this writing, but with little effect.[29] The February 1995 Advertising Law specifically bans all forms of non-hard advertising, but by all accounts and even a cursory monitoring of the media, they flourish.

Take, for example, the article "Be Careful When Buying a Telephone," which appeared in the April 26, 1995, issue of *Guangming Ribao*, the central-level publication designed to serve as a bridge between the party and intellectuals. This article made three rather startling claims: First, some imported telephones had been found to be technically incompatible with the Chinese telecommunications network; second, some foreign companies were dumping "second-hand phones" on the Chinese market; and third, some imported phones had been found to carry the hepatitis virus. One cannot help but suspect that most of *Guangming Ribao*'s well-educated readers would consider each of these claims to be unlikely, especially the third. Why, then, would the paper print the story? Immediately adjacent to the story was a small hard ad for the Sichuan-based Changhong Electronics Company. While it would be impossible to verify, it seems likely that the Changhong Company manufactures telephones, faces foreign competition, and therefore bought the story along with the hard ad in a special package deal.[30]

Li Zirong identifies four reasons why paid news is so difficult to eliminate.[31] First, journalists' income is inordinately low given their level of education and the kind of people with whom they interact in the worlds of business and government. The reporter making 500 yuan a month can easily double his or her income by filing a mere dozen items of paid news each year. Business reporters can become wealthy by Chinese standards, even joining the "car-owning class."[32] And with the urban inflation rate hovering perennially around the 25 percent mark until 1996, "every reporter believes that writing some paid news is unavoidable if our families are to survive."[33]

Second, there is poorly developed professional pride among China's journalists, with most having utterly no sense of themselves as constituting a "fourth estate" whose noble mission is to check government abuse. With corruption becoming rampant in the demoralized post-1989 period, why should journalists not make a little money for themselves? "Everyone else is."[34]

Third, engaging in serious journalism is not only time-consuming and difficult, it is also poorly rewarded and risky. Why take dangerous chances that will result in small payoffs even if they succeed?

Fourth, despite years of discussion, there is still no press law in China to specify improper behavior and corresponding punishments. The February 1995 Advertising Law is considered a step in the right direction, but is still too vague. Moreover, the gap between promulgating laws and implementing them is notoriously wide in China, a country long characterized not by the rule of law but by the rule of men.

"Soft Advertising"

The third kind of advertising—soft advertising—appears on the screen or page as indistinguishable from paid news. For example, a television station might interview a factory manager about how her management style exemplifies the spirit of reform. Interspersed with shots of the manager will be shots of the many fine products the factory has for sale, and at the bottom of the screen will be the factory's address, telephone number, and fax number—the last being absolutely de rigueur. Is this paid news or soft advertising? If the money goes directly to the journalists, it is paid news. But if the money (or most of it) goes back to the station or to one of its subdivisions, it is soft advertising. China's social critics and the Advertising Law lump the two together as "the second kind of advertising" (*di erlei guanggao*), but practicing journalists make a careful distinction between the two. Many denounce paid news, but insist that they have no choice but to sell soft advertising.

The several factors specified above that jointly produce the phenomenon of paid news are ultimately traceable to the desire of individual journalists to increase their material consumption. Such is not the case with soft advertising, which had become by the mid-1990s ubiquitous in Chinese public communication. The rise of soft advertising can primarily be attributed to radical changes in the structure of media units that the propaganda xitong began implementing in the early 1990s. These changes represent a penetration of the 1980s ethos of managerial decentralization and the practice of making economic organizations responsible for profits and losses into subdivisions of the media unit itself.

Consider, for example, the case of Beijing Television.[35] This very important station's 800 programming personnel were divided in April 1995 into 103 "program groups" (*jiemuzu*). Each group was responsible for generating the funds necessary to pay for the great majority of its own operating expenses, the bulk of which were used to produce a single, regularly broadcast program. While the average program group included 7 or 8 members, the groups ranged in size from 1 to 150. The largest groups were responsible for producing the heavily watched, prepackaged morning and evening news programs, and the smaller groups were responsible for producing public affairs, educational, and children's programs.[36] Each of the news and public-affairs groups included at least one director, camera person, video and sound person, and lighting person, as well as one (or more) reporter and editor. Meeting together, group members themselves conceived ideas for news stories and other programs—taking into account the political constraints, of course—and then went out and "shot" the programs on their own.

Although the station paid all of the group members' salaries and arranged for their housing, health care, and various other personal matters—and provided the group with its more expensive equipment—the group itself was forced to pay for all of its daily operating expenses and had to give the station 20 percent of what it raised from soft advertising as a form of compensation for what the station gave the group.[37] Exactly how much the group would be required to raise was determined toward the end of the previous year when group members planned the number of programs they would produce in the following year and estimated how much they would cost. A typical twenty-minute news or public-affairs program might cost 20,000 yuan (U.S.$2,404) to produce and might require three editions per week, or about 150 per year. That means the program group would itself have to raise 3 million yuan (U.S.$360,560) from advertising during the course of the year. The station's advertising department—a completely separate entity whose primary task was to raise the funds necessary to make the big expenditures on salaries, housing, and equipment—did not want to compete with the program groups to attract hard advertising, so the station restricted the groups to selling only 30 seconds of hard advertising per program.

The prices for hard advertising varied, depending on the time of day and the day of the week the program would air, but in almost no case was 30 seconds of hard advertising sufficient to fund the program. Prices for soft advertising tended to hover around 30,000 yuan per five minutes, but those prices also varied. Given the need to pay the station some 20 percent of revenue and to give the group member who attracted the soft advertising a commission (see below)—as well as the need to prepare for uncertainty—groups typically set a target of selling five minutes of soft advertising per twenty-minute program. In other words, about a quarter of the "news" or "public affairs" program would be disguised advertising. Purchasers tended to be state-owned enterprises, collective enterprises, and Sino-foreign joint ventures, most of which enjoy extensive economic property rights to their firms' income—strong incentives to manipulate thought work to cater to potential buyers.

For obvious reasons, few enterprises are willing to purchase soft advertising on programs that do not appeal to large audiences, so the program group had to consider not only what sort of programming would constitute good platforms for factory and store managers to sell their wares, but also what sort would attract large audiences. That meant pressure to insert sex, violence, feudal superstition, and other themes that contradicted the central state's thought-work goals—just as in the case of hard advertising. At the same time, program content had to be selected carefully to facilitate the introduction of factory managers, store managers, and other soft-ad purchasers to the television audience.

Members of the program group did not find producing such programs an easy or pleasant task. Many journalists in particular are well educated and cultured, and they say they find gratuitous sex, violence, and feudal superstition to be distasteful. They certainly loathe having to adopt a serious mien when interviewing factory managers about the amazing properties of their products. Group members often rationalize the inclusion of such content in their programs by arguing that "two 'bad' programs are worth one 'good' program." In other words, it is acceptable to cater to so-called lowest common denominator (*disu*) tastes and the interests of enterprise managers most of the time if some of the time the funds thereby generated from soft advertising can be reinvested back into the production of good programs.

Caution must still be exercised to avoid creating programs that are excessively bad, or whose embedded soft advertising is too "obvious." The state does continue successfully to contain the thought-work effects of soft advertising to an important (if unquantifiable) degree, at least in Beijing. Acting on behalf of the station manager, a committee of retired radio and television xitong cadres monitors (in principle) all programs to make sure that none exceeds the limits of taste or political acceptability.[38] Beijing Television personnel assume the cadres cannot possibly review every minute of every program. But they cannot discount the possibility that their group's program will be selected for review in a given week, so they self-censor from the start.

At the same time, though, the group members must still sell soft advertising and must still produce programs appealing to audience tastes.[39] To help overcome the strains produced by this contradiction, in 1995 the station permitted the group members to take a 4.5 percent commission on all the ads they sell. Over the course of a year, this sum had the potential to become a substantial component of, for example, a reporter's income. To return to the previous example: If the group must raise 3 million yuan a year, and if it is a typical group with five members, then each member must raise 600,000 yuan, out of which he or she may pocket 27,000 yuan, or 2,250 yuan per month. (Recall that the average journalist's salary was only 500 yuan per month in the mid-1990s.)

Of course, there is great variation both within and among groups over how much money individuals can earn, prompting some groups to adopt an informal policy of dividing all proceeds equally among group members. Moreover, informants insist that their primary motivation for selling advertising is not to make money; rather, it is to generate the funding necessary to fulfill their professional desire to create "good" programming. Nevertheless, one cannot help but suspect that soft-advertising commissions are at least a partial solution to the problem of how journalists might benefit materially from China's fast-growing economy in a way that prevents them from becoming thoroughly corrupt and taking the dirtier route of selling paid news. If the journalists were motivated purely out of professionalism and a commitment to their program group, there would be no need to pay them a 4.5 percent commission.

Beijing Television was considered to be an "outlier" in the degree to which it forced program groups to shoulder financial responsibilities, but other stations throughout China are moving quickly toward universalizing the equivalent of program-group systems. CCTV started such a system in 1993—but not in imitation of Beijing Television, a CCTV informant insisted.[40] Guangdong Television has a program-group system similar to Beijing Television's, but in 1995 the Guangdong station did not insist that its groups be fully responsible for daily operating expenses. The Guangdong Television informant was unclear (or unwilling to reveal) whether journalists earned commissions on the ads they sold, but he did acknowledge that there was some sort of material-incentive system in place to encourage station personnel to pull in advertising.[41] Yunnan Television did not have a group system as of 1995, but was expected—along with most other stations nationwide—to adopt such a system by 2000.[42]

Many financially strapped radio stations have also adopted institutions similar to the program-group system. For example, in 1995 each of Beijing Radio's individual substations was treated in a way similar to the program groups at Beijing Television, in that each was required to take responsibility for selling both soft and hard advertising to cover operating expenses. However, the Beijing Radio system was much less "advanced" in this respect than Beijing Television. Beijing Radio's centralized advertising department, which had a division within each substation, controlled all hard-advertising revenues. Income from advertising on the more popular substations (music and news) was used to subsidize operations of the less popular educational and arts substations. The music substation was forced to give the general station about 30 percent of its annual income for redistribution, while the news substation parted with about 20 percent. Activities of the propaganda substations are thereby subsidized, but only at the cost of having to satisfy audience demand by expanding to create new, specialized substations of a more popular nature. No citizen is forced to listen to the propaganda stations, and comparatively few do.[43]

In order to maintain their popularity even the content of the radio news substations has become relatively depoliticized and highly commercialized in the past ten years. News was by far the biggest substation at Beijing Radio in 1995, with more than 100 employees, each of whom was assigned to one of nine program groups.[44] These groups were not individually responsible for profits and losses, however, as were the groups at Beijing Television. They were required to turn over all money raised from advertising to the news substation's centralized advertising department, except for small amounts held back to fund minor costs and purchases. However, the important point is that the program creators were also made responsible for selling advertising, which inevitably influenced program content. Moreover, everyone who sold an ad was rewarded with a 4 percent commission after quotas were filled. Additionally, news personnel who were exceptionally successful at attracting ads were awarded special prizes to further encourage laggards elsewhere in the substation.

In Kunming, the municipal radio station was divided into five departments. The four programming departments (morning, afternoon, evening, and economic information) were all expected to sell soft advertising. The economic-information department was in the best position to sell ads because of its contacts with the business world. As a result, it signs a formal contract each year with the station requiring it to supply a certain (unspecified) amount of money for internal redistribution. Although the Kunming station still relied on the city government to fund half its operating expenses in 1995, the degree of subsidization was decreasing rapidly as the revenue from soft ads sales increased. Fully two-thirds of the advertising revenue at Kunming Radio came from soft ads, despite their illegality. Journalists and other programming personnel found it difficult to overlook the 20 to 30 percent commission that could be earned on ad sales in Kunming, much higher than the 4 to 5 percent figure in Guangdong and Beijing. The higher commission was adopted both to encourage increased enthusiasm for selling ads and to discourage the practice of selling paid news, which was becoming a serious problem in Kunming in the early 1990s. The effect on the content of radio programs was the same as that of soft advertising on the content of television programs: a commercialization of thought work, as the interests of audiences and the individuals and firms benefiting from advertising were put ahead of the statist pursuit of a socialist spiritual civilization.

Soft advertising is classified together with paid news in the February 1995 Advertising Law as the illegal "second kind of advertising" and is said to be "a serious problem that 'the leaders' are very worried about."[45] It is especially problematic in smaller cities and at the county level, where the local government/business elite can monopolize the media and essentially commandeer the thought-work process. This is one reason the Center stresses the requirement that CCTV and the first provincial television station be retransmitted in all localities, that all units with party committees throughout the country subscribe to *Renmin Ribao*, and so on. The problem of sex, violence, and feudal superstition is already considered to be especially grave in the smaller cities and counties, partly, it is alleged, because party-state leaders there are relatively undereducated, uncultured, obsessed with making money, and several steps removed from Beijing's direct supervision. The central party-state can do very little about this situation, other than exhort, unless it reverses the administrative decentralization decisions and property-rights reforms introduced in the early 1980s.

The root of the problem is that decentralization and reform have resulted not only in powerful pressures on—and opportunities for—

media outlets and their members to make more money, but also in the disproportionate enjoyment of material benefits by the higher-ranking individuals within these media outlets. This is a crucial consideration because the higher-ranking individuals are precisely those most responsible for implementing the central party-state's thought-work goals; they are, nominally, the "agents" for Beijing, the "principal." But the foreign car that the television station purchases with its profits "for" the station is much more likely to be put at the disposal of the higher-ranking station personnel than at the disposal of the janitors—though the latter may have plenty of opportunity to drive the car, on errands or as chauffeurs. The car thus becomes not truly public property but, in effect, private property.[46]

The individuals most responsible for implementing the central state's thought-work policies therefore paradoxically face the strongest incentives to violate them by creating spiritually polluting and bourgeois-liberal news stories, plot lines, and programs—which is the kind of media content that readers and audiences most want to consume. Only in that way can more advertising can be sold, more cars be purchased, more banquets be thrown, and more trips be made abroad. Of course, media-unit managers also face incentives faithfully to implement (or at least not to violate) the Center's thought-work goals. In the extreme, Beijing can always marshal its resources to target and fire (or worse) exceptionally deviant media-unit managers. But this is much more difficult as a result of the 1983 administrative reforms.[47] Property-rights reform and administrative decentralization have produced a situation in which the principal faces enormous difficulties in disciplining its thought-work agents.

The higher-level leaders are said to be fully cognizant of the structural forces producing thought-work commercialization and are now reviewing the question of whether such institutions as the program-group system are "logical."[48] They have temporarily concluded that soft advertising can be tolerated as long as it does not overly pollute program content or interfere with the "healthy development of normal advertising," but paid news will be dealt with sternly.[49] This conclusion, however, seems clearly to have been reached out of weakness. Soft advertising and paid news are unintended consequences of the

1980s reforms that simply cannot be easily uprooted. By "temporarily" tolerating soft advertising while the 1995 Advertising Law strictly forbids it, the leadership unwittingly undermines the effort to turn China into a country ruled by law. Who will take the Advertising Law seriously given the fact that media units nationwide are structurally forced and impelled to violate it and the state "temporarily" agrees to this arrangement?

Subsidization of Money-Losing Media Units

Although all important media units nationwide are now either responsible for profits and losses, or expect soon to become so, most of the laggards continue to receive subsidies. None of the important media outlets faces Kornai's hard budget constraint, meaning concretely that none need presently fear the prospect of going bankrupt. But all face pressures to increase income, and all face incentives to increase income as a result of the many new, pleasurable goods and services that can be consumed in today's China as a result of two decades of reform and opening.

The most heavily subsidized medium is radio. In 1982 the entire broadcasting xitong—radio and television together—obtained only 11.5 percent of its income from advertising and "related activities." By 1986 this figure had risen to 20.2 percent.[50] But then "takeoff" began. A 1993 report concluded that, in general, television "receives from the state only one-tenth of what it spends," presumably referring to equivalent-level state administrations.[51] More recent xitong-wide data are unavailable, but all of the television executives interviewed for this research asserted that their stations no longer rely on direct government subsidies, except for a few short-term subsidies for special operations such as satellite transmission.

Radio's situation is far different. Like television stations, radio stations were, from the early 1980s, expected to begin carrying advertising to help stimulate the development of a commodity (eventually market) economy, but as explained above, the radio industry has not been notably successful in this quest. Still, the stations have been required to expand the number of channels of programming they broadcast and to increase their total number of hours on the air, to meet the needs of an increasingly diverse, information-starved society. For example, on the eve of reform, the Beijing People's Radio Station had only three AM channels broadcasting a total of about 50 hours a week. By 1995, in contrast, it had four AM and three FM channels collectively broadcasting 847 hours per week, some seventeen times the late-1970s figure. This expansion has been costly, and while Beijing Radio's income from commercials increased from 250,000 yuan in 1982 (the year the station started carrying ads) to more than 10 million yuan in 1994, this income was sufficient to cover only about 80 percent of the station's operating expenses. The remaining 20 percent was covered by the Beijing broadcasting authority—which, in turn, received most of its subsidies money from the highly profitable Beijing Television.[52]

Most of the flagship party newspapers are now free of regular subsidies—except for the possible hidden subsidies discussed in Chapter 2. This status is partly the result of having been granted guaranteed subscriber bases, partly the result of altering content to attract more readers, and partly the result of branching out into new economic activities such as commercial consulting, advertising, and real estate. *Renmin Ribao*, for example, has been nominally responsible for profits and losses since 1980 and did not receive any money directly from the state from 1980 to 1994. In 1995, however, *Renmin Ribao* was given a special subsidy of about 50 million yuan to cover the cost of expanding the paper from eight to twelve pages.[53] Some 70 percent of *Renmin Ribao*'s remaining income derives from advertising. *Jingji Ribao* (Economic daily) is in a roughly similar situation, except that it receives an apparently smaller subsidy for newsprint and is more popular among readers because of its reputation as an authoritative source of economic information.[54]

The major exception to the prosperity of central-level papers is *Guangming Ribao*. While arguably the highest-quality paper in terms of its proclivity to publish relatively depoliticized, serious discussion of social problems (occasional soft advertising or paid news notwithstanding), *Guangming Ribao* suffers from a stuffy image and so is not particularly popular. The paper suffered greatly when beginning in 1993, the state began requiring individuals, not units, to pay for periodical subscriptions. By 1995 *Guangming Ribao* was receiving about half of its income from advertising, a bit more from the provision of various information services, and the remainder from the central party-state.[55] It is, however, moving toward becoming fully responsible for profits and losses and is expected to attain that status by around the year 2000.

Much more so than in the case of the broadcast media, larger newspaper "establishments" (*she*) have taken to supplementing their advertising revenues by investing in hotels, apartments, stores, and other enterprises with only a tangential connection to publishing. Unlike the younger (television) and weaker (radio) broadcast media, the big party papers have long enjoyed a high bureaucratic status that allows their key personnel to organize and maintain widespread connection networks, purchase property, and engage in other business activities. The papers also possess bloated workforces whose members might as well be put to use doing something constructive instead of—as is common in large Chinese organizations—playing ping-pong in the hallways.

These extra-media economic activities apparently began in earnest only in the early 1990s, in conjunction with the issuance of an SPPA document formally sanctioning them.[56] But by 1995, some 25 to 30 percent of *Renmin Ribao*'s income derived from such sideline activities, and the paper's publicity materials proudly trumpeted the fact, proclaiming as a goal the *she*'s evolution into a "new-style newspaper conglomerate."[57]

Like *Renmin Ribao*, the *Nanfang Ribao* in Guangdong is well placed to make money from real estate, given the 1990s' boom in land prices. But in 1995 *Nanfang Ribao* was also building a new industrial development zone in the city of Dongguan and was heavily involved in the world of finance, using its connections and prestige to borrow money from the state-owned banks and in turn lend that same money at higher interest rates to assorted enterprises with which the *she*'s managers had good connections.[58] Even in the relatively impoverished southwest, *Yunnan Ribao* also engages in such activities; its most important real-estate market is in the relatively prosperous provincial capital of Kunming. *Yunnan Ribao* also takes advantage of its province-wide connections network to buy for export a product in which the region enjoys a global comparative advantage: tobacco. In the mid-1990s one of the *she*'s chief goals was to start exporting more "value-added" tobacco in the form of processed and prepackaged cigarettes.[59]

While advertising obviously exerts both direct and indirect effects on thought work, the propaganda effects of the media selling cigarettes and renting out real estate are much less clear. On the one hand, such activities do increase the financial independence of media units from the state, which probably reduces the state's leverage over their activities. But on the other hand, media content need not be altered to make money from financial services and commodity exports. Perhaps in an ideal world—from Beijing's point of view—media units could end their financial reliance on advertising and come to rely exclusively on sideline activities to achieve and maintain responsibility for profits and losses. Individuals within the media units could then continue to increase their material comfort without having to act as anything other than docile mouthpieces for the central party-state. But revenue from sideline activities currently constitutes only a small proportion of the media units' income, and advertising seems certain to remain a major money earner as China continues its transition toward a market economy.

Brakes on the Causal Mechanism

As explained above, the fact that some media units—such as those in radio—continue to receive subsidies does not prevent them from altering content to cater to market tastes. But the state uses two additional tools to prevent media units from becoming excessively market-oriented in their operations: (1) It continues to categorize them legally and bureaucratically as *shiye*, not *qiye*, units; and (2) It taxes them, both formally through the tax system and semiformally through the media xitong.[60]

DEFINITION OF MEDIA UNITS AS 'SHIYE'

The distinction between *shiye* and *qiye* units is an important one in Chinese bureaucratic parlance. Although both terms can be translated as "enterprise," the term *shiye* connotes cause-oriented enterprises that concentrate on the production and provision of public goods and services, and as a result traditionally require preferential tax treatment and subsidies. The term *qiye*, on the other hand, refers to business-oriented enterprises that produce and provide private goods and services. Because private goods and services are by definition privately consumed, well-managed firms can more easily make a profit from their production and provision and should, it is therefore asserted, pay higher taxes and not receive subsidies.

The Chinese Communist party-state has always categorized units as either *shiye* or *qiye*, and the media have always been categorized as *shiye*, along with libraries, museums, educational institutions, and units devoted to environmental protection and public health. The "cause" that the media are supposed to promote is implementation of the current line in thought work, along with the provision of public-service information such as news, weather, and traffic reports.[61]

But while the distinction between *shiye* and *qiye* units is still quite valid in the case of museums, libraries, and certain other organizations, it is not for most of the mass media. The problem is precisely the belief that, in providing public goods, *shiye* have an inherent tendency to be unprofitable and should therefore be permitted to "eat the emperor's grain," that is, to rely on the government to finance their operations. Obviously, most media outlets today—especially television stations and the larger newspapers—no longer have any need to rely on the emperor for grain, and if released from their public-service duties might eventually be able to out-eat the emperor. As a result, since the mid-1980s, richer media units have been promoting the slogan *shiye danwei, qiye guanli*, suggesting that media units be redefined as cause-oriented in nature and law, but managed like business firms. Clearly, that is how media units now operate in practice, so why not codify the status? There is some evidence that former party chief Zhao Ziyang was willing to entertain the suggestion, but after Zhao's ouster in 1989, the suggestion was put on ice, and the equivalent-level party-state continued to supply even the richer media units with symbolic subsidies so that the fiction of the media remaining pure *shiye* could be maintained.[62]

However, since 1992, pressure to redefine the media's status has resumed, and at least one senior provincial television official asserted in 1995 that the *shiye danwei, qiye guanli* status is now a "goal" that is likely to be achieved "within ten years."[63] But pursuing this goal is not without dangers and costs for the media units. As *shiye*, media units enjoy not only subsidies, however small, but also a preferential tax status.[64]

The new tax system implemented in 1994 requires media units to hand over to equivalent-level tax bureaus only 5 percent of business volume derived from advertising and related activities, in addition to a negotiated profit tax.[65] (Any subsidies the media units receive are not subject to taxation.) This 5 percent figure is much lower than the amount paid by other units in the entertainment business, such as movie theaters and karaoke bars. Their tax rates can be as high as 33 percent.

But the biggest break to media units comes from the lower profit taxes they are permitted to pay. As *shiye*, they frequently assert that the need to supply public goods (especially political propaganda) justifies paying lower profit taxes than *qiye*. Precisely how much lower varies widely from region to region. Typically, in negotiations, media-unit managers will take the average *qiye* tax rate for the region and start subtracting, eventually coming to terms with the local tax officials on how much lower the rate for the media unit should be. There is very little variation on this percentage across the different media within a single province, but there is significant variation across provinces. As a result, some media units pay more profit tax than some pure *qiye*, but only more than *qiye* located in other regions.

On the other hand, if the media were redefined as pure *qiye*, they could in principle abandon the publication or broadcast of political propaganda and other items with little audience appeal and concentrate exclusively on making money. (They would also, of course, have to provide their employees with "social" services such as housing, health insurance, and the like.) In many cases, the additional income gained from sloughing off the political "news" and unpopular arts programs would exceed the increase in taxes. The *shiye danwei, qiye guanli* formulation is the de facto, but not de jure, compromise. The media will continue, however reluctantly, to act as conduits for state propaganda, but at the same time will be permitted steadily to increase the proportion of programs and stories with high audience appeal so that revenues can continue to rise. They will also be permitted to branch out into unrelated economic activities such as real estate and commodity exports. This is what is happening on the plane of reality, but the state still refuses officially to accept the *shiye danwei, qiye guanli* formulation. It does not wish formally to acknowledge its decline in remunerative power over the communications industries, or to consent to a change in the legal status of those industries.

TAXATION

Though they pay at lower rates than do *qiye*, media units must still pay taxes, and many must also give money directly to the bureaucratic organizations that regulate or macromanage them. The latter practice is a legacy of the prereform political economy, when enterprises returned all of their profits to their bureaucratic superiors. In fact, it was only in the mid-1980s that media and other economic units came gradually to be distinguished from the bureaucracy as semi-autonomous organizations.

While CCTV gives only "a little" money each year to the General Bureau of Radio, Film, and Television (GBRFT)—mostly to subsidize the CPRN—"basically all" provincial and municipal television stations, if they are profitable, give money to the equivalent-level radio and television bureau.[66] If they are not profitable, they take a subsidy. The government's finance xitong does not supply funds sufficient to subsidize the many money-losing radio stations (and few money-losing television stations) around the country, so this practice is considered necessary if the poorer stations are to be kept from closing down. For example, in the mid-1990s, the Guangdong Provincial Bureau of Finance gave only about 20 million yuan (U.S.$2.4 million) per year to the provincial Bureau of Radio and Television, an astonishingly scant 10 percent of the Bureau's budget. The Bureau therefore had no choice but to rely on Guangdong Television for the balance of its funding, an amount the source declined to specify, but which obviously must have been about 180 million yuan (U.S.$21.6 million) per year. In Guangdong and elsewhere, the amount to be handed over is negotiated annually, and exactly what percentage of the television station's budget it constitutes varies widely from province to province and, within provinces, from region to region. The Guangdong source declined to reveal what percentage of Guangdong Television's income was represented by the 180 million yuan figure, but a Yunnan source estimated that the nationwide average is 20 to 30 percent of revenue.[67]

Yunnan Television itself is an unusual case. Since 1993, it has been forced to give all of its profits to the Yunnan Bureau of Radio and Television. But after deducting what it "needs for subsidies and various other expenses," the Bureau returns the remaining funds to the station on a monthly basis. Thus, of the 30 million yuan Yunnan Television earned (and dutifully handed over) in 1994, the Bureau gave back 1 million yuan each month, which means that during the year the station was forced to sacrifice 18 million out of its 30 million yuan in profit, or 60 percent—two to three times the national average. This practice was justified as a "temporary" measure to help the many poor regions of Yunnan develop their broadcasting systems. But it was "very sensitive and would be controversial if more people knew about it," because it violates the reform-era line of "separating government from enterprise" (*zhengqi fenkai*).[68]

Guangdong Television distinguishes carefully between payments to the Bureau of Radio and Television—termed "target responsibilities" (*mubiao zeren*)—and payments to the Tax Bureau. With regard to the latter, Guangdong Television paid 5.88 percent of its business volume to the provincial tax bureau: the 5 percent turnover tax plus special, short-term taxes for "city construction" (0.35 percent), "special educational measures" (0.35 percent), and "flood prevention" (0.18 percent).[69] No mention was made of the profit tax, which is always negotiated and which another well-placed source said the provincial Bureau of Radio and Television "collects on behalf of" Guangdong Television and the other electronic media—not to turn over to the tax authorities, but rather to subsidize poorer radio and television stations within the province. In fact, the second source asserted that all of the Bureau of Radio and Television's operating expenses are supplied by the finance xitong—it takes only 20 million yuan a year to run the Bureau—while all of the "taxes" that the Bureau "collects on behalf of" Guangdong Television and the other electronic media outlets are used for intra-xitong, intraprovincial subsidies.

The situation in the world of print is substantially different, because the bureaucratically weak SPPA holds no jurisdiction over the party-owned papers and magazines that dominate the print periodical market. All newspapers, even the flagship party papers, pay taxes, but no paper gives money to the SPPA system. With what appears to be the sole exception of *Renmin Ribao*, the print periodicals' tax rates correspond roughly to the low rates paid by the broadcast media.[70] Most book publishers pay a relatively high turnover tax of 33 percent of business volume to the equivalent-level tax bureau, along with a profit tax of 10 percent. But, in addition, each book *she* is theoretically limited to earning a profit of only about 10 to 12 percent annually; any profits exceeding 12 percent are confiscated by the tax authorities. This institution probably serves as a brake on book publishers concentrating too heavily on catering to the market—though two representatives of the SPPA's Research Institute estimate that up to 15 percent of (legal) book publishers nationwide nevertheless do manage to earn "super-high" profits.[71] At the same time, some book publishers do still give money to the equivalent-level branch of the SPPA, particularly those publishers which "directly belong" to the SPPA. In such cases, the SPPA claims to pass the money on to the tax authorities on behalf of the book publishers, but it is widely assumed that "a portion" of these monies remains within the SPPA system for various uses—some upright, some probably not.[72]

Book distribution constitutes an even more special case.[73] Though technically now a state-owned firm defined as a pure *qiye*, the Xinhua Bookstore functions in many ways like a huge bureaucratic xitong providing *shiye* services. Every county in China has at least one Xinhua Bookstore outlet, and many of the larger towns (*zhen*) also have outlets. This is despite the fact that many of these places are too poor and/or suffer from too low a literacy rate to support a bookstore. Until the early 1980s, all income throughout the massive Xinhua system was ferried up through the hierarchy to the central store in Beijing, where it was redistributed from China's richer locales to the poverty-stricken backwaters. Now, no income is centrally redistributed, but provincial-level redistribution does continue in twelve or thirteen provinces located mostly in western China.

In Yunnan, for example, all Xinhua Bookstores are required in principle to turn over all income exceeding costs to the immediately higher level, which in turn is required to pass the revenues up to the provincial headquarters in Kunming. In practice, each outlet is permitted to retain some 30 percent of its profits, and a cut is taken out at each level as revenue is handed up the hierarchy. The result is that the provincial headquarters receives about 50 percent of Xinhua Bookstores' total intraprovincial profits for redistribution to the money-losing outlets in poorer regions.[74] This ensures that culture flows to backward regions—and state-mandated culture at that, because Xinhua is required to supply all of its outlets, everywhere, with certain politically important books such as volume 3 of the *Selected Works of Deng Xiaoping*. This proviso applies even to those provinces (such as Guangdong and Fujian) where each Xinhua Bookstore is now fully responsible for profits and losses and does not redistribute income.

Ironically, though, throughout the country the provincial-level Xinhua Bookstores must give a certain amount of their annual profits to the provincial-level SPPA bureau. In the case of Yunnan, this amounted to about 980,000 yuan (U.S.$117,783) per year in the mid-1990s. While the Xinhua redistribution system subsidizes the poorer bookstores, the SPPA system subsidizes the money-losing printing establishments and other peripheral publishing enterprises. Many township and village governments have set up collective and/or private printing establishments in recent years (see below), but they are extremely market-oriented and do not willingly provide their services for books unlikely to become relative bestsellers. Therefore, the Center needs to maintain a network of printing establishments that can be paid to take on the propagandistic treatises and tracts that few people will purchase unless compelled to do so.

The collective and private sector—unlike the case of publishing houses and the broadcast media—has become enormously important in the distribution of books, compact discs, videotapes, and audiotapes. None of these collective and private components of "the cultural market" either receives a subsidy or transfers funds to a macromanager to subsidize others. Bookstall owners, karaoke bar proprietors, and similar entrepreneurs do pay taxes, and since 1994 they have been "encouraged" to contribute to "arts foundations" managed by territorial-level branches of the Ministry of Culture (MoC) system. They are not forced to participate, however, and the MoC lacks the personnel necessary to apply significant pressure. Sometimes the taxes that these firms pay are "earmarked" to subsidize dance troupes, museums, and other high-quality (but unpopular) artistic endeavors. But this practice is not institutionalized in the way xitong-based transfer payments are.[75]

Encouraging or forcing thought-work units to subsidize their poorer fellows does act as an effective brake on their becoming overly market-oriented. Like all forms of taxation, forced cross-subsidization limits the full utilization of property rights. The problem is that the tactic cuts both ways. To the extent that government regulators come to rely on media units for funding, the xitong—in theory, an agent of the central party-state—develops a direct interest in media units producing programs and publications with high audience (societal) appeal.

Returning, for example, to the case of Guangdong, it is clear that the provincial Bureau of Radio and Television depends on Guangdong Television for up to 90 percent of its funding. At the same time, the television station legally "belongs" to the bureau; it is not an independent entity. The high degree of mutual dependence that this situation fosters implies a fusion rather than a conflict of interest between the regulator and the operator. The Bureau of Radio and Television faces strong incentives to macromanage in a way that allows the station to maximize its income—subject, of course, to political constraints from elsewhere in the provincial government and from higher levels of the GBRFT xitong. The station personnel, too, want to maximize their income and so must accommodate the bureaucrats to ensure favorable regulatory treatment. They therefore make the "target responsibility" payments, suspecting in some cases that the bureaucrats use at least some of the money received not for subsidizing poorer media units, but for improving the material quality of their own lives.[76] That gives individual bureaucrats a direct, personal interest in the station becoming profitable, in addition to the institutional interest derived from the Bureau's dependence on the station for funding. The result is strong pressure to acquiesce in the creation of programming with high audience appeal, even programming that violates the central state's thought-work goals.[77]

In many cases, the incentive is made even stronger by the fact that there is an overlap in personnel between the stations and their regulators, a phenomenon called *jutaiheyi*, or "bureau and station become one." This institution is more likely to exist at the city level and below, and is nearly universal at the level of the county, where—partly as a result—controlling thought work is considered to be the most difficult.[78] The cities of Kunming, Changsha, and Nanning are well known in the radio and television xitong for their *jutaiheyi* systems, and in Kunming—as elaborated in Chapters 4 and 6—controlling cable television and implementing restrictions on satellite-dish ownership have proved to be eminently unsuccessful. In these cases, the regulator and operator blur the boundaries between (local) state and society to a remarkable degree. As an operator, the television station manager faces strong incentives to air programs that appeal to audiences (society). In the role of the regulator, the manager also faces these incentives, but much more palpably than if the regulator and operator roles were distinct, as they are at the provincial level. When the regulator and the operator literally become one, the likelihood that central-state thought-work policies will be implemented faithfully diminishes considerably. This does not mean that the policies will be blatantly violated or completely ignored, but rather that the regulator/operator will be perpetually motivated to test the limits of the policies in an effort to cater to audience tastes.

The fusion of regulator and operator is not necessarily limited to the government, as distinct from the Communist Party. One high-ranking official with an important Guangdong newspaper reported that in 1993 the central party-state issued a document calling on all media units—including not just television stations but also the big money-making newspapers—to begin turning over a certain amount of their profits each year to the provincial-level *party* propaganda department.[79] This money would be used to subsidize *shiye* units that clearly provided a valued public service but were unable to make money from advertising, such as libraries, museums, and art troupes. At present, all propaganda xitong funds are said to be supplied by equivalent-level Communist Party branches, not directly by government finance bureaus or by media enterprises. All subsidies to the poorer *shiye* come from the government.

Naturally, then, the 1993 proposal has met with controversy, and not only from media units that might see their effective rate of taxation increased.[80] If the proposal is eventually adopted—and by 1995 two years had passed with no agreement on percentages, mechanisms for fund transfers, or any other details (that the source was willing to divulge)—then the party propaganda apparatus would come to have a direct interest in the profitability of media units, similar to the interest of the government's radio and television bureaus. To take a chance on the party's propaganda apparatus becoming dependent for funding on media units could seriously endanger the central party-state's thought-work efforts. Propaganda departments that need or want money—almost all of them, in other words—would face a strong incentive to "turn a blind eye" to programming that violates proscriptions on spiritual pollution and bourgeois liberalization, but which attracts large audiences whose attention can be sold to advertisers.

Commercialization in the Book Publishing Industry

Like their counterparts among periodical publishers and broadcasters, book publishing houses adopted the goal of becoming fully responsible for profits and losses in the early 1980s, and most now no longer receive direct state subsidies.[81] Unlike the other mass media, however, book publishers cannot easily make money selling advertising, whether hard or soft. Instead, to improve their balance sheets, book publishing houses must put out books more likely to be sold, and/or sell some of their SPPA-distributed book numbers (ISBNs) to illegal, underground publishers.[82] To be sure, like other media outlets, most book publishing houses need not fear bankruptcy. They do not, in other words, ultimately face a hard budget constraint. Instead, their motivations are positive. Because they now enjoy extensive economic property rights to the bulk of their income, they face strong incentives both to cater to the market and to sell book numbers to unlicensed publishers. The result is yet another avenue for the commercialization of thought work.

The organizational structure of the publishing houses has not changed fundamentally under reform. They are still state-owned and are still governed internally by party committees. But the behavior of publishing-house personnel has changed markedly as a result of administrative reform and the strong new incentives to make money. The most concrete manifestation of reform in book publishing is the implementation of individual responsibility systems for book editors at "the vast majority" of publishing houses. This institution works as might be expected: Editors are assigned monetary targets at the beginning of each year and are tasked with overseeing the publication of (usually) five books. They must select these five books judiciously in order to reach the monetary targets, and any income exceeding the targets is theirs to keep. For the most part, editors make use of previous-year sales figures to estimate a manuscript's likely popularity and on that basis make their selections for the current year. The most popular books are romances, martial-arts adventures, often sensationalist biographies of important political figures, children's books, and "truly good" books.[83] These books are precisely the kinds most likely to be criticized by the central party-state as violating the proscriptions against sex, violence, feudal superstition, and bourgeois liberalization in the media. But the pressures to generate revenues and the incentives to make money mean that, complaints notwithstanding, editors will inevitably publish them. As one Party Propaganda Department report phrased with disdain, "The customer is God."[84]

Even when the content of a book is quite aboveboard, editors feel pressure to select a title that will increase its appeal to market tastes— even at the risk of distortion:

> A teacher spent most of his life writing a novel entitled *My Mother*, based on the fact that he and his mother had been dependent upon each other for survival for years. After examining the book, a publishing house decided to publish it. But the publishing house believed the title was too ordinary and unattractive and demanded that the author give the book a new title. After several changes, the publishing house was still not satisfied, and in the end it supplied the title: *A 16-Year-Old Lad with a 40-Year-Old Woman.*[85]

The growing market orientation of book publishers has caused "serious" writers to withhold manuscripts and distorted the creative processes of the less serious (but still talented) writers who labor under the assumption that what they write must appeal to large audiences or it will not be published. In other words, quality writers "self-select" themselves out of the book market.[86] This fact is not necessarily problematic from the point of view of the central party-state, however, because good thought work is not necessarily equivalent to good writing. In fact, some would argue that the two are mutually exclusive. But it does mean that in today's climate of extreme money hunger China is much less likely to produce the kind of writer who could rescue the nation's higher culture from the lingering devastation of the Maoist propaganda state. And even if the society were to produce such a writer, he or she would find it very difficult to get published.

A much more serious problem than editors publishing books full of sex, violence, and feudal superstition is the proclivity of publishing houses to improve their balance sheets by selling book numbers. This phenomenon has contributed directly to the formation of what one informant called "the second channel" of book distribution: illegal and semilegal publication and circulation.[87] Although the flow through this second channel has been constricted since a crackdown on selling book numbers began on January 1, 1994 (see Chapter 6), it has not yet been choked off and still constitutes a serious, complex problem for the Chinese state in its efforts to control thought work.[88]

Book numbers are supplied by the SPPA in Beijing, which "creates" the numbers and distributes them through its provincial bureaus. Each number contains at least nine numerals and one or more letters. The first numeral—7, in the case of China—indicates the country of publication. The next three numerals indicate the particular (legal) publishing house. The following five numerals indicate the specific book title. Finally, a combination of one or more letters and numerals indicates the type of book (economics, language, etc.)[89]

Each year, the publishing house sketches out a plan of the books it proposes to publish during the forthcoming year—usually by type, rather than by specific title.[90] On average, each editor publishes five books annually, so the publishing house can simply multiply by five the number of editors in its employ to estimate the number of books it will produce the following year. Before 1994, however, most publishing houses would overestimate this figure and formally submit a request to the provincial SPPA office for more book numbers than they actually needed.[91] There was no reason not to request additional book numbers because they were distributed free of charge and commanded a high price on the black market. As a result, from 1985 to 1994, the actual supply of book numbers in circulation increased by about 15 percent a year while the number of new legal titles published increased by only about 12 percent a year. Some 1,000 to 2,000 book numbers were therefore available for purchase by underground publishers each year.[92] But demand was even greater. The price of black-market book numbers increased an estimated 600 percent from 1990 to 1995.[93] In late 1993, on the eve of the crackdown, book numbers sold for, on average, 8,000 yuan to 50,000 yuan (U.S.$961–$6,009); the variation depended on the riskiness of the proposed publication and its potential for commercial success.[94]

Obviously, the larger publishing houses can significantly increase their revenues by selling a few dozen book numbers each year, a very important consideration now that most of them enjoy extensive economic property rights to house income. In many cases, individual editors can also secure a cut—though apparently not in as formalized a manner as the commissions distributed to broadcast journalists for their efforts in selling soft advertising.

Publishing-house personnel make a careful distinction between selling book numbers outright and engaging in so-called "cooperative publication." In the former case, an illegal publisher will approach either an editor or a higher-ranking publishing house executive with a straightforward request for an exchange: money for a book number. The publishing house may inquire as to the nature of the proposed publication as part of the process of bargaining over price, but otherwise does not concern itself with the final, published product. This violates the publishing house's responsibility as a *shiye* to censor books so that they promote the building of a socialist spiritual civilization or, at the very least, do not violate thought-work proscriptions.

Publishing houses at lower levels in the administrative hierarchy and/or in poorer regions are more likely to engage in the outright selling of book numbers than those closer to the capital or those less desperate. The reason is straightforward: They face strong incentives to make money but can only service populations too poor to buy large numbers of books.

But even higher-level, prestigious book publishers engage widely in "cooperative publication"—though they became somewhat less likely to do so after the crackdown began. In cooperative publication, the publisher takes an active interest in the book project beyond calculating its riskiness and marketability. Typically, the project begins when an author approaches an editor or someone higher-ranking in the publishing house. The author proposes that the house publish the author's book in exchange for the author sharing—or assuming all of—the risk that the book will fail commercially. The author has probably already been turned down by one or more publishers as a result of calculations that the manuscript is either too politically dangerous or is likely to flop commercially. Faced with this situation, the frustrated author does not opt to publish independently, because market entry into the publishing business is controlled by the state and is (formally, at least) highly restricted. The author therefore has no choice but to cooperate with an established publishing house. By selling the book number, the house in turn can ensure itself a basic income from the book. It may then adopt one of several formulas for sharing the responsibility for market failure and the potential benefits of market success, depending on the specific case. But, always, the author assumes more risk than if the house were to publish the book on its own.

The most important players in the illegal publication game are enormous, sophisticated, transprovincial organizations that link illegal publishers with illegal dealers in sprawling, underground networks. The China News Agency described one such organization uprooted in late 1991:

> China recently cracked a large illegal publishing group whose influence had covered 85 counties and cities in 27 provinces, municipalities, and autonomous regions all over the country. A total of 257 units had participated in the related illegal publishing, printing, distributing, and selling. . . . The offenders looked for backers and collaborated with those in legitimate publishing units. . . . Preliminary investigation shows that this group has published 230 illegal publications and printed 1.298 million copies.[95]

Similarly, as Wen Jinhai explains:

> Illegal publishing activities have gradually developed into [large] underground organizations. Such an organization has a clear division of labor. . . . There are many large book dealers controlling underground publishing and marketing across the nation. These dealers hold regular meetings to exchange publishing information, divide territory, and resolve economic disputes. . . . Some live in high-class hotels all year round and

use advanced communications equipment to exercise remote control over underground publishing activities in all localities.[96]

A good example of such a dealer—or "book king," to use Orville Schell's term—is 29-year-old Wang Shuxiang of Hubei province. Wang was sentenced to "death with two years probation" on April 13, 1993, for illegally buying and selling more than twenty book numbers and printing and distributing more than 1.8 million copies of publications with titles like *A Dark Massage House*, *Sex Desires*, and *Elementary Course of Marriage*. On the same date, 40-year-old Li Dasheng was sentenced to twelve years in prison for purchasing book numbers to print and distribute 600,000 copies of publications such as *Sex Swindling Cases*, *A Flesh Deal*, and *The Crazy Bastard*. Both men had made small fortunes in the process of undermining the socialist spiritual civilization, but both constituted only the tip of the proverbial iceberg.[97]

Not all illegal publications are as salacious as *The Crazy Bastard* and the others. Underground publishers frequently copy and reprint legal, above-board publications whose popularity ensures high sales. Undoubtedly the most daring such theft occurred in connection with *My Father, Deng Xiaoping*, the biography of China's senior leader written by Deng Rong, his daughter, and published in September 1993 by the Central Party Literature Publishing House. By February 1994, seven different pirated versions of the book (requiring seven stolen or purchased book numbers) had been discovered, totaling 100,000 illegal copies. The magnitude of the problem of stolen book numbers becomes especially clear when even the daughter of the dictator is victimized.[98]

In December 1991 Liu Zhongde—the deputy director of the Party Propaganda Department and chief antipornography czar—listed several reasons for the flourishing of illegal publications.[99] First, "hostile forces at home and abroad" were pursuing a "peaceful evolution" in China—a de rigueur assertion before Deng's trip to the south in January/February 1992, and current again after Taiwan president Lee Teng-hui's trip to the United States in June 1995. Second, some localities and departments failed fully to grasp the corrosive effects of illegal publications on the socialist spiritual civilization and therefore underestimated the significance of the problem. Third, and relatedly, laws were not being strictly enforced and criminals were being given light sentences.[100] The first three explanations are important, but obvious. The two that follow are much more interesting. But before turning to the final two explanations, it is important to understand the motivations of the printers and distributors, who along with the publishers, constitute integral components of this particular manifestation of thought-work commercialization.

Liu himself revealed that in December 1991 there were nearly 60,000 printing establishments throughout China and only 4,478 (7.5 percent) of them had licenses.[101] The reason there are so many unlicensed printing establishments is that, during the days of the Maoist propaganda state, all party organizations at the prefectural level and above, all of the larger state-run enterprises, and many other organizations were given printing presses and were assigned print workers to produce internal propaganda journals.[102] Beginning in the early 1980s, the many producers of all this printing equipment were suddenly presented with new economic incentives to market and sell as much of it as possible. As a result, supply increased, prices fell, and organizations all the way down to the township level became capable of purchasing it. As early as 1987, township-level printing establishments were implicated in the spread of bourgeois-liberal ideas in the period preceding the December 1986 antigovernment demonstrations. Intoned the *Guangming Ribao*:

> When accepting the orders for printing illegal publications, some township printing houses were merely indulging in seeking "good economic results," or making handsome profits. In fact, they have caused spiritual pollution in our society. . . . The publishing administration departments at all levels should strengthen their management over township printing houses and bring their business under better control. The industry and commerce administration departments and the public security departments at all levels should also make contributions to this work.[103]

But these admonitions failed, and the reason is Liu Zhongde's fourth cause of the problem of illegal publication and distribution: "Economically, the criminals reap colossal profits from speculation and profiteering in illegal publications and [they] use the large amount of money in their control to bribe state functionaries, corrupt cadres, and get them into trouble."[104]

Relatedly, as Wen Jinhai explains, "Once established, a printing house has to pay a certain amount of profit and taxes to the local government. Because of this, the rise and fall of printing houses has a bearing on local economic interests and even on the stability of the local area. Investigating and punishing illegal publications can easily get one sucked into the whirlpool of local protectionism."[105]

At the township level, local government/business elites have developed a fused financial interest in violating the central-state's thought-work goals. Because local administration is several bureaucratic steps removed from Beijing, the central government finds it very difficult to prevent these activities. In the words of one informant, the Center "can control the provincial capitals, but not the places below."[106] This informant argues that the problem is not necessarily that the state is inherently weaker than it was before the mid-1980s—at least, not in absolute terms—but rather that, before the introduction of economic reform, lower-level government officials faced no incentive to violate thought-work goals. Even if effective demand for salacious, illegal publications had existed, there were very few consumer goods to purchase with the resulting profits. By the mid-1990s the situation was far different.

Liu Zhongde alludes to the state capacity issue in his fifth and final explanation of the problem: "Administration has not kept pace with events. Some administrative stipulations have not been implemented properly, and relevant provisions have not been drafted in time when new problems have emerged, providing opportunities for unlawful book merchants."[107]

In this view, the state's coercive apparatus has simply failed to adapt to the rapid societal changes engendered by reform. On the one hand, the efforts that have been made have been undermined by corruption; on the other hand, numerous unanticipated, complex new problems have arisen to which the state has simply failed to generate a coherent response. The result is a loss of central state control over the myriad activities surrounding the production of printed thought work.

In principle, even if the state cannot prevent publishers from selling book numbers or township (and other) printing houses from reproducing illegal publications, it might still be able to prevent retail outlets from selling spiritually polluting materials to the public. The problem here is that the country is now flooded with numerous, legal private and collective book-selling establishments—a reflection of the intentional breakup of the Xinhua Bookstore's nationwide monopoly over book distribution. Many of these private and collective outlets are perfectly willing to supply the populace with spiritual pollution if the price is right.

Immediately following the Fourteenth Party Congress in October 1992, Song Muwen, then the director of the SPPA, "unveiled" an important reform in book distribution to be implemented in 1993. In addition to the Xinhua Bookstore, "other state-run and collective-run bookstores will also have the right to deal with wholesale and retail sales."[108] In fact, Song was only sanctioning a trend that had begun as early as the mid-1980s and by 1993 was already well entrenched. In 1980 various central government agencies responsible for managing the publishing industry had begun issuing a series of documents designed to break up the Xinhua Bookstore's monopoly on distribution. Xinhua was felt to be unresponsive to a pluralizing society's rapidly expanding demand for more varied sources of information.[109]

In December 1991 Liu Zhongde estimated that the distribution reforms had already resulted in the establishment of about 40,000 collective and private bookstores nationwide;[110] by 1997, another source put the figure at 110,000. Some 42 percent of the 260,000 book retailers in operation in China were privately owned.[111] Collective and private stores tend to be much smaller in scale than the Xinhua outlets—sometimes, in fact, they are little more than blankets spread out on sidewalks—but their proclivity to respond quickly to consumer demand with a friendly attitude had resulted in their securing an estimated 50 percent of the national urban retail sales market by 1995.[112]

Everyone interviewed for this study agreed that private and collective bookstores are responsible for the vast majority of sales of illegal publications. Although in principle these stores must obtain licenses from the MoC and SAIC systems, which periodically inspect them to make certain they are not dealing in pornography or other contraband, only rarely do the stores have party committees, nor are they centralized in a nationwide network like the Xinhua Bookstore. Their only concern is to maximize profits while staying out of trouble, not to build a socialist spiritual civilization. They are not components of the propaganda—or any other—xitong. They are willing to buy cheaply reproduced pirated works, pornography, and other illegal items from underground publishers because the low cost of reproduction in the township printing plants means their purchasing price is low—a key consideration for enterprises facing hard budget constraints. At the same time, the private and collective stores can charge relatively high prices for these materials on the open market—also a key consideration, because the retail outlets assume most of the risk of getting caught, and they are the ones who must pay bribes to inspectors from the MoC system, the police, and other agencies to stay in business. Obviously these costs are, at present, acceptably low, because the money to be made from specializing in the private sale of illegal publications has attracted tens of thousands of Chinese citizens into this line of work.[113]

The similar problem of illegal publication, reproduction, and distribution of computer software, videotapes, audiotapes, and compact discs has also been fueled by the rise of private and collective distribution outlets. The Xinhua Bookstores' old monopoly on distribution had also covered vinyl recordings, but no organization ever monopolized the distribution of computer software, tapes, and CDs because these technologies were not disseminated in China until well after the Xinhua monopoly had disintegrated.[114] Because most of the pirated tapes and CDs of concern to the central party-state originate abroad, detailed discussion of this topic is reserved for Chapter 4.[115] It is true, however, that a great many of the karaoke bars and MTVs where pirated tapes and CDs are shown or played are collectively and privately owned. The main point to emphasize here is the close relationship between thought-work globalization and domestic commercialization. Both result partly from administrative fragmentation and property-rights reform, which present duplicators, distributors, and the owners of public entertainment establishments with strong incentives and opportunities to supply the public with the tapes and CDs—the advanced technologies—they demand.

Commercialization in the Film Industry

As a result of reforms introduced in the 1980s and 1990s, film studios, film distribution companies, and individual theaters are all (with a few exceptions) now responsible for profits and losses. They therefore hold effective economic property rights to unit income and face strong incentives to produce, distribute, and show films likely to enjoy high audience appeal. Many film projects are now financed with capital from other Chinese units and from foreigners; a few theaters are also privately owned.[116] As in the case of television, radio, and print, the frequent result is film content that is at odds with state strictures against spiritual pollution and bourgeois liberalization, and very little sense of a mission to build a socialist spiritual civilization.

The incentive to cater to the market can be isolated in the division of property rights among studios, distributors, and theaters. There are three main formulas for the distribution of these rights:

1. The studio grants the distribution company complete rights to sell a film within its region in exchange for a fixed percentage of the film's box-office proceeds.

2. The studio sells the film to the distribution company in exchange for a flat sum of money.

3. The studio sells the film to the distribution company for a flat sum but earns an additional percentage if the distribution company makes a profit. If the distribution company suffers losses, the studio must compensate it accordingly.[117]

Obviously, the studio both enjoys greater rights and assumes greater risks in the first formula, while the distribution company takes the most chances and reaps the most (potential) benefits in the second formula. Rights and risks are more equally shared in the third formula, and for that reason it is now the most popular method in use and is considered likely to become the industry standard. The result is that, whereas before reform neither the studios nor the centralized film distribution company ever cared a whit about a film's potential commercial success, everyone now cares very much indeed: "The customer is God," just as in the case of other media products.

This ethos is expressed straightforwardly and unabashedly by film directors and studio directors. Although film scripts may originate with independent scriptwriters, directors (who actually head large departments), or in-house studio scriptwriting divisions, "whether or not the film will be shot depends, in the first instance, on marketing potential, and only second on artistic value."[118] In a large studio, the writers, directors, and marketing departments all work very closely on a project from the start to ensure that there are no commercial flops among the twenty or so films the studio will shoot each year. Two or three flops can mean financial disaster and reduced consumption for everyone involved. The result is a tendency to fall back on reliable formulas, most of which emphasize sex, violence, and feudal superstition. Few films shown domestically take on politically sensitive issues directly; such films are usually shown only abroad, most notably at international film festivals. But the vast flood of popularistic, "vulgar" films that now inundate China's theaters underscores dramatically the degree to which reform in the film industry has transferred effective—if indirect— power over film content from the state to society.

There is a final manifestation of this phenomenon that should be mentioned. Most individual directors and their entourages now spend only about 40 percent of their working time producing films for the studios to which they "belong."[119] After fulfilling their quotas, directors produce television series, advertisements, and music videos—all of which can earn the directors and their staffs a great deal of money on the side. Precisely how much money varies widely from director to director, but all now hold extensive economic property rights to their own talents and labor, rights over which the state had exercised near-total control before reform. Some of the projects on which directors now spend their "spare time" working are enormous, expensive undertakings, mobilizing talent nationwide. Some even involve cooperation with Hong Kong and/or foreign media companies. The result is yet another avenue by which economic incentives contribute importantly to thought-work commercialization.

The Commercial Side of "Edgeball" Journalism

In the years leading up to the political crisis of 1989, journalists, writers, and other intellectuals were politically engaged and active in pursuing press and publication reforms. But in the years following the 1989 repression, as opportunities to make money multiplied in the booming economy, thousands of journalists and other media personnel abandoned their idealism and "jumped into the sea" of commerce by selling paid news and soft advertising and/or creating media content that appealed primarily to "vulgar" tastes. Today, neither idealistic intellectuals nor statist bureaucrats are satisfied. Thought work is being used in China neither to prepare the ground for a liberal democracy nor to build a socialist spiritual civilization. The public sphere is praetorian.

This picture, though generally accurate, must be modified in two key respects. First, even a casual reading of mainstream Chinese newspapers or a casual viewing of central and provincial television news programs makes clear that, despite the dominant trend, there remain in China numerous journalists who are seriously committed to exposing the country's deep-rooted social problems in an engaging way without, at the same time, deploying hackneyed communist jargon. The myriad issues these journalists take up range from police corruption, industrial pollution, and abuse of migrant workers to the beating of doctors and nurses whose services fail to save patients. This kind of journalism may well be setting the stage for the eventual development of a liberal public sphere, although its practitioners at present constitute only a minority of Chinese thought workers and the institutional setting in which they work is far from supportive.

Second, and much more immediately threatening to the central party-state, is the rise in the aftermath of the Fourteenth Party Congress (October 1992) of so-called "edgeball" journalism.[120] The exiled journalist Zhang Weiguo first described this phenomenon in a report for the Hong Kong publication *Pai Hsing* in March 1993: "Mainland journalists are now initiating a new process of a conscious, courageous, energetic, and ingenious fight for a larger margin of journalistic freedom. . . . The government also seems to be gradually relaxing its high pressure, and reporters and editors who have grown up in the fight against that high pressure have, on the whole, almost regained, or even exceeded, the 1988 level."[121]

Journalists at Shanghai's *Xinmin Wanbao*—a nationally circulated, highly popular "evening paper"—are among the most active and skilled practitioners of edgeball journalism. During the spring and summer of 1993, among other moves, they (1) published a series of stories on the Yang Shangkun family, whose efforts to usurp central leadership positions were quashed by Deng Xiaoping at the Fourteenth Party Congress; (2) revealed an important internal speech by Shanghai mayor Huang Ju before receiving authorization; and (3) gleefully reported Tiananmen dissident Wang Dan's early release from prison in 1993.[122] Similarly, in April 1993, the Xi'an paper *Shengcai yu Shenghuo* (Fortune and life) published an article commemorating Hu Yaobang, the relatively liberal Communist Party leader whose death in April 1989 sparked the Tiananmen demonstrations.[123]

Edgeball journalism did not long escape the attention of senior propaganda commissars in Beijing, who made it a key target of their multifaceted crackdown on heterodoxy that began in August 1993. Minister of Propaganda Ding Guan'gen himself attacked edgeball book publication in a speech made during the autumn of 1993. His comments suggest a keen understanding of how the "game" is played:

> Most typical are biographies that eulogize the deeds of Comrade Xiaoping or other proletarian revolutionaries of the older generation. On the surface, nothing seems to be wrong with them, but on looking closer, we can see that the authors may be using the "April 5th Movement" of 1976 as a foil for the political disturbances of 1989, or criticizing the "Gang of Four" antiparty clique on the surface while actually totally negating and censuring the way our party handled the 1989 disturbances.[124]

Of course, allegorical criticism has long played an important role in the Chinese political process, particularly during the Communist period. What makes post-Fourteenth Party Congress edgeball journalism different from, say, Wu Han's veiled criticisms of Mao on the eve of the Cultural Revolution, is the fact that now such daring criticism is thought to sell books and newspapers, and that is one of the key motivations for publishing it. No less an authority than Ding Guan'gen himself acknowledged at the beginning of the omnidirectional crackdown that advertising publications as "politically extremely sensitive" helps publishers increase sales.[125] Thus, among the books discovered and banned in connection with the 1994 anti-pornography campaign were at least three titles of a "reactionary" nature: *4 June Poems*, *Deng Xiaoping and His Secret Empire*, and *Mao Zedong and His Women*.[126]

The powerful incentives to make money introduced with the 1980s' reforms had by the 1990s begun interacting with the tradition of allegorical and indirect political criticism to produce the politically corrosive phenomenon of edgeball journalism. People enjoy reading it, apparently because of the thrill of being privy to inside information, and journalists enjoy writing it, because it allows them to play an exciting role in politics. Politically conscious journalists can therefore harmonize their interests with money-minded media outlet managers. The only loser is the central party-state.

Telecommunications and Thought-Work "Societalization"

To a much greater extent than the mass media, telecommunications are inherently "societalizing" in their implications for thought work because they directly transfer from the state to individuals and groups in society the power to initiate, send, and receive messages. Anyone with access to the telecommunications network can formulate a message and send it to anyone else on the network, in the form of phone calls, faxes, or e-mail. As discussed in Chapter 2, the number of Chinese citizens enjoying network access is increasing at an unprecedentedly rapid rate, with each household, on average, expected to own a telephone by the year 2020. Continuing advances in technology have expanded the volume and variety of information that can be transmitted on the network, while expansion of the use of optical fiber (which emits very little radiation) and automatic switching equipment makes the network very difficult for the Chinese state to police.

Even more than the mass media, the telecommunications industry has, since the early 1990s, witnessed a legal, if still limited, effective privatization. This has been fueled by both the deep decentralization of the Ministry of Posts and Telecommunications (MPT) xitong and the mushrooming demand for horizontal telecommunications capability spawned by the spread of the market economy. The "Provisional Arrangements for Approval and Regulation of Decentralized Telecommunications Services" promulgated by the State Council on November 1, 1993, explicitly permit numerous state-owned and collective-owned enterprises to offer the public telecommunications services, provided the enterprises first obtain a license from the MPT and comply with a list of not especially restrictive requirements.[127] As discussed in Chapter 5,

Liantong and Jitong—the two major alternative service providers to China Telecom, the MPT provider, are state-owned firms—but firms whose higher-ranking personnel (in particular) enjoy significant economic property rights to firm income. What is especially noteworthy about the November 1993 "Arrangements" is that "collective" firms are also explicitly permitted to enter into the telecommunications business, and "collective" is often a euphemism for "private."

Only China Telecom, Liantong, and Jitong are permitted to supply the public with basic telecommunications services. Collective and private firms concentrate on specialized services such as mobile cellular, paging, on-line information, and VSATs.[128] So many of these firms had entered the telecommunications market by the spring of 1993 that the State Radio Regulatory Commission (SRRC)—the body charged with managing the electromagnetic spectrum—was forced by signal-interference problems to step in and more rigorously regulate the assignment of spectrum space.[129]

In 1993 it took only about 1 million yuan (U.S.$120,187) to set up a paging station servicing 1,000 subscribers, an initial investment that could be recouped in a year.[130] As a result, an enormous array of companies entered the paging and mobile cellular markets, usually in alliance with territorial-level government bodies, and some supplied their customers not only with notifications of phone calls but also with news and "information with a sensual or superstitious flavor."[131] Other companies, meanwhile, began offering a large variety of on-line information that included everything from pornography to weather forecasts, a "burst of value-added services" thought by multinational telecommunications analysts to be on the verge of takeoff into exceptionally rapid growth by 1995.[132] About 1,000 VSAT networks were in operation by mid-1993, a figure expected to increase tenfold by the year 2000.[133] Some twenty MPT-licensed domestic companies supplied VSAT services in 1995, and the number was projected to grow to several hundred by century's end.[134]

Meanwhile, a radical decentralization of decision-making authority within the MPT system (discussed in Chapter 5) has resulted in territorial-level telecommunications bureaus-cum-operators securing extensive economic property rights to their units' income. Reforms introduced in the 1980s allowed the territorial-level bureaus to retain up to 90 percent of after-tax profits.[135] Except in poorer regions, it was not especially difficult to make a profit providing telecommunications service because demand was strong and the local bureau enjoyed a monopoly. Between 1989 and 1993, the price for local telephone service increased 30 to 100 percent nationwide, with the variation attributable to the fact that the MPT in Beijing had lost the ability to prevent some of the subunits of its xitong from engaging in predatory pricing.[136] Installation fees ranged from 2,000 yuan to 6,000 yuan (U.S.$240–$721),[137] and the wait for a phone ranged from six months to a year.[138] The installation fee was paid upon application, so the telecommunications bureau earned interest on the subscriber's prepaid fee for up to a year before the subscriber was hooked into the network.[139] The only way to speed up the process was to pay a bribe.[140] All of this meant strong incentives to supply the public with telecommunications services, regardless of the consequences for state control over thought work.

Now that Liantong and Jitong have officially begun operations, the telecommunications bureaus no longer enjoy monopolies on long-distance and value-added services, but they do still retain one very important competitive advantage: They continue to combine the functions of regulator and operator in one agency. Because even Liantong and Jitong must secure the local telecommunications bureaus' approval to access the public network—and because the myriad array of other telecommunications service providers must secure similar approval for their operations—there are obviously serious conflicts of interest. The MPT system has been under enormous pressure since the early 1990s to "separate regulation from enterprise" (*zhengqi fenkai*), with the Ministry of Electronics Industry (MEI) and possibly the People's Liberation Army (PLA) applying the bulk of the pressure.

The MPT's response has been to separate regulation from enterprise in form but not in fact. In 1994 the MPT spun off one of its divisions— the Directorate General of Telecommunications (DGT)—as a "financially independent enterprise-bureau."[141] In other words, the functions that were supposed to be split—enterprise and bureau—were actually combined, with an oxymoronic new term coined to describe the organization: *qiyeju*. The organization was given the English name "China Telecom" and was even supplied with a fancy logo that looked suspiciously like the AT&T logo. Few were fooled by this move, and the MPT xitong continues (as of this writing) to resist separating regulation from operation, instead concentrating on making money—as well as, of course, building China's telecommunications infrastructure. The big winners of the MPT's successes are not only the xitong personnel who can increase their material consumption, but also Chinese society, whose members secure from the state a significantly greater measure of power in originating, sending, and receiving all manner of communications messages.

Radio-Television "Hotline" Programs: The Birth of a Liberal Public Sphere?

One of the most important developments in Chinese thought work since the Fourteenth Party Congress is the combination of mass media and telecommunications in the form of numerous—by now virtually ubiquitous—radio and television "hotline" programs, on which listeners with access to telephones can ask questions and offer opinions. Guangdong's Zhujiang Radio carried the first regular hotline program when it began broadcasting in December 1986. For the next few years, most of the topics discussed on hotline shows nationwide concerned the arts and entertainment, not social issues—although there was some serious attention given to inflation during 1988. Until 1992, political pressures deterred listeners from raising politically sensitive issues, and too few people had access to telephones for call-in shows to become broad platforms for serious public discussion.

But a confluence of important forces caused this situation to change dramatically in the mid-1990s. Rapid development of the telecommunications system provided more and more individuals with the tools to participate. The political temperature was turned down in the wake of the Fourteenth Party Congress. The state continued to try rigorously to restrict media content—even launching the crackdown on heterodoxy in 1993—but in general the period after the Fourteenth Party Congress was significantly relaxed in a way that helped facilitate both the spread of hotline programming and the broadening of its content to include politically sensitive issues.

Now, however, it is questionable whether the central party-state could reverse itself and shut the programs down—at least without paying an enormous political price. The simple fact is that call-in programs are, like edgeball journalism, extremely popular, and as part of the commercialization trend have migrated throughout the radio-television industry. The Shanghai broadcasting authority established China's first specialized hotline station—the Oriental Radio Station—in the fall of 1992, but almost all stations at higher levels in the administrative hierarchy now "open the phones" frequently throughout the day in a bid to maintain high listenership. For example, in Guangdong, the Zhujiang Radio economic station's special hotline program, "Social Hot Topic," airs each morning, Monday through Saturday, from 7:30 to 8:30. The format is as follows: A specialist on some current, pressing issue speaks for about five minutes and then listeners are invited to call in with their comments. "Social Hot Topic" is extremely important to Guangdong Radio's financial health because some 44 percent of all Guangzhou adults listen to at least some of the program every day, and occasionally the broadcast reaches 60 percent of adults. This is in Guangzhou City alone; an unknown number of listeners from the surrounding suburbs also tune in. As a result, "Social Hot Topic" is a magnet for advertisers and serves also to increase listenership for Zhujiang Radio's other programs. All of Guangdong Radio's substations have hotline programs; on average, for all stations, the phones are open an amazing one-third of the broadcast day.[142]

While the topics discussed cover everything from public health to job hunting to the lives of singers and actors, they seem to be growing steadily more political.[143] This is evident from the translations of Guangdong programs supplied periodically by the United States Foreign Broadcast Information Service (FBIS). During the week of July 4–10, 1993, for example, callers to Zhujiang Radio's "Social Hot Topic" program raised the following politically and socially sensitive issues (among others): discrimination against members of the floating population, discrimination in the workplace against non-party members, deluxe new housing projects designed exclusively for the rich, heavy military vehicles causing damage to city roads, police "fining people just for the sake of it," air pollution, and trafficking in women and children.[144] In December 1993 a Ms. Liu called to say that "she often comes across motorcades on highways around Baiyun Airport and, whenever such motorcades pass by, the police never fail to drive other road users out of the way. She says most motorcades are convoys for high-ranking government officials who claim to be servants of the people. She compares these motorcades to emperors' and senior mandarins' convoys in imperial China of the past."[145]

Some analysts speculate that China's call-in shows are on the verge of evolving into an electronic, liberal public sphere, in which citizens critically discuss political and social problems in a serious way, generating a societal public opinion that state leaders must recognize as a legitimate and important input into the policymaking process. For example, noting that "the call-in and live-interview format has been getting listeners all across the country accustomed to the notion of open discussion," Schell suggests provocatively that "it is not difficult to imagine the role that such shows might play should some future wave of national protest sweep the country."[146] Relatedly, Zhang Xiaogang makes the important point that "the increasing availability of telephones has enabled listeners to raise anonymous questions" on the programs without fear of being traced by the authorities.[147]

The comments translated by FBIS make clear that call-in shows do sometimes broadcast critical comments remarkably similar in nature to what might be heard in the proverbial coffeehouses of the liberal public sphere. But no caller is ever permitted to voice opinions that violate the four cardinal principles. A two-line screening process prevents that from happening. The first line is an editor who answers the phones and discusses with callers what topics they propose to raise. Editors deem politics paramount in their calculations, though they are also concerned with expanding the variety of topics addressed so that listeners do not become bored and turn elsewhere. The second line is a seven-second electronic delay that allows engineers to cut off callers willing to lie to the editor. In most cases, it is true, callers are cut off, not because of the politically sensitive nature of their comments, but rather because "they are acting crazy, saying nonsensical things," and the like. Most callers know and respect the political limits and censor themselves. But the call-in show always has the option to censor.[148]

It therefore seems clear that, at present, China's call-in shows cannot be considered components of a liberal public sphere. Most of what they broadcast appears to be fluff, the listeners censor themselves or are censored by engineers, and the state reserves the right to shut the shows down completely should that prove "necessary," not acknowledging the shows' legitimacy as independent sources of public opinion. Thus, the MRFT specified in May 1994 that the social role of call-in program hosts is to "propagate the party's and government's principles, policies, and new measures and . . . dismiss the masses' misgivings, vent their feelings, enhance their confidence, and play a correct role in guiding public opinion."[149] Of course, the reason the MRFT felt the need to specify these responsibilities is precisely because sometimes the shows get out of hand. Their hosts do not always faithfully implement the state's thought-work goals, yet neither do they service an independent civil society. They reinforce public-sphere praetorianism, like most other components of the thought-work enterprise.

CHAPTER FOUR

The Globalization of Thought Work

Thought-work globalization is a special variant of commercialization that can be defined as the gradually increasing penetration of China's mass media and telecommunications networks by symbols originating from places outside Beijing's legal jurisdiction (this includes Hong Kong, which is administratively autonomous under Chinese sovereignty and of course quite distinct culturally). These symbols take many forms: Internet messages, faxes, shortwave radio broadcasts, television programs, films, videotapes, and even books and periodicals. Most originate in the United States, Hong Kong, and Taiwan, but an increasing number of other societies' media products also penetrate the Chinese symbolic environment now as the country becomes ever more tightly linked into the highly automated, worldwide communications web.

Just as in the case of thought-work commercialization, all three independent variables—administrative fragmentation, property-rights reform, and technological advance—contribute to thought-work globalization, but items of high technology (computers, modems, fax machines, satellite dishes, and videocassette recorders) play an especially prominent role in globalization processes. The simple reason is that externally originated communications messages must travel relatively great distances to reach China and therefore must first be made "transportable." Yet clearly administrative fragmentation and property-rights reform also contribute importantly to globalization, primarily because external messages are usually supplied to meet marketplace demands. Globalization in this sense is a variant of commercialization, but its effect is distinct. Chinese citizens enjoy increasing access to "alternative meaning systems" that can be used to challenge the domestically prevalent meaning systems, and in particular, the meaning systems that the central party-state seeks to promote.[1]

Telecommunications Globalization

The data presented in Chapter 2 suggest in a striking way the magnitude of thought-work globalization specifically via telecommunications since China's political crisis in the spring of 1989. Possibly the most important piece of data in this regard is the fifteenfold increase in long-distance telephone calls per capita—including transborder long-distance calls—between 1989 and 1996. By the end of 1993 residents of 876 Chinese cities could make direct-dial, automated calls to 198 countries and regions around the world, and the number of international direct-dial circuits increased to 24,000 from only 78 in 1978.[2] The majority of international calls and fax exchanges are probably aimed purely at facilitating economic cooperation among firms and firm subsidiaries in Guangdong and Hong Kong and in Fujian and Taiwan.[3] The central party-state, however, can do little to prevent its citizens from using telecommunications linkages to acquire politically propagandistic information from abroad, except in the case of suspect individuals specially targeted.[4]

This fact would likely become painfully clear to the Chinese authorities in the event of another political crisis. Many scholars and commentators attribute a strategically central role to fax technology in informing dissidents about the declaration of martial law in Beijing on May 21, 1989, and the Tiananmen massacre June 3–4.[5] As presented in Chapter 2, 2,600 fax machines were in use throughout China in 1989, a figure that increased at least five times by the end of 1993. All informants at multinational telecommunications firms agreed that the 12,276 fax machine figure for 1993 (the most recent year a figure was reported) vastly underestimated the true number of machines in use even at that early date, because a registration system the Center introduced in the aftermath of the 1989 crackdown disintegrated within a year. By the mid-1990s anyone could purchase a fax machine and simply plug it into a telephone jack.[6] Meanwhile, the number of fax messages sent increased by a staggering 2,300 percent between 1989 and 1996—from 240,000 to 5.6 million.

Another important development in the globalization of Chinese thought work—the political significance of which has yet to be tested—is the linking of the country to the Internet starting (in earnest) in October 1994. Worldwide, the number of computers—as distinguished from individual users—connected to the Internet increased 51 times between 1990 and 1995, from 130,000 to 6.64 million.[7] Except for a few dedicated linkages with research institutes in Europe and the United States, China was not an early participant in the rapid growth of the Internet.[8] Part of the problem was technological—there were simply too few computers in China to support early Internet access.[9] The other part was bureaucratic/political—the Ministry of Posts and Telecommunications (MPT) was struggling mightily to maintain control over computer networks and the value-added telecommunications services they would support in its ongoing turf battles with the Ministry of Electronics Industry (MEI).

In July 1993 the MPT unveiled Chinapac, the China Public Packet Switching Data Network, a computer-based network suitable for data transmission, e-mail, and other value-added services that initially linked 30 provincial capitals and the city of Chongqing, and reached more than 500 cities by late 1994. There were, at first, some 5,500 domestic Chinapac ports, and subscribers could (in theory) make connections to external networks through international gateways in Beijing and Guangzhou.[10] However, MPT subdivisions demanded exorbitant rates for access to the outside world. For example, the Beijing Telecommunications Authority charged U.S.$5,000 a month for a dedicated line linking Chinese subscribers to the Internet in the United States.[11] Not surprisingly, there were few takers: There were only 8,000 subscribers nationwide by late 1994.[12] Most of the multinational corporations leased their e-mail and data-transmission lines from foreign telecommunications providers.[13]

But in 1994 the MPT lost its monopoly over computerized telecommunications networks, and the door to the Internet opened wide. First, the State Council approved Jitong's proposed "Golden Bridge" project, which would include Internet access among its services. This immediately increased the pressure on the MPT. Second, the State Education Commission approved the creation of two academic networks: CERNET (the China Education and Research Network, based at Qinghua University) and CASNET (the Chinese Academy of Sciences Network). CERNET in particular is expected eventually to link hundreds of thousands of scholars and students at universities all over China with their counterparts in the outside world, including Hong Kong, Taiwan, and the United States.[14] CASNET duplicates CERNET in some respects, but its area of operation is limited to Beijing. Soon after its founding, Jitong revealed that one of its primary missions would be to merge CERNET with CASNET under the Golden Bridge, so that a unified second, larger network could be formed to counterbalance the MPT's Chinapac.[15]

Under the pressure of competition, the MPT began enthusiastically to promote the development of Internet usage via Chinapac in the second half of 1994. It signed an agreement with the U.S. telecommunications company Sprint on August 30 for access nodes to the Internet through Beijing and Shanghai. These nodes would be used not only by Chinapac, but also by CERNET and CASNET.[16] During the late fall and early winter, the technical term "Chinapac" was suppressed and replaced by "Chinanet" as the MPT developed a marketing plan to promote its own Internet service.[17] Initially this service would be available only in Beijing, and to stimulate interest, the Beijing Telecommunications Authority suspended a huge red banner on the front of its headquarters building with the word "INTERNET" written in large white letters. The first subscribers were granted free access during a promotional period beginning in February 1995, and by mid-April 400 Beijing individuals and units had opened accounts. By late June, when access spread to Shanghai and Guangzhou and the promotional period ended, more than 1,000 individuals and units had subscribed to the MPT's Internet service nationwide, with the number of regular users (including those on CERNET and CASNET) estimated at more than 40,000.[18]

By the end of 1995 MPT officials expected to have 10,000 Internet subscribers—both individuals and units—on Chinanet, concentrated in the cities of Beijing, Shanghai, Guangzhou, and Nanjing.[19] Factoring in CERNET and CASNET subscribers, Xinhua reported that some 40,000 units and individuals had secured access by August 1996.[20] But just a little more than a year later—in October 1997—the Ministry of Public Security (MPS) estimated that as many as 620,000 Chinese citizens had secured access to the Internet, with the number expected to reach 4 million by 2000—an astonishingly rapid rate of growth.[21] A key factor fueling this takeoff was increased computer sales. The 1 million computers sold in China in 1995 represented a 20 percent increase over 1994, and the annual increase was projected to rise to 40 or 50 percent from 1996 to 2000. About 10 million Chinese urban families were expected to own computers by the century's end.[22]

Management of the Internet, though fragmented horizontally, is centralized vertically in Beijing. That is, regardless of the service to which an individual or unit subscribes, approval must come from the relevant central agency in the capital. For example, potential Shanghai subscribers to Chinanet can submit applications in Shanghai, but must obtain approval from the Ministry of Information Industries (MII)—the successor to the MPT—in Beijing before receiving an account. This practice is consistent with the maintenance of MII authority over all transprovincial and international long-distance telecommunications. The primary function of the practice, however, is simply to route revenue to the MII, not to control the content of e-mail and other messages. The MII can deny accounts to suspected "bad elements," but once individuals and units secure accounts, the MII and other central agencies can no more easily monitor e-mail and Internet transmissions than they can monitor telephone calls and faxes.[23]

They cannot, for example, prevent Chinese people from reading *Tunnel* (*Suidao*), an electronic antiregime magazine established in the summer of 1997 by an anonymous organization of Chinese intellectuals living in the United States.[24] *Tunnel*'s mission is to use the Internet to undermine state control over specifically political thought work, and its editors hope that after they have tunneled enough wormholes into the dictatorial edifice, it will collapse. The editors both originate articles themselves and solicit articles from people living in the PRC who dare not publish their opinions inside China.[25] The editors compile these articles into files and send them via e-mail to *Tunnel* subscribers throughout China and the world, asking that they be downloaded, photocopied, faxed, and otherwise further distributed.

Hence, it seems likely that early in the 21st century, millions of Chinese citizens will be able to exchange text, images, and sound—some of it political and expressly antiregime—with interlocutors throughout the world. The globalization of thought work via integrated mass media and telecommunications will have advanced to a seriously troubling state from the point of view of the propaganda commissars in Beijing. Whether it will contribute to the formation of a liberal public sphere or merely reinforce public-sphere praetorianism remains to be seen.

The Legal and Semilegal Importation of Television Programs

By the mid-1980s the growing gap between audience demand and China's own television production capabilities had forced the nation's numerous new television stations to turn to the international market to buy or otherwise acquire programming—first legally and eventually not so legally. The stations were also positively motivated to acquire externally produced programming because its popularity guarantees large audiences whose attention can be sold to advertisers—the crux of the connection between thought-work commercialization and globalization. American and Hong Kong producers dominate the international market for television because of early entry and longstanding comparative advantage; as a result, by the early 1990s Chinese airwaves had become inundated with American and Hong Kong films and teleplays. One Ministry of Radio, Film, and Television (MRFT) survey conducted in October 1993 found that fully 74 percent of television programs broadcast at the provincial level and below originated abroad.[26]

More than a few Chinese leaders and thinkers are unhappy with this situation. Consider the words of Marxist theorist Liu Renwei, writing colorfully in the authoritative *Qiushi* in March 1996:

> [Western] mass media dump their cultural products in an explosive manner so that the sky of the Third World is shrouded in a pestilential atmosphere. Singing stars, dance stars, movie stars, comic stars, and sexual stars are in a complete mess contending for vulgarity and striving for favor. Mysterious cases of murder, scandals of sexual stars, gothic fiction, legendary romance, punk rock and roll, and midnight film and

television shows all appear on the stage clamorously. The agile and fierce American cowboys, the affected English gentleman, the befuddled life of pleasure-seeking, the supercilious display of power and influence, the fairy tale of the ever existing Western Paradise . . . blot out the sky and land with their gloomy shadows.[27]

Despite the prevalence of such sentiments in high places, the central party-state's best efforts to prevent the influx of foreign television programs from completely escaping control have not been notably successful, precisely because of the contradictions presented by the combination of administrative fragmentation, property-rights reform, and technological advance.

The American Columbia Broadcasting System (CBS) established the typical pattern for Sino-foreign television exchanges in 1982 in a barter deal with Central China Television (CCTV). Under the terms of this agreement, CBS provided CCTV with 64 hours of programming (with programs that varied from *60 Minutes* to the *Tournament of Roses Parade*) in exchange for 320 minutes of commercial air time on CCTV.[28] The Chinese side would not, therefore, be forced to sacrifice scarce foreign-exchange reserves to acquire popular programming, nor would it have to incur the risks and headaches of program production. It would need only allow foreign suppliers a certain amount of advertising time on Chinese television. Very soon after, numerous American and Hong Kong companies entered the Chinese market on similar terms, and almost immediately they began evading the Center and dealing directly with provincial and municipal stations. From 1982 to 1986, for example, Shanghai Television imported more programs than did Central China Television. By 1991, while only 12 percent of CCTV's programs originated abroad, an estimated 25 percent of programs nationwide did, and foreign and Hong Kong shows were more apt to air at the provincial level and below during prime time, maximizing their potential social impact.[29]

Officially, only the Beijing, Shanghai, Guangdong, and Fujian provincial television stations are allowed to import directly from abroad without central oversight. Before the mid-1980s, almost all other lower-level stations complied with the central government's "requirement" that they obtain external programming only from CCTV's would-be monopolistic Import Distribution Company. Officially, the lower-level stations are still "encouraged" to import only through this constricted channel, but "almost none of them" do.[30] In principle, although lower-level stations (except the Beijing, Shanghai, Guangdong, and Fujian provincial stations) may negotiate with external providers directly, they are required to submit samples of the programs they would like to import to the General Bureau of Radio, Film, and Television's (GBRFT's) Social Management Department for approval before any deals are finalized.[31] But again, "almost no" stations follow this procedure. Why? Because "the stations' judgment matured, so they were granted more decision-making authority." That is the official answer.[32] But no source could point to a specific policy document that bestowed this authority upon the lower levels. What appears to have happened instead is that the lower-level stations—motivated by the desire to increase audience size and sell more advertising—simply took the authority, and Beijing lacked either the capacity or the will to recover it. The result is "a sense that Beijing's control is eroding."[33]

Informants confirmed that the Guangdong provincial television station enjoys full autonomy to import programs from abroad, without submitting samples to the GBRFT in advance. There are vaguely defined and weakly enforced limits, however, on both the number and content of foreign programs that may be imported, though precisely how these limits are enforced is unclear. Without revealing the exact figure, the Guangdong source acknowledged that the permitted number of imports "increases a little bit each year"—despite the Center's efforts begun in the summer of 1993 to reduce the proportion of television programs originating abroad.[34] In Yunnan, meanwhile, informants acknowledged that, on paper, the provincial station is not permitted to import programming directly from abroad, and that all imports must first be approved by the GBRFT. In reality, however, the GBRFT "trusts" Yunnan Television to make wise decisions, and rarely interferes. The only constraint on Yunnan Television that prevents it from directly importing more programs than it does is money. As explained in Chapter 3, Yunnan Television is forced to give a very large percentage of its profits to the provincial Bureau of Radio and Television; as a result, the station imports only the cheaper, second-rate programs, in addition to those supplied free by the U.S. and other embassies. However, it also airs a large number of foreign and Hong Kong programs acquired from the domestic exchange networks discussed in Chapter 5.[35]

In the early years, selling to Chinese stations was not profitable for foreign suppliers. Ad rates were low because audience sizes were small, and the incomes of those audiences were usually not sufficient to purchase foreign consumer goods. But after 1989, demand for foreign programming began to rise sharply as the spread of cable television increased the number of channels available to twelve to fifteen per city. Responding to the market signals, as many as 150 foreign and Hong Kong companies were actively competing to sell or barter programs to Chinese stations by the mid-1990s.

Each of the dozen or so notably successful ventures typically cultivates an informal, ephemeral network of 30 to 40 Chinese stations, to which it supplies a steady stream of programming with ads included. Unlike networks in the United States, these Chinese networks are highly unstable in composition; key personnel at the 30 to 40 member stations must constantly be kept "happy," meaning concretely that they must be paid individual compensation. The fact that the supplied programs do contain segments for local ad insertion and should attract large audiences is an insufficient incentive to hold the networks together.[36] At the same time, none of the stations can be trusted to carry the ads that foreigners sell, despite the fact that foreign-inserted ads usually amount to no more than 90 seconds per hour of programming, while the Chinese side might sell up to 8 1/2 minutes of advertising per hour. The foreign suppliers must therefore hire special Hong Kong–based monitoring firms to roam China, checking up on the network stations.[37]

A good example of a company well placed to become a dominant player in the China market is Hong Kong's Television Broadcasts International (TVBI). As the international arm of TVB—which caters exclusively to the domestic Hong Kong market—TVBI has access to an enormous stock of Chinese-language films and teleplays, and the company continues to churn out some 700 hours of new programming each year.[38] TVBI has been active in China since 1987, supplying programs to television stations and cable systems at all levels in the hierarchy.[39] Unlike most of the other big players, TVBI barters only about half the programs it exports to China; it licenses the other half to the Chinese stations in exchange for cash. (The stations must pay in U.S. dollars, increasing the incentive to sell ads to foreigners—another form of thought-work globalization.) The biggest markets are Guangdong, Shanghai, Nanjing, and Beijing—the markets with the richest populations. Each year, TVBI supplies its Chinese buyers with an increased number of hours of programming, although informants were unable or unwilling to provide precise data. Like other companies, TVBI must constantly contend with purchasing stations that delete TVBI-sold ads to insert locally sold ads. And like other companies, although TVBI does not sell directly to the domestic Chinese exchange networks, it must monitor the domestic exchanges that take place to guard against TVBI-owned programs being pirated or resold.[40]

The company's provincial- and municipal-level partners provide TVBI and Hong Kong and other foreign suppliers with guidelines to what sorts of programs would be undesirable. Programs with excessive sex, violence, and/or destabilizing political ramifications should obviously be avoided—though it is not always clear to the Hong Kong program providers where the lines are to be drawn. Although historical dramas are enormously popular in Hong Kong and Taiwan, Beijing bans the importation of dramas that might exacerbate interethnic group tensions, such as those which depict Manchus or Central Asians in a poor light. Some of this material does, however, slip through, despite strenuous efforts by the external suppliers not to offend. (They almost always provide the Chinese side with preview tapes first.) Other programs are considered undesirable, not because of central-state concerns, but because Chinese audiences simply do not enjoy watching them. Into this category would fall horror movies, science fiction, American westerns, and programs that deal with adolescent romance. Also in this category are films or teleplays with extremely bitter plots: "They've been through a lot there," one source sighed.[41]

Especially in recent years, Hong Kong–based companies have entered China to engage in the coproduction of films and teleplays with various mainland counterparts.[42] From this trade, Hong Kong companies gain access to scenery and architecture not available in a semi-Westernized city-state, while the Chinese side learns the latest production techniques. There are two main types of coproduction. In the first type both the Chinese and the Hong Kong side put up some of the resources to create a product that will air both inside China and abroad. In this type of coproduction the Chinese side owns the rights to the programs when they air in China, and the Hong Kong side owns the rights when they air abroad. In the second type of coproduction foreigners simply hire Chinese actors and other personnel and use Chinese facilities, but the resulting film or teleplay will circulate only outside China. The Chinese side will be compensated for its contributions, but will not hold any rights to the programs produced. This second type of coproduction tends to predominate. In either case, central approval is not needed for Hong Kong firms to engage in coproduction, though it is required for purely foreign firms to coproduce in China.[43]

Except for short-term arrangements, no foreign or Hong Kong firm is permitted on paper to own or operate any share of any component of the Chinese public communications system, including television production facilities.[44] But one Hong Kong firm whose representative insisted on anonymity has succeeded in establishing a joint venture with "a Guangzhou government body" to produce programming and develop its own network within China—something nominally illegal.[45] A special relationship between the Hong Kong firm and the People's Liberation Army (PLA) facilitated this apparently unprecedented arrangement—which was approved by the MRFT in August 1994.

The "X Network" (a pseudonym) produces programming within the safe confines of a PLA base in Guangzhou. In exchange for political and possibly even physical protection, the X Network funds and manages a school on the grounds of the compound where high-level PLA officers learn military doctrine. The source would not comment on whether the PLA (or a section of it) also derives direct pecuniary benefits from the network; nor would he comment on exactly how this unusual arrangement was made. He did say that within the joint venture there is no party organization and no representative of the party's propaganda apparatus—not entirely unusual in joint ventures—but that a member of the Guangdong Provincial People's Congress does sit on the X Network's board of directors. Beyond proudly showing off photographs of the well-equipped studio in a military compound surrounded by high walls topped with barbed wire, the source would only say that the PLA connection "has been a big help."[46]

By May 1995 the X Network—then only nine months old—already had fifteen member stations located mostly in the "first and second tier" municipal markets of Beijing, Shanghai, Tianjin, Nanjing, and so on. By the end of 1995 the Network hoped to have 25 member stations. Its long-term goal was 60 to 80 stations. The larger the number of member stations, the more difficult it is to monitor broadcasts—an essential fact that assuages the concerns of advertisers who fear that member stations will block out their expensive commercials. It also becomes difficult to establish orderly marketing arrangements after the number of member stations exceeds about 80—naturally, each station wants a monopoly on the Network's programs within its region. Additionally, the commercial power of potential audiences begins to fall off markedly after the top 80 markets are penetrated. Few foreign advertisers expect to sell substantial amounts of their consumer products in China's poorer border and mountainous regions.[47] Of course, pirated copies of the X Network's programs may end up being broadcast in some of the poorer regions, facilitating the spread of thought-work globalization China-wide. However, from the perspective of the X Network, this is not a serious problem as long as the big-market stations are purchasing its programs and airing them with the ads included.

It is perhaps not surprising that the X Network chose to establish its headquarters in Guangzhou. This liberal, prosperous, commercial metropolis located just a short drive from Hong Kong enjoys a unique status in the globalization of Chinese thought work—evidence that there is some regional variation in declining central control, even if from a larger perspective the phenomenon exists China-wide. Importantly, both the Guangzhou municipal and Guangdong provincial cable networks have full permission to retransmit Hong Kong television programs, including news programs—a privilege that no other system in China has. The justification for Guangzhou's special status is this: Since its residents can see Hong Kong television anyway, even with simple antennas, why not retransmit the programs at a higher technical quality, insert ads, and make money? Officially, cable systems north of Guangzhou (where Hong Kong signals cannot easily be picked up) are not permitted to retransmit Hong Kong television, but by all accounts they do it anyway. These smaller systems' managers can point to the fact that if the provincial cable network succeeds in linking the whole province—a policy initiative discussed in Chapter 6—then everyone in Guangdong will eventually have access to Hong Kong television. Why should the smaller systems refrain from providing the service a few years earlier?

One of the most important facts about the legal retransmission of Hong Kong television in Guangdong is that the Hong Kong television stations retransmit completely uncensored news programs from Taiwan several times a day. These and most of the Hong Kong news programs devote serious and unbiased attention to political and other developments in Taiwan and elsewhere around the world. Naturally, this presents a dilemma to the Guangdong radio and television authorities: How far should the globalization of manifestly political thought work be allowed to go? It appears obvious, awkward, and heavy-handed to block out Taiwan and Taiwan-related news, yet to allow such news to penetrate the PRC's symbolic environment could have seriously adverse political consequences.

Before May 1995, when Taiwan president Lee Teng-hui's controversial trip to Cornell University was announced, the Guangzhou municipal cable station always blocked out Taiwan and Taiwan-related news, while the provincial station only occasionally did. After that date, however, both cable stations began blocking out Taiwan-related news regularly. Whenever Taiwan news was about to be broadcast—or, more often, a few seconds into the story—color bars would suddenly appear across the screen and all would be silent until the offending story or broadcast had ended. This action was taken for Cantonese, Mandarin, and even English broadcasts. It points to the potential power, as discussed in Chapter 6, of the centralizing cable television networks to assist the central state in achieving its thought-work goals, at least in the limited sense of keeping out patently offensive news stories. Nothing is done to censor the other news, however, nor to block out the decidedly bourgeois-liberal and spiritually polluting films, teleplays, and variety shows that frequently can be seen on Hong Kong television.

With this one important exception, cross-border television news does not yet play a significant role in the globalization of Chinese thought work. The focus remains on meretricious entertainment, reinforcing public-sphere praetorianism. Although some stations at the provincial and subprovincial levels illegally retransmit some of the signals of the Cable News Network (CNN) and possibly other satellite news providers, most municipal and provincial stations rely on CCTV for international news.[48] In fact, there is little incentive to compete with CCTV to provide international news for the simple reason that most audience members, just like audiences in the United States, assertedly do not want to watch it.[49] CCTV provides international news in its role as a central-level *shiye* whose market is "guaranteed" by the requirement that all CCTV-1 broadcasts be retransmitted throughout China. CCTV obtains most of its international news copy from the Xinhua News Agency, but it also obtains some foreign news from its own bureaus in Hong Kong and Washington. Video comes from a variety of sources, including CNN and Reuters Television (formerly VISNEWS).[50] Because CCTV can carefully edit this tape, images seriously at odds with official proscriptions rarely enter China via this route.

But the reason lower-level stations face little incentive to supply the populace with international news is not because the central party-state is especially powerful, but because it is a money-losing proposition.[51] Administratively and technically, the lower-level stations could easily import foreign news from satellite and other sources, but they generally lack the economic incentive.[52]

Satellite Television

All of the companies currently supplying external television to China legally send their products into the country on tape, using private couriers. To date, none dares to use satellite facilities to transmit into China, not only because of the great sensitivity with which Beijing views satellite broadcasting, but also because it would be impossible to prevent nonsubscribers from stealing the programs off the air. The relevant satellite footprints cover all of China, so suppliers would have to encrypt their broadcasts and supply customers with decoders. It is possible they would also have to supply the authorities with decoders in exchange for permission to broadcast. This would give rise both to a greater likelihood that the authorities would find objectionable elements in the programs and to the danger that some of the authorities themselves might pirate external programs, particularly those authorities fused into close relationships with the television stations they macromanage. Another consideration is the high cost of broadcasting by satellite. To date, the major players in the broadcasting market are satisfied with videotape, but as giant entertainment companies like Disney and Time-Warner join Rupert Murdoch's News Corporation in attempting to penetrate the huge Chinese television market, satellite broadcasting might prevail.

Several satellite systems currently beam television programs into China. The most well known are Asiasat, PanAmSat, and—perhaps surprisingly—the mostly Chinese-owned Apstar. Asiasat's position on transborder broadcasts is representative: If a receiving country finds any of the content objectionable, then it is that country's responsibility to prevent its people from seeing it. Asiasat claims no responsibility— though it does require prospective customers both to reveal what they plan to broadcast before transmitting it and to keep out pornography. Until April 1994, Asiasat carried the BBC World Television News Service on its northern and southern beams for STAR-TV, and it continues to carry the BBC on its southern beam; but Asiasat never censored or blocked out any of the BBC's broadcasts. Technically, it would be a simple matter for Asiasat to shut down one transponder in a group of transponders should the Chinese government make the request. But as of this writing Beijing has never made such a request, reserving its pressure for STAR-TV, the primary program provider. It would be somewhat awkward for Beijing to complain about Asiasat—the state-owned China International Trust and Investment Corporation (CITIC) owns a large chunk of Asiasat's stock.

Moreover, several important Chinese organizations are Asiasat customers. This is perhaps not surprising, given that Asiasat targets China as the major market for its northern-beam services. In 1995 sixteen Chinese customers leasing 6 1/2 transponders constituted about half of Asiasat's overall customer base. These customers ranged from CCTV and China International Radio to telecommunications users such as *Renmin*

Ribao and the People's Bank of China. Asiasat also leases transponders to the Yunnan and Guizhou provincial television stations, ostensibly as a more efficient alternative to microwave transmissions in these mountainous regions.[53]

Following the explosion upon launch of Apstar-2 in January 1995, Apstar lost several customers, but Apstar-1—launched the previous summer—continued to provide transponders to several different external television providers whose signals Beijing might not wish the Chinese people to receive. These providers included CNN, Turner Network Television, Home Box Office, the Discovery Channel, Disney, and Reuters. This raises the question of a serious contradiction: How could a firm majority-owned by Chinese government bureaucracies act as a conduit for television programs (including news) that threaten to undermine efforts to build a socialist spiritual civilization, programs that inundate China with spiritual pollution and bourgeois liberalism? Apstar's response is staunchly to defend the right of the Chinese government to keep out unwanted broadcasts, but Apstar—like Asiasat—also points out that blocking unwanted broadcasts is the exclusive responsibility of the Chinese government, not of satellite companies: "We supply satellite services to our customers, period." Therefore, interactions with the party propaganda department or even the MRFT are "irrelevant." Reports that Apstar reserves the right to shut down transmissions of anything the Chinese government finds offensive are "a private matter between Apstar and our customers," and at any rate no such right had been exercised as of the spring of 1995.

The most well-known satellite television provider in Asia is STAR-TV, which in the mid-1990s leased its transponders exclusively from Asiasat. The STAR-Asiasat relationship has deep roots. Li Ka-shing, whose Hutchison-Whampoa group is one-third owner of Asiasat, founded STAR-TV shortly after the launch of Asiasat-1 in April 1990 and began transmitting one channel experimentally the following April. By December 1991 STAR-TV was offering five channels, 24 hours a day, on Asiasat-1's northern beam (targeted at China): (1) BBC World Television News (dropped in April 1994),[54] (2) MTV-Asia (also eventually dropped, but replaced with STAR's own Channel V music-video provider), (3) Prime Sports, (4) Star Plus (a family-oriented channel featuring American, British, and Australian films, talk shows, and other entertainment), and (5) the Phoenix Chinese Channel (featuring films and teleplays produced in the PRC, Hong Kong, and Taiwan). With the exception of Prime Sports, almost all of the programs on the other four channels were either originally filmed in Mandarin or subsequently dubbed into Mandarin; STAR-TV, unlike CNN and some of the more recent arrivals to Asia, does not have trouble attracting Chinese audiences because of a language barrier.[55]

Because of the attractiveness of the programming and the ease with which satellite dishes could be purchased, STAR-TV claimed in February 1993 that already 4.8 million Chinese homes—around 20 million people—could receive its signals.[56] Even though the 4.8-million figure represented only 3 percent of the television homes in China, many more people probably watched the STAR programs when they visited friends and relatives whose homes were equipped with satellite dishes. People with dishes were likely, of course, to be socially influential "opinion leaders" active in diffusing new worldviews, values, and action strategies derived from STAR-TV, particularly given that the telecommunications network was also developing quickly at this time.

In any event, audience size continued to expand rapidly. In the fall of 1993 STAR-TV commissioned Frank Small and Associates to conduct a survey of 22 Chinese provinces (in 12 of them, only major urban centers), which found 30.4 million homes (about 120 million people, some 10 percent of the population) capable of receiving STAR-TV, a sixfold increase in less than a year.[57] The breakdown by major cities is provided in Table 6. There seems to be a clear tendency for larger percentages of television homes to have access to STAR-TV the farther the region is from Beijing (the simple correlation is 0.552), and the more mountainous the region is (e.g., in the southwest). Residents of coastal regions do not seem to be more likely to have access to STAR-TV, nor do residents of richer regions (in the latter case, the correlation is -0.484). Mountainous terrain—which provides a good justification for installing satellite dishes—seems to be the most important variable in explaining access. But other variables are also likely to be important, even if they cannot easily be specified.

In December 1994 no less authoritative a body than China Statistics

TABLE 6

Homes in China with STAR-TV, Autumn 1993

City	STAR-TV homes	Percent of total TV homes	City	STAR-TV homes	Percent of total TV homes
Chongqing	3,172,000	85%	Qingdao	209,000	12%
Chengdu	1,662,000	72	Hefei	199,000	21
Zhengzhou	1,017,000	72	Nanjing	143,000	11
Kunming	831,000	95	Tianjin	131,000	6
Guangzhou	723,000	49	Harbin	123,000	9
Changsha	536,000	39	Shanghai	103,000	3
Nanning	510,000	80	Nanchang	80,000	9
Xi'an	405,000	26	Shenyang	57,000	4
Changchun	396,000	25	Xiamen	40,000	14
Guiyang	342,000	88	Dalian	35,000	3
Shijiazhuang	329,000	46	Taiyuan	30,000	5
Jinan	310,000	23	Ningbo	19,000	1
Beijing	283,483	9	Hangzhou	7,000	1

SOURCE: Frank Small and Associates, via STAR-TV.

Consultants Limited, the official marketing arm of the PRC's State Statistical Bureau, reported survey results that found 64 percent of two- and three-star hotels in China capable of receiving satellite broadcasts, and 88 percent of these hotels retransmitting STAR-TV. (Only 11 percent carried CNN, which is usually seen only in four- and five-star hotels.) The average occupancy rate of the 330,000 rooms available at the two- and three-star hotels was 71 percent, and 70 percent of the guests were Chinese business travelers.[58] (An unknown number of the remaining 30 percent were Chinese tourists.) Not surprisingly, these hotels tend to be concentrated in the political and economic centers of Beijing, Shanghai, Jiangsu, and Guangdong. Although exact figures are impossible to calculate from the data provided, it is obvious that a significant number of Chinese citizens have access to STAR-TV through hotel rooms. As economic development races ahead and new, horizontal-exchange relationships are forged in the market economy, the need for travel increases. An unanticipated by-product is exposure to externally derived worldviews, values, and action strategies, which can then be widely disseminated by the well-connected, mobile individuals endowed with the status and resources required to travel and with access to the rapidly expanding telecommunications network.

The Globalization of Radio Thought Work

As explained above, the Center places at least nominal restrictions on lower-level television stations' legal importation of foreign and Hong Kong films and teleplays—though the limitations are not very effective. But at present, Beijing does not overtly restrict radio stations from importing anything. Throughout China, all radio stations, at any level, may import programs directly from abroad.[59] As a result, while the Central People's Radio Network (CPRN) exchanges programs (mostly classical and popular music) with 40 to 50 foreign countries and regions, numerous provinces and cities have been conducting Sino-foreign professional exchanges since the early 1980s. These exchanges encompass both the provision of programs and business visits by high-ranking personnel from each side to the other's headquarters. As in the case of CPRN, most of the programs exchanged are musical.[60]

For example, some 30 percent of the music Beijing Radio broadcasts originates outside China. Beijing Radio has full authority to decide how much and what kind of music to import and rarely faces interference from the central party-state.[61] Beijing Radio is not constrained by copyright restrictions in its importation of music in the way that television stations are sometimes limited in their importation of films and teleplays. People are willing to listen to the same music repeatedly, while they are not willing to watch the same TV programs repeatedly. Recording companies want radio stations to play their music at no charge, as often as possible, as a kind of free advertising. Because the Chinese market for tapes and compact discs is potentially gigantic, record companies do not complain when Chinese radio stations play their music without permission or compensation. Because this music is technically well produced and for other reasons highly popular, Chinese stations have every incentive to play as much of it as their audiences will support. Of course, the stations must also take into account government monitors' degree of tolerance for externally produced music, but rarely do central propaganda commissars complain about radio music in the way they complain about television programs.[62]

It will probably come as no surprise that Guangdong Radio broadcasts a great deal of external music, the vast majority originating in Hong Kong. Officials at Guangdong Radio would not provide precise figures, but the fact that the populations of both Guangdong and Hong Kong speak (and sing in) Cantonese facilitates a huge inflow of Hong Kong CDs and tapes—or perhaps a trickle of imports followed by large-scale, internal piracy. Official contacts are not required for Guangdong Radio to acquire external music: Its representatives can easily purchase CDs and tapes, pirated or otherwise, on the street. The same is true, to a lesser extent, in other parts of the country, including the mountainous and landlocked southwestern city of Kunming. There, the city-level station can easily fill its airwaves with substantial amounts of external music purchased from local dealers, even though it imports nothing directly from abroad because of severe financial constraints.[63]

On occasion, even radio call-in programs can facilitate thought-work globalization. The most dramatic example of this phenomenon occurred during the summer of 1993, when the controversial Hong Kong radio personality Pamela Pak briefly hosted a live call-in show from 11 P.M. until midnight on the Beijing People's Radio Station. Pak was infamous in Hong Kong for addressing some of society's most sensitive problems, generating the most controversy for her frank discussion of sex. She began her Beijing program on June 27, 1993, and immediately stunned listeners: "Wives phoned in saying they hated their husbands; husbands called up in a dilemma over whether or not to leave their wives for their mistresses; and a lot of soldiers complained about their low social status and the brutality of officers. . . . The children and teenagers who call[ed] into the programme show[ed] themselves to be incredibly rude and spoiled, threatening to beat their parents if they did not [get their way]."[64] But in exposing the seamier side of life in the Chinese capital, Pak soon got herself into trouble with the authorities. The highest leaders in the party's Central Propaganda Department (CPD) were apparently unaware that Pak's program even existed until late July. One observer suggested only half in jest that the old men who run the CPD are already fast asleep by 11 P.M. At a meeting on August 2, however, the CPD discussed Pak's program and decided to cancel it, ostensibly for the legalistic reason that Hong Kong and Taiwan residents are not permitted to broadcast live on the mainland. Pak was notified of the decision on August 6, when CPD officials suggested that she supply Beijing Radio with a prerecorded program to replace the canceled live call-in show. Pak declined and no longer broadcasts within China. She had become a victim of the first salvos in the omnidirectional crackdown on heterodox thought work (discussed in Chapter 6). Her case demonstrates that the central party-state does remain an important player in the thought-work market, even though its force is often held in reserve and can sometimes be paralyzed temporarily.[65]

Another example of thought-work globalization, though not nearly as controversial as the Pak case, is the joint live broadcasts of Radio-Television Hong Kong (RTHK) and Guangdong's Zhujiang Economic Radio Station.[66] Underscoring, as with cable television, the regional distinctiveness of Guangdong, these stations, from 1991 to 1993, jointly produced 26 live public affairs call-in programs focusing on problems related to trade and investment. All topics were carefully discussed ahead of time. Editors at the studios in both Guangzhou and Hong Kong screened the calls to make certain that listeners' questions and comments were consistent with the topic at hand, but they did allow the expression of complaints on such mildly controversial issues as red tape and corruption. Eventually, the principals decided to abandon this program in favor of a more popular series on Cantonese music. They insist, however, that the decision had nothing to do with politics. Although the cancellation was announced in late 1993, during the early phases of the omnidirectional crackdown, it assertedly resulted from the calculation that both stations' most important consideration must be to create financially viable programs. Still, a precedent had been set for joint Sino–Hong Kong broadcasts of hotline programs, a precedent that could easily be resurrected in the post-reversion period.[67]

Perhaps cognizant of the possibility of a merger of the symbolic environments of Hong Kong and Guangdong, agents of the Chinese state have on occasion reacted with fury when Guangdong residents telephone Hong Kong talk shows to express their opinions on Chinese affairs. For example, in December 1992 RTHK broadcast an interview with the dissident Wang Ruowang and afterward opened the phones. A listener from Foshan telephoned to express his support not only for Wang but also for the Hong Kong United Democrats, the chief opposition party in Hong Kong, whose leaders were outspokenly advocating, in defiance of Beijing's wishes, high levels of autonomy and democracy for the territory. *Wen Wei Po*, a Hong Kong newspaper controlled by the Chinese Communist Party, subsequently launched a strongly worded attack on RTHK:

> Now that RTHK has conducted a meticulous plot and arranged for an important villain who has been flagrantly advocating the overthrow of the Chinese government to make long remarks on the radio, now that it has incited the audience in Mainland China to praise and support the United Democrats of Hong Kong, . . . now that it has put into effect [former governor Chris] Patten's anti-China line, then what is the difference between its nature and the proposed "Radio Free China" or "Radio Free Asia?"[68]

Criticism like this gets the attention of Hong Kong's broadcasters and communicates to them in a not-so-subtle way the limits they should not transgress. But Hong Kong's broadcasters cannot prevent Chinese citizens from telephoning talk shows, something that occurred on the RTHK programs about once a month in the mid-1990s. Nor do they wish to silence their mainland listeners.[69] The combination of mass media with advanced telecommunications makes it very difficult for the Chinese state to manage thought work as rigorously as the leadership would like to, particularly in the region of Guangdong, which itself is becoming linked ever more closely with other regions of China.

Shortwave Radio

With the exception of occasional call-in shows, almost no external public affairs or news programs enter China as a result of legal importation by official radio stations. Legal importations are usually limited to music and other forms of art and entertainment. Audiotape of foreign news events is centrally supplied by the GBRFT's China International

Radio Station. Hong Kong and foreign popular music and entertainment probably exert an indirect effect on politics as a result of the gradual changes those media induce in listeners'—especially young listeners'—worldviews, values, and action strategies. But the more direct impact on politics within the sphere of radio thought work comes from the news and public affairs broadcasts of the Voice of America (VOA), the BBC, and—after September 1996—Radio Free Asia (RFA).[70]

Chinese citizens have probably always listened to the VOA and BBC, although surveys were out of the question until the mid-1980s. To achieve wider coverage while avoiding the extensive construction of costly intermediate retransmission stations, the CPRN broadcast only on shortwave from its inception in the early 1950s until the early 1970s.[71] There are no reliable data on the number of specifically shortwave receivers in use in China, but presumably if the central party-state wanted its message to be heard, it would have insisted that receivers be equipped to receive CPRN broadcasts. On the other hand, it is possible that the CPRN's broadcasts were received locally by retransmission stations, which then converted them into AM signals. One source estimates that there were only 12 million shortwave receivers in use in China in 1975, but already 100 million AM receivers in use.[72] During the Maoist era, the retransmission stations were occasionally warned not to accidentally retransmit external shortwave broadcasts.[73]

But while not having access to shortwave receivers might prevent Chinese citizens from listening to most foreign broadcasts, it does not prevent them from listening to the VOA, because the VOA also broadcasts on the AM band. The VOA's regular Chinese listenership has held steady at about 19 million people—some 2 to 4 percent of the adult population—since 1985, when the VOA commissioned the first in a series of semisecret audience surveys.[74] It is thought that listenership rises sharply during periods of crisis; for example, the number of listeners might have reached 60 million in May and June of 1989.[75] The regular listenership is concentrated in the urban areas and consists almost entirely of intellectuals, students, government officials, and business people—precisely the sort of opinion leaders now also using the Internet. The VOA has in fact specially targeted the business community in recent years with new programs that explain the functioning of international markets, the principles of management, and other practical mat-ters. The VOA's audience in all demographic subgroups is significantly larger than that of the BBC, primarily because the VOA's Mandarin broadcasts (eleven hours a day) exceed those of the BBC in number.[76]

One potential avenue for the entry of VOA programs into China has failed. Though successful in other countries, the "placement program"—in which the VOA supplies prepackaged programs to receiving-country stations for free broadcast—has flopped in China. Important progress was made in 1988 when the Chengdu municipal radio and television authorities agreed to serve as the hub of a network of VOA affiliates that would supply stations throughout China with English-teaching programs. Plans were also made to publish an accompanying textbook. But Tiananmen destroyed this project, and it was not resumed even in the relatively liberal period following the Fourteenth Party Congress (October 1992). The Chinese central party-state has thus obviously been successful in controlling this particular avenue of thought-work global-ization. There is a strong incentive for stations to carry VOA programs, because many of the music programs in particular could serve as excel-lent platforms for the insertion of locally sold advertising. But because Beijing singled out the VOA for heavy, sharp, and sustained criticism after the Tiananmen massacre, it is simply too dangerous, too closely associated with the concept of "peaceful evolution," to serve as a real-istic partner.[77]

The Uncontrolled Tide of Tapes and Compact Discs from Abroad

Particularly at lower levels of the administrative hierarchy, Chinese television and radio stations turn to the "cultural market" of tapes and CDs to fill their schedules with foreign and Hong Kong programming. In the hundreds of collective and privately run music and video stores that line the streets of almost every major Chinese city, media managers and the public at large can easily purchase cheap, pirated copies of for-eign and Hong Kong videotapes, audiotapes, and CDs. When a televi-sion or radio station manager is forced to take responsibility for profits and losses and motivated to consume the income from his or her effec-tive economic property rights, what better way to keep costs down?

The same logic applies for China's thousands of karaoke bar and MTV proprietors, whose inputs—in the form of pirated music and videos—cost far less than the admission prices charged to patrons. Here again it is clear how thought-work globalization is, in key respects, a variant of thought-work commercialization.

Individual Chinese citizens do not typically purchase CDs or rent videotapes, because CD and videocassette players are too expensive. Thus, of the estimated 10 million legally copyrighted CDs and tens of millions of pirated CDs sold in China each year, the lion's share is purchased by radio stations and karaoke establishments.[78] Similarly, the vast majority of videocassette purchases and rentals are made by MTVs and by lower-level broadcast and cable television stations.[79] In principle, then, if the central government could control the lower-level television and radio stations and the karaoke bars and MTVs, it could shut down this particular avenue of thought-work globalization. Specific efforts to manage the cultural market are discussed in Chapter 6. For now, let it be said that clearly the administrative, technological, and economic variables driving all forms of thought-work commercialization, globalization, and pluralization are overwhelming the Center's best efforts in this regard. Thus, Thomas Gold writes that the CPD found in a 1991 survey that more than 80 percent of the most popular 600 songs played in karaoke bars originated outside the mainland.[80] A year later the Ministry of Culture (MoC) put the figure at closer to 95 percent, and even those songs recorded in the PRC are now heavily influenced by Hong Kong and Taiwan styles and themes, which include consumerism, individualism, and liberalism.[81]

The state does have mechanisms in place designed to channel the importation of foreign tapes and CDs. One or two publishing houses in each province are given exclusive permission to import and distribute such products, with all proposed video imports requiring (in principle) approval by the GBRFT's Audio and Video Recordings Management Office.[82] But the problem is not typically the behavior of state-designated importers and distributors, who tend to abide by the law. The problem is with the numerous illegal and semilegal producers and distributors of CDs and tapes who function in much the same way as the illegal book and periodical publishers discussed in Chapter 3.[83] One Chinese journalist described the linkages between these organizations and overseas CD pirates: "It is said that some audio industry businessmen from Hong Kong and Taiwan . . . rope in people in charge of CD factories on the mainland, give bribes to local cadres, and ask factories to produce pirated audio tapes and CDs semi-overtly."[84]

A corresponding process results in pirated videotapes being conveyed into China (these are called, colloquially, "water tapes," indicating their origins abroad). It should be emphasized that the co-conspiring Chinese factories are not the publishing houses authorized by the state to import tapes and CDs; rather, they are collective and private enterprises usually receiving some sort of illicit though official backing, typically from a township government or elements of the military.[85] Most of the factories are located in Guangdong, but because of the rapid development of China's transportation industry in the past twenty years, illegal tapes and CDs from abroad can now be found in every major Chinese city, including mountainous and landlocked Kunming.[86] But while official publishing houses will not typically reproduce illegal recordings, official distribution outlets will happily sell them. Judging from their low prices, illegal CDs can be purchased even in the stores of joint-venture hotels, including some American joint-venture hotels.[87]

Film Imports

The shattering of the film-distribution monopoly discussed in Chapter 5 has contributed not only to thought-work pluralization and commercialization but also to globalization. Before January 1, 1993, a centralized, state-owned company managed the circulation of all films in China, domestic and foreign. Under the 1993 reform, film-production studios secured the right to sell directly to newly decentralized provincial and subprovincial film-distribution companies, and even to individual theaters. But the centralized Import-Export Company did retain its monopoly over the importation and distribution of foreign films, including those originating in Hong Kong.

During the 1980s and early 1990s, the Company was restricted to importing about 60 films a year, half from Hong Kong. The justification for this restriction was both to prevent the globalization of thought work from getting out of hand and to allow time for China's infant (technically and commercially) film industry to develop. The Company chafed under these restrictions because its employees now held effective economic property rights to the firm's income. Clearly, there were giant rents to be reaped from monopolizing the supply of enormously popular, externally produced films. As a result of immense but opaque Company lobbying pressures, MRFT officials finally agreed in April 1995 to drop the 60-film-per-year restriction, ostensibly for the primary purpose of stimulating China's own film industry via increased competition.[88]

As of this writing, it is too early to anticipate the full consequences of this reform, but film industry officials predicted it would certainly lead to an increased influx of films from abroad.[89] These officials pointed out that over 70 percent of lower-level television programs originate externally and that "water tapes" are enormously popular at China's numerous MTVs. What is to stop the Company from flooding the country with cheap foreign and Hong Kong films to reap the enormous rents?

Of course, the fact that the Company is centralized will in principle make it easier for the GBRFT to screen out overtly dangerous or spiritually polluting political films. But there is concern at the top that the extreme market orientation of the distribution company and of China's theaters will result in the importation of only cheap, low-quality foreign films, not the numerous high-quality films that even some of China's highest leaders acknowledge foreigners sometimes create, and which can be used to elevate the Chinese people's artistic sensibilities. These concerns prompted the MRFT to demand an apparent concession from the Company in exchange for lifting the limit on the number of foreign imports: While the Company may import as many films as it wishes, it must import at least ten "good" foreign films each year, with "goodness" to be defined in negotiations with MRFT officials.[90]

Ironically, though, the first "good" film imported under this policy was *The Fugitive*, the American suspense film starring Harrison Ford as Richard Kimble, a physician falsely accused and convicted of killing his wife. On the way to the execution grounds, Kimble escapes in the pandemonium that follows a miraculous bus accident. He is then pursued relentlessly by a tenacious State, personified in the hyper-dedicated U.S. marshal Philip Gerard. The MRFT's decision to import *The Fugitive* probably resulted from a calculation that the film is not only technically well produced but is also an action thriller devoid of overt politics. A moment's reflection, however, will make the covert politics clear. It is certainly plausible that large numbers of Chinese citizens would identify with an upstanding American wrongly condemned by his government to death and then relentlessly hounded and chased. They may first conclude that the American system is unjust—a perception probably consistent with the Center's thought-work goals. But in the United States, at least, the innocent man secures his freedom in the end, while in China the execution would have probably long since taken place. While the exact situation with regard to *The Fugitive* is unclear, the subtleties and complications of media effects imply that even the Center's best efforts to manage and control public communications can easily backfire.

Thought-work globalization will increase not only as a result of lifting the limitations on the number of film imports. In response to the new competition from technically superior Hong Kong, American, and European studios, China's own formerly protected filmmakers will likely enter into more coproduction arrangements to "improve the quality" of their films.[91] It seems likely that in the process of absorbing foreigners' technical skills, many of the more subtle themes of overseas films will also seep into—cultural nativists might say "pollute"—Chinese films. Foreign themes have proved popular. Of course, Chinese filmmakers will not willingly give up their own form of comparative advantage in competition for the domestic film market: a deeply rooted, almost intuitive knowledge of the stories and themes most likely to appeal to Chinese audiences. Because globalization is not only partially fueled but also conditioned by commercialization, the producers and importers of foreign media products must to some degree adapt to Chinese tastes. But as in the case of television programs, the tastes adapted to are those of society, not the state—excepting the overtly political.

The Trickle of Imported Print

One of the original hypotheses of this study was that there would be very little globalization of thought work via the print medium. It is technically and administratively much easier for governments to control the importation of bulky paper products than it is for them to control smaller CDs and tapes, to say nothing of invisible electromagnetic radiation. Moreover, with the important exception of the printed products produced by overseas Chinese (especially in Hong Kong and Taiwan), there is likely to be very little demand for externally originated books and periodicals, for the simple reason that comparatively few Chinese citizens can read English and other foreign languages. This hypothesis was confirmed.[92]

Nevertheless, the Center is still forced to make strenuous efforts to contain and channel the globalization of printed thought work; it is not content to rely on language barriers alone. Efforts at channeling actually began during the very early years of the regime with the founding of the publication *Cankao Xiaoxi* (Reference news), a daily compilation of foreign news reports translated accurately into Chinese by presumably trustworthy journalists at the Center's Xinhua News Agency. In January 1957, on the eve of the Hundred Flowers Movement, Mao Zedong revealed that *Cankao Xiaoxi*'s minute circulation of 2,000 would soon be increased to 400,000 so that even non-Party members could read it:

> This is a case of a Communist Party publishing a newspaper for imperialism, and it even carries reactionary statements vilifying us. Why should we do this? The purpose is to put poisonous weeds and what is non-Marxist and anti-Marxist before our comrades, before the masses and the democratic personages, so that they can be tempered. . . . The publication of *News for Reference* [*Cankao Xiaoxi*] and other negative teaching materials is "vaccination" to increase the political unity of the cadres and the masses.[93]

Whether the vaccination effect was achieved is an unanswerable question, but in any case by 1982 *Cankao Xiaoxi*'s circulation had risen to a staggering 25 million copies per day—by far the largest circulation of any paper in the world. By 1993 *Cankao Xiaoxi* still boasted the largest circulation of any paper in China, but by that time the number of copies per day had fallen dramatically to a still quite-respectable 8 million. The reason for the decline was apparently the general relaxation of the requirement that Chinese organizations (especially those with party committees) throughout the country subscribe to all of the Center's most important official publications. Following the Fourteenth Party Congress (October 1992), they were required to subscribe to only one central paper and one provincial paper. But given this fact, it is worth noting that *Cankao Xiaoxi*'s circulation of 8 million remains much higher than the 1.7-million circulation of *Renmin Ribao*, the flagship publication of the central party-state.[94]

Still, *Cankao Xiaoxi*'s falling circulation would seem to indicate that, if anything, there has been a relative "de-globalization" of printed thought work. Fewer people seem interested in acquiring accurate news about the outside world, or even in acquiring accurate news about China reported by journalists abroad. The problem would appear to be twofold. First, *Cankao Xiaoxi* is a "serious" paper competing in a marketplace dominated by fluff-filled evening and weekend papers whose goal is to satisfy the Chinese media consumer's desire for more entertainment. Second, most citizens in a huge, continental country like China seem inherently to have little interest in the outside world other than as a source of amusement and curiosity (compare this to the generally low interest of most Americans in foreign affairs). Interest should increase as more Chinese units become directly and indirectly linked into the webs of the global economy, and units more tightly linked probably are more likely to subscribe to *Cankao Xiaoxi*.[95] But these units and simply curious individuals today have access to many avenues other than *Cankao Xiaoxi* to increase their knowledge about the outside world: satellite television, telecommunications, travel, and so on. *Cankao Xiaoxi* no longer enjoys the monopoly on accurate information about the outside world that it did in the decades before reform.

Nor for that matter does the Xinhua News Agency still enjoy an airtight monopoly on the provision of news about the outside world to lower-level Chinese periodicals. While Tsan-kuo Chang, Chin-hsien Chen, and Guo-Qiang Zhang found in a 1989–90 survey of party-controlled provincial and municipal papers that "all the news about the outside world and China's relations with foreign countries" was supplied by Xinhua,[96] cracks in this edifice of control had already begun to appear by the early 1990s. As discussed in Chapter 5, the wealthier newspapers higher in the administrative hierarchy now occasionally send reporters abroad to produce feature stories—though no non-central paper has bureaus established abroad. At the same time, the

CPD complained in late 1993 that in pursuit of markets "some newspapers even reprinted materials from the overseas press in violation of the state's relevant regulations."[97]

Most of the papers that dare to reprint foreign stories are among the numerous new, radically market-oriented publications that units with only weak links to the propaganda xitong began establishing in the mid-1980s—although some lower-level, party-controlled papers also sometimes illegally reprint overseas newspaper articles. The motivation in either case is to increase readership by appealing to audience tastes. While most Chinese citizens, most of the time, do not wish to consume foreign news, many do apparently enjoy reading foreign fluff and sensationalistic news and are more willing to purchase those papers that reproduce it. This fact underscores the linkages between commercialization and globalization and the praetorian nature of the Chinese public sphere. The phenomenon takes on an extreme form when illegal, underground Chinese publishers reprint foreign pornography, which apparently is quite a common occurrence.[98]

As mentioned above, the Chinese government does, of course, permit the importation of some foreign-language newspapers and news periodicals, though it strictly limits their circulation to expensive hotels and Chinese government and academic units.[99] Importantly, no Chinese-language newspaper or news magazine may be legally imported from abroad, except for certain Chinese-controlled Hong Kong publications such as *Wen Wei Po* and *Ta Kung Pao*. The obvious aim of this restriction is to keep politically critical Hong Kong and Taiwan periodicals out of the country, and the restriction is apparently quite successfully enforced—although in May 1996 Shenzhen authorities were forced to mobilize 100 public security personnel to seize some contraband Hong Kong papers smuggled in by train and bus.[100]

The central party-state also strictly forbids domestic print media outlets at all levels of the hierarchy from entering into joint ventures with foreign and Hong Kong publishers.[101] There is strong demand on the Chinese side for cooperation with outside publishers because the highly market-oriented Chinese media managers believe they can secure significant competitive advantages by adopting advanced production techniques and styles of reportage from Hong Kong and elsewhere. At the same time, foreign publishers would like to use joint ventures as Trojan horses to invade the Chinese print media market.

One of the most active firms in this regard is *Sing Tao*, the Hong Kong daily whose English-language sister publication is the well-known *Hongkong Standard*. Both papers are highly respected, and both made important forays into the Chinese domestic media market in the early 1990s that came crashing to a halt when the crackdown on heterodox thought work began in late 1993.

Sing Tao did succeed in establishing a joint-venture entertainment magazine with several official and semi-official Guangzhou organizations—a venture that survived the crackdown. But a more important effort to establish a daily business paper with a publishing house in Shenzhen failed in November 1993. The Shenzhen partner (whose identity a *Sing Tao* source declined to reveal) successfully secured approval from the CPD to publish the paper in the heady months following the Fourteenth Party Congress. *Sing Tao* thereupon established a Shenzhen office, purchased equipment, hired personnel, and otherwise prepared to publish the paper, only to receive the disturbing news a few months later that the Center had suddenly withdrawn its approval.[102]

One *Sing Tao* informant explains the dynamics as follows: Provincial- and municipal-level media administrators believe that the units under their jurisdiction can be made more competitive and profitable with the injection of foreign funding, technology, and expertise. These bureaucrats lobbied successfully in the post-October 1992 period to obtain the approval of middle-ranking propaganda commissars in Beijing to set up the joint ventures, only to have them canceled when word of the arrangements reached Minister of Propaganda Ding Guan'gen and head of the Hong Kong–Macao Affairs Office Lu Ping. Both Ding and Lu took the Trojan horse metaphor almost literally, believing that allowing Hong Kong newspapers and magazines into China would lead very quickly to an uncontrollable flood of unacceptably political print publications. They believed other Hong Kong publishers would imitate *Sing Tao* and set up their own joint ventures with other mainland publishers—with the consequence that the "cancer" of thought-work globalization would metastasize throughout the entire Chinese body politic.[103]

Even seemingly innocuous forms of cooperation have been prohibited. For example, one problem in transporting English-language newspapers to four- and five-star hotels is that they must be printed in Hong Kong or Tokyo and then put on planes bound for some 30 large Chinese cities, where they arrive early in the afternoon on the day of publication. At that point, the papers are put on delivery trucks, which then must wend their way very slowly through maddeningly thick traffic jams. As a result, the papers arrive at the hotels no sooner than twelve hours after publication. Strictly speaking, they are therefore no longer "news" papers.

But from September 1994 to January 1995, the *Hongkong Standard* was able to solve this problem and secure a competitive edge over other English-language papers in the city of Beijing by striking a deal with the official *China Daily* to use its comparatively advanced printing facilities to print the *Standard* right in the capital. The obvious result would be quicker delivery to points of sale. But in January, *China Daily* managers "regretfully" informed their *Standard* partners that the paper's workload had suddenly become too heavy—the arrangement would have to stop. Once again, *Sing Tao* officials suspect that lower-level propaganda officials originally gave the go-ahead for this innocent arrangement—the paper would circulate in China anyway, only earlier—but were subsequently overruled by higher-ranking personages in the CPD. Their motivation, again, was fear of the Trojan horse, fear that allowing the spark of Sino–Hong Kong (or Sino-foreign) joint ventures in print could set off a prairie fire that eventually would consume China in a globalization of printed thought work.[104]

The manner in which foreign books are imported also reflects the interaction of thought-work commercialization, globalization, and pluralization. While certain government agencies and research institutes in the past enjoyed unrestricted authority to import books and other publications of a technical nature clearly relevant to their legitimate activities, all other imports were monopolized by the General Book Import-Export Company, located bureaucratically under the State Press and Publications Administration (SPPA), and before 1987 under the SPPA's predecessor in the MoC.[105] But beginning in the late 1980s, big bookstores in the provincial capitals and certain other large cities began importing books on their own, without first seeking or receiving any special approval from the SPPA. As a result, by 1995 at least 30 bookstores nationwide freely imported books directly from abroad. Neither the SPPA nor any other bureaucracy plays any role whatsoever in approving these imports; they are too vast in number to be examined one by one.[106] The bookstores themselves must be relied upon to exercise political judgment over what books would be permissible to import. In most cases, it appears, the stores are cautious, tending to import books more likely to be spiritually polluting than bourgeois-liberal; that is, relatively apolitical romances, adventures, and classic works.[107] The main source of the really "bad" books remains the numerous, transprovincial, underground publishing and distribution networks whose linkages extend to Hong Kong and whose activities are discussed in Chapter 3.

The globalization of thought work is inextricably linked with the commercialization and pluralization of thought work, and all contribute importantly to China's public-sphere praetorianism. While pluralization is most clearly associated with administrative variables and commercialization with economic variables, the variables that most potently explain thought-work globalization are clearly technological. Powerful broadcast satellites, small satellite receiving dishes, automated telecommunications switching equipment, and optical-fiber transmission equipment are inherently difficult for any government to control. This point is most obvious in the Chinese state's struggles to regulate satellite television and the Internet.

But technology alone does not explain thought-work globalization. Beijing might well be able to turn back the globalization tide if it did not have to contend with the powerful economic incentives that tempt media units and Chinese individuals (often illicitly) to import foreign communications messages, and if it were not saddled with a fragmented bureaucracy that is technically underequipped and lacking in skilled personnel. But the cold reality of the interaction of these administrative, technological, and economic variables is something that the state cannot wish away. The struggle thus continues as praetorianism takes deeper root.

CHAPTER FIVE

The Pluralization of Thought Work

China's leaders are significantly more satisfied with the thought-work messages created and circulated by central-level media outlets than with those created and circulated by outlets lower in the administrative hierarchy, to say nothing of those originating abroad.[1] Satisfaction is not complete, of course, and the growing market orientation of even Central China Television (CCTV), the Central People's Radio Network (CPRN), and *Renmin Ribao* is a source of concern. But compared to the content of media outlets at the provincial level and especially at the subprovincial level, the content of the central outlets is generally satisfactory. This is perhaps not surprising given the fact that the capital's propaganda cadres monitor the central outlets relatively easily and directly appoint the outlets' leading personnel.

The problem is that Chinese citizens no longer need consume the offerings of the central media outlets as they had no choice but to do under the "communication compression" of the Maoist propaganda state. Today the people of China have a much wider variety of message sources from which to choose, whether in broadcasting, print, or telecommunications. This proliferation of sources is the meaning of the term "pluralization," the third major manifestation of declining central control over thought work. Pluralization undermines Beijing's control in two ways. First, it provides the Chinese populace with a greater degree of choice over what messages to consume, often leading to consumption patterns that do not include official, central messages. Second, it multiplies the number of points at which the Center must apply power or authority to interdict objectionable messages, such as those which flooded the country's telecommunications networks in May and

June of 1989.[2] A degree of pluralization was expected and desired when communication reforms were introduced at the beginning of the 1980s, but it quickly escaped control when combined with commercialization and globalization. It began to crowd out the Center's messages, frequently in favor of spiritual pollution and bourgeois liberalism—undermining the socialist spiritual civilization and contributing importantly to public-sphere praetorianism.

Pluralization results from an expansion in the number of both media channels available within society and the sources of content that feed those channels. If the number of channels had increased while all content continued to originate with the Center, then obviously there would have been no pluralization, only a "loudspeaker effect." But the number of sources has also increased dramatically under reform, and even though the Center does retain influence over what messages will be circulated through the new channels—because of its general influence over society—it cannot exert as much control as it could under the Maoist propaganda state, and it cannot exert as much control as its official spokesmen assert would be desirable.

All three of this study's causal variables—administrative fragmentation, property-rights reform, and technological advance—contribute to pluralization. This is an important point to stress because at first glance pluralization looks very similar to administrative fragmentation, suggesting the possibility of tautological reasoning. But as this chapter seeks to demonstrate, administrative fragmentation is only necessary, not sufficient, to cause pluralization. For example, without technological advance—such as the widespread diffusion of telecommunications technologies—many fewer message sources would be competing to structure the symbolic environment. And in the absence of property-rights reform, lower-level media outlets would face much weaker incentives to replace centrally supplied media content with more popular materials either locally created or acquired from elsewhere in China and abroad.

Pluralization has not been absolute, of course. In particular, Chinese-style pluralization should not be confused with the liberal "pluralism" that prevails in the thought-work markets of industrialized democracies. That sort of pluralism exists in a well-functioning, institutionalized public sphere, not a praetorian public sphere. China's situation is more disorderly and cacophonous. Thus, the Hong Kong daily *Sing Tao* reported in June 1997 that Chinese authorities were worried that "excessive" propaganda in society might lead to "noise," and that even a single mistake made by a book, article, or television program could "result in regional instability and affect or interfere with the overall situation."[3] Ongoing state efforts to eliminate "bad" messages from the thought-work market, though far from completely effective, are somewhat effective, and the general climate of political repression does deter people from publicly circulating messages that directly challenge the legitimacy of Communist Party rule. But media and telecommunications consumers do have access to a far greater variety of communications messages than ever before in Chinese history. The variety is so great that all the "noise" prevents the Center's messages from getting across. Efforts to build a socialist spiritual civilization and crack down on heterodoxy can thus be seen as desperate attempts by the central party-state to reassert its relevance in the thought-work market and not be completely marginalized by the forces of commercialization, globalization, and pluralization—which together are "contaminating" the Chinese symbolic environment with a flood of distracting messages.

Television

More than 80 percent of Chinese households owned a television set in 1996, up from nearly none in 1978. About a billion people counted themselves regular television viewers, and while the mere handful of viewers in 1978 could only watch the programs of 32 stations, the billion in 1996 could watch programs broadcast by 880 (licensed) stations.[4] Moreover, these 880 stations originated 66 percent of the television hours they broadcast in 1996, not content to rely exclusively or even predominantly on the offerings of CCTV.[5] The 54 teleplays produced throughout China in 1982 increased to 983 in 1996 and totaled more than 550,000 hours of programming.[6]

In fact, Chinese viewers have access to many more than 880 television stations. By 1995 nearly 2,000 county-level retransmission stations (*zhan*) had been illegally converted into semi-autonomous broadcasting stations (*tai*) originating their own programming. Moreover, the number of such stations was increasing at an 18 percent annual rate.[7] It is not known what percentage of county-level stations' program hours are (illegally) originated locally, but the stations did face sharp criticism at the January 1994 propaganda conference because of the spiritually polluting nature (and often overseas origin) of many of their programs. According to informants, this criticism "did not have much effect."[8]

Why do broadcast administrations at the county level persist in setting up program-originating stations despite the Center's evident disapproval? First, it should be noted that the Center apparently has not devoted significant resources to cracking down on the county stations, and complaining and cajoling can only go so far. But the reason that significant resources would be required for a crackdown is precisely because of the interaction of administrative fragmentation, property-rights reform, and technological advance. The original decentralization policies of the early 1980s gave lower-level authorities the right to regulate broadcasting in their regions.[9] Once they had secured this right, the lower-level authorities faced strong incentives to expand the number of broadcasting stations under their jurisdiction because they held effective economic property rights to the profits that could be made from fees and advertising. Programming was cheap because of the easy availability of videotapes and satellite feeds.[10]

The result of these developments is a marked multiplication in the number and variety of televised messages available to a society that only two decades ago was mired in communication compression. Of parallel importance, audiences can consume these copious programs in the privacy of their own homes—no longer under the watchful eyes of work-unit propaganda commissars who helped the audiences "understand" the programs in small group study sessions. As reported by Jinglu Yu, as early as 1987 only 3 percent of China's then 590 million television viewers watched programs at public viewing places; 83 percent watched in their own homes; and the remaining 14 percent watched in the homes of friends and relatives.[11] Thus, no longer can the state micromanage the "multistep flow" of images and ideas diffused by the many new television offerings available in a climate of pluralization, commercialization, and globalization.

This is not to say, of course, that the Center has given up on efforts to get its own messages across, or that it completely fails to do so. There is a television hierarchy in China, at the top of which sits CCTV. This entity "belongs" to the General Bureau of Radio, Film, and Television (GBRFT), which itself answers directly to the highest organ (on the government side) of central-state power: the State Council. But the reality of administrative fragmentation means that CCTV enjoys only "guidance relations" (*zhidao guanxi*) with lower-level stations, and "guidance relations" do not imply significant power. Essentially, CCTV can offer suggestions to the lower-level stations about what sorts of programs they should carry but can do nothing to force them to comply.[12]

The only rigorous requirement is that all stations everywhere set aside one frequency to broadcast all of CCTV Channel 1's broadcasts, which in 1996 featured 33 hours of propagandistic news per week, in addition to various other educational, entertainment, and sports programs.[13] Forcing the lower-level stations to carry CCTV-1 is perceived as important, not only to helping the central party-state inculcate appropriate worldviews, values, and action strategies, but also to ensuring that CCTV itself retains a large, stable audience whose attention can be sold to advertisers.[14] At present, lower-level stations need not retransmit CCTV channels 2 (oriented toward economic information), 3 (entertainment), and 4 (international), but they are "encouraged" to retransmit them. Otherwise, CCTV must rely on satellites and its own microwave network to increase the audience size for these channels.

But importantly, many subprovincial stations ignore even the requirement to retransmit CCTV-1. Minister of Radio, Film, and Television Ai Zhisheng addressed this problem at the January 1994 propaganda conference and made a point of noting that Party Propaganda Minister Ding Guan'gen "is personally concerned about it."[15] The chief culprits, Ai said, are county-level television stations and unsanctioned, small-scale cable networks—as ubiquitous in urban China as the semi-piratical county stations are in the countryside. The reason the small-scale cable networks—which typically service only an apartment complex or a work-unit compound—do not retransmit CCTV-1 is similar to the reason the county stations do not retransmit it. Their channel capacity is restricted and they prefer to transmit the more titillating programs

their subscribers want to watch, which usually means pirated videotapes often of a pornographic nature.[16] With regard specifically to the
county-level stations, as Ai explained in January 1994, most have only
one channel, and they want to use that channel to broadcast programming with high audience appeal so that they can sell more advertising.[17]

At the time Ai spoke, a crackdown on the lower-level stations was in
the works, as part of the overall crackdown on heterodox thought work
that had been launched the previous autumn. Shortly before the propaganda conference the Ministry of Radio, Film, and Television (MRFT)
jointly drafted a document with the Central Propaganda Department
(CPD) that would require county-level stations first to retransmit
CCTV-1, then the first channel of the provincial station, and finally their
own programs. If implemented, the plan would result in no county-
level station legally broadcasting its own programs unless it had the resources to set up three separate channels. First priority would go to dis-
seminating the messages of the central party-state, and second priority
would go to those of the province. In addition, even relatively well endowed county-level stations that could set up three channels would not
be permitted to create their own programming. Any programs to be locally originated would have to be purchased or acquired through domestic barter networks and approved by (unspecified) higher-level authorities. The reason, Ai stated, was simply because otherwise the
county-level stations would continue to create and air "things in poor
taste" and thereby violate the proscriptions against spiritual pollution.[18]
The deeper reason was to keep the power over the origination of symbols from descending to levels lower than the Center could effectively
monitor and control.

Radio

Before the takeoff of television began in the early 1980s, radio served as
the chief instrument by which the Center reached hundreds of millions
of illiterate peasants and workers with its messages of revolution and
development. But since the advent of reform, radio's role as a tool for
thought work has receded significantly in importance. By the early
1990s urban residents were more likely to own a television set than a

radio receiver, and the situation in the countryside was undergoing a similar transformation as the old radio-loudspeaker networks fell into disuse and wealthier peasants began purchasing television sets. Nationwide, the number of radio receivers per household reached a peak of 0.85 in 1987 and then began a steady decline to 0.66 in 1992. In that year, for the first time in Chinese history, the number of television sets in use surpassed the number of radio sets. By 1996 there were 65 black-and-white television sets for every 100 rural residents but only 29 radio receivers.[19]

At the same time as listeners were "tuning out" Chinese radio, however, the number of licensed stations—or sources of radio messages—was increasing from 93 in 1978 to 1,244 in 1996.[20] In addition, the higher-level stations began carrying several more channels of programming than their Mao-era predecessors had; listeners enjoyed a wider variety of radio choices than ever before. The MRFT officially expected most urban residents to have access to six or seven radio channels early in the 21st century, and rural residents to have access to five or six channels.[21]

The total number of radio programs produced legally at the municipal level and above also increased dramatically under reform, from 282,000 hours in 1985 to 2.9 million hours in 1996. About 77 percent of radio programs were written, produced, and broadcast by the individual stations themselves, at all levels of the hierarchy.[22] At the same time, the population coverage rate increased from 64 percent to 84 percent, extending the expanded listening options to residents of regions previously unserved by radio, especially mountainous and desert areas. The population coverage rate was expected to reach 90 percent sometime early in the 21st century.[23]

Radio is part of the same xitong as television and is organized in an analogous, semihierarchical structure. Like CCTV, the CPRN is directly subordinate to the GBRFT. The same relationship exists between provincial administrations and provincial radio stations, and in principle between all other equivalent-level regulators and operators throughout the country, just as in the case of television. Before the 1980s Chinese radio was highly and effectively centralized, under the slogan "Take the central station as the basis and the local stations as supplementary." As with television, lower-level stations were forced to retransmit highly stylized central propaganda during the Cultural Revolution decade, a policy that inhibited their evolution into pluralistic sources of programming. All of this changed during the 1980s, however—particularly after the important March/April 1983 radio-television work conference. Lower-level stations were given progressively more autonomy to create and air programs of their own choice, to hire talent directly from society, and to raise funds for equipment purchases and capital investments. At the same time, they were instructed to sell advertising in order to promote the development of the commodity/market economy and to achieve eventual economic self-sufficiency. In this respect, radio stations differed little from television stations, even though they ended up facing many more difficulties on the road to economic self-sufficiency because they were not as attractive to advertisers.

The Center, to make certain that its messages continue to reach all four corners of China, "requires" provincial-level radio stations to retransmit all broadcasts of the CPRN's first and second channels; but in this case, unlike the similar mandate regarding CCTV-1, no provincial-level station complies. The provincial-level stations restrict themselves instead to retransmitting only the two daily, half-hour "united news broadcasts" that air in the morning and evening. The Center's policy of making certain that "its" voice (the CPRN's programs) is heard around the clock, nationwide, is clearly important to its thought-work goals, but provincial broadcasting authorities can actually dissent from the stricter requirement without appearing to violate the main thought-work line. They point out that direct CPRN broadcasts throughout the country already reach nearly 70 percent of the population—a figure that they, at least, consider to be sufficiently high. Complying with the regulation to retransmit CPRN channels 1 and 2 would only increase the potential central audience by some 10 to 15 percent. That seems unwarranted to the lower-level stations in light of the fact that they can make a great deal of money by broadcasting more appealing programs and selling advertising on the channels that "should" be used to retransmit CPRN.[24]

From the perspective of the Center, however, 10 to 15 percent of the potential listening audience is a huge number of people whose attention state propagandists and advertisers consider important. The CPRN believes that nearly 300 million people a day hear at least part of the united news broadcasts, a fact that underlines the potential to increase audience size by relying on administrative fiat.[25] While it is true that the CPRN's broadcasts can already be heard in the wealthier parts of the country, and that the 10 to 15 percent increase from faithful implementation would come only in the poorer desert and mountainous regions, that is not the real issue. CPRN may argue that it is necessary for Beijing, Shanghai, Guangdong, and other wealthy regions to retransmit CPRN channels 1 and 2 only to help convince the poorer regions to comply, but this does not appear to be the station's primary concern. The CPRN wants channels 1 and 2 to supplant existing broadcasts in the richer regions in order to expand its audience size among people with higher purchasing power and in regions of comparative political importance. This outcome is precisely what the regional stations seek to avoid.

But because the CPRN has only a "guidance" relationship, not a "leadership" relationship, with the lower-level stations, it cannot force them to retransmit the central programs. The GBRFT governmental bureaucracy is more hierarchical, but is still subordinate at the regional level to the regional governments (it may be even weaker in the wake of the March 1998 governmental reorganization). The net result is that most regional stations do faithfully retransmit the united news broadcasts while none retransmits all of CPRN channels 1 and 2. Many stations selectively retransmit from these two and the other five CPRN channels while illegally substituting their own advertising, blocking out the CPRN ads. This practice is illegal and infuriating to the CPRN, but is not patently political in the way that a refusal to retransmit the united news broadcasts would be. Some stations would definitely prefer to carry local news instead of the CPRN broadcasts, because "that's the only news that the vast majority of our listeners want to hear," but very few stations actually fail to comply with this particular central demand.[26] Precisely where the line is to be drawn between the kind of mandates that receive unquestioned obedience and those which are ignored is unclear to the outsider, but it is apparent that pluralization via radio has increased significantly since the days of high centralization under Mao, partly as a result of the expansion of channels and partly as a result of noncompliance with central retransmission demands.

Atrophy of the Radio Loudspeaker Network

A key component of Mao's strategy for achieving central-state penetration of rural society was to wire the countryside for radio broadcasting by loudspeaker, a centerpiece of the Chinese propaganda state. Until the 1980s this policy proved highly successful, so as early as 1964 it was reported that approximately 95 percent of China's peasants were within earshot of a loudspeaker, whether at home or in public facilities such as government buildings.[27] Moreover, Chinese sources claim that this form of state penetration of society was actually quite well received by its target audience. "The masses say: 'Wired broadcasting doesn't use [our] electricity, we don't need to turn [the loudspeakers] on, we can hear them when we eat, we can hear them when we work, we can hear them when we're walking around, we can hear them when we lay down to rest—it's most convenient and practical.'"[28]

But apparently not everyone among the masses agreed that this situation was pleasing. The proportion of individual peasant households connected to the loudspeaker network fell from 65 percent in 1974 to 43 percent in 1984.[29] The total number of loudspeakers in use decreased from a peak of 113.7 million in 1977 to only 82 million in 1991.[30] The chief reason was competition from the new, decentralized television industry. In areas with especially high levels of television set ownership, wired radio networks have "basically disappeared," as a result of the concrete fact that lower-level broadcasting authorities have, since the late 1980s, put more and more of the locally controlled microwave frequencies needed for loudspeaker broadcasts to use in the more lucrative activity of retransmitting television signals, particularly—today—provincial satellite broadcasts.[31] As a result, the population coverage rate of the loudspeaker network—a measure of infrastructural capacity of centralized thought work—fell from about 80 percent in the early 1980s to 45 percent in 1995.[32]

Even in those regions that still make extensive use of the loudspeaker network, the disestablishment of the commune system has created a variety of problems reflective of the logic of collective action—assuming that the loudspeakers can be considered a "public good," not a public annoyance. Most importantly, the wire stations cannot maintain equipment because they lack funds. The Party's Document No. 37 of 1983 mandated that subscribing households each pay a one-yuan fee for equipment maintenance after disestablishment of the communes, but it is apparently difficult to extract the payment from village residents who, if they desire, can hear the broadcasts from the speaker at the village government headquarters whether they pay or not. It would be better to save the money and use it eventually to purchase a television set.[33] The loudspeaker stations are permitted to sell advertising, but interest on the part of the business world is low because the audiences are small and their buying power is weak. To increase audience size, station managers now carry many more locally originated programs, all the way down to the level of the township. From the point of view of the central party-state, however, this measure only counters the weakening of its voice with intensified pluralization. In any case, the localization efforts seem unlikely to "save" the loudspeaker network, the fate of which now rests with a merger of cable television and cable radio. But that too seems unlikely to happen within the next decade. Regions still relying on the loudspeaker network are too poor to afford cable television, and the pattern thus far has been to deploy the resources previously used for the loudspeaker system to replace it with a local television infrastructure, not to bring the two forms of broadcasting into a complementary relationship.[34]

The rural areas also have access to wireless radio broadcasting, of course, and this segment of the radio industry has fared reasonably well under reform—at least in comparison with wired broadcasting. During the 1980s, when urbanites began abandoning private radio ownership in favor of television sets, millions of peasants purchased their first radio receivers. Only 17 out of every 100 peasant households owned a radio set in 1978, but the figure increased to 54 out of 100 by 1985.[35] One important stimulus to the peasants was probably the localization of radio content, begun in 1984 in connection with an All-China Work Conference on Rural Broadcasting. The Center hoped that this reform would "provide the township party committees with an effective propaganda tool," apparently failing to perceive it as yet another step down the path toward pluralization.[36] The number of township-level radio stations increased from nearly zero in 1982 to 40,000 in 1992, and during the same decade, the number of county-level stations increased from zero to 2,452 as the former county retransmission stations (*zhan*) were converted into fully functioning radio stations (*tai*).[37]

From one perspective, these developments do exemplify the relative economic health of rural broadcasting, but they also represent serious pluralization of thought work. County-level stations in particular have become very active in creating programming—even news programming—with strong local appeal. They make easy use of local dialects and speak distinctly to local tastes and concerns. The old, centralized loudspeaker network was devoted to bringing the culture of the center to the periphery, whether "culture" meant revolutionary consciousness or birth control. The new, decentralized, broadcast networks reinforce the strength of local cultures—without completely determining their content, of course. The full implications of this retreat of the central party-state from rural thought work were apparently not understood when China's leaders implemented the reforms of the early 1980s, and in fact the full implications are probably not understood even today.

Internal Program-Exchange Networks

Individual television and radio stations producing exclusively for protected local markets could not (and cannot) satisfy the mushrooming demand for media fare in China. Expansion in the number of hours broadcast has far outpaced expansion in the number of talented personnel capable of creating programming that attracts large audiences. Additionally, it would not be economically efficient for each provincial station, for example, to create all of its own programming. As a natural result, several semiformalized exchange networks have sprung up that allow television stations in particular to augment their programming stock by trading their programs for programs produced by other stations. The central party-state officially supports these networks but also tries to restrict the scope of their operations.[38] But in general the networks function free of Beijing's interference, a reflection of the fact that in the radio and television xitong, horizontal administration takes precedence over vertical administration.

The October 1980 radio-television work conference anticipated the impending shortage of programs and, as a result, formally encouraged local stations both to produce their own programs and to exchange programs with other stations.[39] After 1980 stations could no longer passively rely on the Center to provide programming the way they were forced to do during the Cultural Revolution. The days of communication compression were over. As a result, in 1980 seven city-level television stations immediately came together to form the first significant exchange network, the Cooperative Association of Urban Television Stations. By the time the Association celebrated its tenth anniversary, it had expanded to include more than 170 member stations. Between 1985 and 1990, Association members exchanged 1,783 hours of programming and "cooperated in a planned and systematic way" to produce eight serial programs on special topics, totaling 416 episodes.[40]

The All-China Provincial-Level Television Station Cooperative Association was also organized shortly after the October 1980 work conference, and by 1995 all 35 provincial-level stations had joined. This group meets every autumn to settle program-exchange deals for the following year. Typically, group members exchange whole series of programs, dramatically reducing the production burden on individual stations. For example, about half of Beijing Television's programs are acquired from the Association, and in exchange Beijing Television barters away or sells about one-third of the programs it produces. Although the programs thus acquired by Beijing Television do not usually air in prime time, they nevertheless constitute a significant contribution to the station's overall program stock. For stations that lack the talent of Beijing Television, programs acquired from the exchange network are not only used in prime time; they also serve as central components of the stations' strategy for increasing audience size.[41]

Despite the fact that the central party-state officially supports the activities of the program-exchange networks, it is concerned that the networks could evolve into powerful, semi-autonomous organizations threatening the Center's overall thought-work project in a way that no individual television station could do on its own. As a result, although the Center exercises no direct authority over the networks, it does try in other ways to restrict their activities. For example, it forbids the networks' member stations from broadcasting live outside their regions—unless they broadcast by satellite, as discussed in Chapter 4. As networks, member stations may create entertainment programs, but they may not create news and public-affairs programs. They may, however, exchange news and public-affairs programs created by individual member stations.[42]

Of special concern to the central propaganda leadership is the participation of numerous new county-level stations in program networks. Apparently the county-level stations had by the early 1990s become a lucrative market in which municipal and provincial stations could dump their old programs. (The higher-level stations are much better staffed and equipped to produce programs than county-level stations.) Worse, the county stations had begun turning to pirated or smuggled overseas videotapes to fill their schedules, and then bartering the tapes in exchange for municipal and provincial programs. Given the rapid growth of the number of county-level stations, there is concern that they could—through these practices—evolve into a major artery for the globalization of thought work. They could become entry points for foreign programs that, once inside China, could circulate freely within the exchange networks, completely out of the central state's control. Minister of Radio, Film, and Television Ai Zhisheng raised this issue at the January 1994 propaganda conference. Ai complained that in 1993 provincial-level stations broadcast almost 4,000 hours of programming each week, but produced (as opposed to originated) only about 800 hours per week, which means that only 20 percent of their programs were produced in-province. Although Ai did not reveal what proportion of the remaining 3,200 hours of programming originated abroad, he did complain that if provincial-level stations do not begin to produce more of their own programs—and exchange them with other domestic stations—then stations at all levels of the hierarchy will have little choice but to turn to foreigners to fill the gap.[43]

In December 1994, Ai's successor, Sun Jiazheng, called for the establishment of central- and provincial-level "program exchange centers" throughout China to address this problem. These centers would be managed by the central state (*guojia*), in an effort to keep track of what the county-level stations were buying and selling.[44] However, this "call" did not have the force of law, and as late as the summer of 1995 was not expected to be heeded.

Like television stations, most radio stations now also exchange programs with their equivalent-level counterparts—and sometimes directly with foreign stations—but what they exchange consists primarily of entertainment programs, not news and public-affairs programs. Except for the CPRN's programs, radio news and public affairs are highly localized in content, a fact which itself contributes to pluralization. For example, the Beijing People's Radio Station receives only 10 percent of its news from other regions of China and 20 percent from the Xinhua News Agency (which carries both domestic and international news).[45] Beijing Radio is the station servicing the capital, the residence of hundreds of thousands of well-educated people from elsewhere in China who staff the offices of the central government. If even the audience of Beijing Radio is largely uninterested in anything other than local news, the situation in less cosmopolitan, less educated locales can easily be imagined.[46] There, stations under pressure to raise money from advertising face little incentive to supply audiences with external news now that they can make their own programming choices. They would certainly be willing to supply other stations with "news" from their own regions, because such "news" could be bought or otherwise used as platforms for selling soft advertising to local firms interested in accessing external markets. But that would probably require accepting other regions' "news" in exchange.

Chaos in the Cultural Market

The term "cultural market" refers to an array of activities associated with the buying, selling, renting, and public exhibition of videotapes, audiotapes, compact discs, films, and certain print publications whose primary social function is to provide entertainment. Both the concept and the reality of the cultural market emerged only in the late 1980s. Before then, the technologies that allow for mass reproduction of video and audio recordings had not yet been widely disseminated in China.[47] Nor had the reforms yet resulted in incomes rising to a level sufficient to create an "effective demand" for cultural market goods and services. The cultural market is thus a new, chaotic arrival on the Chinese political-economic scene, something to which the state has yet to generate a coherent, effective response. This also contributes importantly to thought-work pluralization.

In December 1982 the State Council gave the MRFT primary responsibility for planning the overall development of the audio/video industry. The MRFT would approve the units that would be allowed to produce and sell audio/video products, regulate the industry and ensure that state policies are enforced, and manage imports of audio/video products.[48] This probably did not appear to be such a difficult task at the time, since the old China Record Corporation continued to monopolize audio-video production, and the vast majority of the population was too poor to purchase its products.

But a decade of 10 percent annual economic growth and market-oriented reforms changed this picture dramatically. By April 1991 there were 190 licensed audio/video production companies scattered throughout China, 94 publishing houses printing literature to accompany audio/video products, 200 dubbing and processing units, and thousands of distribution units and projection centers.[49] The newer technology of the compact disc developed more slowly. The Xianhe Corporation of Shenzhen was the only CD-production facility in existence as late as 1992, but by early 1994 the figure had jumped to 25 factories and 30 production lines.[50] These outfits "belonged," not only to units within the MRFT system, but also to units within the Ministry of Culture (MoC) system, the State Press and Publications Administration (SPPA) system, and—in the case of semilegal and illegal production—the systems of the Ministry of Electronics Industry (MEI) and the People's Liberation Army (PLA). It therefore became impossible for the MRFT to manage development of the audio/video industry as envisaged by the State Council in 1982. General administrative decentralization policies implemented from the early 1980s had resulted in lower-level units within almost all systems being granted vast new authority to engage in a byzantine array of economic activities. A significant number of such units perceived audio/video production to be a quick path to riches. In the mid-1990s these units devoted themselves to inundating China with tapes and compact discs from a variety of sources, most notably Hong Kong, Taiwan, and the United States.

The film industry, meanwhile, remained highly centralized under the MRFT xitong until January 1, 1993, when a major new reform shattered the monopoly of the China Film Distribution and Screening Company.[51] Before 1993, China's 21 central- and 13 provincial-level film-production companies were required to sell all of their full-length feature films to the Company in exchange for a fixed fee of 900,000 yuan (U.S.$108,168). At the same time, the Company was required to purchase every film the studios produced.[52] All films, once purchased, were distributed down through the Company hierarchy to the county level and below. Individual theaters could only purchase films from the equivalent-level Company branch in their region.

But the January 1993 reform both decentralized the Company and granted studios the right to sell directly either to the newly autonomous, lower-level companies or to the theaters—at any level in the hierarchy. In the prevailing pattern today, the studios sell directly to the provincial-level companies, thereby achieving rough market parity. There are 30 to 35 studios and 30 to 35 provincial-level companies. Once the companies have purchased a film, they own exclusive rights to sell it within their area of operations. Thus, if the Jiangsu provincial distribution company buys rights to a film, all the theaters in Jiangsu that wish to show it must buy from the Jiangsu company. They may not turn to extraprovincial sources. Occasionally, and with increasing frequency, studios sell directly to the theaters (some of which are large chains, but always restricted to specific regions). But this is difficult because both the distribution companies and an estimated 80 percent of the theaters are macromanaged by the MoC xitong, which discourages competition among its component members. Nevertheless, a clear pluralization of film sources has followed automatically from the 1993 reform.[53]

Film pluralization interacts with commercialization and globalization to cause consternation among some leaders at the central level, but in general (domestic) films are not considered to be as serious a problem as audio- and videotapes and CDs, because Chinese studios only produce about 150 films a year.[54] Most of the vastly more numerous tapes and CDs are "consumed" at public establishments—karaoke bars, dance halls, restaurants, MTVs, and the like—because the typical Chinese household cannot afford a videotape or CD player. These public establishments are regulated primarily by the MoC system, but secondarily by the public-security and industry and commerce systems. A large but ultimately unknown proportion of these establishments entertains customers with illegal video- and audiotapes pirated on a massive scale from foreign, Hong Kong, and Taiwan imports. As a result, customs officials also play a role in managing the cultural market. Hence, the number of bureaucracies responsible for regulating—or enjoying rights to participate in—this market totals at least eight: the MoC, the GBRFT, the Ministry of Public Security (MPS), the State Administration of Industry and Commerce (SAIC), the SPPA, the Ministry of Information Industries (MII), the PLA, and the Customs Administration.

As detailed in Chapter 6, the central party-state has responded to this radical fragmentation of audio/video communications management by creating small coordinating groups and launching periodic mobilizational crackdowns, both with decidedly mixed success. Hence, the pluralization of communications messages in the form of tapes and discs continues unabated, fueled by the full complement of administrative fragmentation, property-rights reform, and technological advance.[55]

Periodical and Book Proliferation

Official Communist Party newspapers dominated propagandistic public communication during the Cultural Revolution decade. In 1970 there were only 42 newspapers nationwide, and radio stations were forced to rebroadcast newspaper content and Xinhua News Agency dispatches at the expense of their own programs. The newspapers and Xinhua adhered strictly to the prevailing political line and excelled only in reportage about abstruse theoretical issues. They were thus the very antithesis of the highly audience-oriented, pluralistic media of today.

All of this began to change in the late 1970s. First, as Table 7 makes clear, the number of newspaper and magazine titles increased enormously under reform, as did the annual number of book titles published. The result is a much greater variety of information available in print today than at any time in Chinese history.[56] Of course, politically radical and highly pornographic materials are usually available only from underground sources, but even the official world of print has ex-

TABLE 7

Periodical and Book Publication, 1970–1996

	Newspapers		Magazines		Books	
Year	No. of titles	Copies printed per capita	No. of titles	Copies printed per capita	No. of titles	Copies printed per capita
1970	42	5.60	21	0.08	4,889	2.16
1978	186	13.28	930	0.79	14,987	3.92
1985	698	18.88	4,705	2.42	45,603	6.30
1986	791	18.03	5,248	2.23	51,789	4.84
1987	850	18.74	5,687	2.37	60,213	5.72
1988	829	18.66	5,865	2.30	65,961	5.60
1989	852	13.86	6,078	1.63	74,973	5.20
1990	773	14.04	5,751	1.57	80,224	4.93
1991	812	15.25	6,056	1.78	89,615	5.30
1992	875	16.14	6,486	2.01	92,148	5.41
1993	943	16.25	7,011	1.98	96,761	5.00
1994	1,015	14.84	7,325	1.84	103,836	5.01
1995	1,049	14.77	7,583	1.93	101,381	5.22
1996	1,083	14.67	7,916	1.89	112,813	5.85

SOURCE: Guojia Tongjiju, ed., *Zhongguo Tongji Nianjian, 1997*.

perienced a remarkable pluralization of content over the past twenty years. As the director of the SPPA's Newspaper Department put it in early 1993, "The Chinese press has already changed from the past single-purpose party committee organization reports to a diversified and multifunctional newspaper complex in which party reports are just one major factor."[57]

Indeed, this diversification is even more advanced than Table 7 suggests, because the table omits data concerning the numerous trade, commercial, and professional periodicals published ostensibly for internal audiences only, but in fact available to anyone. Some 5,000 of these internal (*neibu*) newspapers and 10,000 *neibu* magazines were published in 1993.[58]

Table 7 also indicates that the number of newspaper, magazine, and book copies per capita has leveled off at about fifteen papers, two magazines, and five books per person per year. Further increase of these figures is restricted by both the rising cost of paper and limitations on demand. Indeed, the number of print media copies per capita was actually much higher in the mid-1980s than in the mid-1990s, before the cost of paper began to rise alarmingly and before video and audio started competing with print for the favor of Chinese media consumers.

Growth in the number of periodical titles has itself been of concern to the central party-state, simply because the more numerous the sources of communications messages, the more difficult they are to control. The Center's voice is all too easily crowded out. By the time of the December 1986 student demonstrations, the number of newspaper titles had increased from 186 (in 1978) to 791, while the number of magazine titles had increased from 850 to 5,248. Although all of the new periodicals had official "backers" (*guakao*)—that is, sponsorship by other, nonmedia units—and the vast majority of the backers were governed internally by Communist Party committees, the degree of discipline in the system had by the mid-1980s waned to the point that the numerous new nonofficial papers could easily get away with publishing a significant amount of material that many party-state leaders in Beijing found objectionable. Linking the demonstrations as well as other manifestations of spiritual pollution and bourgeois liberalization with periodical proliferation, the central party-state in January 1987 created an important new bureaucratic organization for the express purpose of regulating the numerous new nonparty print publications. This organization is the SPPA, or *Xinwen Chubanshu*. Under it was established a system of bureaus (*ju*) in provincial capitals and a few large cities, but not below.[59] A *shu* is lower in rank than a *bu* (ministry), but because the SPPA's jurisdiction would be limited to nonparty publications, it was deemed unnecessary and even undesirable to give it the status of a *bu*—despite the fact that broadcast media and telecommunications were managed by *bu* from the early 1980s.[60]

The conservative Du Daozheng was named the SPPA's first director, at the same time as the conservative Wang Renzhi assumed the party post of Minister of Propaganda.[61] In an April 1987 interview Du announced five important-sounding SPPA chief tasks, the most important of which was to license publications by granting their publishing houses book numbers (ISBNs and ISSNs).[62] By controlling book numbers, it was believed, the SPPA could control the total number of publications. Table 7 reveals that, in the aftermath of the 1986–87 political crisis, the SPPA initially succeeded not only in slowing the growth in new periodical titles, but even in cutting the number of, in particular, newspaper titles from 850 in 1987 to 829 in 1988. The number of magazine and book titles continued to rise, however, as no effective, centralized mechanism for allocating book numbers had yet been developed. The buying and selling of book numbers became common as publishing houses were made responsible for profits and losses. By the early 1990s the proliferation of print media was, once again, out of central state control and has basically remained so ever since.[63]

A key problem is that, once in possession of ISSNs, periodical publishers need not reapply. In principle, the SPPA's provincial bureaus investigate all publishing houses annually, but "very few" are closed or even censured for the content of their publications. The reason for this is unclear given the frequent complaints of senior Chinese leaders about spiritual pollution, but it seems likely to be because of the SPPA's inherent bureaucratic weaknesses as a *shu*. The SPPA system is (assertedly) slightly more centralized than the GBRFT system, but its provincial bureaus frequently come under strong pressure not to shut down print media outlets that for whatever reason enjoy provincial government support.[64] In any dispute, the bureaus have only a *shu* above them from which to seek political assistance. The SPPA grants book and/or periodical numbers directly to only a few large publishing houses that "belong" to it bureaucratically. All other publishers apply to provincial or municipal bureaus with close ties to the territorial administration. Below the provincial level, the SPPA is hamstrung even more severely by the fact that it has no representation; the hierarchy penetrates down only to the level of the provincial capital. As a result, it became obvious in the early 1990s that the creation of the SPPA as a means to rein in the proliferation of print media had failed. The multiplication of the communication channels with which the Center had to compete for the attention of the citizenry continued.[65]

The Ebbing Primacy of 'Renmin Ribao' and the Xinhua News Agency

Under Mao, the twin pillars of thought-work centralization were *Renmin Ribao* and the Xinhua News Agency.[66] As the official organ of the Communist Party Central Committee, *Renmin Ribao* acted as the chief conduit of official interpretations of all political, economic, social, and cultural events—domestic and international—to party members and society at large throughout the country. Although lower-level newspapers and radio stations did have some flexibility in news selection—at least in the period before the Cultural Revolution—their editors and managers carefully scrutinized *Renmin Ribao* for signals as to what stories should be carried and how they should be presented.[67] At the same time, the Xinhua News Agency monopolized the provision of all extraregional news to every media outlet in the country. That is, although newspapers and radio stations did enjoy some autonomy in selecting the news of their regions, they were forced to accept Xinhua dispatches for all news of other regions, including news from abroad.[68] In this way, the Center could ensure itself a firm grip on the basic contours of thought work throughout the country, particularly given the rudimentary nature of the media and telecommunications technology that prevailed under Mao.[69]

Notably missing from the Maoist structure was a centralized censorate. As Judy Polumbaum writes, China, unlike other Soviet-style propaganda states, has no

> formalized, institutionalized, and universalized prepublication censorship apparatus. . . . The Party sets the overall tone and direction for the press implicitly through general policy statements, and more directly by specifying instructions and priorities for the press via documents and bulletins transmitted from propaganda authorities to news organizations and their Party administrators, editors, and reporters. How directives and guidelines are interpreted in practice is largely up to local Party committees and news organizations themselves.[70]

This system is referred to as the "editor responsibility system" and applies also to the broadcast media and to film. Editors are appointed by territorial-level party committees, not by the vertical party propa-

ganda apparatus. The editor responsibility system could function effectively to maintain central control over thought work under the "societal
totalitarianism" of Mao, but the record indicates that it is far too "loose"
to be reliable when charisma becomes (poorly) routinized. Discipline
flags, then is tightened up again during campaigns, but slips a notch
with each turn of the cycle. By the early 1990s Chinese reporters and
others in the media were even discussing the sensitive phenomenon of
editors—and indeed the very individuals responsible for managing
thought work within media units—becoming "unit oriented" as opposed to "xitong oriented." That is, they had become more concerned
with advancing the material interests of their particular newspaper,
television station, or radio station than with building a socialist spiritual civilization.[71]

Under Mao and in the early years of Deng, *Renmin Ribao* and the
Xinhua News Agency could at least "set the agenda" for Chinese
thought work—thereby playing the role of a censor in exerting a centralizing effect. But in today's setting of administrative fragmentation,
property-rights reform, and technological advance, *Renmin Ribao* and
Xinhua can only set the agenda for a very few politically active individuals. While it may be true that Minister of Propaganda Ding Guan'-
gen himself still reads and approves all *Renmin Ribao* editorials every
day—underscoring their continued importance to the central party-
state[72]— assertions such as that of Guoguang Wu that *Renmin Ribao* still
enjoys "'hegemony' in shaping Chinese public opinion" are simply un-
sustainable, the vain wishes of central-state leaders notwithstanding.[73]
Renmin Ribao's circulation fell from 7 million copies per day in 1979 to
only 1.65 million in 1993.[74] Moreover, at least during the first six months
of 1992, only 2.5 percent of *Renmin Ribao*'s subscribers were individuals.
The other 97.5 percent were units, whose leaders felt compelled to subscribe to the paper whether anyone in the units reads it or not.[75] Fewer
people now are exposed to *Renmin Ribao* than at any time since the mid-
1950s, and even those who are exposed to it also consume competing
media messages from numerous other sources that simply did not exist
before the reform era. To many members of the populace, the Center's
voice has become only one of many in a huge, often dissonant chorus.[76]

Renmin Ribao officials interviewed for this study acknowledged the decline in circulation without providing exact figures, but professed not to be concerned for either political or economic reasons. First, all units with party committees must still subscribe, and second, all "important" cadres and officials (including business elites) must still read *Renmin Ribao* to "get ahead" in the system.[77] At the same time, however, *Renmin Ribao*'s editors have radically altered the paper's style and content to make it more readable and appealing to general audiences in the hope of eventually increasing circulation again—an attempt to substitute commercialization for pluralization. All but the central news is now presented in a much less ponderous fashion than before (even if it remains highly politicized), and there is much more reporting on culture, the arts, and even sports. As discussed in Chapter 3, *Renmin Ribao*—like most other media outlets—is fully responsible for profits and losses, and its staff faces strong incentives to increase audience size so that more advertising can be sold. And despite its falling circulation, the paper has had much success selling advertising because it does enjoy a "captive audience" of coerced subscribers and because large enterprises find it politically useful to support the paper financially.[78]

But in light of the falling circulation figures, the assertion that *Renmin Ribao* is a "must read" for cadres, officials, and business people seems likely to be an overstatement for all but a tiny elite. In 1993 the State Council ordered that, thenceforth, all personal subscriptions to party and government journals must be paid for out of personal funds and may no longer be subsidized by subscribers' units. As a result, *Renmin Ribao*'s circulation immediately fell by 28 percent, while *Guangming Ribao*'s fell 43 percent and *Qiushi*'s fell 27 percent.[79] Clearly, a significant number of former subscribers believe they can easily do without these central-state publications.[80] *Renmin Ribao* and the flagship provincial party papers continue to maintain guaranteed minimum subscriber bases as a result of their role as conduits of official political pronouncements and interpretations, and undoubtedly individuals in politically important positions still at least scan the headlines. But the fact that many units will not subscribe unless forced to do so—and the fact that content must be altered to make the paper more appealing—exemplify the advanced state of thought-work pluralization (i.e., decline of central hegemony) that had set in by the early 1990s. The Center must now contend with numerous competitors for the attention not only of the citizenry at large but even of the political elite.[81]

The difficulties facing the Xinhua News Agency also illustrate waning central power over the symbolic environment. While *Renmin Ribao* is an official organ of the Communist Party Central Committee, Xinhua belongs directly to the highest governmental body, the State Council. Xinhua's voluminous dispatches—sent down through a massive hierarchical network that penetrates into every corner of China—therefore carry the force of officially prescribed interpretations of all the key daily events affecting the country, domestic and foreign.[82] But interviews with journalists and editors suggest that most Xinhua dispatches no longer inspire any particular awe.

Until the early 1980s Xinhua accompanied each of its dispatches with the equivalent of an "A," "B," "C," or "D" rating to indicate its importance ("A" being the most important).[83] Except for the period of greatest Cultural Revolution communication compression, Xinhua subscribers did enjoy some flexibility in selecting the stories they would print or broadcast, particularly stories in the "C" and "D" categories. However, as stated above, if the lower-level media outlets did choose to cover an extraregional event, they were required to use the official Xinhua reportage and were not permitted to change even a single character. In 1982 and 1983, however, the leaders of the propaganda xitong decided to end the practice of ranking news items, thereafter permitting the subscribing media outlets themselves to determine newsworthiness. Only in exceptional cases does Xinhua now identify stories as "must-carry" news, affixing them with the term *jiyao* ("extremely important").[84]

Media outlets may also now freely cover stories from outside their regions (sometimes even from abroad) if their audiences seem likely to be interested.[85] They no longer need rely exclusively on Xinhua for extraregional news that they consider to be especially important. This fact is frustrating to Xinhua, but less for political reasons than for economic reasons. Put simply, Xinhua can no longer reap the benefits of a monopoly on extraregional news, though it does still enjoy a near-monopoly on foreign news.[86] The result is pluralization in the form of a dramatic drop in the proportion of media outlets' news originating with Xinhua. While the absolute amount of "extremely important" news is estimated to have remained constant since the early 1980s, the size of the average newspaper has quadrupled, so that Xinhua copy now represents only about 10 to 20 percent of all the news covered—and it tends to be the news less likely to be read, precisely because it is the dull, politicized news that the central party-state regards as "extremely important."[87]

However, the breakdown of Xinhua's monopolistic rights to the supply of extraregional news has so far resulted in only potential economic loss. The agency is not earning any money from providing the service anyway. The reason is simply that subscribers consistently and almost unanimously refuse to pay. In principle, the subscribers have been required to pay ever since the early 1980s, but in practice very few have ever paid a dime. They face very little incentive to pay because the "extremely important" news that they pass on for the central government is itself a kind of sacrifice; that space could be used to publish popular news and therefore increase ad revenues. Subscribers know that the central government will not cut off the supply of Xinhua dispatches as punishment for their refusal to pay, and no alternative sanctions have yet appeared. Early in 1995, Xinhua did secure a promise that "from now on" the flagship provincial party newspapers, at least, will pay their assessed fees, but the agreement did not apply to any other media outlet. In the meantime, the agency remains heavily reliant on the central government for subsidies, while searching for new ways to generate income by diversifying into video production, economic consulting, advertising, and public relations. In line with the trend, Xinhua is now under strong pressure to become fully responsible for profits and losses and is responding by metamorphosing into a general information-services conglomerate.[88]

In view of all these difficulties, Minister of Propaganda Ding Guan'gen in February 1995 called upon the chief editors of the party papers to "assume the main responsibility for giving shape to a unifying force," such a force being necessary to counter the pluralization of communication sources under reform. Party papers in particular should "promptly publish major news released by the Xinhua News Agency and reprint important editorials and articles from *Renmin Ribao*," the latter because significantly fewer people now read *Renmin*

Ribao itself.[89] Eighteen months later, a frustrated Ding attacked on another front. The CPD issued a circular calling on managers of newspaper posting boards to post "mainly" the central and local party papers, including *Renmin Ribao*. Those posting boards devoted to other newspapers should be built only in less strategically located places, and certainly not on major streets or in major plazas.[90]

Pluralization via Telecommunications

As discussed in Chapter 2, China's telecommunications industry has since the mid-1980s developed so rapidly that the country is well on its way to "leap-frogging" into an advanced, broadband, digital system that could prove the envy not only of the developing world but even of those developed countries with sunk costs into relatively antiquated copper wire–based systems. But the ultimate result will probably be not simply an enhanced information exchange that improves economic efficiency but also numerous new problems in managing thought work. Chinese citizens will deploy the telecommunications system to communicate with each other and with residents of foreign countries and regions about all manner of subjects, not only by voice but also by fax, e-mail, and the Internet. Such a development will even more dramatically multiply the number of points at which the Center must interdict undesirable thought-work messages and thus contribute to deepened thought-work pluralization. Eventually everyone with access to a telephone and more advanced technologies will be able to generate and circulate their own thought-work messages: pluralization in the extreme.

Chapter 2 also discussed the State Council's 1993 approval of the creation of two new enterprises to compete with the Ministry of Posts and Telecommunications (MPT). These two enterprises would provide alternative telecommunications services, a development that may improve efficiency of information flows but only at the expense of intensifying pluralization. The new companies, Liantong and Jitong, are building their networks partly by linking together the preexisting "private" networks owned by certain energy and transportation ministries. Because Liantong and Jitong are likely to contribute to an intensification of the trend toward pluralization—as well as the trends toward commer-

cialization and globalization—and because these processes exemplify in
a particularly powerful way the effects on thought work of administrative fragmentation, property-rights reform, and technological advance,
a relatively detailed examination of the formation of Liantong and Jitong will help to focus analytical attention on the linkages between the
causal variables and loss of central state control over thought work.

The idea of connecting preexisting private networks to form alternative public networks first emerged around 1990.[91] The general consensus is that the idea originated with Hu Qili, a very high-ranking party
member demoted to Minister of the Electronics Industry after aligning
himself with the disgraced Zhao Ziyang during the 1989 political crisis.
One story has it that Hu conceived the idea of an alternative to the MPT
simply as a result of having repeated difficulties making long-distance
calls. In truth, the idea seems likely to have emerged from a combination of factors related to Hu's vision of the information industries playing a potentially determinative role in the trajectory of China's all-
around 21st-century development.[92] Hu believed that the MEI should
take primary responsibility for transforming China into an information
society, and that the MPT—under its long-time, not-notably-visionary
Minister Yang Taifang—was holding the country back by acting passively in the face of new challenges and demonstrating more concern
for shoring up its bureaucratic position than for forging ahead energetically with bold new ideas.

Hu himself was far from averse to playing bureaucratic politics. In
fact, some speculate that one of his chief motivations in pursuing the
development of alternative telecommunications networks was simply
to get even with the MPT. The MPT consistently refused to source its
equipment from the MEI system—despite the dominant role in telecommunications equipment production that the State Council's Leading Group for the Revitalization of the Electronics Industry had assigned to the MEI in 1985.[93] Moreover, the MPT was thought to be
actively discouraging multinational telecommunications equipment
providers from cooperating with the MEI, threatening them with economic discrimination unless they promised to work exclusively with
the MPT. Given the generally poor state of China's telecommunications
infrastructure at the time—and given the money to be made when the

country's telecommunications industry finally "took off"—Hu considered this behavior to be outrageous, nothing less than evidence that the MPT "would rather give advantages to foreigners and sell China out than cooperate at home"—an old proverb that implies treason. The depth of the animosity is palpable.

Hu had many potential allies in his quest to develop alternative public networks, most notably the ministries with underused private capacity and nationwide organizations—such as the Bank of China and *Renmin Ribao*—that could benefit from advanced telecommunications services. Because of the cloud of Tiananmen, however, Hu remained restricted in his political maneuvering until 1992. It was only after the Fourteenth Party Congress in October 1992 that Hu was able formally to propose before the State Council the idea of linking the underutilized private networks into alternative public networks.[94]

Hu suggested two networks, each to be run by a separate company affiliated with the MEI. The first company, Liantong, or "the United Telecommunications Company," would provide alternative long-distance services to the Chinese public; it was expected to become "the MCI of China." The thinking behind Liantong was simply that competition in the telecommunications industry would stimulate the MPT (and Liantong itself) to provide better service. The second company, Jitong, or "the Auspicious Telecommunications Company," would concentrate on providing value-added services such as electronic data transfer, electronic mail, and video-on-demand. Hu and his associates could argue that Liantong would aid China's economic development primarily by acting as a competitive stimulus to the MPT. But the rationale for creating Jitong was not only that value-added services would constitute an integral component of the envisioned information society, but also that advanced data-exchange networks would be enormously helpful to the Center's efforts to reassert control over the macroeconomy.

Initially, yielding to intensive lobbying by the MPT, the State Council rejected Hu's proposals, but during the winter and spring of 1993, Hu carefully targeted and eventually secured the crucial support of three key proponents: Premier Li Peng, who enjoyed close connections with the energy ministries that had spare telecommunications capacity; Vice Premier Zhu Rongji, in charge of overall macroeconomic management;

and Vice Premier Zou Jiahua, whose primary portfolio was macroeconomic planning. Hu also benefited initially when longtime MPT minister Yang Taifang retired in April 1993 and was replaced by the relatively junior (and ultimately underestimated) Wu Jichuan, whose status in the governing hierarchy was far lower than that of Hu.

During the first half of 1993, Hu and his associates at the MEI developed a more detailed set of plans for Jitong, the project likely to have the most appeal to the State Council. In July 1993 Hu presented these plans to the Council as the three "Golden Projects": Golden Customs, Golden Card, and Golden Bridge.[95] Golden Customs, to be built first, would electronically link all customs offices and all enterprises engaging in foreign trade. This project would ensure the Center a steady flow of timely, accurate information on foreign trade, and would "help check malpractices regarding licenses, quotas, settlements of foreign exchange, and taxes."[96] Golden Card, meanwhile, would link 300 million Chinese consumers into an electronic banking network, including credit card and ATM services. It would establish the groundwork for an eventual transition to a cashless society, in the process giving the Center much more control over the money supply and therefore inflation.[97] Golden Bridge, the master project, would link all government bodies, large- and medium-sized industrial and commercial enterprises, educational and research institutions, other important organizations, and even individuals into a pan-China intranet and, externally, to the Internet, providing subscribers with "virtual private networks" for data, e-mail, and video exchanges, both domestically and internationally.

The idea behind Golden Bridge—indeed, the basic mission of the entire Jitong enterprise—was nothing less than to transform the fundamental structure of Chinese society, to break down the barriers among vertical xitong and between cellularized regions to build a new, multicentric (but fully interconnected) "societal xitong." Specifically to appeal to the central government, Golden Bridge would in the process "link up the State Council and national economic administrations throughout 500 cities in China for the purpose of comprehensive control and adjustment."[98]

The State Council approved the creation of Jitong in June 1993 and of Liantong in December 1993. The two companies actually were assigned different bureaucratic statuses. Jitong "belonged to" (*shuyu*) the MEI, while Liantong "belonged to" the State Council. They each had up to 30 different shareholders, representing a broad cross-section of China's high technology industries. But both companies were closely associated—both in the minds of industry officials and in reality—with Hu Qili's MEI.

Perhaps not surprisingly, no MPT-affiliated firm purchased shares in either Liantong or Jitong. In fact, the MPT had been bitterly opposed to the creation of alternative telecommunications providers from the start. Under Yang Taifang, the MPT succeeded in delaying their approval, but the relatively junior minister Wu Jichuan could not hold the line.[99] In the first few months after his appointment, Wu adopted what one foreign telecommunications businessman dismissed as "an ostrich strategy"—he simply refused to believe that the MPT's monopoly would ever be broken. By early 1994, after the State Council had made its decision, Wu's attitude shifted to a different kind of complacency: "We don't care; let them go ahead and try to build their networks." Wu saw both Liantong and Jitong as "a mixed bag of disparate units with little knowledge of telecommunications." By the summer of 1994, however, when Liantong and Jitong staged gilded inaugural ceremonies at the Diaoyutai State Guest House and several of China's senior leaders attended, Wu was left almost literally speechless by the magnitude of his bureaucratic defeat. At the Liantong inaugural in July, Wu "was flustered, ruffled, unable to make polite comments."[100]

At the same time, however, Wu was quietly launching a bureaucratic counteroffensive that soon gathered strength and eventually—much to the astonishment of many insiders—succeeded not only in preventing Liantong and Jitong from becoming serious competitors, but even put the MEI out of business. Wu had many good cards to play. First was the obvious fact that, lingering dissatisfaction aside, the MPT had a remarkable record in developing China's telecommunications system after 1985. Second was the equally obvious fact that neither Liantong nor Jitong could survive if they were not granted access to the MPT-controlled public network; the MPT had little incentive to grant this access. Beginning in the spring of 1994, Wu adopted the two-pronged strategy of more widely publicizing the MPT's many successes, and foot-dragging on efforts by Liantong and Jitong to secure terms for interconnectivity.

But the competition became intense in the fall of 1993, when the MPT unveiled Chinapac, the public packet-switching network that would fulfill precisely the same functions as the MEI's Golden Projects. China-pac had been in the works for years, and its formal coming-out ceremony appears to have been timed purely as a rejoinder to Hu's July presentation before the State Council. During the late fall and winter, Wu and his staff wrote numerous articles trumpeting Chinapac and the MPT's undeniable successes, both for industry journals and for the general press. By the spring of 1994 the term "Chinapac" was suppressed in favor of "China's Information Superhighway," a more grandiose appellation than even "the Golden Projects." In April Wu convened a symposium on the Information Superhighway, inviting foreign telecommunications dignitaries and securing wide publicity. At the symposium, Wu asserted straightforwardly that the Information Superhighway would be "based on the country's public telecommunications network," not on the private networks being gathered together by Jitong.[101]

Shortly thereafter, the MEI struck back, securing broad publicity for a pilot Golden Bridge project in Shanghai. "China will build a modern nationwide economic information network this year" on the basis of the Shanghai project, Xinhua reported, implying that Golden Bridge was proceeding much faster than the MPT's Information Superhighway. Golden Bridge was "aimed at meeting the needs of social and economic development and facilitating state macroeconomic regulation and decision-making."[102] Wu, too, had emphasized the contributions of the MPT's Information Superhighway both to the functioning of the socialist market economy and to central state efforts to reassert macroeconomic control. The battle had been fully joined.

In May 1994 Vice Premier Zou Jiahua stepped in to settle this particular phase of the MPT-MEI conflict with an appearance at the All-China Meeting of Directors of Post and Telecommunications Bureau Chiefs in Beijing. At the end of this conclave, Zou exercised his powers to "sum up" the meeting by making the following declaration:

> In light of the principles of making overall planning, combining departments with localities, letting each level assume responsibility for itself, and joining efforts to build communications facilities, . . . the MPT should conscientiously formulate the strategic principle for China's communica-

tions development and draw up the long-term plan and the fiscal-year plans for the nation's telecommunications development. . . . [However,] not only should we successfully build the public communications network throughout the country, but also we should give full play to the role of special networks.[103]

Clearly, Zou was trying to smooth over the bitter differences between the MPT and the MEI. He recognized from his higher-level vantage point that cooperation between the two emerging telecommunications systems would be essential to building both the "societal xitong" that would buttress the market economy and the Information Superhighway that would, inter alia, strengthen the Center's control over the macroeconomy. Zou succeeded during the fall of 1994 in forcing the MPT and both Liantong and Jitong to agree in principle that the secondary telecommunications providers would be granted access to the MPT's public network. From the perspective of the Center, constructing two completely separate networks would have constituted an outrageous waste of societal resources.[104] The only sticking points—and they have proven to be major sticking points—are the terms of access, and in particular, the cost.

Probably in recognition of his company's relative weakness as a bargaining partner, Liantong's first chairman, Zhao Weichen, immediately adopted a humble facade, publicly acknowledging at every opportunity that Liantong was the MPT's "little brother," and that the MPT enjoyed full rights to macromanage the telecommunications industry.[105] But the MPT responded to this "concession" by contemptuously asserting its superiority as the government department charged with macromanaging the telecommunications industry, not a mere business association like Liantong.[106] Liantong had only conceded the MPT's right to set broad standards and goals for the industry, not to order the company around as a second-class organization. But the MPT—bitter and frustrated at losing its monopoly—was exceptionally reluctant to accept anything less than acknowledgment of its inherent superiority.

But Liantong's basic gripe was not the disrespect the MPT relished heaping upon it. It was instead the fact that the MPT enjoyed enormous commercial and political advantages over its competitors as a result of its status as both an operator and a regulator. Since the late 1980s, the

State Council had been pushing the MPT to "separate regulation from operation" (*zhengqi fenkai*) by severing the ties that linked the MPT as regulator with the MPT as operator at all levels of the administrative hierarchy. This topic is discussed in Chapter 3, but it bears repeating that the MPT's failure to implement the *zhengqi fenkai* policy—a failure that one high-ranking MPT official fully acknowledged (albeit using euphemistic terminology)—made it very difficult for Liantong and Jitong to achieve effective market entry.[107] The MPT could always produce a new regulation or a simple declaration biased in favor of the operators within its own xitong.

With an eye to resolving these serious difficulties, Vice Premier Zou in December 1994 convened the first meeting of a special "small group" composed of MPT and Liantong personnel at the assistant minister level to work out a formula for allowing the secondary carriers access to the public network. By May 1995 this group had met ten times and had little or no progress to report for its efforts.[108] Any objective assessment of the situation would make it clear that the MPT was intentionally deploying delaying tactics. For example, at every meeting MPT officials raised questions about Liantong's technical standards, despite the fact that Liantong had secured the assistance and advice of up to 100 foreign firms and experts in building its network. The MPT also often avoided resolving important issues, saying, "For that, you need to get the approval of telecommunications authorities at the local levels." But when Liantong would then open up discussions with the Beijing, Shanghai, Tianjin, or Guangzhou municipal telecommunications authorities, they, in turn, would apologetically assert, "Sorry, but we need approval from Minister Wu's office before we can proceed on that."[109] As a result of these infuriating roadblocks—all the more galling given the State Council's obvious high-level support—Liantong officials in the spring of 1995 pessimistically predicted that it could take up to ten years to offer fixed-line telecommunications services to the Chinese public. In any event, Liantong did finally start offering fixed-line services in the city of Tianjin on July 18, 1997, by which time the company had built mobile telephone networks in 76 cities and had established a nationwide paging network of 100,000 subscribers.[110]

In the meantime, Hu Qili and the MEI had hit upon a risky new strategy for dealing with the MPT, a strategy that could have far-reaching implications for the overall development of all of China's communications industries—including the mass media. While negotiations on Liantong-MPT and Jitong-MPT interlinking continued within the small group at the Center and in several locales, the MEI began actively promoting the creation of a Telecommunications Commission that would answer directly to the State Council—on the same level as the State Planning Commission, State Education Commission, and others. Modeled somewhat on the U.S. Federal Communications Commission, the Telecommunications Commission would supersede in rank all of the telecommunications- and media-related bureaucracies and would impose authoritative solutions when disputes among them arose. The MPT would be completely divested of its regulatory responsibilities and transformed purely into an operator, competing on a "level playing field" with Liantong, Jitong, and perhaps other providers in the future.[111]

Unfortunately for the MEI, this strategy backfired spectacularly. The State Council did indeed create a new high-level ministerial body to govern telecommunications development in the organizational reforms of March 1998: the MII. Both the MEI and the MPT were turned into MII bureaus. But the problem from the MEI's vantage point was that the first new Minister of Information Industries was none other than Wu Jichuan, and the new ministry simply took over the old MPT building in Beijing. In other words, it appeared as if the MPT was simply absorbing the MEI and assuming a new name.[112]

But the abolition of the MEI does not necessarily mean that Liantong and Jitong will not go forward. In fact, the rationale for creating the new super-ministry was precisely to reduce jealously between the MPT and MEI so that genuine competition within the telecommunications industry could finally be introduced. Whether Wu's perspective will change now that he sees the world from a higher vantage point is of course impossible to say, but it does seem likely that negotiations over interconnectivity will now proceed much more smoothly than before, and that Liantong and Jitong do have a future.

As stressed above, one of Hu Qili's key "selling points" in convincing the State Council to sanction alternative public networks had been that Jitong, in particular, could strengthen central-state control over the macroeconomy. The question then naturally arises: Will the rise of secondary telecommunications providers strengthen or weaken the central party-state? Might their services not actually counter thought-work pluralization, if not necessarily thought-work commercialization and globalization?

There is a long tradition in planned political economies of frustrated bureaucrats desperately embracing high-technology solutions to planned systems' inherent inefficiencies. If only powerful computers and advanced information systems could be installed, then the planning process could be perfected and there would be no need to take the political risks of implementing fundamental reforms.[113] It was clearly to this strain of thinking among Soviet-trained apparatchiks such as Li Peng, Zou Jiahua, and Zhu Rongji that the more reformist-minded Hu Qili appealed. At the same time, neither Hu nor Wu Jichuan ever failed to underscore the benefits of advanced telecommunications to developing the socialist market economy, the sacred term promoted by Deng Xiaoping and his allies after the Fourteenth Party Congress.

But technology by itself cannot determine sociopolitical outcomes. It can only contribute to sociopolitical outcomes in interaction with other components of the social setting. Given the general trend toward decision-making fragmentation in all institutions of contemporary Chinese life, it seems highly unlikely that modern telecommunications will be able single-handedly to restrengthen the central party-state. Instead, modern telecommunications more likely will interact with elements of the overall fragmentation process to produce even more fragmentation.

Specifically in the issue-area of thought work, the result probably will be continued pluralization, commercialization, and globalization. Competition among alternative providers of telecommunications services will only speed up the dissemination of the telephone and even more advanced technologies throughout Chinese society. Indeed, within a year of Liantong's formal establishment, the wait for a fixed telephone fell from one year to three months in the city of Beijing.[114] Presumably after Liantong is fully up and running, the cost of both domestic and international long-distance calls will fall—unless, of course, the new MII bureaucratically stifles competition. The end result would be more Chinese citizens communicating more frequently with each other and with people abroad, completely out of monitoring range of the central party-state.[115] Similarly, the Internet and other value-added services that Jitong and China Telecom will provide will result in more Chinese citizens exchanging information with each other and with people abroad.

Because even the public network is highly automated and decentralized, the number of points at which the central party-state must interdict the flow of undesirable messages will continue to increase. Given the Center's large budget deficits and the general fragmentation of authority, China's current pattern of telecommunications development seems likely to contribute to a deepening of public-sphere praetorianism, not a restrengthening of the central party-state. Eventually it might contribute to the creation of a genuinely liberal public sphere, but that would be far in the future.

CHAPTER SIX

The Struggle to Reassert Control

The political upheaval of spring 1989 finally brought into sharp focus the causal path linking administrative fragmentation, property-rights reform, and technological advance with the commercialization, globalization, and pluralization of thought work. Indications that spiritual pollution and bourgeois liberalization could unsettle the post-Mao political order first appeared as early as 1983, but to most leaders the early indicators seemed mere minor irritants that could be handled administratively with a few jailings here, a few party expulsions there.[1] Only in 1989 did a wide spectrum of China's leaders finally realize with a shock the extent to which lost control over thought work could threaten the regime's integrity.

As Deng Xiaoping himself admitted in a June 9, 1989, meeting with martial law officers in Beijing, "It wasn't that we didn't talk about the four cardinal principles, political thought work, and opposing bourgeois liberalization. It was that we lacked consistency and thoroughness, failed to take action, and actually didn't talk enough. The problem wasn't with the four cardinal principles themselves, but with the fact that we didn't uphold them thoroughly, lacking in education and political thought work."[2] Three months later, on September 16, Deng elaborated, "The turmoil has been a good lesson for us. For many years, a few comrades among us have buried their heads in the concrete details of their work, not concerning themselves with political developments, not taking thought work seriously. . . . But following this turmoil, everyone's mind is clear."[3]

Still, the leaders were loath to acknowledge an organic connection between the reduced ability to control communications flows and the basic "line" of the post-Mao period: economic reform and opening to the outside world. Clearly, as explained in the preceding chapters, without reform and opening it is extremely unlikely that the Center would have lost any significant control over thought work. In particular, if production units had not been made responsible for profits and losses, the economic incentives contributing to thought-work commercialization, globalization, and pluralization would simply not have been present. But to point out publicly the causal connections between reform and opening and the loss of control over thought work would have been exceptionally taboo, if not politically dangerous, as long as Deng Xiaoping was in power. As a result, a collective cognitive dissonance appeared to prevail in Zhongnanhai. The leadership would seek to build both a material civilization and a spiritual civilization, even though achieving the first probably makes achieving the second impossible. Having to choose between a material and a spiritual civilization is an extremely unpleasant prospect, so the leadership—publicly at least—denies the reality of a fundamental contradiction.

Only in the aftermath of the Fourteenth Party Congress (October 1992) did some leaders and intellectuals finally begin gingerly to probe the connections between the administrative, economic, and technological forces unleashed by reform and opening and the loss of control over thought work. While continuing to deny the existence of the fundamental contradiction, some leaders did quietly begin to acknowledge the difficulties of building a socialist spiritual civilization and countering spiritual pollution and bourgeois liberalization under the conditions of "the new situation"—a euphemism for the multifarious effects of reform and opening. Importantly, however, the official response was not to reverse reform and opening, but instead to launch an omnidirectional crackdown on heterodox thought work beginning late in the summer of 1993 and continuing as of this writing.[4]

This "natural experiment"—whose goal is dramatically to reinvigorate state control over society in the thought-work issue-area—will help to answer the question of whether, in fact, any country can shift from a planned economy to a market economy at fin-de-siècle levels of communications technology without giving up the propaganda state. Initial indications in China are that the Center, if vigorous and well disciplined, can remain an important force in the thought-work market, but can no longer come close to monopolizing it as in the period before reform. The result is a radical constriction of the Center's ability to shape the citizenry's worldviews, values, and action strategies, which both reduces the state's capacity to attain goals in other issue-areas and plants the seeds of a potential legitimacy crisis.

Soon after the Fourteenth Party Congress, Minister of Culture (until 1998) and Deputy Director of the party's Central Propaganda Department (CPD) Liu Zhongde emerged as perhaps the leading, and certainly the most trenchant, analyst of the contradiction between maintaining control over thought work and making the transition to a market economy. In the process, Minister Liu established the fundamental intellectual rationale for the omnidirectional crackdown: the concept of "managing the cultural market" administratively. Liu argued on the eve of the crackdown—in *Qiushi*, the party's chief theoretical journal—that

> if cultural products are chosen by the market, under certain social and
> historical conditions, harmful "cultural trash" will inundate the market
> and poison the people. Our regulation and control of cultural products
> and cultural markets through such means as laws and policies should be
> more direct and forceful. . . . [But] cultural construction is a long historical
> process requiring long-term accumulation. . . . Because the quality of
> people's thinking and general education as well as the general mood of
> society are not ideal at present, divorce and even deviation between social
> benefits and economic results will exist for a protracted period of time.[5]

Six months later, Liu was forced also to pay homage to the Fourteenth Party Congress line of building a socialist market economy, by asserting that the "construction of the socialist cultural market should (1) be in accordance with the general laws of a market economy and (2) be in accordance with the demand for establishment of a socialist spiritual civilization: Neither can be cast aside."[6]

The "divorce and even deviation between social benefits and economic results" about which Liu wrote in the summer of 1993 refers to the tendency of producers of all manner of cultural products—television programs, films, newspaper articles, and so on—to cater to the so-called lowest common denominator (*disu*) tastes of the market. This is all in the process of putting personal economic gain ahead of the public, moralistic goal of building a socialist spiritual civilization—empirical facts discussed repeatedly in this book. In analyzing the problem, Liu tacitly acknowledged the reality of thought-work commercialization and expressed both the central party-state's frustration and its determination to reverse the situation.[7] As *Ming Pao* reported in December 1993, "Top CPC leaders had reached a consensus of opinion [at Beidaihe in the summer], and agreed that while building the market economic structure, they must never relax efforts in propaganda work, but new management methods must be adopted to tighten control."[8]

To discuss this new policy thrust, the leadership convened in Beijing in January 1994 the highest-ranking propaganda work conference to be held in the country since March 1957. The conference's 181 participants included all members of the Politburo Standing Committee as well as other Politburo members with portfolios related to propaganda; party committee assistant secretaries from every provincial-level administrative unit; propaganda ministers from every provincial-level administrative unit; representatives of every unit of the central propaganda and cultural system; representatives from the central political departments of both the People's Liberation Army (PLA) and the People's Armed Police; and high-ranking representatives of the women's, labor, and youth mass organizations. At the same time, and also in the city of Beijing, seven other propaganda-related meetings were held, bringing the total number of propaganda system cadres "networking" in Beijing and discussing the new line on thought work to 1,143.[9] Senior leader Deng Xiaoping (in the form of a *Renmin Ribao* commentary) was there to "greet" the assembling delegates. The paper quoted Deng as saying that conference delegates should recognize that "ideological and cultural departments must produce more spiritual fruits for the people and resolutely stop the production, import, and circulation of poor-quality products."[10]

High-ranking propaganda officials in attendance at the conference echoed Liu Zhongde's concerns about the need to manage the administration of the cultural market more rigorously. For example, Yu Youxian, the director of the State Press and Publications Administration (SPPA), wrote in *Renmin Ribao* that

under the conditions of the socialist market economy, the press and publications will, for a long time to come, face the question of how to properly
handle the relationship between social benefits and economic results. . . .
We must persist in putting social benefits in the most important position
and, with this as the prerequisite, unify economic results with social benefits. At the same time, it is necessary to adopt measures related to structure
and rules to eradicate the influence of "money worship."[11]

Similarly, Ai Zhisheng, the minister of Radio, Film, and Television,
asserted that "although spiritual products also possess a commercial
nature and must therefore be governed by the law of value, in comparison with material products, they especially need to be macro-regulated
and under no circumstances can their production and distribution be
allowed blindly to follow market signals."[12]

That is the fundamental meaning of the concept of administratively
managing the cultural market, the guiding ethos behind thought-work
policy in the aftermath of the Fourteenth Party Congress. The most important manifestation of this ethos—as explained in the pages that follow—is indeed the omnidirectional crackdown on all forms of heterodox thought work. The concept is also used in the narrower sense of
policing the market for videotapes, audiotapes, and compact discs. But
the concept is particularly important and interesting in the broader
sense of serving as the intellectual rationale for continued state intervention in the production and circulation of all forms of propagandistic
public communications—even after the transition to a market economy.

Macromanaging "Televised Thought Work"

Loss of control over the flow of television programs into and through
China is a source of great consternation in Beijing. As argued in Chapter 1, even apparently innocuous arts and entertainment programs can
slowly undermine the best efforts to build a socialist spiritual civilization, and in the long run can contribute to fundamental transformations
in the nature of the polity. Most high-ranking Chinese propaganda officials seem keenly aware of this fact and are deeply concerned. For example, at the beginning of the omnidirectional crackdown, Minister of
Radio, Film, and Television Ai Zhisheng argued that numerous and

complex problems facing the television "enterprise" (*shiye*) demand serious and urgent administrative attention—in a way consistent with the developing ethos of managing the cultural market:

> It is imperative to be strict in controlling satellite ground reception stations. It is imperative to run cable television stations properly . . . and it is imperative to keep these stations under strict control. All areas should attach importance to relaying CCTV [Central China Television] programs. It is imperative to augment control over the broadcast of overseas programs. The permit system for teleplay production should be earnestly implemented [to counter unsanctioned private production]. Unauthorized production teams should be halted. Control over advertisements should be magnified.[13]

Ai's remarks indicate that the leadership was especially worried about the pervasiveness of Hong Kong and foreign television programs on Chinese airwaves. As discussed in Chapters 3 through 5, these programs enter the country on videotape and via satellite, and once inside China circulate freely (if often illegally) through the nation's flourishing internal program-exchange networks. By the summer of 1993, probably during the annual conclave at Beidaihe, the leadership concluded that this situation had become intolerable.

As a result, according to the respected Hong Kong newspaper *Ming Pao*, the CPD issued an order in early August proclaiming that, "henceforth, radio and television stations at the national and local levels must substantially lower the proportion of programs from outside the mainland. . . . [They] should be strictly limited to 20 percent of ordinary television programs, and should account for less than 30 percent of cable-television programs."[14] Two months later, Minister Ai declared that "we should be very strict in controlling broadcasts of imported programs. On this issue, we should avoid putting economic returns above all other issues. The effect of movies and television programs on the teenager should not be neglected."[15]

Subsequently, at the January 1994 National Propaganda Conference, Ai revealed the results of a survey conducted by the Ministry of Radio, Film, and Television (MRFT) of 13 provincial and 33 city television stations the previous October. The survey found that an astonishing 74 percent of the programs these stations carried during the survey period originated abroad. The majority of these programs were "in poor taste," Ai complained, saturated with "violence and sex."[16] This was one of the reasons why, in the summer of 1993, the MRFT issued new stipulations requiring that thenceforth at least 80 percent of television programs airing at all levels of the administrative hierarchy must be programs produced in China. Skepticism notwithstanding, a reduction in the proportion of Hong Kong and foreign programs from 74 percent to 20 percent of all programs aired could be achieved, Ai argued, if only lower-level stations would imitate CCTV, whose externally originated programs amounted to only 2.2 percent of the total aired.

The problem, of course, is that in the 1980s the central party-state had made television stations at all levels of the administrative hierarchy responsible for profits and losses and in the process had created powerful incentives for stations to cater to audience (societal) demand, as opposed to the demands of the central party-state. For resource-starved smaller stations, the temptation to turn to cheap, popular, pirated videotapes originating abroad has proved overwhelming. CCTV is blessed with a wealth of creative talent that very few provincial stations can match, let alone the hundreds of stations at the municipal level and below. CCTV has also been granted a huge, virtually guaranteed audience in exchange for conveying the Center's view of the world in newscasts and certain other programs, while lower-level stations must compete to attract audiences. Given these pressures and incentives, lower-level station managers calculate that, if what the audiences want to see are violent and titillating programs produced by foreigners and overseas Chinese, and if these programs can be purchased inexpensively in the form of pirated videotapes sold on the street or bartered in internal exchange networks, then it is worth the risk of offending central leaders to broadcast such programs. In fact, it is highly unlikely that anyone in Beijing will know what programs are being aired below the provincial level anyway.

Presumably the crackdown that began in August 1993 should have addressed some of the problems that concerned Minister Ai, but the difficulties that his successor, Sun Jiazheng, bemoaned in December 1994 sound strikingly similar to Ai's list of fourteen months earlier. First, Sun said that although by the end of 1994 land-based television signals covered 83.3 percent of China, only half the population was then capable of receiving CCTV Channel 1, primarily because many lower-level stations consistently defy the requirement that this channel be retransmitted everywhere, all the time. Second, lower-level stations—especially smaller-scale cable networks—carry far too many "mediocre" programs, purely to increase audience size. Third, and relatedly, the lower-level stations and networks carry far too many foreign (including Hong Kong and Taiwan) programs. "Several tens" of foreign television signals penetrate China's borders, Sun asserted. In fact, foreigners are willfully carrying out a "cultural infiltration" of China that should be resisted but that lower-level television stations instead unpatriotically assist for the purpose of making money.[17] There is therefore a clear contradiction between television stations catering to market demand and the state mandating that they help build a socialist spiritual civilization. Building a socialist spiritual civilization requires supplying audiences not necessarily with what they want, but with what the central party-state wants them to have.

Although no follow-up study of the results of the foreign television crackdown has yet been published, interview informants asserted that, if anything, the percentage of externally originated programs on Chinese television stations is probably rising. Thus, the MRFT was forced to reiterate its call for a reduction in foreign programs in November 1996, and even demanded that "the airing of television plays from outside the border during prime time should be suspended for the time being."[18] The only possible exception to the general ineffectiveness of the foreign television crackdown might be in "eight key cities and regions" assertedly targeted by Beijing for especially rigorous thought-work management—Beijing, Shanghai, Guangdong, Xinjiang, Tibet, and three other regions.[19] But so far there is no evidence that the percentage of externally originated programming is actually falling in these areas, though it apparently does remain comparatively low in Beijing, where central government cadres find television easy to monitor. The percentage of external programming in Guangdong is thought to be rising slowly from an already high base, because that province is adjacent to Hong Kong, the source of most external programming (foreign or otherwise).[20] And, as explained in Chapter 4, Hong Kong television broadcasts are legally retransmitted over Guangdong's cable networks.

Efforts to Control the Importation of Satellite Television

Even during the 1989–91 period, before STAR-TV was born, Beijing was actively taking steps to prevent the importation of external television signals, an effort apparently motivated by the Tiananmen-induced concern that thought work was escaping control. In May 1990 the MRFT, Ministry of Public Security (MPS), and Ministry of State Security (MSS) jointly issued an "order" (*mingling*) that banned the use of dish antennas to receive any signals other than those originating within China, unless official permission had been granted.[21] But at least in the Guangzhou area, where dish antennas are not necessary but are helpful for receiving Hong Kong television broadcasts, the 1989–91 crackdown was woefully ineffective:

> Public antennas set up by government departments and their directly subordinated units were removed; however, the more the prohibition was stressed, the more serious was the trend in setting up private antennas by the people. . . . Even the electronics experts in the Army went out privately to provide anti-jamming services to the people, and their work quality and reputation are among the first class.[22]

In late January 1992, one month after STAR-TV first began broadcasting, the service ran into serious (but temporary) difficulties in China. The MRFT and the Beijing Public Security Bureau ordered at least some of the 50 Beijing-area hotels then receiving STAR-TV to pull the plug.[23] No new restrictions were placed on CNN at this time, however (as had been the case from June 4 to October 1, 1989), apparently because STAR-TV carried the BBC World Television News in both English and Mandarin, while CNN's broadcasts were exclusively in English. In addition, the other STAR channels (notably MTV-Asia) offered glances of comfortable lives of conspicuous consumption in Taipei and Hong Kong, lives to which few Chinese citizens could then aspire, potentially increasing dissatisfaction with the communist government only weeks after the collapse of the Soviet Union.

But the restrictions were lifted (or their effectiveness faded) over the course of 1992, after Deng Xiaoping's "trip to the south" ushered in a period of relative liberalism in Chinese life. The period between summer

1992 and summer 1993 was in general a harmonious one in the Beijing–STAR TV relationship, which even included a November 1992 "summit meeting" between Ding Guan'gen—soon to be named chief of the CPD—and Richard Li, son of Li Ka-shing and in charge of STAR-TV.[24]

It was on July 26, 1993, that Rupert Murdoch's News Corporation purchased a 63.6 percent stake in STAR-TV from Hutchison-Whampoa, which would retain the remaining 36.4 percent stake until July 1995, when Murdoch took full control.[25] On August 20, 1993, the State Council adopted Decree No. 129 of 1993, "Provisions on the Management of Ground Receiving Equipment for Satellite Television Broadcasting"—a key component of the omnidirectional crackdown. The provisions were not officially promulgated until Premier Li Peng signed the decree on October 5, 1993. During the interim seven weeks, Murdoch made his inflammatory declaration that "advances in the technology of telecommunications have proved an unambiguous threat to totalitarian regimes everywhere."[26] Although some speculated that this statement was what spurred Beijing into launching the crackdown, obviously that is not possible, since its provisions were finalized before Murdoch made the remark. Instead, the omnidirectional crackdown, in all of its manifestations, appears to have been planned during the summer 1993 leadership retreat at Beidaihe, and was probably mooted even before Murdoch bought his STAR-TV shares.

Decree No. 129 attacked the satellite-dish problem on all fronts. Production of satellite dishes would be restricted to "enterprises designated by State Council administrative departments in charge of the electronics industry" (Article 4). The sale of satellite dishes would be restricted to "units designated by the industrial and commercial administrative departments of provincial, autonomous regional, and municipal people's governments in conjunction with administrative departments in charge of internal trade, radio, television, and electronics" (Article 5). To import preassembled satellite dishes would require a certificate from the MRFT; to import electronic components would require a certificate from the Ministry of Electronics Industry (MEI) (Article 6). Individuals would be banned completely from importing, installing, or using satellite dishes unless they could cite "exceptional circumstances" (Article 9). Units wishing to install satellite dishes would have to first apply to the equivalent-level radio and television bureau, and their applications would have to be approved by the provincial-level bureau (Article 8). Previously installed satellite dishes would have to undergo the examination and approval process within six months (i.e., by April 5, 1994). Individuals in violation of these regulations could be fined up to 5,000 yuan (U.S.$601) and units up to 50,000 yuan (Articles 10 and 11). The straightforward purpose of the provisions, according to Article 1, was "to promote socialist spiritual civilization."[27]

In February 1994 the MRFT promulgated a set of rules for the implementation of the State Council's October decree.[28] The most important component of this set of rules was the stipulation that units wishing to install satellite dishes merely to watch domestic Chinese television have only to secure the approval of the equivalent-level and next-highest-level radio and television bureaus. On the other hand, units wishing to install dishes to watch externally originated programs must obtain the approval not only of these divisions of the radio and television xitong but also of equivalent-level and next-highest-level state security bureaus. Separate licenses are thus required to receive foreign as opposed to domestic broadcasts, and foreign broadcasts are defined as an issue in state security. In those rare cases when individuals apply for permission to purchase and install satellite dishes, they may apply only for licenses to receive domestic broadcasts; no individual may legally import external signals. The problem, of course, is that CCTV and several provincial stations use Asiasat platforms to broadcast into China—as does STAR-TV—and it takes only minor technical adjustments to configure a dish to receive all the offerings of a single satellite. Consequently, after obtaining domestic licenses, units can easily supply their customers with STAR-TV if they are willing to take the chance of getting caught.[29]

In the months immediately following the State Council's October 1993 decree, various Chinese personages sought both to justify its measures in terms of socialist spiritual civilization and to reassure foreigners that the measures did not imply that China was closing its doors completely to foreign television. Vice Minister of the MRFT Wang Feng, for example, asserted on October 15 that managing "the reception of television programs transmitted via satellite from outside the national boundaries is a question of national sovereignty. . . . Considering the necessity of inspiring patriotism among the citizenry, of protecting the excellent cultural heritage of the Chinese nation, of promoting socialist spiritual civilization, and of maintaining social stability, we are totally justified in enacting some necessary provisions."[30]

Similarly, *Renmin Ribao* editorialized on January 16, 1994 (one week before the National Propaganda Conference), in the following terms: "Setting aside what kind of subtle influence the values, morals, and cultural patterns publicized by these [non-Chinese] television programs will have on our country's audience, especially young people, speaking just in terms of safeguarding the country's sovereignty, it is absolutely necessary for us to manage according to law the reception of satellite television programs."[31]

From the start, pundits were predicting that the satellite-dish crackdown would fail. Lincoln Kaye, the *Far Eastern Economic Review*'s China correspondent, suggested four reasons: (1) issuing licenses for the millions of dishes already in use would take too much administrative time and effort; (2) dismantling the dishes already in use would also require too much time and effort; (3) few of today's Chinese citizens are willing to "inform" on their neighbors as they had done regularly under the Maoist propaganda state; and (4) satellite dishes are easy to make and profitable to sell.[32] At most, the crackdown would raise the price of dishes for consumers and/or cut into the supplying firms' profits, depending on elasticity of demand. In any case, there was little likelihood that STAR-TV would vanish from Chinese living rooms. The state was simply no longer capable of organizing society in a way sufficiently thoroughgoing to bring about such an outcome. The Beijing government could throw stones in the path of thought-work globalization, but could not completely stop its progress.

Six months after the crackdown began, some dish manufacturers reported that, initially, the heavy publicity surrounding promulgation of the new rules had produced a drop in sales to individuals, but that work units continued to buy steadily.[33] The implication was that obtaining the necessary license was not particularly difficult for work units, which routinely install dishes to set up small-scale cable networks. At the January 1994 National Propaganda Conference, Ai Zhisheng acknowledged that "after the regulations were passed, although most people embraced them, there has been some obstructionism." He also underscored the Center's frustration by stating that "we *hope* that every place and every department will rigorously uphold and thoroughly implement the measures." He implicitly linked thought-work globalization with property-rights reform by asserting that "the flood into our country of imported programs can ultimately be attributed to the phenomenon of 'looking at everything with money in mind.'"[34] That might have meant the economic incentives facing small-scale cable operators and satellite-dish producers and dealers, or perhaps corruption by the bureaucratic agencies issuing the licenses.[35]

A year later, the picture was somewhat more complicated. Different respondents gave different answers to the question of how effective the crackdown had been; no answer seemed definitive. One respondent suggested that the crackdown had probably been effective in limiting sales of new satellite dishes, but that very few of the millions already installed had been dismantled.[36] A problem with this view, however, is that dishes were still visibly on sale in China's major cities. The fact that the price in the spring of 1995 had fallen to about 2,400 yuan (U.S.$288) from 4,000 yuan in the spring of 1993 might have meant weaker demand, but it could also have been an indication that factories were producing ever more satellite dishes and flooding the market. Another respondent suggested that as long as people had the money to buy, dish dealers were not asking to see licenses.[37] But even if the dealers do demand to see licenses before selling equipment to receive domestic television signals, the buyers can easily reconfigure their dishes to watch STAR-TV (and other foreign offerings) once they arrive home.[38]

A more sophisticated view is that the crackdown experienced more success in the big cities than in the suburbs, smaller cities, and countryside, and that among the big cities, the crackdown was more successful in the "eight key cities and regions" possibly targeted by the central government for especially strict thought-work management. One Hong Kong source said that she understood the government was tacitly permitting satellite-dish ownership in the countryside, because the countryside cannot easily be wired for cable television and because peasants are thought to be easier to control than city dwellers, even if external television does change their action strategies and worldviews.[39] Relatedly, when the Voice of America (VOA) was preparing to begin broadcasting its weekly satellite-TV program to China in the summer of 1994, investigators sent out to determine the effectiveness of the crackdown discovered that dish dealers were still easy to find, but that they had been chased from the inner cities to the suburbs, where the police are fewer in number and are less disciplined.[40] Even Chinese officials acknowledged that illegal viewing of STAR-TV continued, and that the problem is worse outside the big cities. But the reasons they posit are superficial and even tautological: Cadres in the suburbs, smaller towns, and countryside "are not hitting hard enough," "their educational levels are too low," and so on.[41]

The STAR-TV audience data discussed in Chapter 4 indicate that just before the crackdown began, a startling 95 percent of homes in Kunming equipped with television were capable of receiving STAR broadcasts (see Table 6). This figure far exceeds the 49 percent of homes in Guangzhou and the 9 percent of homes in Beijing capable of receiving STAR-TV; in fact, it was the highest percentage in the nation. But the figure is not necessarily an exaggeration. Officials in Kunming confirmed that more than 90 percent of the population probably was watching STAR-TV in the months before the crackdown began, but they insisted the number had dropped dramatically by 1995. The reason, however, was not the crackdown—satellite dishes were simply reregistered, not ripped out—but rather the fact that the novelty of STAR-TV had worn off and a state-run municipal cable-television system had been put in place. Still, only half the Kunming population had entered the official cable network by mid-1995, with not many more expected to join, so the number of STAR viewers in the city undoubtedly remained very high, even if the exact figure is unknown.[42]

Kunming is not a city on the central government's purported "eight key cities and regions" list, but perhaps it should be. One of the oddities of Kunming and indeed much of southern China (including the sensitive region of Tibet) is that its residents are capable of receiving both Asiasat-1's northern and southern beams. When Rupert Murdoch decided to placate Beijing by dropping the BBC World Television News Service from the northern beam in April 1994, he continued to carry it

on the southern beam. Anyone in Kunming capable of watching STAR-
TV can, as a result, also watch the BBC News, though the fact that it is
not broadcast in Chinese would presumably deter most viewers from
tuning in.[43] On the other hand, during a national political crisis, Kunming viewers and others in the southern footprint might pause if they
stumbled upon the BBC transmitting images of people demonstrating
in Tiananmen Square. Such images would fuel the curiosity necessary
to generate inquiries both interpersonal and via the fast-developing
telecommunications network, stimulating a potentially rapid dissemination of information about future political demonstrations throughout
China.[44]

That the Chinese government would find STAR-TV's five channels
threatening is particularly interesting in light of the long list of new players now offering—or planning soon to offer—satellite television services
to Asia. The list includes not only CNN, but also the Asian Business
News network, the Discovery Channel, HBO, Disney, TVB, other Hong
Kong and Taiwan broadcasters, and many more. One industry official
predicted in January 1994 that by 2005 there could be 500 satellite-TV
channels available in the Asia-Pacific region.[45] Other insiders caution that
the 500-channel prediction is based on an analysis of projected satellite
launches and the prevailing television-to-telecommunications transponder ratio, not on an analysis of the potential television market, and so
probably is inflated. Even if 500 channels were to become available, they
argue, only 50 to 100 would be in Mandarin, and many of these would
require decoders to receive.[46] Still, 50 to 100 is a large number, and among
the offerings is expected to be one or more 24-hour Mandarin news
channels modeled on CNN.[47] Hence, despite the crackdown, Beijing's
difficulties in staving off the globalization of "televised thought work"
are likely to become significantly more formidable in the near future.

The Cable Television "Solution"

Chinese officials within the radio and television xitong are aware of the
500-channel prediction and are concerned. They know that satellite
dishes are expected to become smaller and less conspicuous, and that in
the long run it will be impossible for the state to prevent people from

installing them. "If they become as small as teacups or rice bowls, how could we control them?" asked one official rhetorically.[48] The strategy for dealing with the problem is threefold: First, the state will temporarily ban individuals from installing dishes and try to limit the number of units installing them. Second, it will crack down hard on smuggled videotapes. If China's entertainment industry can be protected now, in its infancy, then perhaps by the time the dissemination of satellite dishes completely escapes state control (if, indeed, it ever does), the industry will be sufficiently developed to meet the needs of Chinese viewers. Third, all incoming television signals will be routed through cable networks—not through the thousands of semi-autonomous small networks that now crisscross the urban landscape, but rather through "centralized" (within cities and eventually provinces) state-run cable networks. This policy emerged only after 1990. Before then, cable television developed erratically, completely out of the central government's control.

The industry does not have a long history in China. Although the first cable network was established as far back as 1964—when closed-circuit television facilities were installed in the Beijing Hotel—it was not until the 1980s that the number of cable subscribers became significant. This is not surprising, since before 1980 there was little on Chinese television worth watching, and nothing comparable to STAR-TV available by satellite. During the 1970s many work units set up small-scale cable systems within their residential compounds. These efforts were motivated primarily by the fact that most urban Chinese live in sky-scraping apartment buildings that block or distort broadcast signals. The State Council approved a resolution in 1980 calling for all new apartment buildings to include small-scale cable systems so that the state could be assured of easy access to the minds of the citizenry. As a result, by the end of 1984, although there were some 300 small-scale cable networks spread across urban China, the largest such network linked only 30,000 households.[49]

During the late 1980s, the administrative districts (*qu*) of many Chinese cities began to link work-unit cable systems together into larger networks. By 1990 work units were operating 782 cable systems, whereas districts had established only 314.[50] Meanwhile, several bureaucracies argued over the question of which one would be permitted to macro-manage the cable industry. In 1990 the State Council ruled in favor of the MRFT's xitong in its "Temporary Measures for Regulating Cable Television," and immediately the MRFT declared that all cable television networks of whatever size and type must apply to the MRFT for a license.[51] This was the first step toward linking all cable television stations together within each city. Later in 1990, at a National Cable Television Management Conference, MRFT officials formally unveiled the goal of eventually linking all city networks together within each province.[52] The result, it was hoped, would be 35 cable systems only one step removed from direct central control.

But following STAR-TV's first broadcasts in December 1991, the number of cable systems increased rapidly, completely outstripping the state's efforts to license and regulate them, let alone efforts to implement the "one city, one network" policy. Data on the growth of the cable industry are inconsistent and sporadically supplied, but the overall number of systems increased from 1,300 in 1991 to 3,200 in 1995. What is unclear is the average size of these networks. Presumably they have been getting larger, since the MRFT had licensed 1,200 systems by April 1995—though 2,000 networks were still without licenses at that late date. The total number of subscribers in licensed systems was reported to be about 15 million at the end of 1992 and more than 30 million by early 1994.[53] But there is no way of knowing how many millions of people have access to cable through the 2,000 unlicensed networks. Some of these networks are small and their subscribers restricted to unit members, but others have spread out into surrounding communities and absorbed tens of thousands of subscribers.[54]

Originally, the MRFT had hoped to have all cable systems licensed by 1993; in 1995, the target date was pushed back to 1999. Unlicensed systems tend to be concentrated in the south, but every province has them. Not surprisingly, these networks do not apply for licenses chiefly because they retransmit STAR-TV, pornographic videos, and other contraband materials.[55] In the spring of 1995 the state seemed to be backing down from the demand that all unit systems merge into citywide systems. "It's okay for units to have their own systems as long as they don't violate the law," said one informant.[56] In fact, acknowledging the legitimacy of separate unit systems would appear to be essential if hotels and apartment buildings that service foreigners are to continue to retransmit CNN and other channels that Chinese citizens may not legally receive.

Today's biggest political struggles in the cable-television industry are not between cities and independent-minded work units, but instead between cities and independent-minded administrative districts. At least in the larger metropolitan areas, the districts have succeeded in unifying most work-unit systems, but most cities cannot unify the districts. The majority of the district systems obtained their cable licenses in the late 1980s, before the "one city, one network" policy direction was adopted. The licenses were granted without expiration dates, giving the districts a powerful tool to use in negotiations with the new city networks. In most places where a solution has been found, the district networks share profits with the municipal system and enjoy varying degrees of autonomy in selling advertising, collecting subscriber fees, and originating programming. Outcomes have ranged from a high level of centralization (Shanghai) to profound fragmentation (Tianjin), with most places falling somewhere in between.

Meanwhile, in the suburbs, the smaller towns, and the countryside, thousands of retransmitting stations—built during the 1980s to ensure that CCTV and provincial broadcasts reach every corner of China—have evolved into semi-autonomous, program-originating cable networks even more prone than their urban counterparts to supply subscribers with STAR-TV, pornography, and other politically unacceptable items.[57] At the January 1994 National Propaganda Conference, MRFT officials expressed the concern that if managing counties' broadcast stations had proved difficult under the "four levels operate [television]" slogan, managing even lower-level cable stations might be impossible if they are permitted to originate their own programming. Vice Minister of the MRFT Wang Feng acknowledged that "the vast majority" of small-scale cable and retransmitting stations were already capable of originating their own programming, and that most of the programming consisted of low-quality (technically and in terms of content) videotapes, often smuggled in from Hong Kong and/or pirated. Thus, Wang said, cable networks at levels lower than the administrative district would be forbidden from originating their own programs—but not until sometime "in the future." The policy would have to be implemented "step by step."[58]

Clearly, the effort to centralize the cable industry, whether in the cities or the provinces, was running into serious difficulties. These difficulties were spawned by the financial opportunities inherent in catering to viewers in a way that violates the center's thought-work goals, the easy availability of satellite and cable technology, and the administrative fragmentation that had begun in the 1980s.

It is primarily the rise of numerous, unsupervised cable networks (and lower-level television stations) that is fueling the enormous demand for foreign programming. The Center recognizes this fact, but nevertheless struggles administratively to prevent the lower-level networks from importing foreign films and teleplays.[59] As Yu-li Liu writes:

> All the films and dramas produced in foreign countries, including Taiwan, Hong Kong, and Macao, have [in principle] to be examined and approved by the Local Management Department of the MRFT. They must be centrally introduced by the Chinese Television International Corporation [i.e., CCTV's *Guoji Gongsi*], then uniformly provided to cable television stations and centres by programme supply organizations at the provincial level. . . . [But] because [approved] supply falls short of demand, cable-TV stations and centres have to find [alternative] channels for purchasing programs.[60]

As a result of this problem, the MRFT issued a new set of regulations in February 1994 reiterating that cable operators were not permitted to deal with foreigners directly, but must instead work through CCTV.[61] These rules applied to all cable stations, including those at the municipal and provincial levels, even in Beijing, Shanghai, Guangdong, and Fujian, whose broadcast stations have permission to import directly from abroad. Nevertheless, a year later, foreign suppliers interviewed in Hong Kong indicated that cable networks remained willing to negotiate with them directly, and that negotiations with some of the larger networks were in fact under way. Few foreigners want to work with the smaller networks of such concern to Beijing, however, because they are relatively uninteresting to advertisers and would be difficult to police. The smaller networks must therefore obtain their Hong Kong, Taiwan, and foreign programs illicitly, which from Beijing's point of view is an entirely different sort of cultural management problem.[62]

In the months preceding the omnidirectional crackdown, globalization via cable networks ascended to new heights when, on May 4, 1993, the provincial Beijing cable station—under the nose of the central party-state—dared to retransmit some of the programs of STAR-TV's Chinese Channel. Two days later the MRFT ordered Beijing Cable to stop the broadcasts.[63] This was before the rules had been codified; Beijing Cable was probably testing them. Similarly, but on a smaller scale, the cable network of a Heilongjiang textile printing and dyeing plant decided to begin retransmitting overseas videotapes and satellite programs on July 22, 1993. These activities continued for about two months, until Premier Li Peng signed the decree restricting the use of satellite dishes, after which provincial authorities punished the textile plant and publicized it as a negative model.[64] Meanwhile, as stated above, the Hong Kong newspaper *Ming Pao* reported that in early August 1993 the CPD demanded a reduction in the proportion of externally originated cable-television programs to 30 percent. (There is no indication what the percentage may have been when the demand was made.)

In the winter of 1994, shortly after the close of the National Propaganda Conference, the Beijing cable network once again got itself into trouble by offering live retransmissions of the American sports network ESPN. On February 8, 1994, the State Council issued an order suspending the retransmissions on the grounds that they violated the new restrictions on importing satellite-television programs.[65] Beijing Cable was permitted to resume carrying ESPN two months later, but not live; all programs first had to be recorded and edited. Apparently it was the principle of disallowing live retransmissions that the State Council wanted to stress. Sports would appear to be fairly harmless, but the central state could not afford to sanction the precedent of live retransmissions from abroad.[66] By early 1995 ESPN was claiming an audience of 5 million homes in China, but it is not clear what percentage (if any) of the cable stations supplying ESPN carried it live.[67]

At the National Propaganda Conference, some television and cable-network managers inquired directly of MRFT officials whether it would be permissible to record satellite programs and then air them after they had been vetted. "No," was the curt answer of Vice Minister Wang Feng, who proceeded to instruct the delegates to get on with the task of implementing the October 1993 State Council directive. Wang reminded his audience that the MRFT had established a centralized program-exchange network for cable systems in October 1992, and suggested that if the networks were facing program shortages they should make use of this network. CCTV would remain the sole legal conduit for programs originating abroad, whether recorded from satellite or imported on videotape. Wang pointed out that the MRFT actually had reaffirmed this line in the fall of 1993, but "quite a large proportion of provinces and cities aren't taking it seriously."[68]

In the spring of 1994 at least one-third of the programs airing on licensed cable-television stations still originated abroad. This prompted a new set of MRFT regulations in April that explicitly banned all retransmissions of Hong Kong, Macao, and Taiwan television programs (except in Guangdong) and the transmission of all unauthorized videotapes and films on cable networks. Violators faced stiff fines and other punishments. At the same time, the MRFT announced that no overseas organizations would be allowed to set up or operate cable networks in China, either independently or in joint ventures. This was an especially big blow to Hong Kong's Wharf Cable, which had entered into an agreement with the Chengdu government to set up a municipal cable service there. As a result of all these moves, Sun Jiazheng—who succeeded Ai Zhisheng as Minister of Radio, Film, and Television in May 1994—claimed in a December 1994 speech that investigative teams dispatched to twenty provinces had determined that the problem of cable networks relaying external satellite television programs had been "brought under control." Of course, this assessment could not have taken into account the estimated 2,000 networks that had yet to be licensed and the unknown number of privately owned satellite dishes.[69]

A monopolistic, centralized urban cable network has yet to be established. China has seen both a fair degree of centralization (Shanghai) and a high degree of fragmentation (Tianjian). The dominant pattern is exemplified by the case of Guangzhou, a city that is crisscrossed by two "centralizing" networks, one belonging to the Guangzhou City Television Station and the other to the Guangdong Provincial Television Station.[70] For provincial capitals to have two centralizing networks is not unusual. Despite the fact that the MRFT has called for the establishment of only one centralizing network per city, about 75 percent of the provincial capitals have two. The reason is a combination of administrative confusion, political squabbles, and the strong desire of both the provincial- and municipal-level television regulators to make money from cable. The city of Beijing has two centralizing cable systems, but in the case of Beijing and most other provincial capitals the municipal network tends to have many more subscribers than the provincial network, primarily because the goal to centralize within cities was articulated before the goal to centralize within provinces.

In the case of Guangzhou, however, the municipal and provincial networks were roughly balanced in power as of mid-1995, the municipal network linking together 300,000 households and the provincial network 200,000. There was no clear division of territory between the two systems. A pattern of cross-hatching prevailed, characterizing even individual apartment buildings, where some residents subscribed to the municipal system, others to the provincial system.

In short, the Center's efforts to meet the challenges presented by satellite and other external television providers by channeling their broadcasts through gradually centralizing cable networks are running up against serious obstacles. Work units, district stations, and competing transdistrict stations all vie for the profits to be made from catering to China's growing market for cable television, and the state lacks the capacity to force implementation of the centralizing policy. Continued difficulties suppressing STAR-TV viewership and the airing of spiritually polluting and/or bourgeois-liberal teleplays and films are the result. It would therefore appear that managing the television corner of the cultural market is not meeting with notable success.[71]

Videotapes, Periodicals, and "Pornography"

The Center's first formal effort to regulate the new technology of videotape came in August 1985, when the State Council officially prohibited private individuals from establishing MTVs. Only organizations with party committees would be allowed to show videotapes publicly, and they would first have to obtain certification from territorial-level offices of the MRFT, the Ministry of Culture (MoC), the State Administration of Industry and Commerce (SAIC), and the MPS. The primary concern was to curb the viewing of spiritually polluting and bourgeois-liberal tapes imported from Hong Kong and abroad. But videotapes and the technology to use them continued to spread rapidly with the deepening of the market economy and the increase of disposable income. The Center soon found it impossible to enforce its ban on the public display of videotapes in privately owned establishments.

The next step, then, was to try to block the circulation of the tapes, particularly those originating abroad. The MRFT convened a conference on the video menace in Hefei from June 16 to June 21, 1987. This conference was followed by a four-month crackdown on the buying and selling of illegal tapes that ended inconclusively on the eve of the Thirteenth Party Congress (October–November 1987).[72] As a result, videotapes and the technology to use them continued to disseminate rapidly throughout Chinese society in 1988, under the conditions of an overheated economy.

But the nationwide antigovernment demonstrations the following spring finally forced the government to take serious, sustained action against not only illegal videotapes from abroad but all forms of heterodox thought work appearing within the cultural market. On August 24, 1989, the Party Center and State Council jointly convened the All-China Teleconference on Rectifying and Cleaning Up Book, Periodical, and Tape Markets, to launch what would become the first in a series of campaigns against broadly defined "pornography." Declaring that "sweeping away pornography is an integral component of the struggle against bourgeois liberalization," the senior Party leader in charge of propaganda, Li Ruihuan, delivered the keynote address to the teleconference and set the tone for the eight-month campaign that followed:

> Especially in recent years, there've been far too many publications [on the market], with counterrevolutionary books and periodicals that promote bourgeois liberalization and suffer from serious political mistakes unworthily occupying prominent market positions, alongside a torrent of books, periodicals, and tapes of an obscene, pornographic, violent, and feudal-superstitious nature. If these publications and tapes aren't thor-

oughly suppressed, they will produce serious spiritual pollution and social dangers. . . . Rectifying and cleaning up book, periodical, and tape markets is closely related to our country's efforts to achieve long-term stability.[73]

In early September Li made a trip to four southern provinces to oversee implementation of the campaign. The same week, the Party Center and State Council jointly issued an eight-point circular designed both to underscore the seriousness of the campaign and to clarify for lower-level cadres the definition of pornography and how cadres should handle pornography dealers. The definition was capacious, encompassing politically "bad" materials as well as what is commonly regarded as pornography. The purveyors, it was declared, should be dealt with sternly. However, their stern treatment should be meted out "according to law." Cadres must not go so far as to destroy the liveliness and diversity of the cultural market, and they should not resort to the terrorist tactics of Maoist mass campaigns.[74]

But the first step in dealing with the problem was simply to reduce the number of periodical titles in circulation, as well as the number of publishing houses that produced them. A circular issued on October 4, 1989, declared that a periodical should be suppressed under any one of nine conditions. For example, most party and government departments publishing more than one periodical would be required to eliminate all but one; publications covering the arts, entertainment, commercial activities, and legal affairs should be "consolidated"; and central and provincial party papers should (with a few exceptions) stop publishing supplementary pages and editions that pander to "vulgar" tastes. At the same time, publishing houses with a reputation for specializing in obscenity and/or counterrevolutionary periodicals should be shut down; even central government organizations should be restricted to maintaining only one publishing house per agency.[75] The limited results of this initiative are evident in the data presented in Table 7. The number of legally published newspapers fell from 852 in 1989 to 773 in 1990, whereas the number of legally published magazines fell from 6,078 in 1989 to 5,751 in 1990. But growth resumed almost immediately, and by 1992 there were more periodical titles in circulation than in 1989.

The Center resorted a second time to the tack of trying to restrict bad thought work by limiting or even reducing the number of periodical titles and publishing houses during the early stages of the omnidirectional crackdown. SPPA Deputy Director Liang Heng revealed in April 1994 that "approval for new newspapers and periodicals basically has stopped this year. If provinces and units wish to run new newspapers and periodicals, they should reduce the original newspapers and publications, . . . the purpose being to promote the good and eliminate the bad."[76]

Many units with no natural connection to the communications industry had taken to publishing highly market-oriented periodicals "just for the sake of making money." These units competed directly with the traditional, state-sanctioned publishers both for market share and for costly inputs such as paper. As a result, the SPPA was able to rally mainstream publishers in support of the new restrictive regulations. The SPPA was, in effect, promising the preexisting publishing houses that they would be allowed to satisfy all of the future increases in demand for printed information without having to worry about competition from new, upstart publishers. Because demand was expected to continue to grow and present potentially profitable opportunities, the mainstream publishers naturally rallied to support this particular SPPA policy, while continuing willfully to violate certain other, inconvenient policies, such as the ban on selling book numbers.[77]

In any case, the restrictions proved ineffective. The number of newspapers published grew from 943 in 1993 to 1,015 in 1994—an 8 percent increase—and of magazines, from 7,011 in 1993 to 7,325 in 1994—a 4 percent increase. By 1996 the number of newspapers published had reached 1,083, and of magazines, 7,916.[78] "Basically stopping" the establishment of new journals actually allowed for continued increases at the same rates as before. Meanwhile, a Hong Kong source estimated that there were an additional 20,000 nominally *neibu* (internally circulating) publications in open circulation in 1996.[79]

Regardless of the exact figures, the policy of constricting the number of periodical channels to control thought work had clearly failed. "It's relatively easy to set up a new periodical," one informant explained, "and many units want to set up periodicals because the market for information is strong and growing."[80] There is thus much money to be made from going public with *neibu* periodicals, and no unit within the propaganda xitong—least of all the bureaucratically weak SPPA—holds legal jurisdiction over the thousands of units now entering this business.

Nominally *neibu* publications became the target of an intensive new phase of the omnidirectional crackdown in the months immediately following the Sixth Plenum of October 1996. The CPD issued orders in January 1997 for governments below the provincial level to shut down 80 percent of externally circulating *neibu* periodicals by the end of 1997; the remaining 20 percent would be brought into the propaganda xitong and supervised by the SPPA. The chief targets of this new phase of the crackdown would be publications of "excessively poor quality" and those with a circulation of less than 20,000. A newly established Central Committee work group would coordinate the implementation of these draconian measures—essential because the SPPA is unrepresented below the provincial level (except for a few large cities) and the units whose publications would be targeted for elimination are not organized within the propaganda xitong.

The CPD also announced in January 1997 a plan to reduce the number of officially approved, openly circulating periodicals by 20 to 30 percent during 1997, claiming that it had already cut the figure by 5 percent in 1996—an assertion belied by official State Statistical Bureau data. After the 1997 reductions, the CPD would fix the total number of approved periodicals at least through 1999, with new periodicals approved only to replace old ones going out of business.[81]

It did not take long, however, for the CPD to back down from these excessively ambitious plans, suggesting that they might have been motivated partly by CPD minister Ding Guan'gen's desire to signal his political support for Jiang Zemin as Deng Xiaoping's death approached. Sources revealed in May 1997 that, instead of trying to reduce the total number of approved periodicals by nearly 2,000 in 1997 (i.e., 20 to 30 percent), only about 300 would be forced to cease publication. No mention was made of the possibility that they would actually be replaced—except for the converted erstwhile *neibu* publications. Jiang Zemin's Sixth Plenum speech stressing the socialist spiritual civilization appears to have created an atmosphere reminiscent of 1958, in the sense that in an overheated political environment relevant departments publicly announced unattainable goals from which, just a few months later, they were forced to back down.[82] The omnidirectional crackdown would of course continue, and the state would continue to try vigorously to reassert control over thought work, but the rhetoric would be cooled down and the specific targets would be scaled back.

The second basic tactic for rectifying and cleansing the book, periodical, and tape markets is specifically to target undesirable materials, destroy them, and punish their producers and sellers. This tactic always works in the short run in a highly visible way. For example, the campaign launched in August 1989 resulted in 185,000 bad books and magazines and 33,000 bad audio and video recordings confiscated in Shanghai alone by the following spring. Massive hauls were taken in on October 1, 1989 (National Day) and January 1, 1990, when thousands of citizens were mobilized across the city to search street stalls and seize contraband materials.[83] Nationwide, by the early summer of 1990 mobilized citizens and the authorities together had confiscated "several million tons of obscene books" and more than a million videotapes. Nearly 800 individuals had been arrested for producing and/or peddling pornography and other banned cultural products.[84]

In fact, the first campaign was so "successful" that a second one was launched toward the end of 1990 and continued into the spring of 1991. The CPD's Liu Zhongde claimed at a December 1991 National Antipornography Work Conference that the second campaign, too, "scored remarkable successes," resulting in nearly 7 million printed publications and 50,000 videotapes seized and burned. More than 3,000 illegal publishing operations and 2,946 book and audio-video shops were shut down. The irony was that Liu was trumpeting the successes of the 1990–91 campaign to stimulate enthusiasm for yet another campaign in 1991–92.[85] Obviously, if the first two campaigns had been fundamentally successful, there would have been no need to conduct a third campaign.

By 1993 the originally annual campaigns had evolved into a single, ongoing campaign, as the state began gradually to institutionalize its ineffective response to the pornography menace. To coordinate the activities of the several bureaucracies mobilized during campaigns, shortly after the Fourteenth Party Congress the Party Center established the Leading Small Group to Sweep Away Pornography, led by the CPD.[86]

The small group brought together representatives of the SPPA, the MoC, the MPS, and other units with a hand in suppressing pornography. By mid-1993 comparable antipornography committees had been established at all levels of the hierarchy down to the county.[87]

Meanwhile, in October 1993, at the start of the omnidirectional crackdown, the MoC convened the first All-China Cultural Market Management Work Conference in Beijing. While details of this meeting are vague, one concrete result was the adoption of a system whereby providers of cultural goods and services must first obtain certification (a *xukezheng*) from the equivalent-level Bureau of Culture before applying for a business license from the SAIC xitong. This move clarified that "spiritual" goods and services are to be considered different from "material" goods and services, and provided that suppliers of spiritual products must subject themselves to at least an initial inspection by a unit of the propaganda xitong before going into business.[88]

In 1995, the Center's serious new efforts to eliminate pornography and other undesirable products from the cultural market were obviously running up against profound difficulties.[89] What might be called "unsystematic, experimental" efforts to procure pornography (in the conventional sense) in Beijing, Guangzhou, and Kunming illustrate some of these difficulties. From street vendors in nearly every Chinese city today, one can easily purchase magazines that tell sexual tales, but contain no photographs (except for suggestive covers). Purchasing photographic pornography, however, is much more problematic. Almost always, photographic pornography is hidden behind the counters. As one official with the central government explained, "There's plenty of that kind of stuff around, but because you're a foreigner and don't have a relationship with the street vendors, they aren't going to show it to you."[90] This statement—made before the "experimental" efforts began—proved to be entirely correct in the cases of Beijing and Guangzhou, but not in the case of Kunming.[91]

A street stall vendor in Kunming said "of course" he sells photographic pornography, "but would you please come back in twenty minutes?" He went away to his apartment and returned with a selection of three magazines that would probably be classified in the United States as "erotic" rather than "pornographic." The photographs were of unclothed women in provocative poses, but were decidedly mild in comparison with what is sold in, for example, Hong Kong. "We have other kinds, too," the vendor said, "including some from foreign countries. But you'll have to come back tomorrow night. I have to order it from the distributor. He keeps it at a warehouse nearby, but I wouldn't be able to find him tonight."[92] A foreigner caught with pornography in China could easily get into trouble, so there would be no tomorrow night. However, it would have been rude not to purchase at least one magazine in exchange for the vendor's troubles.

The magazine decided upon cost 41.90 yuan (U.S.$5) and was actually not a periodical; according to the publication information, the single edition had been issued in January 1994 by the Shanxi People's Fine Arts Publishing House. It was affixed with a book number and included a few paragraphs of opening text, with lines like, "The body is God's most beautiful work of art." All of the women were said to be Chinese, and all of the photography was done in China. (This was stated with pride.) The magazine was distributed by the Chongqing branch of the Xinhua Bookstore.

Although certainly not a representative sample of all the pornography available in China, this single magazine did illustrate several important points. First, the widely made assertion[93] that pornography is chiefly imported from abroad and is far more rampant along the coast seems questionable in light of the fact that this particular magazine was (assertedly) published in Shanxi, distributed by a Chongqing-based bookstore, and purchased in Kunming—while all of the photographs were of Chinese women posing at Chinese sites. Second, the magazine was technically well produced, expensive, and affixed with a book number, which suggests that the domestic pornography-producing industry is reasonably well capitalized. It is said that much Chinese pornography consists of poorly reproduced, pirated versions of Hong Kong magazines, but clearly that is not always the case. Third, the magazine was published in January 1994, several months after the beginning of the omnidirectional crackdown. Obviously, not everyone was deterred by the crackdown, particularly by the campaign to sweep away pornography. Finally, the fact that it proved easy to purchase pornography in Kunming and impossible in Guangzhou and Beijing was consistent with other evidence (such as the STAR-TV viewership data presented in Chapter 4) that thought work is relatively less controlled in the southwest. This would appear to lend credence to the rumor that the Center had targeted "eight key cities and regions" for especially rigorous control of thought work, and that Kunming is not on the list.

Under the general rubric of managing the cultural market, controlling the new technologies of videotapes and compact discs has proved even more difficult than controlling pornographic print. One problem is that it is not entirely clear which bureaucracy should take primary responsibility for regulating even the legal importation of videotapes. The three chief candidates would be the General Bureau of Radio, Film, and Television (GBRFT); the SPPA, and the MoC. The MRFT was originally given the responsibility because of the similarity between videotapes and film and because of the fact that many television stations transmit imported videos as a key element of their programming strategies. But numerous organizations in the SPPA system such as bookstores and publishing houses reproduce and sell videos, while MTVs, karaoke bars, and—below the provincial level—bookstores and theaters are macromanaged by the MoC. The fact that units of the PLA and the Ministry of Information Industries (MII) are heavily involved in producing video and audio equipment and allegedly in pirating tapes and CDs obviously complicates the picture even more, as does the fact that during crackdowns the police and customs administrations have to be mobilized and their activities coordinated with the other bureaucracies, frequently transregionally. Hence, as Minister of Culture Liu Zhongde acknowledged in the spring of 1996, "Illegal audio-visual products have not yet been exterminated; intellectual property rights are still being infringed upon; . . . pornographic and reactionary audio-visual products remain despite efforts to exterminate them; distribution by state audio-visual distribution units is in a state of chaos."[94]

Cracking Down on the Buying and Selling of Book Numbers

As discussed in Chapter 3, before 1994, publishing houses typically requested more book numbers from the provincial SPPA bureaus than they needed to ensure a surplus to sell to underground publishers. In

September 1993, at the beginning of the omnidirectional crackdown, central officials planned a "resolute rooting out of the corrupt behavior of buying and selling book numbers."[95] At a joint conference convened in October, the CPD and SPPA decided that the best way to do this would be to restrict the supply of book numbers to five per editor per publishing house, effective January 1, 1994, with the result that the number of new books published each year could be capped at 70,000.[96] Publishing houses are limited in the number of editors they can hire by the party-state's personnel system (even though they now do have much greater choice over precisely whom to hire). The new restrictions seemed promising.

By mid-1995, however, officials in the publishing world estimated that the number of books tagged with illegal ISBNs had fallen only about 20 percent as a result of the new restrictions, even though the price of the average number had risen three to four times. It is considered likely, however, that publishing houses and their editors are now being "comparatively more careful" in examining the manuscripts that potential ISBN purchasers propose to publish, a development that should be regarded as a positive effect of state action. Moreover, the number of new titles published in 1994—at least as officially reported—was indeed below 70,000, and the next year it fell by 14 percent.[97]

However, in January 1997, a few months after the Sixth Plenum, the SPPA formally "reissued" eleven regulations "on strictly prohibiting the buying and selling of ISBNs." Although it is true that the reissued regulations appear to have been "fleshed out" from earlier, similar dicta—for example, by specifically prohibiting publishing houses from encouraging editors to sell book numbers to meet quotas under the "editor responsibility system"—the simple fact that the SPPA felt no choice but to reissue the regulations 3 1/2 years into the crackdown indicates quite clearly that the crackdown was running into difficulties.[98]

How can the selling of book numbers persist despite the new limitations? One reason is that publishing houses, when requesting book numbers from the provincial SPPA office, usually submit lists of only the categories of books they plan to publish. They do not submit lists of specific titles; often, in fact, they do not even know the titles in advance. It becomes quite an easy matter to substitute new books for less commercially promising ones in the original plan. Usually, a substitution will require less work on the part of the publishing house's editors and will result in the author or underground publisher taking on a greater share of the commercial risk. Of course, the publisher risks that the sold book number will be discovered. But so many books are now published in China that the odds of being discovered are not especially high, particularly given the incentive of book dealers to hide especially dangerous publications and to bribe inspectors responsible for managing the cultural market.[99]

Another problem irritating both to the state and to publishing houses is that a large number of book numbers are simply "stolen" each year; more precisely, the numbers are copied from authorized publications already on the market and then affixed to illegal publications. (Numbers are also frequently fabricated.) For example, in the mid-1990s the Yunnan People's Publishing House each year discovered about 70 to 80 of its book numbers affixed to publications that none of its editors—apparently genuinely—knew anything about. The books were found all over China, not just in Yunnan—pointing to the truly widespread, transprovincial nature of the problem. Typically, inspectors in the MoC system would discover the illegal books circulating outside the province and then telephone the Yunnan People's Publishing House to make further inquiries. Inside Yunnan, the house's own personnel would occasionally stumble upon illegal publications while browsing through bookstores or while casually examining the offerings of street vendors. Whenever such cases are discovered, the house sues if a culprit can be identified, but only in a very few cases can a culprit be found.[100] Obviously, restricting the supply of book numbers is unlikely to solve this problem.

In any case, in the estimate of two Chinese analysts interviewed for this study, the restrictions cannot last in their present form because the demand for information of all sorts—including that supplied by books—continues to grow rapidly. To meet this demand, either the currently existing publishing houses must be allowed to publish more books or new publishing houses must be established. But, as discussed above, the Center currently is trying to cap the growth in periodical and book titles and sees an expansion in the total number of publishing houses as inherently threatening. To establish a new house requires only the permission of the provincial-level SPPA office, over which the provincial government wields much more control than does the SPPA at the Center. Increasing demand for books nationwide creates strong incentives for the provinces to compete with each other in establishing more publishing houses to meet the demand—a situation that could easily spin out of the Center's control. This problem is a structural one too deep for the weak SPPA bureaucracy to root out.[101]

Efforts to Regulate Telecommunications Flows

The omnidirectional crackdown on heterodox thought work did not initially encompass China's telecommunications networks, which continued as of 1995 to be viewed primarily as instruments for the transmission of technical and commercial information, not as tools of propaganda. Yet in China as elsewhere, telecommunications are rapidly merging with the mass media to provide all manner of value-added services that are clearly propagandistic in nature, including e-mail capability, fax services, and Internet access (where one can download on-line information including pornography).[102] Even *Renmin Ribao* is transmitted electronically, via satellite, from Beijing to more than 30 sites around the country for printing.[103]

The reasons few people at the Center perceived telecommunications as potentially threatening to thought work are complex. First, historically, the telecommunications network was woefully underdeveloped and was in fact used almost exclusively for technical and administrative purposes. For this reason, telecommunications is not now, nor has ever been, organizationally a part of the propaganda xitong.[104] The result of this legacy is that the vast majority of the documents and instructions issued by the CPD to mass-media outlets throughout the country do not reach the hundreds of official and semi-official companies and organizations supplying the public with telecommunications services. If telecommunications companies continue to branch out into the provision of propagandistic communications messages, a major restructuring of the xitong system would be needed before the CPD could, with facility, directly influence the operations of these companies.[105]

But incorporation of telecommunications providers into the propaganda xitong is not at this writing on the (public) agenda and would undoubtedly be resisted vigorously by individuals working in the telecommunications industry. Their position is that telecommunications companies provide only the means to supply the population with communications messages, not the messages themselves. Thus, even when telecommunications companies transmit pornographic images to their customers from the Internet and other sources, "that is not our problem." Anything available in the cultural market should be fair game for transmission. Telecommunications companies cannot be expected to judge the healthiness or political correctness of every message they transmit; propaganda is not their job.[106] As one informant phrased it, "Pornography and counterrevolutionary spiritual products are everywhere, but not every unit can be a part of the propaganda xitong. Should the transportation departments become part of the propaganda xitong? Should they be held accountable when bad people use the roads and railways to transport pornography?"[107]

To people in the telecommunications business, keeping pornography and other undesirable cultural products out of the symbolic environment is a problem for the police and the departments charged with managing the cultural market. Importantly, in this regard, the State Council gave the MPS and the MSS joint responsibility for "safeguarding computer information systems," including value-added telecommunications, on March 1, 1994. The regulations make clear that "safeguarding" means involving the MPS and MSS in inspecting the networks' content: "No organization or individual may use computer information systems to engage in activities that endanger national or collective interests, as well as the legitimate interests of citizens."[108]

"Exactly," said one official from the Ministry of Posts and Telecommunications (MPT). "The public and state security organs are responsible for pornography and counterrevolutionary propaganda; they are not our concerns." However, this official had to admit that cooperating with the MPS and MSS would be essential if the agencies were to police the nation's telecommunications networks successfully. Obviously, some degree of cooperation takes place every time a telephone is tapped. But specifically with regard to value-added services, there had been no discussion on how to cooperate as of spring 1995. At least two of the four Internet providers had not yet even met with security officials to discuss the special threats to propaganda that this service presents, because "it's too early" and "there aren't many subscribers yet."[109]

A second reason telecommunications services were not initially included in the crackdown is simple ignorance on the part of propaganda officials about how contemporary telecommunications can be used to engage in thought work. Members of the foreign business community, in particular, often express amazement at how rapidly the Center is allowing telecommunications to develop, given this potential. In the words of a Beijing-based vice president of one of the world's leading telecommunications firms: "The leaders are just asleep. They have no idea what's going on."[110] Similarly, an American academic who lectured in China on telecommunications security found "an extraordinary degree of ignorance" about these issues, even among telecommunications engineers.[111] Another analyst suggested that this ignorance is particularly profound among older engineers and those living outside the big cities. Value-added services are "booming" everywhere, but the only people who realize the significance of this development for thought work are a few dozen young, foreign-trained managers and engineers in Beijing, Shanghai, and Guangzhou. Most of these young managers and engineers are ideologically predisposed to favor an increased liberalization of information flows, and so are not likely to try to put a stop to it.[112]

Only in 1996 did the Chinese authorities, finally grasping the significance specifically of the Internet, target telecommunications services in general as part of the omnidirectional crackdown. On February 4 the State Council promulgated a new set of regulations governing Internet access provision aimed primarily at limiting the number of providers to the current four: China Telecom, Jitong, the State Education Commission, and the Academy of Sciences.[113] These regulations resembled the set issued in the autumn of 1993 to force the nation's numerous new suppliers of other kinds of value-added services to register with the MPT—an effort that, some observers believe, was motivated more by the MPT's desire to guarantee its xitong a cut of the profits than by a concern that propaganda was escaping control. However, the February

1996 Internet regulations do specifically address the thought-work problem by expressly forbidding the use of the Internet to transmit or receive undesirable communications: "Units and individuals engaging in Internet business . . . shall not make use of the Internet to conduct criminal activities—including activities prejudicial to state security and the leakage of state secrets—or to produce, retrieve, duplicate, and disseminate information prejudicial to public order, and pornographic materials."[114]

At the end of February the MPS issued a "circular on recording the use of Internet information" that required Internet subscribers to register with their local MPS-xitong office.[115] Precisely what sort of information subscribers would be required to supply was not reported, but presumably it would include their e-mail addresses and servers—the better to track down suspected violators of the State Council's new regulations. Subsequently, upon realizing that Internet users in China can avoid the need to register with either the MPT or the MPS by simply dialing in to Hong Kong or foreign Internet servers, the MPT in the spring formulated a package of measures designed specifically to outlaw this practice, warning that the ministry will "closely monitor the inflow and outflow of on-line messages."[116]

In the summer of 1996 the CPD itself became involved in Internet issues, marking the first time in recorded Chinese history that telecommunications had been brought within the purview of the propaganda xitong. CPD Minister Ding Guan'gen had journeyed to Singapore in September 1995 to study how that culturally repressive (but economically advanced) city-state manages communications flows. In July 1996 Ding returned to the Lion City, this time reportedly "to study ways of screening out material on the Internet that is not in line with official ideology."[117] While precisely what Ding discussed with his Singapore hosts was not reported, it seems more than coincidental that two months later the Chinese government began trying to use telecommunications technology to prevent its citizens from accessing external Internet Web sites containing news, pornography, information supplied by exiled human rights groups, and other dangerous material. Singapore had implemented a similar set of measures the previous year.[118]

Finally, in December 1997 the MPS promulgated a new set of "Regulations on the Security and Management of Computer Information

Networks and the Internet."[119] These regulations are completely consistent in spirit with the earlier restrictions, but more explicit. They outlaw, for example, nine specific uses of the Internet, including "inciting
to overthrow the government or the socialist system," "harming national unification," "destroying the order of society," and "injuring the
reputation of state organs." Naturally, pornography is outlawed, as is
"feudal superstition." In fact, the list is so long and nebulous that just
about any imaginable use of the Internet might be illegal given creative
interpretation.[120]

The problem is that, at present, it does not seem possible technically—or at least "techno-bureaucratically"—for Beijing to control the
Internet. One foreign expert interviewed in 1995 asserted that Chinese
propaganda officials "don't know how to control [the Internet], and they
don't even know they don't know how to control it."[121] The 1996–97 regulations make clear that now, at least, they know they need to control it.
But one official with the MEI's telecommunications division acknowledged in 1995 that "neither the Ministry of Public Security nor anyone
else in China currently possesses the technology to police today's
telecommunications networks because they're too sophisticated."[122] Foreign and Hong Kong telecommunications equipment providers believe
that technology to monitor value-added telecommunications flows "to
a degree" will soon become available. For example, it might be possible
to use new filtering technologies to prevent a few exceptionally undesirable Internet messages from entering or circulating within China. But
this technology will be "extremely expensive," and not until 1997 did
Chinese bureaucracies evince either a knowledge of its existence or a desire to purchase it.[123]

Beijing's experiences trying to block domestic access to forbidden
foreign Web sites are illustrative of the difficulties a propaganda state
faces in adapting to new telecommunications technologies. Starting in
the autumn of 1996, the Center ordered the MPT to deny Chinese Internet subscribers access to a long list of external Web sites, including that
of the VOA. As Figure 2 makes clear, the government scored a smash-
ing success with this tack, sharply reducing the ability of Chinese citizens to directly access the VOA site and download its files. Both the
number of weekly Web site hits originating in China and the number of

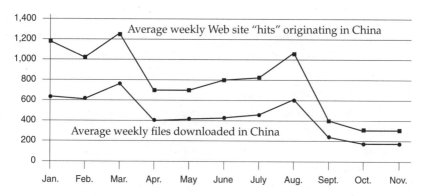

FIGURE 2. Use of the Voice of America Web Site in China, 1996 (data from Voice of America)

files downloaded dropped sharply after the implementation of the new restrictions in September.

But the key phrase is "direct access." Blocking direct access to Internet Web sites is relatively easy to accomplish as long as the service providers are limited in number and are directly subordinate to the central authorities. The central state has only to develop a list of banned sites and order the MII to deny access to their Internet addresses.

There are, however, two main problems with this approach. First, the number of sites that might contain "bad" information increases daily, even hourly. Many of these sites' webmasters simply copy files from other sites and recirculate them. There is no way that the Chinese government—or any other government—can possibly keep on top of this rapidly changing situation. They can certainly continue to update the list of banned sites, but can effectively concentrate only on those sites known to be purely bad, such as major Western, Hong Kong, and Taiwan news outlets and famous pornographic sites.

The second major problem, about which the Chinese state can currently do nothing, is that acquaintances or even strangers in other countries and regions can easily access sites blocked from China, download their files, and then retransmit the files into China as e-mail messages. Once inside China, these files can circulate endlessly along the domestic e-mail network, or can be printed out and subsequently faxed and/or photocopied; the effort to deny access to the files will have failed. This is exactly the strategy of *Tunnel*, the subversive e-mail magazine—though it originates its own material. Of course, state efforts to deny access will have had some effect, inasmuch as accessing the banned information will have become more costly and difficult, and Chinese citizens will know that they must exercise caution about what they upload and download. But still the information will circulate.

Fundamentally, the most difficult problem in this regard is the extremely decentralized nature of China's telecommunications network, both in technological and in administrative terms. By 1994 the system was 97 percent automated, which means that almost all transmissions are now handled by hundreds of computerized switching centers, completely free of direct human intervention.[124] Moreover, almost all of the major trunk lines now, or soon will, consist entirely of optical fiber, which according to one authoritative source "cannot be hand tapped with intercepting splices, and do[es] not radiate electromagnetic signals which can be read remotely."[125] Thus, the number of centers at which information must be intercepted increases rapidly with each passing year. If in 25 years the Chinese network is composed entirely of optical fiber, then it is possible that all messages will have to be intercepted at the telephone or modem of the individual sender/receiver. "Technobureaucratically," that would mean that, in effect, the state could monitor any message, but not all messages.[126]

But even individual monitoring will become more difficult if encryption technology is disseminated in China. At this writing, agencies of the U.S. government and Congress continue to debate a proposal to lift restrictions on the sale of encryption technology abroad. Also in debate are requirements that all encrypted messages sent domestically include a code that would allow the federal government, under certain circumstances, to "decrypt" the messages of suspect individuals.[127] If this technology reaches China, and the MPS and MSS cannot crack the codes, then individuals and organizations with the means to purchase the technology will be able to send and receive even politically subversive messages at will, with little fear of central government intervention. Given the difficulties the Chinese state faces in enforcing its restrictions on satellite dishes—which sit conspicuously atop apartment buildings—it seems unlikely that it could fare any better trying to control small devices attached to telephones.

Additional Elements of the Omnidirectional Crackdown

The most visible components of the omnidirectional crackdown on heterodox thought work, which began in the summer of 1993, are the efforts to restrict access to external Internet Web sites, staunch the dissemination of satellite dishes, sweep away pornography, and curb the sale of book numbers. Additional, integrally related components of the crackdown package include the following measures:

The discouragement, and eventually the elimination, of illegal book sales and the privately owned sector of the book retail trade. Specifically, publishing houses are banned from selling books to privately owned bookstores. Before this restriction was implemented in late 1993, publishers faced strong incentives to sell to privately owned bookstores because, according to industry regulations, they could take 80 percent of the volume of subsequent retail sales. If they sold to collectively owned bookstores, they could take 70 percent of retail sales, but if they sold to the Xinhua Bookstore, they could take only 30 to 40 percent of retail sales. The purpose of the ban is clearly to choke off the privately owned bookstores' lifeline, to force them into selling only illegal books, with the hope that eventually the illegal book market can be isolated among the private dealers and destroyed. The purpose of allowing collective bookstores to retain only 30 percent of the volume of book sales is to discourage entry into this market. But national policymakers do not want to restore the old Xinhua monopoly, so they cannot completely shut down the collective bookstores. Given the advantageous terms of exchange, publishing houses continue eagerly to sell to the collective stores, and somehow private dealers also manage to secure supplies; undoubtedly, a proportion of their products is pirated. Industry officials estimate that, nationwide, Xinhua retains a hold on about 50 percent of the retail book market, but that legal publishers sell 60 to 70 percent of their books to Xinhua. If these figures are correct, then clearly the collective and private dealers are obtaining some books illegally.[128]

The strengthening of party organizations within publishing houses, "particularly those dealing in humanities and general publications." Minister of Propaganda Ding Guan'gen announced this measure in the fall of 1993. Ultimately ("before too long"), all editors and principal associate editors are to become "the responsible persons of their unit's party committee or party branch." But the first step will simply be for all press and publication management departments in all localities to "compile statistics on their party organizations as quickly as possible in order to provide the leadership with some firsthand information."[129] Central policymakers sense that publishing houses are slipping from party control, partly, it would appear, because they do not even have complete information on the question of exactly who is running the publishing houses.

The certification of key personnel in the publishing industry. This measure, announced jointly by the CPD, SPPA, State Education Commission, and Ministry of Personnel, states that, beginning in 1997, chief editors of book and periodical publishing houses, the directors of audiovisual copying enterprises, Xinhua bookstore managers, and various other key individuals in publishing will have to undergo special training courses before taking up (or resuming) their positions. Starting January 1, 1999, individuals not in possession of training certificates would be forbidden from working in key publishing-industry positions.[130]

A widening of the readership of 'Renmin Ribao,' the citadel of thought-work orthodoxy. The Party Center issued a circular in August 1993 urging localities to increase subscriptions to *Renmin Ribao* and urging the post office to improve its delivery.[131] Then, in January 1994, the CPD issued a set of "suggestions" reminding party organizations throughout the system that all individual party members had to subscribe to at least one party paper or journal. Moreover, "party organizations should give periodical written tests to cadres with party membership to check their knowledge about major domestic and international events and use the test results as one of the criteria for their promotion or job assignment."[132]

Informants at *Renmin Ribao* would not comment on this "suggestion," and other individuals interviewed seemed to be completely unaware of it. The latter fact would seem to indicate that "suggestions" are not necessarily to be taken seriously, even when they are issued by the CPD. Perhaps for this reason, the CPD is reported to have again "ordered" party cells throughout the system to subscribe to key party papers in October 1996—though this time not mentioning examinations.[133]

The eventual elimination of paid news and soft advertising. The CPD and SPPA jointly convened a conference in Beijing in August 1993 that resulted in the circular "Improving Professional Ethics in Journalism's Ranks and Forbidding Paid News." In fact, the circular banned all forms of compensated journalism, including "soft advertising."[134] But apparently the results were unsatisfactory, because in May 1996 the CPD issued yet another circular banning paid news: "We should be soberly aware that 'paid news' has not been totally banned, despite repeated orders. At present, 'paid news' is staging a comeback to a certain degree in the form of individual or invisible behavior, and the people involved are forming a social stratum. This warrants great attention, and effective measures must be adopted to solve the problem."[135] As discussed in Chapter 3, paid news and soft advertising were also formally forbidden in the February 1995 Advertising Law. But all informants agreed that "it's just as big a problem today as it was before."[136]

A ban on the unauthorized domestic republication of articles from overseas periodicals. This "special instruction," issued by the CPD in October 1993, applied even to the dispatches of Zhongguo Xinwenshe, the state-owned news agency whose primary mission is to provide propaganda for the outside world. Zhongguo Xinwenshe's dispatches "do not suit domestic readers," the special instruction explained.[137] (The extent of the republication of overseas news, either before or after the reiteration, is unclear.)

The detection and elimination of political "error" in newspapers and magazines with subnational distribution. A special group of retired propaganda xitong cadres, formed in early 1996, was especially concerned with publications backed by units relatively low in the administrative hierarchy.[138]

The implementation of new restrictions on Hong Kong and foreign films and television programs circulating in China. In January 1994 the Center decided to reduce the number of coproductions involving Chinese, Hong Kong, and foreign film producers. At the same time, efforts would be made to restrict internal circulation of coproduced films.[139] Subsequently, in July 1996 it was reported that the CPD had ordered the MRFT to suspend for an indefinite length of time the program to import "ten good films" a year from abroad, precisely because the propaganda chiefs (including Ding Guan'gen himself) were "rather nervous at the situation of the swarming of U.S. video and film culture into the mainland."[140] At the same time, the *Far Eastern Economic Review* reported that the CPD had ruled in March 1996 that two-thirds of all films shown in Chinese theaters must henceforth be of Chinese origin.[141]

The demand that guesthouses and hotels "comprehensively relay" central and provincial radio and television broadcasts. This would discourage retransmitting only STAR-TV and the more salacious local offerings, or using their in-house closed-circuit networks primarily to relay suspect videotapes.[142] With the deepening of the market economy has come increased domestic travel, and the state apparently wants access to its citizens' minds both when they are at home and when they are on the road.

An intensification of the practice of providing the populace with social models for emulation. No less an authority than the Xinhua News Agency reported that the number of models publicized in 1995 "increased substantially," and featured the "leading model cadre" Kong Fansen: "[Kong] dedicated himself entirely to the snow-capped plateau [of Tibet]. His deeds collectively reflected the lofty spirit of outstanding party member cadres during the new period. His deeds touched the hearts of millions of people."[143] Other model personages of 1995 included Han Suyun, the "good military wife"; Sai Erjiang, the "heroic policeman"; Tian Peifa, the "outstanding rural teacher"; and Li Runwu, the "good, honest cadre." What is unclear is the extent to which (if at all) these models inspired China's citizens to change their behavior, or even, indeed, whether they paid them the slightest attention or even knew of their existence.

The Positive Side of the Coin: Building a "Socialist Spiritual Civilization"

As the intensification of the provision of models would suggest, throughout the omnidirectional crackdown the party-state continued the positive efforts begun in the early 1980s to build a socialist spiritual civilization. There has in fact always been a positive side to communist propaganda. Thus, Mao waxed philosophic about the utopia soon to be created in China during the euphoria surrounding the Great Leap's early successes,[144] and Deng Xiaoping in October 1979 called upon writers and artists to "try harder to portray and help foster the new socialist man" so that the country could achieve the four modernizations while upholding the four cardinal principles.[145]

The first public use of the phrase "socialist spiritual civilization" appears in a document issued jointly by the party's CPD and the Ministries of Education, Culture, Public Health, and Public Security on February 28, 1981. The document promoted a new public-morality campaign called the "five talks and four beautifuls" (*wujiang simei*).[146] This campaign continued well into the mid-1980s and at some point along the way acquired, in addition to the five talks and four beautifuls, three "ardent loves" (*re ai*): ardent loves for the motherland, for socialism, and for the Communist Party. These were the shorthand slogans that the party-state adopted to summarize the contents of the socialist spiritual civilization it hoped eventually to build.

During the mid-1980s, the venerable Chen Yun, while simultaneously overseeing a party rectification drive, presided over the drafting of a programmatic statement on building a socialist spiritual civilization that was eventually adopted at the Sixth Plenum of the Twelfth Central Committee (September 1986). This document, which established building a socialist spiritual civilization as an important "policy direction" of the party-state, asserted both the "strategic position" of building a socialist spiritual civilization in achieving the party's other goals—including the four modernizations—and that building a socialist spiritual civilization was one of the party's "fundamental responsibilities," a self-evidently essential task. What constituted a socialist spiritual civilization was, however, vague and capacious—as it remains today. The programmatic statement declared variously that the Chinese people should promote harmony among ethnic groups, solve problems with a scientific spirit, work hard, adopt lofty ideals, respect old people and soldiers, combat bureaucratism, protect public property, fight feudal superstition, and reduce wasteful spending on weddings and funerals. Naturally, all of these things should be accomplished in a Marxist way, and in a way consistent with the four cardinal principles.[147]

By the early 1990s it had become clear that not only was China not making progress toward building a socialist spiritual civilization, but that in fact corruption, prostitution, and numerous other nefarious phenomena were, if anything, making Chinese society less spiritually civilized.[148] The leadership—as explained above—finally began discussing publicly the contradictions between shifting to a market economy and maintaining control over thought work, which was seen as organically linked to building a socialist spiritual civilization.

At the January 1994 National Propaganda Conference, Jiang Zemin delivered a keynote address on these matters noteworthy in two respects. First, he acknowledged that "the new situation" presented the party-state with tough new challenges in controlling thought work that required new (unspecified) measures, an apparent reference to managing the cultural market and the omnidirectional crackdown. Second, he called on the assembled cadres to develop *"specific* measures for the building of a spiritual civilization within two to three years according to the new situation."[149]

At least some of the Center's new "specific measures" were finally announced in October 1996 at the close of the Sixth Plenum of the Fourteenth Central Committee. Declaring that "we must resolutely prohibit any action that creates and spreads cultural garbage" so that "a marked improvement in the quality of people" can be realized, the plenum's final resolution established the following concrete goals for building a socialist spiritual civilization:

1. All provincial-level units must establish "a group of model cities and urban areas" by the year 2010, in addition to "civilized villages and townships" in the countryside.

2. Advanced collectives and individuals must be publicized as models.

3. Effective fundraising mechanisms must be set up to finance "spiritually uplifting" but unpopular arts not supported by the market, while the percentage of government budgets devoted to financing fine arts must grow at a rate "no less than that of revenue."

4. The national radio and television infrastructure should be expanded, "with emphasis placed on increasing the coverage provided by national and provincial radio and television broadcasters."

5. The Party Central Committee will establish a "committee to guide spiritual civilization construction."

6. Potentially most importantly, "in the assessment and evaluation of Party and government leading bodies and major leading cadres, not only their achievements and capabilities in promoting material civilization will be taken into account, but also their successes in leading the building of spiritual civilization."[150]

As of this writing, it is too early to evaluate the effectiveness of these "specific measures," but it is clear that they depart little from earlier specific measures to build a socialist spiritual civilization, and for that matter sound similar to Chiang Kai-shek's notably unsuccessful New Life Movement of the 1930s.[151] The only possibly significant difference is the call to link cadre promotion to the efforts to build socialist spiritual civilization. But whether this call will be implemented thoroughly (or at all) remains to be seen.

What did happen in the months immediately following the Sixth Plenum was that almost every provincial-level party committee issued reports outlining how they were implementing Jiang's guidelines with great enthusiasm. The city of Beijing, for example, adopted five concrete measures, all with a very stale air about them: It (1) promoted a "Beijing Citizens' Pledge of Civilization," (2) launched "an all-out drive to learn from the exemplary deeds of [one] Li Suli" and other model individuals, (3) constructed some cultural facilities to promote patriotism, including a museum to commemorate the War of Resistance Against Japan, (4) increased the number of road signs and billboards promoting "the public interest," and (5) adopted a "five best literary works project" to encourage the development of spiritually healthier books, essays, dramas, films, and television programs.[152] These actions did not depart significantly from those taken sporadically in the years prior to the Sixth Plenum and cannot reasonably be construed as anything new.

In May 1997 Jiang, Ding Guan'gen, and their allies did succeed in establishing, as an organ of the Party Central Committee, the "Central Guidance Committee on Spiritual Civilization Construction," as vowed at the Sixth Plenum. While precise composition of the Guidance Committee is unclear, most major political figures attended its inaugural session, and Jiang delivered the keynote address. This would appear to indicate the Guidance Committee's importance and Jiang's seriousness about pursuing the spiritual civilization line, and would also reinforce the prevailing interpretation of the renewed emphasis on building a socialist spiritual civilization as one of Jiang's tactics to consolidate personal political power.

In fact, as early as 1994 it had become apparent that Jiang was trying to deploy the spiritual civilization issue to stave off attacks from such would-be challengers as Qiao Shi. Jiang apparently had a falling out with propaganda czar Li Ruihuan in late 1994 and stripped from him the primary responsibility for macromanaging thought work, handing this authority over to the relatively loyal Ding Guan'gen.[153] Over the course of 1995 and into early 1996, Jiang found himself obliquely criticized by Deng Liqun and other remnant Maoists for being soft on thought work. Qiao Shi then jumped enthusiastically into the game, arguing that Jiang's alleged weakness on the Taiwan issue had been a key factor contributing to Lee Teng-hui's success in securing a visa to visit the United States in June 1995.[154] This criticism is thought likely to have stimulated not only Jiang's heightened emphasis on the socialist spiritual civilization campaign but also his efforts to harness and ride the tiger of nationalism, for example by sanctioning the 1996 publication of the xenophobic book *China Can Say "No."*[155]

But to underscore an important point: The problem of thought work is significantly more than an issue in intra-elite politics; it is in fact an issue in state-society relations. In this regard, it is important to remember that the omnidirectional crackdown began in the summer of 1993, while Li Ruihuan was still macromanaging thought work. Many leaders other than Jiang are concerned about controlling communications flows. Jiang, a gifted political entrepreneur, can use both the omnidirectional crackdown and the efforts to build a socialist spiritual civilization to enhance his political support among comrades in the "selectorate" who ultimately will determine his political fate.[156] Of course, Jiang's strategy of staking his political future on the success of building a socialist spiritual civilization is one fraught with risk, since the chances of its success seem exceedingly slim. Administrative fragmentation, property-rights reform, and technological advance appear quite likely to continue slowly, but inexorably, to undermine state control over thought work, the crackdown and new efforts to build a socialist spiritual civilization notwithstanding.

It is too early to evaluate with finality the effects of the omnidirectional crackdown on heterodox thought work. But all of the initial evidence, though scattered and incomplete, suggests that the Center has not been able to use either the specific measures of the crackdown or the broader initiative of asserting administrative control over the cultural market to resume its prereform domination of thought work. The administrative, economic, and technological forces fueling China's public-sphere praetorianism appear too powerful to overcome. It is significant, however, that the Chinese state continues to assert the right and responsibility to shape its citizens' worldviews, values, and action strategies, and refuses to acknowledge that control over thought work might well have to be sacrificed in exchange for economic development and integration into the world economy.

China's leaders seem to be only dimly aware of the profundity of the trade-off, and do not discuss publicly its implications in depth. Precisely what they would do should the omnidirectional crackdown conclusively fail is an interesting question, but present indications are that failure will come only slowly and undramatically, and will be punctuated by limited successes in a way that masks the need to take more drastic action. Business as usual will then likely resume, and the forces undermining Beijing's control will continue to take their toll.

CHAPTER SEVEN

Thought Work and the Transition from Authoritarian Rule

To recapitulate the major finding of this book: A combination of administrative fragmentation, property-rights reform, and technological advance has produced a serious reduction in the Chinese central party-state's ability to control thought work or public communications flows. Thought work has become commercialized and globalized, its sources pluralized. Efforts by the state to reassert control are not completely without effect, but generally fail to achieve their goals. The attempt to build a socialist spiritual civilization appears certain to fail. Yet neither are forces in civil society using thought work to generate a political challenge. China's public sphere is praetorian and the polity unfocused and aimless.

What, then, are the larger implications of this study? In particular, how should previous scholarship on democratization, the state-society relationship, and China's political future be assessed in the light of this study?

Communication and Transitions

The collapse of totalitarian and authoritarian regimes around the world since the mid-1980s is a development of enormous importance, not least for students of comparative politics and international relations endeavoring to explain why, when, and how such transitions take place. Yet strangely enough, in the light of this study, to date, very little of the transitions literature has focused on the ancien régimes' success (or lack thereof) in managing propagandistic public communications. This is despite the fact that, as argued in Chapter 1, the costs of remaining in power, and securing compliance over the broad range of issue-areas about which governments are concerned, are likely to be significantly lower the better they manage thought work. At the same time, controlling specifically telecommunications appears to be strategically vital to preventing regime opponents from coordinating protest activities on the street, as they did in Thailand in 1992.

O'Donnell, Schmitter, and Whitehead define "transitions from authoritarian rule" in the following terms: "Transitions are delimited, on the one side, by the launching of the process of dissolution of an authoritarian regime and, on the other side, by the installation of some form of democracy, the return to some form of authoritarian rule, or the emergence of a revolutionary alternative."[1]

Generally speaking, scholars who study transitions can be divided into four categories: (1) those who believe that polities interlock functionally with economic, social, and cultural systems and so must constantly adjust to maintain balance; (2) those who stress the strategic choices of the elite, relatively isolated from the larger forces in society; (3) those who emphasize the interplay of competing social groups; and (4) those who suggest the importance in transitions of overwhelming pressures from abroad.

The traditional legitimacy theories (e.g., economic crises causing regimes to lose public support, thereby convincing them of the need to negotiate their way out of power) belong in the first category, whereas the rational-choice theories best exemplified by Adam Przeworski's work belong in the "strategic choice" category.[2] In the "interplay of competing social groups" category fall various Marxist theories and, in particular, Barrington Moore's classic *Social Origins of Dictatorship and Democracy*, concerned more with the "original" transitions from authoritarian rule in the eighteenth and nineteenth centuries than with recent transitions.[3] Finally, the "external pressures" category includes a number of theories ranging from works that emphasize the need of elites to legitimize externally imposed austerity programs by seeking public support to those which make sweeping claims about the spread of the democratic-statist model everywhere, such as can be found in the works of Stanford sociologist John Meyer and his students.[4]

But in overlooking states' efforts to control public communications flows, these otherwise often powerful approaches miss two potentially decisive factors. First, there is the possibility that cross-border communication flows will interact with elements of domestic political crises to produce "transitionary moments." This seems to have happened in several East European countries in the fall of 1989, the Soviet Union in August 1991, and Thailand in May 1992. Second, long-term, glacial changes in people's worldviews, values, and action strategies can contribute to the creation of situations in which existing political orders no longer seem either legitimate or tenable to the citizenry or to large sections of the ruling elite, situations out of which the political crises that precede transitions emerge. Meyer perhaps comes closest to this conception in his emphasis on the spread of the norm of the modern state worldwide since the nineteenth century, but even he pays little attention to how the dissemination of advanced communications technologies can both spread the values of the global culture and actually undermine state builders' authority.[5]

In general, the transitions literature, as it currently exists, assigns to the mass media only the most passive role in the democratization process. It ignores telecommunications entirely. At best, state policy toward the media is used as a barometer of liberalization; at worst, the media are treated cursorily or ignored altogether. Very rarely are media organizations or media effects evaluated as potentially independent causal factors in the processes of transitions. The unstated assumption permeating the transitions literature is that the media already exist semi-independently within a submerged, but still vibrant, civil society. The media may have been repressed for years or even decades, but they have never lost their elemental independence and can often draw on a glorious past to put pressures on regimes to liberalize and eventually democratize.[6] But in the case of China, where a transitionary crisis emerged in the spring of 1989, the media were absorbed by the state in the 1950s and—cut off from their past—lost all institutional autonomy. Partly for this reason, the Chinese transition failed. Clearly, the Chinese media do not exist as elements of an independent, politicized civil society. Yet what they do in violating the Center's thought-work policies does gradually undermine the government's authority, weakening state power over society. During crises, the media might even be used to quickly undermine the government's authority. But all of these subtle and complicated possibilities are quite beyond the bounds of the existing transitions literature, even though they obviously demand serious attention.

Specifically on the question of telecommunications, the silence of the transitions literature is deafening. The only partial exception is to be found in the work of Samuel Huntington, notably in his 1991 study of democratization, *The Third Wave*. Huntington argues, as the name of his book would suggest, that there have been three waves of democratization since the early nineteenth century (1828–1926, 1943–62, and 1974–present), and that during the third wave "demonstration effects" have played a much more important role because of the "tremendous expansion of global communications and transportation that occurred in the decades after World War II and particularly the blanketing of the world by television and communications satellites in the 1970s."[7] Although Huntington conflates telecommunications with the mass media and exaggerates the role of satellites in the television broadcasting of the 1970s—satellite television only began to "blanket the world" in the 1990s—his work is important in at least drawing attention to the central role of transnational communications in fueling political change. But unfortunately, Huntington declines to take his analysis further by exploring the causal processes in depth.

The notion of "demonstration effects" implies a rather mechanistic stimulus-response causality in which the dictator in Country "Y" democratizes as a direct result of the democratization efforts of the erstwhile dictator in Country "X." The dictators in both countries may be coming under pressure from a mobilized society politicized in part by media images and telecommunications messages received from abroad. But it is impossible to say, because surprisingly, given his groundbreaking work on political participation in *Political Order in Changing Societies*, Huntington passes over the opportunity to examine in detail the processes by which media and telecommunications development might be spawning increased political participation, or otherwise influencing elite decision making. Huntington is content instead merely to imply exceptionally powerful media effects without subjecting the notion to serious examination or explanation: "The impact of the demonstration effects did not depend significantly on the existence of economic and social conditions favorable to democracy in the recipient country. As the snowballing process went on, indeed, that process itself tended to become a substitute for those conditions."[8]

Such a statement borders on technological determinism, because it implies that wherever advanced communications equipment becomes available, democratization will certainly occur. But surely the situation is more complicated than this. The structural conditions in which individuals and groups fight for democracy vary enormously from country to country and exert a profound impact on the outcome. Telecommunications and the mass media are likely to play important—if hitherto understudied—roles in democratic transitions, but only in interaction with other variables. Certainly that is a key conclusion to be derived from the present study.

Although China itself remains formally authoritarian, massive changes are taking place at a subterranean level that suggest some sort of in-progress transition, a transition whose end is uncertain but whose uncertain trajectory itself makes China an important case to study. At present, the Chinese public sphere is praetorian, but what are the long-term implications of the state losing control over its citizens' worldviews, values, and action strategies? Could these subterranean transformations again suddenly burst to the surface in a crisis, as happened in nearly 200 Chinese cities in 1989? Could an "electronic public sphere"—a genuinely liberal public sphere—develop, linking advanced telecommunications networks with radio call-in shows whose audiences eventually demand the overthrow of the Communist Party? Do advanced telecommunications networks facilitate the growth of transregional (and/or transnational) political action groups exerting even more pressure on the state?

The Generation of Public Opinion and Social Networks

Telecommunications and the mass media can certainly play crucial roles in the generation of public opinion and social networks outside state control. All of the important Chinese leaders who spoke at the National Propaganda Conference in January 1994 called for the party-state to "correctly guide public opinion."[9] The people were known to have held opinions even in the days of Mao, but not until 1989, it seems, did China's leaders come to realize with a shock that the citizenry is capable of generating a genuine public opinion. This genuine public opinion is defined not as aggregates of individuals secretly holding to their thoughts, but instead as "people recognizing a problem, producing conflicting ideas about what to do, considering those alternatives, and trying to resolve the matter by building consensus for a line of action."[10] Members of society in alliance with disaffected elements of the party-state were clearly doing just that during the spring of 1989, and China's repressive leaders recognized the ominous link between the autonomous generation of public opinion and the reduced prospects for continued authoritarian rule.

But because public opinion is closely associated with the twin concepts of civil society and the public sphere,[11] it is important to clarify that telecommunications and media development facilitate the generation of all manner of social networks and groups, not just those civicly concerned with building democracy and solving sociopolitical problems. Recently in China, as state power has declined in a variety of spheres, sociologists have turned their attention to the resurgence of criminal gangs. The well-known exiled democracy activist Su Xiaokang asserted in the summer of 1992 that the Ministry of Public Security (MPS) had counted some 1,800 underground societies, gangs, and illegal associations active in China; the largest such groups included tens of thousands of members whose activities spanned several provinces. Some groups controlled agricultural production, some tax-farmed, and some—typically southeastern hill clans—actually administered territory. They also often formed alliances with overseas gangs to ferry drugs, guns, and prostitutes into and out of China.[12]

Sun Hui and Wu Mengshuang, writing a year later in the Shanghai journal *Shehui* (Society), described how these unofficial—but certainly not civil—societies operate:

> [They] oppress whole towns by bullying the businessmen; eat and drink their fill without paying; forcibly take whatever they desire; wantonly insult women; extort money and items from sources public and private. . . . [They] employ various means to bribe, entice, and corrupt personnel of party and government organs, and in particular public security and justice workers,

into acting as protective umbrellas. . . . They represent a wicked force that challenges the political power of the people and the laws of the state.[13]

One of the most interesting aspects of these gangs is precisely their reliance on advanced telecommunications facilities to manage their far-flung activities. As Sun and Wu write, "Underground criminal societies generally possess modern means of transportation and advanced communications facilities. For example, the underground criminal society headed by Wu Jiazhen in a certain suburb of Yancheng, Jiangsu Province . . . has set up communication links by purchasing a radio station and walkie-talkies, and it has installed a tower antenna over twenty meters high in front of the entrance to its headquarters building."[14]

So closely are gangsters associated with high-tech telecommunications in China (including Taiwan and Hong Kong) that the popular term for a mobile telephone is not *xingdong dianhua*—the technical term—but rather *da ge da*, literally "big brother big," connoting important personages in the underworld.

It is axiomatic in political and social analysis that the line between gangs and revolutionary movements can sometimes be quite thin. The validity of this assertion is not restricted to China. The government of Pakistan claimed in July 1995 that some 1,000 people had been killed in Karachi during the previous year by the Mohajir Qaumi Movement (MQM), a group claiming that the Islamabad government was discriminating against its Urdu-speaking citizens. Pakistani authorities were convinced that the MQM militants' use of mobile telephone and paging systems—used to scurry around Karachi staging urban guerrilla attacks—was making it impossible for government forces to act against them effectively. As a result, the government requested Karachi's mobile phone companies to switch off their systems for a short-term crackdown beginning at midnight on July 3. The companies complied, the crackdown commenced, and the violence subsequently subsided (though did not end entirely).[15]

Potential for the Emergence of a Chinese Civil Society

The spring 1989 antigovernment demonstrations and subsequent Tiananmen massacre constituted a watershed not only in Chinese politics, but also in the *study* of Chinese politics. Particularly after the East European communist regimes collapsed in the autumn of 1989, many scholars began to interpret Chinese politics from the perspective of civil society models. The existence of a vibrant civil society was asserted in the transitions literature to have contributed fundamentally to the democratization of large parts of Southern Europe and Latin America; now, civil societies were argued to have contributed crucially to the collapse of communism in Eastern Europe. Given how close the Chinese Communist regime apparently came to collapsing in the spring of 1989, might not a civil society also be blossoming in China—part of a global trend—even if it was repressed in the immediate aftermath of the massacre? And if so, would democratization not be China's ultimate fate, the current cold spell notwithstanding?

Many scholars optimistically embraced this view in the early 1990s.[16] Consider the words of McCormick, Su, and Xiao: "The 1989 Chinese Democracy Movement is best understood as the expression of a fundamental conflict between a state with totalitarian intentions and an emerging civil society. . . . If the growth of civil society is a long-term trend which began over a century ago and is still underway, then the Leninist state established in 1949 can be seen as an interruption rather than the inevitable and unavoidable expression of Chinese culture."[17] The present study suggests that such a view is incorrect.

The key problem with applying the civil society concept to China is fundamental and obvious. There is little evidence that the semi-autonomous groups emerging in Chinese society—often with the help of advanced communications technologies—meet the classic criteria for a civil society, specifically the requirements that (1) such groups enjoy a sphere of legal autonomy acknowledged and guaranteed by the state; (2) the groups in turn acknowledge the state's legitimacy as the primary rule-maker and rule-enforcer in society; (3) the groups energetically pursue the political interests of their members, albeit within frameworks constructed in negotiations with the state; and (4) the groups partake of the political dialogue that should be flourishing in a liberal, well-structured public sphere.[18]

Scholars determined to find civil society in China have too often ignored these definitional requirements, simply stretching the meaning of the term "civil society" until it becomes capacious enough to encompass Chinese reality. Thus, Gordon White distinguishes "political civil society"—the classic concept—from Chinese civil society, which is characterized by "a change in the balance of power between state and society in the latter's favor, a clearer separation between the spheres of 'public' and 'private,' far greater scope for the expression of individual and group interests, and the ability of social interests and organizations to acquire greater autonomy from and influence over the state."[19] With Chinese collaborators, White did discover a mushrooming of new social organizations in Xiaoshan city, Zhejiang province, during the 1980s. But these organizations were not involved in politics other than as relatively passive "transmission belts" for the state, and appear to have had little influence on policy, other than at the margins. Moreover, White himself is well aware of the problem: "At the present stage, the independence and the influence of the associations are too weak to allow us to call them 'pressure' groups or even 'interest' groups. As organizations they are far too deeply penetrated by the state. . . . And yet there is movement."[20]

Language like this implies that even though there is no political civil society in China at present, eventually the outcomes associated with political civil societies will occur, because some sort of irreversible process has been set in motion. But White and other inventors of what might be called the "civil society with Chinese characteristics" concept fail to demonstrate why this should be the case, why the logic of fin-de-siècle Chinese society should be the same as that of classical, political civil society. Nor do they demonstrate that the former necessarily leads to the latter.

White and his fellows are far from alone in embracing a capacious definition of civil society. Following the intellectual trail blazed by Alexis de Tocqueville, many scholars assert (or assume) that the formation of any unofficial group, no matter how apolitical, can ultimately contribute to democratization. Robert Putnam summarized this body of thought in his highly influential study of Italian democracy:

> Participation in civic organizations inculcates skills of cooperation as well as a sense of shared responsibility for collective endeavors. Moreover, when individuals belong to "cross-cutting" groups with diverse goals and

members, their attitudes will tend to moderate as a result of group interaction and cross-pressures. These effects, it is worth noting, do not require that the manifest purpose of the association be political. Taking part in a choral society or a bird-watching club can teach self-discipline and an appreciation for the joys of successful collaboration.[21]

The relative autonomy gained by social groups in China and the attendant pluralization of society uncovered so painstakingly by White and others are undoubtedly significant; indeed, those are fundamental assumptions of this book. But the application of the civil society concept to these developments and the implication that China is destined for democratization are highly questionable. Clearly, alternative networks and groups have emerged in Chinese society over which the state has difficulty exerting control, but the logic that governs their evolution and political impact may well differ significantly from the logic of civil society—though precisely in what ways is admittedly difficult to discern.[22] In the Italian case, Putnam is unable to sort out the independent causal effects of different kinds of groups because apolitical joining is highly correlated with political joining. In China, apolitical joining is on the rise, but political joining is not; at present, then, it cannot reasonably be argued that a genuine Chinese civil society is taking shape. By a similar logic, although the shoots of a liberal, structured public sphere may be present in the proliferation of radio call-in shows, access to the Internet, and even karaoke bars and MTVs, they have not yet matured and could possibly be crushed back into the ground by a vigorous new authoritarianism. For the present, China's public sphere remains praetorian.

Several other factors highlighted in this study also suggest the dubiousness of applying the civil society concept to China. First, and most important, all Chinese media outlets continue to be governed internally by Communist Party committees. Although media personnel may well be becoming more "unit-oriented" in their behavior, their units are most certainly not recognized by the state as autonomous institutions with rights of their own; to the extent that they enjoy autonomy, it is de facto, not de jure. Yet as explained above, the acknowledged institutional autonomy of social groups is an integral component of the definition of a civil society. Semi-autonomous media organizations are also assumed to be important factors in civil society–based explanations of transitions from authoritarian rule (though they are not systematically studied). Some Chinese media organizations—most notably the *Guangming Ribao*—can boast a prestigious precommunist past, but not a shred of their original autonomy survived absorption by the party-state in the 1950s. These organizations are simply in no position to play the political role of some of the prestigious Latin American newspapers that clung tenaciously to a semi-autonomous status during years of harsh repression.

It is true that some media-related organizations in China are not governed directly by party committees—some teleplay- and film-production companies, advertising agencies, and telecommunications service providers, for example—but these organizations still do not enjoy recognized autonomy within the Chinese system. The government always reserves the right to repress these organizations at the slightest provocation, even if it does not necessarily possess the will or the capacity. At the same time, it is true that the party is trying to limit arbitrary governmental interference in the business activities of communications (and other) firms, but with decidedly mixed results. The party-state still clings to the right to interfere "if necessary," regardless of the prevailing line. Therefore, the Chinese media cannot be considered components of a genuine civil society.

This assertion may seem somewhat at odds with this study's fundamental assumption that the central party-state is losing control over thought work. If party committees still govern the media, then how can the Center be losing control? The key is to recognize the difference between civil society and other forms of unofficial society. Civil society is inherently political. Its members constantly participate in politics. They discuss it in the media and at public places such as coffee houses or tea shops, and they coordinate their antigovernment activities using telecommunications. Clearly, the Chinese state retains a great deal of control over the circulation of open, public, political communications, such as the political news broadcast by the major television stations and radio stations and printed in the large-circulation newspapers. Yet as discussed throughout this study, a vast volume of information now originates outside this system—for example, from abroad (in the form of shortwave radio broadcasts, the Internet, and satellite television) and internally (in the form of illegal underground publications, faxes, and other telecommunications messages). Moreover, lower-level media outlets often decline to recirculate or rebroadcast central news; instead, they supply their audiences with local news and amazing tales (frequently fabricated) from abroad. Other news and quasi-news circulates in the form of voice and fax via the fast-developing telecommunications network, and by the "grapevine," which has always existed in China but which now is extending its reach and becoming much more efficient as a result of telecommunications development. Even if the central party-state remains capable of controlling the "most important news," this information constitutes an ever-shrinking segment of the overall volume of information that the Chinese people consume.

But what audiences turn to instead—what they demand from the media and what the media eagerly supply so that they can sell advertising—is not the political news required to feed a civil society, but rather meretricious entertainment. Reforms introduced in the media have produced a society awash in titillating, violent, and (on the surface) apolitical entertainment. While it is likely that much of this entertainment contains subtle political messages likely to exert a long-term impact on the Chinese people's worldviews, values, and action strategies, nothing about it justifies asserting that a liberal, structured public sphere is in the process of emerging now. Yet such a public sphere is central to the classical definition of a civil society. At the same time, while it is also true that there is much good journalism in China today—seriously exposing deep-rooted social problems—and though callers to radio hotline programs do sometimes broach sensitive subjects, far too much journalism is tainted by soft advertising and paid news, and the bulk of the discussion on call-in shows concerns singers' and actors' private lives. Thus, if a Chinese public sphere is emerging, its presence is currently overshadowed by vast volumes of relatively apolitical messages.[23]

A related problem with the civil society models is that they imply that when a state loses political power, that power is automatically reconcentrated by competing organizations that use it to participate vigorously in politics, especially in the public sphere.[24] But in the case of Chinese thought work, power is only becoming dispersed—to individuals with access to the telecommunications network, to the richer businesses and factories that can afford to purchase advertising, to embryonic television networks linked up with foreign program suppliers, and to the purely foreign advertisers and program providers based in Hong Kong and abroad. Thought work is becoming commercialized, globalized, and pluralized in an apparently patternless mosaic. The potential is in place for it to be reorganized into a concentrated political force, but so far there is little indication that anything like that is taking place.

Civil society models also imply that all of the groups that emerge with the decline of state power are politically engaged, liberal, and restrained in their demands. They partake of the "civic culture," and they acknowledge the legitimacy of the state as the ultimate public authority. But the present study suggests that this kind of group is only one of the kinds to emerge with the decline of state power. An array of other groups not so civil also emerges, and in fact in China the "uncivil" type has been much more prominent than the largely nonexistent civil type. The typical gang leader in China today moves from city to city, hotel to hotel, always using mobile telephones to stymie the police in their efforts to track him down. (He is also very likely to derive his worldviews, values, and action strategies from Hong Kong films and teleplays about triads.) Clearly, such groups' activities are not the kind conceived by theorists of civil society. In the extreme, even the activities of large-scale revolutionary movements can be facilitated by weakened state power over thought work, and revolutionary groups are not usually known for partaking of the civic culture. The gradual fusion of the mass media with telecommunications to the point that even video images can be transmitted over the "phone" network only enhances the potential for groups of all types to appear on the scene, and for some of them to make the polity completely unsafe for democracy.

Thought Work: Irreparably Shattered?

What, then, are the implications of this book for China's political future? At least in the short to mid-term, a frustrated central party-state

operating in a climate of thought-work commercialization, globalization, and pluralization will continue to lash out against change sporadically, inconsistently, and ineffectively. Much of this reaction—such as
the jamming of the Voice of America (VOA) and the harassment of
Hong Kong and foreign journalists—will heighten international tensions. All of it will heighten tensions within Chinese society and with
lower-level governments.

At the same time, continued telecommunications development will
facilitate the emergence of numerous new social networks linked with
individuals and groups abroad whose worldviews, values, and action
strategies differ sharply from those Beijing wants to inculcate in the
minds of the Chinese people. These transnational networks will include
everything from human-rights groups to criminal gangs. In a general
sense, the transfer of control from the state to society over the structuration of China's symbolic environment will continue. But barring a
political crisis similar to that of spring 1989, Beijing will continue to
control the most sensitive political information. As a result, the population will be saturated with colorful and exciting entertainment, but little serious and honest discussion of pressing social problems. Building
a socialist spiritual civilization in this context will be impossible, but so
too will be building a liberal democracy. Therefore, unless and until a
new political crisis develops—a crisis capable of marrying the mass
media with telecommunications to generate the formation of an electronic public sphere—control over thought work is likely to remain
chaotic, uninstitutionalized, and not channeled for political purposes;
in short, it will remain praetorian.

Such a situation seems already to prevail on the international level,
where existing communications regimes are inadequate to deal with
the challenges posed by new technologies and cascading globalization.
Far too many pundits predict that reducing the barriers to transnational
information flows will lead smoothly and ineluctably to a liberal world
of universal similarities in which steadily growing mutual understanding mitigates international conflict to the point at which war becomes
obsolete. Other, even more optimistic pundits predict that the development of cross-border communications will inevitably produce a "global
civil society" whose eventual end can only be worldwide democratiza-

tion. But blind optimism of this sort ignores the fact that many states now feel seriously threatened by the chaotic globalization of information flows and attribute their insecurities to the machinations of other states. China frequently accuses the United States of using the VOA, Radio Free Asia (RFA), and other tools to effect a "peaceful evolution" of the Chinese polity into a condition of bourgeois liberalism. Cuba, Vietnam, and North Korea agree.[25]

In sum, for the foreseeable future, transborder images and information appear likely to flow in an unsystematic, praetorian manner similar to the situation prevailing inside China's borders. Governing elites everywhere face the challenge of managing propagandistic public communications flows in a way consistent with the long-term goals of state- and nation-building. The net result may be positive or negative, comforting or disturbing, depending on the specific sociopolitical settings with which globally free-floating symbols interact—and depending on the observer's own values. In some settings, transborder communications flows may contribute to democratization, development, and the attainment of social justice; in others, they may contribute only to disorganized violence. The fracturing of state-centered communication patterns is fostering change everywhere, but nowhere are the consequences of change self-evident.

Reference Matter

For full authors' names, titles, and publication data on works cited in short form in these notes, see the Bibliography, pp. 283–320.

CHAPTER 1. "THOUGHT WORK" IN THE PRAETORIAN PUBLIC SPHERE

1. Reprinted in Deng Xiaoping, *Fundamental Issues*, p. 36.

2. The *New York Times* journalist Nicholas Kristof has also reported hearing of Chinese children demanding to be read their rights, but the Beijing psychologist claimed to have observed such games firsthand. See Kristof.

3. At least in Western scholarship, the term "thought work" was formerly used to denote efforts by party-state cadres at the lowest rungs of society to impart "correct" understandings of state policy in highly controlled small study groups. The classic treatment is Martin King Whyte's *Small Groups and Political Rituals in China*. Today, however, "thought work," along with the term "propaganda" (*xuanchuan*), is used in official Chinese discourse to refer more broadly to all efforts to structure the symbolic environment, whether intentional or not. On this process of "structuration," see Giddens.

4. North, p. 53.

5. See Skinner and Winckler.

6. See Hoare and Smith.

7. See Alexander, pp. 281–301.

8. Scott; see also Selbin.

9. Geertz, p. 216.

10. See Anderson.

11. Kenez; see also Siebert et al.

12. The book is based on documentary analysis and 72 interviews conducted in Taipei, Hong Kong, Beijing, Guangzhou, Kunming, and Washington. In the text and notes, the interviews are numbered 101–72. Some interviews concerned more than one topic; thus, telecommunications was the subject of 17 interviews, television the subject of 33, radio the subject of 19, print the subject

of 27, the "cultural market" the subject of 7, and film the subject of 5. Most topic interviews were conducted in Beijing (42), followed by Hong Kong (34), Guangzhou (11), Kunming (10), and Washington (1). Subjects in all sites provided extensive information about other sites; in particular, subjects in Beijing and Hong Kong tended to be well informed about the thought-work situation in other parts of China.

13. For excellent studies of evolving ideology, see Goldman; Brugger and Kelly. For thoughtful analyses of changing popular culture, see Gold; Zha.

14. The terms "central party-state" and "the Center" refer in this book to the Beijing-based, higher-level networks and hierarchies charged specifically with managing propaganda. Precise composition of these networks fluctuates, but they always include higher-ranking officials in the MII, MoC, and SPPA, as well as the Communist Party's Department of Propaganda. For purposes of brevity, this book frequently uses the terms "state" and "Beijing" in lieu of the cumbersome "central party-state," though not without recognition of the fact that the state is a hierarchical organization that may take different forms and play different social roles across levels of the hierarchy and regions.

15. See Habermas; Siebert et al.

16. The classic works in this genre include Lerner; Pye; Deutsch; Schramm, *Mass Media and National Development*; Schramm and Lerner. Many communications scholars subsequently came to see "dependent" systems as constituting another alternative to authoritarian and liberal systems, or that liberal systems could themselves be dependent. See, for example, Smith; McPhail.

17. Huntington, *Political Order in Changing Societies*.

18. The term "telecommunications" refers to messages sent point to point by an electronic medium over relatively long distances, whereas the term "mass-media communications" refers to messages—electronic or otherwise—sent from a single point to large audiences. Traditionally, telecommunications denoted primarily telephony, but in the 1980s, as the capacity of telecommunications transmission systems expanded, telecommunications lines began to be used to transmit messages containing a great deal more information than the traditional telephone call, telegraph, or fax. Marriage of telecommunications with the computer soon allowed for sophisticated forms of electronic data interchange, electronic mail, and eventually the Internet.

19. "Pluralization" in this sense must be distinguished carefully from the "pluralism" of liberal public spheres.

20. Of course, state actions also influence the *inputs* to the symbolic environment generated by all the new sources, but to a much less significant extent than in the past.

21. Yet this argument is made forcefully by, among others, Strand; McCormick et al.; White.

22. The socialist spiritual civilization concept is vague and complex, but one

high-ranking propaganda cadre explained in 1995 that its basic components include putting the collective good above individual self-interest, and esteeming education, science, and fine art. Interview 160.

23. Buci-Glucksman, p. 43.

24. Liu Renwei.

25. See Nathan, chapters 7–9.

26. The list derives from numerous formal and informal discussions between 1994 and 1998.

27. "Strengthening Propaganda and Ideological Work."

28. "Resolution of the CPC Central Committee on Certain Important Questions."

29. The terms "commodity fetishism" and "penetration" are Marxian and, especially, Gramscian; see Hoare and Smith. On the processes by which telecommunications can contribute to the formation of a societal public opinion, see Price; Price and Roberts.

30. Keohane and Nye adopt the sanguine but sober view in *Power and Interdependence*. The findings of the present research are more consistent with Rosenau's argument—at times optimistic and at times pessimistic—in *Turbulence in World Politics*.

31. Thus, shortly after RFA began broadcasting in the autumn of 1996, the flagship *Renmin Ribao* compared it with earlier American military intervention in Asia and editorialized, "The Asian people have long experienced the 'freedom' of the United States; who will accept such 'freedom' any longer? In the minds of some Americans, the United States is good in everything and all other countries are no good; it seems that the United States has the right to intervene in the internal affairs of other countries and force its value concepts and patterns on other people. Such a mind-set makes the United States easily forget its own disgusting conduct." See Gu Ping.

CHAPTER 2. THOUGHT-WORK INSTITUTIONS UNDER REFORM

1. See Victor H. Mair, "Language and Ideology in the Written Popularizations of the *Sacred Edict*," in Johnson et al., pp. 325–59.

2. Rowe, "The Public Sphere in Modern China," p. 314.

3. Leo Ou-fan Lee and Andrew J. Nathan, "The Beginnings of Mass Culture: Journalism and Fiction in the Late Ch'ing and Beyond," in Johnson et al., pp. 360–95.

4. Wright.   5. Ting, pp. 10–11.

6. Ibid., pp. 15–19; Eastman.   7. See Teiwes.

8. Meisner, pp. 41–42.

9. Teiwes, p. 84. The number of papers was reduced from about 1,800 in the mid-1930s to 655 in 1956.

10. Frederick T. C. Yu, p. 155.

11. Whyte, "Small Groups and Communication in China."

12. On the multistep flow, see Rogers. Already the communists had forced China's traditionally semi-autonomous intellectuals into exclusive state service. See Timothy Cheek, "The Honorable Vocation," in Saich and van de Ven, pp. 235–62. This idea of integrated control is an important theme that illuminates the discussion later in this chapter about "communication compression" and the transformative effects of reform-era telecommunications development.

13. See Teiwes, p. 16.

14. J. Chang, "The Mechanics of State Propaganda," in Cheek and Saich, pp. 76–124.

15. See Alan P. L. Liu, pp. 115–16.

16. Ibid., p. 55.

17. Joint Publications Research Service, "Translations," p. 65.

18. Mao, "On the Correct Handling of Contradictions Among the People," in *Selected Readings*, p. 378.

19. Quoted in Frederick T. C. Yu, p. 16.

20. *Dangdai Zhongguo de Guangbo Dianshi*, vol. 1, p. 65.

21. Ibid., p. 43. Similarly, the number of newspapers in circulation fell from 343 in 1965 to 42 in 1970; the number of magazines fell from 790 in 1965 to 21 in 1970; and the number of books published fell from 20,143 in 1965 to 4,889 in 1970. Guojia Tongjiju, *Zhongguo Tongji Nianjian, 1997*, p. 705.

22. Clandestine reception of foreign shortwave radio broadcasts did occur during the Cultural Revolution, as well as some circulation of banned books, but the audiences seem likely to have been very small.

23. Frederick T. C. Yu, "China's Mass Communication in Historical Perspective," in Chu and Hsu, pp. 49–50.

24. Alan P. L. Liu, pp. 105–7.

25. There is, of course, widespread suspicion that the Lei Feng character never actually existed. But other model individuals and units have existed and still do exist, even if the gloriousness of their deeds is exaggerated.

26. Alan P. L. Liu, p. 110.

27. Television began in 1958 but its diffusion was extremely limited until the 1980s.

28. See Oksenberg.

29. For a vivid account of the Democracy Wall movement, see Garside.

30. Deng, "Uphold the Four Cardinal Principles," in *Selected Works*, pp. 174–79.

31. Baum, pp. 105–6.

32. Deng, "Bourgeois Liberalization Means Taking the Capitalist Road," in *Fundamental Issues*, pp. 114–15.

33. Deng, "Concerning Problems on the Ideological Front," in *Selected Works*, p. 368.

34. Deng, "The Party's Urgent Tasks on the Organizational and Ideological Fronts," in *Fundamental Issues*, pp. 30–35 (emphasis added).

35. At the time, Hu was Deng's hand-picked successor but faced opposition from military and other senior leaders who did not respect him. The reasons for his dismissal are therefore too complex to specify. See Harding, pp. 202–36.

36. Deng, "Take a Clear-Cut Stand Against Bourgeois Liberalization," in *Fundamental Issues*, pp. 164–65.

37. For a much later explanation, see Jiang Yaping.

38. Informants repeatedly asserted that such thinking lay behind leadership decision-making in the early 1980s; see, e.g., Interviews 111, 119, 133, and 138. But none of the informants took direct part in the decision-making process. Their knowledge comes instead from attending work conferences, reading documents, and otherwise exchanging information with fellow thought workers.

39. This calculus is documented in the early chapters of *Dangdai Zhongguo de Guangbo Dianshi*, vol. 1.

40. *Dangdai Zhongguo de Guangbo Dianshi*, vol. 1, p. 66.

41. Interview 166; see also the discussion in Lynn T. White III, "All the News," in Chin-Chuan Lee, pp. 88–110.

42. *Dangdai Zhongguo de Guangbo Dianshi*, vol. 2, p. 15 and p. 477.

43. See also the later "Regulations on Radio and Television Management."

44. *Dangdai Zhongguo de Guangbo Dianshi*, vol. 2, pp. 296–99.

45. The term *xitong*—literally, "system"—refers to a cluster of bureaucracies responsible for implementing (and, to a degree, formulating) policy over a set of interrelated issue-areas. There are four or five main xitong, including foreign affairs, finance and economics, and—most important for this study—education and propaganda. Xitong are organized into loose, interpenetrating hierarchies, so that within any single organization there can be representatives from more than one xitong. But most organizations are primarily identified with one xitong. The xitong serve as trellises for networks of intensive interaction. When someone in China says that he or she "works in the '*x*' xitong," the flavor sometimes resembles the English "I work in the '*x*' industry." For an authoritative explanation, see Lieberthal.

46. Interviews 123, 137, 159, and 170.

47. In March 1998, the MRFT was slightly downgraded to a "general bureau" directly under the State Council, in a reform likely to compromise its already anemic authority vis-à-vis provincial governments.

48. Film was not brought under the MR(F)T system until 1985, when jurisdiction over the state-owned, provincial-level film-production studios was transferred from the MoC. According to the informants in Interviews 124 and 135, the reason for giving the MRT jurisdiction over film-production studios was to facilitate improvement in the quality of television by allowing the new medium more easily to draw upon the talents of China's many gifted film directors and actors.

49. Lieberthal and Oksenberg discuss the conflicts between *tiao* and *kuai* in great detail in *Policy Making in China*. On the creation of the MRT, see Xing-zhengyuan Xinwenju, pp. 205–7.

50. Zhu and Wang, p. 65.

51. The country was flooded with unofficial Red Guard publications during the 1966–69 period, but these appear never to have been regulated by the MoC (or any other bureaucracy).

52. Interview 140.

53. Interview 142. Outside of a few large cities, the SPPA enjoys no representation below the provincial level.

54. Thus, domestic Internet Web sites are regulated by the MPT, despite their obviously propagandistic nature. See "Control of Public Multimedia Communication Tightened."

55. At this writing, the MPT and the MEI are being reorganized as bureaus under a new MII, in a dramatic administrative reform announced in March 1998. But it appears the MPT faction will dominate the new ministry, since the first minister is erstwhile MPT chief Wu Jichuan, and the new ministry's headquarters is the old MPT building on West Chang'an Road. The reorganization is therefore likely to make little difference for the functioning of the MPT system and in particular is unlikely to strengthen the center vis-à-vis the localities. It certainly will not affect the xitong status of telecommunications' units.

56. Abler, "Hardware, Software, and Brainware," in Brunn and Leinbach, p. 36.

57. The MPT's history is thoroughly reviewed by Zita; see also Ante Xu.

58. See Table 1.

59. Tan.

60. Ding Lu. The taxation rate for the provincial-level telecommunications bureaus was reduced from 33 percent to 10 percent in 1986, but there appears to be great variation in the tax rates of subprovincial telecommunications authorities. See Ure.

61. Lin Sun, "Funding Telecommunications Expansion."

62. See Zita, pp. 11–12. Of course, the MPT would also produce telecommunications equipment—a source of much contestation between the two ministries that would eventually figure in the creation of two alternative telecommunications service providers: Liantong and Jitong.

63. By the early 1990s management of the equipment-producing factories in both the MPT and MEI systems had been transferred to the localities, a reform initiative that contributed to a voluminous increase in the production of all manner of communications equipment and its dissemination throughout society, outside of direct central control. In 1994, both the MPT system and the MEI system each had more than 100 companies churning out communications equipment across China, often with important assistance from multinational in-

vestors (Interview 132). One source estimated that "about half" of all the telecommunications equipment in China is produced in each system. But the source also asserted that today the factories are much more likely than before to orient themselves toward the interests of the regions in which they are located than to the xitong (Interview 144).

64. Zita, p. 14; see also Li Guangru.

65. Interview 121.

66. Interviews 110, 114, and 116. There was even some talk in the mid-1990s that the MPT xitong would be broken up into 38 independent regional telephone companies (along the lines of the 1984 AT&T breakup). Nothing of the sort had occurred as of 1998, however, even though the de facto power of the localities continued to increase. Interview 132; see also "China: Breaking Up."

67. Oksenberg; Zita, p. 33.

68. See Kornai, especially pp. 110–30. Large firms in capitalist economies sometimes face similar incentives.

69. Data cited in Xie Liangjun, "Telecommunications Expansion Unabated." On interconnectivity, see Zita, p. 33.

70. See Fei Chang He.

71. See Ding Lu.

72. Many of the wealthier provinces simply refuse to supply the MPT with as much revenue as it demands, and in fact are rumored to be supplying less and less with each passing year. Privately, MPT officials acknowledge the increasing difficulties securing provincial compliance, but they decline to provide detailed figures (Interview 132).

73. Interview 132.

74. Interviews 121 and 131. Poorer regions cannot afford to flout MPT requests with quite as much impunity because of their reliance on the intra-xitong transfer payments.

75. There is private ownership of some small-scale telecommunications, advertising, and film/television production companies, as well as bookstores.

76. Barzel, p. 2.

77. Kornai, pp. 64–67.

78. Ibid., p. 66; see also Andrew Walder, "Corporate Organization and Local Government Property Rights in China," in Milor, pp. 54–56.

79. Because the state remains the legal owner, firms and managers do not have the right to alienate the property.

80. Numerous scholars have written about the complexity of the Chinese state-enterprise relationship in recent years. A few particularly important examples include Oi; Kuen Lee; Groves et al.; Thomas G. Rawski, "Progress Without Privatization," in Milor, ed., pp. 27–52; Walder, "Corporate Organization"; Walder, "Local Governments"; Whiting; Putterman; Steinfeld.

81. Walder, "Local Governments as Industrial Firms," p. 58.

82. Rawski, in Milor, ed., p. 44. Profit is defined as sales revenue minus costs and turnover taxes. See also Groves et al.

83. Several informants asserted that managers in media and telecommunications firms do enjoy such "fringe benefits," but the informants always declined to discuss the issue in detail. This reluctance suggests another problem with the Groves et al. study: It is based on managers' self-reports to the Economic Structure Reform Commission. The reason this is problematic is simply because the managers would likely understate any personal benefits resulting from reform, particularly those acquired in ways whose propriety (or legality) might be questionable.

84. See Hayek.

85. As detailed in Chapter 3, the advertising industry grew at a 40- to 50-percent annual rate after the mid-1980s. Part of the reason is because firms throughout the Chinese economy have been made somewhat responsible for profits and losses and so face strong incentives to increase their sales through the use of persuasive messages in the media.

86. See, for example, "National Hi-Tech Project."

87. Multinational corporations and nongovernmental organizations are perfectly willing to help China "digest" this technology by providing advice on precisely which items should be procured and training on how to use it. See, for example, "State to Join with Overseas Companies to Develop Internet"; "Asian-Net Launches 'Massive' Internet Training Program."

88. Particularly in the countryside, however, there is great inequality. The informant in Interview 117 estimated that about 90 percent of farm households in the coastal regions own television sets, but that only 70 percent own sets in Central China, and a mere 25 percent own sets in the barren western reaches of the country.

89. Yu Huang.

90. The number of transponders available in the Asia-Pacific was expected to double with the launch of 80–100 additional satellites by 2000. Interview 107.

91. See *Media Asia* 20(1), 1993, a special issue devoted exclusively to satellite communications in the Asia-Pacific region.

92. The other two co-owners of Asiasat are the (PRC) state-owned China International Trust and Investment Corporation (CITIC) and the Anglo-Hong Kong Cable and Wireless Group, whose major subsidiary is Hong Kong Telecom. Each of the three principals holds one-third of Asiasat's shares.

93. Asiasat obtained its license in Hong Kong from a body that answered to the British government. Now, the Hong Kong Special Administrative Region (SAR) government issues these licenses, with Beijing's precise role uncertain.

94. Interview 107.

95. This history is detailed in Ren Xianglin; *Dangdai Zhongguo de Guangbo Dianshi*, vols. 1, 2; Yang Xueming.

96. These figures refer to the registered, legal satellite dishes, and include those used for various telecommunications services such as "very small aperture terminal" (VSAT) transmissions. (Estimates of unregistered dishes and those used only for television follow.) Of course, each dish devoted to receiving television broadcasts is capable of serving thousands of individual households connected to a cable network. See Yang Xueming, p. 93; Li Qiongmu; "Spokesman Gives Update on Satellite Communications."

97. The precise size depends on location.

98. The 1993 figure is cited in "China Without Borders"; the 1995 figure is based on personal observations.

99. Crothall and Hughes.

100. A former MEI official, Li Qingliang, revealed these figures at a spring 1993 conference held in Hong Kong. They are much higher than the official figures reported by the State Statistical Bureau, but the latter include only licensed satellite dishes. See Manuel, "Consumers Purchase 500,000 Satellite Receivers."

101. Cited in Wang Li.

102. Guojia Tongjiju, *Zhongguo Tongji Nianjian, 1997.*

103. An MTV is an establishment that provides semiprivate rooms equipped with videotape players. Small groups of customers can select what they want to view from the MTV's tape library. "KTV," meanwhile, is another term for karaoke bar.

104. Cited in Wang Li.

105. See Chen Yunqian; Zhao and Liu. It is important to note that this growth started from a very low base. ITU data indicate that countries at China's level of economic development in 1992 "should" have about 3 telephones per 100 people, but China had only 1.63. The reasons for this discrepancy can be traced to the alternately vertical and cellular Maoist political-economic system, whose architects neither required nor desired significant cross-regional or cross-xitong communication.

106. Interview 103.

107. Interview 114; Chu Baoping, "Growth in Telecommunications, Post Industry Discussed"; Liu Manjun; "PRC Estimates Post, Telecom Industry Growth in 1998." A long-term goal well within reach at current rates of growth is 40 telephones per 100 people by 2020, which equates to more than 1 phone per household. See McGregor and Keller.

108. Guojia Tongjiju, *Zhongguo Tongji Nianjian, 1997.*

109. "Urban Residents Increasingly Installing Private Telephones"; "Report Views Telecommunications Usage Nationwide."

110. "Telecommunications Sector on Major Investment Program"; "Telecommunications Industry Grows 30 Percent in 1997."

111. Interview 114; "Cellular Mobile Phone Calls Available in Qinghai."

112. Interview 132; "Number of Radio Pager Customers Soars."

113. Interview 132; see also Weinstock, Apostolous, and Chen.

114. Guojia Tongjiju, *Zhongguo Tongji Nianjian, 1994*, p. 487; see also "Tele-communications Minister on Improvements."

115. She and Yu, p. 30.

116. Interview 132; see also Zita, p. 31.

CHAPTER 3. THE COMMERCIALIZATION OF THOUGHT WORK

1. "Vulgarization" of media content is documented, discussed, and lamented in issue after issue of such publications as *Xinwen Zhanxian*, *Zhongguo Jizhe*, and *Xinwen yu Chuanbo Yanjiu*, as well as in mainstream publications. For a good overview in English, see Fang Zhen. Key Chinese citations include Xu Renzhong; Zhu Mingzuo; Sun Xupei; Zhang Yongjing; Song Muwen; Zhou Yanwen. Even the intellectually oriented *Guangming Ribao* now feels the need to encourage its journalists to appeal more to audience tastes by "deeply penetrating a topic but presenting it in a simple way," and most party papers now publish special, entertainment- and lifestyle-oriented "weekend editions" to expand readership. The prevalence of sexual themes and gratuitous violence on television and in films is evident even to the most casual viewer.

2. Of course, "society" is a complicated entity consisting of numerous individuals, groups, and organizations unequal in their ultimate influence over the content of media messages. (Measuring the exact distribution of influence is a difficult exercise beyond the scope of this study, for which it suffices that the central party-state's influence is declining.) Additionally, not all messages that cater to audiences are inconsistent with central-state preferences. Judging from the long list of official complaints and efforts to crack down, however, many such messages are inconsistent—sometimes radically—with official preferences.

3. For a good overview of audience research in China, see Chen Chongshan.

4. As explained elsewhere in Chapter 3, almost everyone working in the mass media interviewed for this research acknowledged the media's extreme market orientation, sometimes with praise, sometimes with criticism. But it was impossible to examine the exact, microscopic details of particular editorial decisions being made—except in the case of soft advertising and paid news. It is also often unclear exactly how media units spend their increasing revenues. Most informants claimed that units can use significant proportions of their increased revenues to improve the material living conditions of unit employees, usually by distributing bonuses and fringe benefits. But they were typically vague as to exactly how these processes take place, sometimes implying that they were not completely above-board.

5. *Dangdai Zhongguo de Guangbo Dianshi*, vol. 1, p. 37. No mention is made of Liu's thoughts on the propriety or necessity of print-media outlets selling ads.

6. Yu, p. 19.

7. *Dangdai Zhongguo de Gongshang Xingzheng Guanli*, pp. 191–95 and 584–601.

8. Interview 138.

9. See Ma Dawei; Stross.

10. Interviews 111, 120, and 138. The euphemism used at the beginning of the reform era was "socialist commodity economy."

11. Interviews 111 and 138; see also Lu Lin; "Official Views Ad Boom Among Enterprises."

12. Liu Renwei.

13. *Dangdai Zhongguo de Gongshang Xingzheng Guanli*, p. 192.

14. Ibid., pp. 593–94.

15. See Guo. Even if county-level stations are included in the calculation, 1,985 television stations shared the 4.48 billion yuan in television advertising revenue in 1994, an average of 2.256 million yuan per station. At the same time, 2,509 newspapers shared the 5.05 billion yuan in revenue accruing to that industry in 1994, at about 2.013 million yuan per paper. The per-station revenues of the television industry would triple if county-level stations are excluded. (There are no data available for advertising on cable-television stations; only recently and reluctantly did the authorities permit cable stations to carry ads.)

16. The precise figures are unavailable. No informant was willing to reveal exactly how much revenue his or her media unit earned each year, possibly because trumpeting success would make tax avoidance more difficult.

17. Interview 128.

18. Ibid.

19. The term "station" in this usage refers not to an independent station but to a separate substation of the existing broadcasting authority. A provincial capital might have six or seven substations, each broadcasting on a different frequency. Only one of these stations will be an economic station; in addition, there will be a news station, an arts station, an educational station, a music station, and so on. The individual substations are *not* each financially autonomous; revenues from the more popular stations are used to subsidize the others.

20. On the rise of the economic stations, see Guo, pp. 2–3. In the summer of 1994, there were said to be 70 to 80 economic stations nationwide. See "Directors of Economic Broadcast Stations."

21. Interview 161. This interview is the source for most of the information on the Zhujiang Economic Station.

22. For good overviews of the history of paid news and soft advertising, see Min; Wang Ruiming; Liu Zuyu.

23. Li Zirong.

24. Yun, p. 38.

25. Interview 120. This informant mentioned three American companies she

"knew" to be involved in the practice, but no company representatives were willing to comment.

26. Also in the spring of 1993, a company directly subordinate to *Renmin Ribao* was discovered to be selling illegal passports. See Lu Yu-sha; Shao Huaze.

27. "More on State Council Circular on Advertising."

28. Interview 138; see also Guojia Gongshang Xingzheng Guanliju and Guojia Jihua Weiyuanhui; "Government to Adopt a National Ad Agency System."

29. Zhonggong Zhongyang Xuanchuanbu and Xinwen Chubanshu; Li Zirong; "Campaign Launched to Educate Journalists on 'Press Ethics.'"

30. A *Guangming Ribao* source staunchly denied that any of his paper's reporters ever sells news, although he did admit that they are encouraged to "keep an eye out" for advertising opportunities. Interview 139.

31. Li Zirong, p. 55.

32. Liu Zuyu.

33. Interview 108. Of course, not every reporter writes paid news.

34. This is the argument of the informant in Interview 115.

35. Information on soft advertising at Beijing Television was supplied by the informants in Interviews 125 and 137.

36. Lavish entertainment programs are the responsibility of midsized groups, but these projects usually involve hiring writers, directors, and actors assigned to other units who are allowed to work freelance on a contractual basis.

37. Before the summer of 1995 the station funded about 10 percent of the groups' daily operating expenses, but planned to phase this funding out completely. No other station in the country has gone this far, but Beijing Television is considered to be a trendsetter whose example others will follow.

38. Interview 125. Occasionally, famous directors and not-yet-retired radio and television personnel join the watchdog groups, which are known simply and euphemistically as the "Radio and Television Study Committees" (*Guangbo Dianshi Xuexi Weiyuanhui*). Similar committees perform the watchdog function in Guangzhou and Kunming, but informants there were unwilling to discuss the committees' activities other than to state that the committees are locally constituted. Interviews 159 and 170.

39. Indeed, not only must the television station personnel take into account the views of the Study Committee and develop programming useful for selling soft ads, they must also face the fact that the station conducts weekly surveys to measure program popularity. The results of these surveys—which violate the most basic principles of the theory of sampling design—become an important factor in determining whether station personnel will be promoted. Interview 125.

40. Interview 123. There is sharp competition between Beijing Television and CCTV not only for the attention of the capital's audience, but also for the rich

pool of media talent living in this relatively affluent, educated, and cultured city. For example, Beijing Television personnel complain about the fact that CCTV is permitted to publish the authoritative *Radio and TV Guide* (*Guangbo Dianshi Bao*). The *Guide's* editors insist that Beijing Television supply them with programming information three weeks in advance, during which time, Beijing Television is convinced, CCTV officials strategically schedule programming in a way designed to maximize the central station's competitive advantage. Far from being harmless and amusing, this sense of competition underscores the enormous pressure on television stations even in the capital to attract large audiences.

41. Interview 159.

42. Interview 170.

43. High-ranking station informants quietly acknowledged this point while declining to provide precise data.

44. These groups are called *bu* (departments) at Beijing Radio, but their operations are very similar to those of the *zu* (groups) of Beijing Television.

45. Interview 137.

46. Xinhua reported on May 8, 1996, that, nationwide, extrabudgetary funds—over whose expenditure enterprises exert significant (if varying) authority—now total about 300 billion yuan (U.S.$36 billion) a year. The rules for spending this money are not always clear, prompting the Ministry of Finance to establish a hotline so that citizens can report enterprise personnel who use extrabudgetary funds "to buy luxury cars and houses or to speculate in real estate and stocks," or otherwise to embezzle. Precisely how much of the 300 billion yuan is, in this way, effectively privatized was not reported.

47. No instance of a media-unit manager being dismissed for transmitting excessively market-oriented media content was discovered in the process of this research—except for underground purveyors of pornography and "reactionary" materials. Personnel changes in major media outlets usually result from complex changes in the overall political situation such as occurred in May/June 1989, not from the secular trend towards content commercialization, globalization, and pluralization. But the threat of removal from office exists and almost certainly acts as a brake on content becoming excessively market-oriented, if for no other reason than content could be used as one of many subsidiary weapons to attack vulnerable editors and station managers during the next political change.

48. Interview 138.

49. Ibid.

50. See Zhu and Wang, p. 73.

51. Problems Unit, Literature and Art Bureau, CPC Central Committee Propaganda Department.

52. Interview 127.

53. Interview 143. This subsidy constituted about 21 percent of *Renmin*

Ribao's projected 1995 turnover. Two *Renmin Ribao* representatives justified the subsidy on the grounds that the state itself had demanded the expansion in number of pages so that the proportion of popular material in the paper could be increased and its ongoing decline in readership reversed. At the same time, the state regulates *Renmin Ribao*'s subscription price and apparently its advertising rates—yet another justification for funding the expansion with a subsidy. Without the subsidy, it would be impossible for the paper to increase its purchases of newsprint, the cost of which has risen appreciably since the institution of a price-deregulation scheme in 1987. (About half the supply of newsprint is still distributed by the state.) Interview 109; see also Xingzhengyuan Xinwenju, p. 198.

54. Interview 111.

55. Interview 139. The informant would not reveal the precise amount of the subsidy.

56. Interview 142. No copy of the document could be located, but at any rate it was probably unnecessary to obtain SPPA approval because the flagship party papers are not subservient to the SPPA system. The director of the SPPA, Yu Youxian, openly praised and encouraged the print media diversification trend in his speech before the Beijing propaganda conference in January 1994. Yu, "Jianchi Fangxiang, Shenhua Gaige."

57. Interview 143.

58. For example, in the spring of 1995 *Nanfang Ribao* extended loans to two concrete-producing factories. A portion of the loans would be repaid in kind, which meant that the *she* would have later to use its connections to sell concrete to construction firms. But this would be "no problem." Interview 162.

59. Interview 172.

60. These tools for maintaining control should be distinguished from the steps taken to reassert control discussed in Chapter 6.

61. Interviews 153 and 159.

62. Interviews 112, 153, and 159. When the media began diversifying in the early 1990s, the situation became even more complex. Because almost all of the major media units now own distinct advertising agencies—and many dabble in real estate and other business activities—some divisions of media *shiye* are now treated as *qiye* for taxation and other purposes. While *shiye* units may therefore establish *qiye*, no *qiye* may establish a *shiye*; it would be impossible, for example, for a construction company to set up a television station. The only exceptions are in-house or intra-xitong media and educational institutions that in principle may not offer their publications or services to the general public.

63. Interview 159.

64. Interview 166.

65. Interviews 123, 125, 159, and 166. Details of the new tax system were published by the Xinhua News Agency on December 13, 1993, and translated in

FBIS Daily China Report, December 16, 1993, pp. 27–29. Most money-making media units were required to pay a profit tax even before 1994. (Profit is defined as sales revenue minus costs and turnover taxes.)

66. Interview 159. None of this money goes up the xitong, however; i.e., none of it leaves the county, city, or province in which it is collected. The higher-level regulators must turn to the higher-level media outlets to secure their additional income.

67. Interview 166.

68. Interview 170. Note that this informant thus regarded Yunnan Television as a business enterprise, or *qiye*, even though it was defined by the central party-state (and treated by the provincial state) as a *shiye*.

69. Interview 159.

70. *Renmin Ribao* pays an annual turnover tax of fully 51.5 percent of its business volume, which amounts to about 125 million yuan (U.S.$15 million). Although *Renmin Ribao* informants refused to release this information, it could easily be calculated from the separate statements informants made and from the *she*'s publicity materials. Interview 143.

71. Interview 142.

72. Interviews 140, 142, 168 and 169.

73. Most of the information for the following two paragraphs was supplied by the informant in Interview 168.

74. But of Yunnan's approximately 300 Xinhua outlets, only fourteen, in three regions, were losing money in 1995. That is why the lower-level stores are permitted to retain 30 percent of their profits, and why many of the stores throughout the province are becoming rich.

75. Interview 167.

76. One Chinese informant said that though all of the money television stations give to their regulators is supposed to be used to subsidize poorer members of the radio and television xitong, it is permissible to use "a little of it" to upgrade the regulators' lifestyles (Interview 166). A foreign source close to Shanghai Television said that she understands the Shanghai Bureau of Radio and Television annually sets targets for money Shanghai Television must pay to the Bureau; the station is permitted to keep and report as profits only those receipts in excess of the funds given to the Bureau. The justification for this sort of treatment is that Shanghai Television has become "too profitable," not that there are other broadcasting outlets in Shanghai that require subsidies. Shanghai has suburbs, but unlike Yunnan and Guangdong it is not a huge province with wide gaps between rich and poor regions. Exactly how the money handed over to the Bureau is spent, therefore, is a mystery, but some of it is thought to go toward improving the lives of the regulators (Interview 146).

77. Although the logic of this pressure is clear in theory, more research will be needed to test how it operates in fact. Unfortunately, (mis)use of funds given

by enterprises to bureaus is an area about which it is very difficult to obtain systematic, reliable data.

78. Interview 166. On controlling county-level televised thought work, see, in particular, Minister of Radio, Film, and Television Ai Zhisheng's speeches at the January 1994 national propaganda conference, republished in *Quan Zhongguo*, pp. 121–26 and 313–27.

79. Interview 162. The informant was unable (or unwilling) to provide a copy of the document, and it could not be located in any published source.

80. Ibid. However, precisely who besides people in the media industry opposes the proposal is unclear.

81. Interviews 109, 115, 140, and 169. The publishing houses that still require subsidies are located mostly in the poorer regions of China, particularly in areas with dense concentrations of minority populations.

82. Some publishing houses with special status are granted virtually guaranteed markets and so do not have to take either of these paths. A good example would be The Commercial Press in Beijing, which holds, if not a monopoly, at least an overwhelmingly dominant market position in the authoritative translation of serious foreign works, both artistic and scholarly (Interview 140). At the same time, almost no publisher sells serial numbers—ISSNs, as opposed to ISBNs—because they have to be used and reused for as long as the serial is in publication (Interview 109).

83. Interview 115. This informant could not give a precise definition of a "truly good" book, but implied that truly good books are those that chance crossing the line of political acceptability not by sensationalism, but by critically and honestly analyzing the dynamics of the political-economic system. See also Problems Unit.

84. Problems Unit, p. 19.

85. Nan Lin.

86. Interviews 109 and 115.

87. Interview 109; Schell. The "second channel" first appeared in the mid-1980s and has grown enormously since then. Orville Schell writes of three channels of book distribution, distinguishing between patently illegal underground publishers and sellers and those who have government permission to publish and distribute certain kinds of works but who exceed their mandate.

88. One source estimated that 10 percent of all books published in China in the year before the crackdown were tagged with bought or stolen book numbers, and that 80 to 90 percent of pornographic and bourgeois-liberal books were so tagged (Dong). Schell puts the figure at closer to 33 percent (Schell, p. 30). The problem is geographically quite widespread: 280 underground publishing houses were shut down and more than 1.5 million "reactionary or pornographic" books and tabloids were confiscated in 183 cities across China during 1993 (Tian Tian).

89. Interview 140.

90. See "State Issues Regulations on Publishing Industry."

91. The central SPPA office issues book numbers directly to only ten publishing houses (the ten houses it centrally macromanages).

92. Guojia Tongjiju, *Zhongguo Tongji Nianjian, 1995,* p. 647; "Government Clamps Down on Book Registration Numbers."

93. Interview 109. This increase was in nominal, not real, terms.

94. Ibid. The more sex, violence, feudal superstition, and political dissent, the greater the commercial potential of the book and the higher the political risk of publishing it. Consequently, higher scores on these factors all result in the book numbers to be sold costing more. Of course, for exceptionally risky books the underground publisher might not even bother to purchase a book number. But this is dangerous because books without numbers can easily be spotted in stalls and bookstores by even the laziest inspectors.

95. "Crackdown on 'Largest' Case Reported."

96. Wen, p. 33.

97. "Beijing Punishes Illegal Publishing Activity."

98. Li Ren.

99. Liu was promoted to Minister of Culture after the Fourteenth Party Congress (October 1992).

100. "Propaganda Official on Antipornography Efforts."

101. Ibid., p. 26. Only 300 of the printing houses were state-owned. See also Ma Chenguang.

102. Yan Shan-ke.

103. "Strictly Ban Illegal Publications."

104. "Propaganda Official," p. 25.

105. Wen, p. 35.

106. Interview 120. See also "Printing Industry Management Regulations."

107. "Propaganda Official on Antipornography Efforts," p. 25.

108. "Press, Publications Reform to Be Deepened."

109. For detailed discussions, see *Dangdai Zhongguo de Chuban Shiye*; Zhongguo Chuban Kexue Yanjiusuo.

110. "Propaganda Official on Antipornography Efforts," p. 26.

111. Interview 168; "Censors to License Private Bookstands."

112. Interview 168. The Xinhua Bookstores retain their monopoly over educational materials for students at the high-school level and below, and they tend to enjoy larger market shares in poorer regions where effective demand is too weak to support collective and private outlets facing hard budget constraints.

113. Interview 168. Various private book, compact disc, and tape sellers openly acknowledged the need to pay frequent bribes in Interviews 163 and 165.

114. Interview 168.

115. Of course, spiritually polluting tapes and compact discs are also pro-

duced domestically, and are often affixed with stolen or purchased identifying numbers akin to ISBNs. See "Ban Transactions in Publication Numbers."

116. Interviews 124 and 135.

117. Interview 135. Similar formulas are used to divide property rights and responsibilities between provincial-level distribution companies and their lower-level counterparts, between distribution companies and theaters, and between studios and theaters on those rare occasions when the studios sell to the theaters directly.

118. Ibid.

119. Ibid.

120. The term "edgeball" derives from table tennis. When the journalist "hits an edgeball" (*da ca bian qiu*), he or she strikes the ball in a way that causes it just to scrape the edge of the table. Propaganda commissars cannot possibly get to the ball, so the point goes to the journalist.

121. Zhang Weiguo, "Reporters and Editors." See also Shih.

122. Zhang Weiguo, "Reporters and Editors," p. 37.

123. Ibid., p. 37.

124. Quoted in Shu.

125. Ibid., p. 18.

126. Fang Yuan, "A Number of Books and Underground Publications Are Banned." Five of the nine kinds of contraband books and journals seized in an autumn 1994 Beijing raid "were of a reactionary sort." See "Beijing Raids Underground Publishing House."

127. Interview 132.

128. The term "VSAT" is an acronym for "very small aperture terminal." VSATs are private satellite networks that link together the offices of multinational corporations, banks, airlines, and other business and government organizations whose activities are scattered across large territories.

129. Wang Yanrong, "Radio Stations to Be Surveyed, Registered."

130. See Lin Sun's analysis in "Mobile Communications Takes Off in China."

131. "Paging Services Prohibited from Distributing News." There were 2,100 officially approved paging companies in operation at the end of 1996. See also "Number of Radio Pager Customers Soars."

132. Interviews 102, 103, 114, and 122; see also the "Circular Concerning Cracking Down on Unauthorized Radio Stations."

133. See Yao Yan, Cao Zhigang, and Yu Renlin; "Spokesman Gives Update on Satellite Communications"; "Nation's Banking System to Invest 1 Billion Yuan."

134. Interview 147.

135. For a good historical overview, see Ding Lu.

136. Interview 110; see also Lin Sun, "Funding Telecommunications Expansion."

137. The MPT regulates tariffs successfully and fixes domestic tariffs at a low rate nationwide, but even in the case of tariffs, local telecommunications bureaus are able to increase their incomes by adding assorted surcharges to subscribers' bills. Interviews 110, 114, and 131.

138. The MPT's official goal was to reduce the wait to less than one month by 2000. See Liu Manjun.

139. Interview 131. It should be stressed that MPT system officials certainly did not use all of the rents they secured from predatory pricing on personal consumption. In fact, the rapid nationwide growth of China's telecommunications industry indicates that a significant proportion of the rents was reinvested. The precise proportion would be impossible to calculate given available data, but one multinational telecommunications analyst insisted that it was "undoubtedly very, very high." Interview 114.

140. Interviews 102, 103, 114, and 131; see also Zhao and Liu.

141. Interview 132.

142. Interview 161.

143. *Guangming Ribao* complained in 1994 that some call-in shows are political to the point of broadcasting "content deviating from the principles and policies of the party and the government." See Kuang Zong. All informants interviewed about the matter for this study agreed that hotline programs are becoming significantly more political with each passing year.

144. "Review of Guangdong Radio 'Hotline' Program," July 14, 1993.

145. "Review of Guangdong Radio 'Hotline' Program," January 5, 1994.

146. Schell, p. 30.   147. Zhang Xiaogang, p. 213.

148. Interviews 127, 161, and 166.   149. Kuang Zong, p. 38.

CHAPTER 4. THE GLOBALIZATION OF THOUGHT WORK

1. In a 1996 study, Joseph Man Chan found that, in Guangzhou, the higher the degree of exposure to Hong Kong television, the more likely a person was to agree that "money is the best indicator of one's achievement," "premarital sex is acceptable," "one may have to pursue personal interest at the expense of public interest," and "the gap between rich and poor is acceptable." All such sentiments contravene the requisites of the socialist spiritual civilization. However, as in many media effects studies, Chan's conclusions are compromised by difficult questions regarding self-selection biases. Chan, "Penetrating China's Cultural Shield."

2. Interview 132; Wu Jichuan, "Telecom Sector Expands International Cooperation"; She and Yu; Zita, p. 31.

3. In 1994, some 15,000 telecommunications messages—by fax and voice— were being transmitted between China and Hong Kong at peak times during business days. See Clifford, "Communications: China Calling." Telecommuni-

cations exchanges between the mainland and Taiwan increased by 20 to 30 percent annually in the period 1989–95, and by 1996 there were some 38,000 fax and voice exchanges between Taiwan and Fujian each day. Yuan; "Fujian, Taiwan Telecommunications Links Rising."

4. The extent to which Chinese public and/or state security officials are able to monitor telecommunications transmissions is a controversial issue. Knowledgeable sources told Kenneth Lieberthal that, technically, all transmissions can in principle be monitored; but telecommunications engineers in Hong Kong and Beijing told another foreign scholar that, technically, that would be impossible. The key point is that technology is always embedded in administrative, economic, and cultural settings, and it seems highly unlikely that the Chinese state is "techno-administratively" capable of monitoring all telecommunications transmissions throughout the country, even if its agents can monitor a significant number of transmissions—and can certainly monitor the transmissions of known or suspected dissidents. Private communications.

5. See, for example, Martz; "The Information War," in *Asiaweek*, June 23, 1989, p. 30.

6. Interviews 102, 103, 110, 114, and 122.

7. Thousands of individual users can be connected to a single computer. See Markoff, "AT&T May Have Edge in Future on Line."

8. Researchers at the Chinese Academy of Sciences' Institute of High Energy Physics were the first Chinese citizens to access the Internet—at least from the mainland—connecting in 1988 to the European Centre on Nuclear Research. See Zuo.

9. *Renmin Ribao* reported that as of 1995 there were "over 12,000 large, medium-sized, and small computers and over 2 million microcomputers of various types" in China. See Liu Cai.

10. "Opening of Public Switching Data Network Reported"; Gao Tao.

11. Cited by Zheng.

12. Gao Tao, p. 1.

13. Interview 114.

14. "Computer Network to Connect Universities"; He Jun, "Computer Network to Link 1,000 Universities."

15. Interviews 122 and 141.

16. Interview 122; see also Li Yan.

17. Actually the terms "Chinanet" and "Chinapac" are not completely synonymous; rather, Chinanet is being built on the back of the Chinapac system with expertise from the American computer firm AsianInfo. See Laris.

18. Zuo; "Public Security Ministry Circular on Internet Use." After the end of the promotional period, Internet access charges were 100 yuan (U.S.$12) per month for six hours of use and 600 yuan per month for 40 hours of use.

19. Interview 134; see also Tacey.

20. "'Infohighway Space' to Start Operation at Year End."

21. Wang Jing; "The Great Wall Wired."

22. "Internet Becomes Part of Daily Life." But at least until a decade or so into the 21st century, the most active Internet users are expected to be students, professors, and business people involved in external trade and investment. See Faison, "Chinese Cruise Internet, Wary of Watchdogs."

23. Interview 122. Efforts by the central party-state to prevent the importation of undesired Internet information are discussed in Chapter 6.

24. See *Tunnel*'s inaugural declaration, available upon request at voice@earthling.net. See also "Cyberspace Magazine Fights for Freedom of Expression."

25. Fifty issues had been sent out by early 1998. The February 10, 1998, issue included such articles as "The Equality of the Masses and Elites," "China's Rent-Seeking and the Redistribution of Wealth," "The Difficulties of Workers Who Have Lost Their Jobs," and "Another Side of the Southeast Asian Financial Crisis."

26. Cited by Ai Zhisheng in "Zai Quanguo Guangbo Yingshi Xuanchuan Gongzuo Huiyishang de Jianghua," in *Quan Zhongguo*.

27. Liu Renwei.

28. Jinglu Yu, "The Structure and Function of Chinese Television, 1979–1989," in Chin-Chuan Lee.

29. Hong.

30. Interview 123.

31. Interview 126.

32. Interview 123.

33. Karp, "Do It Our Way."

34. Interview 159.

35. Interview 166.

36. Interviews 148, 149, 150, and 156. Not a single external television supplier would admit to having paid bribes to Chinese buyers, but all external television suppliers claimed that "almost everyone else" does pay bribes. Representatives of smaller companies made the reasonable suggestion that it is primarily the larger companies that pay bribes. They have the capital to secure a stranglehold over markets at an early date and then keep entry costs high for subsequent, would-be competitors.

37. Interview 148.

38. Most of these programs are in Cantonese, but can easily be dubbed into Mandarin (with Chinese subtitles).

39. This is despite the fact that cable stations are nominally forbidden to import directly from abroad.

40. Interviews 103 and 106.

41. Interviews 106 and 146; quotation from Interview 146.

42. Purely foreign companies also engage in coproduction, but not as extensively as Hong Kong companies.

43. Interviews 106 and 146.

44. In 1994 the Center reaffirmed its ban on permanent joint ventures in teleplay and film production on the mainland. See "AFP Reports on PRC Film Industry." But one source asserts that foreigners may, and enthusiastically do, invest in joint ventures to produce and distribute videotapes, audiotapes, and compact discs. However, in such cases, the foreigners' role is supposed to be restricted to transferring technical knowledge, not determining content—except, of course, for products to be imported. Interview 133; see also Wu and Fong.

45. In the spring of 1995, Rupert Murdoch secured approval to establish a coproduction facility in Tianjin, but apparently only for sports programs. Interview 145; see also Keenan.

46. Interview 150. The X Network's license was granted by the Guangzhou Administration of Industry and Commerce. Once initial approval was secured, the Network no longer needed any contact with the MRFT. The Network itself owns all the rights to the programs created at the PLA facility.

47. Ibid.

48. Interview 152.

49. Interviews 119, 123, 159, and 170.

50. Interview 123.

51. This is the straightforward assertion of the informants in Interviews 119, 123, 159, and 170.

52. One very well-placed CNN source believes that provincial and municipal stations download and rebroadcast CNN International's signals with increasing frequency, but there are no data to support the claim. Interview 152.

53. But numerous cable systems throughout China retransmit the Yunnan and Guizhou signals, stimulating a race that resulted in some twenty provinces broadcasting via satellite by the end of 1995—most on domestic satellites. Interestingly, it took Guangdong Television several more months to begin satellite broadcasting because CCTV was furiously lobbying the State Council to force Guangdong Television to broadcast by satellite only in Cantonese. The motivation was purely commercial, but CCTV's request was said to be receiving a favorable hearing because the central party-state feared the specter of Mandarin-language news from Hong Kong being broadcast nationwide (Interviews 123 and 153). In any event, when Guangdong Television finally did begin broadcasting by satellite in July 1996, most of the programs were in Mandarin, but did not include Hong Kong news ("Guangdong Satellite Broadcasting Trial Begins"; "Guangdong Starts Satellite Television Transmission").

54. In the summer of 1994 the BBC revealed plans to broadcast news bulletins into China by satellite starting within 12 to 24 months, but nothing concrete has materialized as of this writing. See Holden.

55. See Hughes; Kishore; Manuel, "STAR TV Renews Attempt to Enter Mainland Market."

56. Cited in Georgette Wang.

57. Interview 104. No surveys were conducted in Tibet, Xinjiang, Inner Mongolia, Ningxia, Gansu, Qinghai, Hubei, and Hainan. About 20 percent of the homes had access to STAR via small-scale cable networks. See Jordan.

58. Interview 104.

59. Interviews 127 and 128. Station managers know that certain exceptionally political programs should not be imported, and very few stations are thought to take programs from the VOA and the BBC.

60. *Dangdai Zhongguo de Guangbo Dianshi*, vol. 2, pp. 340–41.

61. Of course, Beijing Radio's managers are cognizant of the kinds of music that it would obviously be "incorrect" to import, and they have to exercise more caution than their counterparts in regions relatively distant from the capital, where central-level bureaucrats cannot "tune in."

62. Interview 127.

63. Interview 166.

64. Crothall, "Authorities Cancel Radio 'Phone-In Show.'"

65. Ibid.; Interview 127.

66. RTHK is Hong Kong's public radio and television program creator; none of the programs in the "joint venture" was designed to make money. In fact, they all cost RTHK money.

67. Interview 154.

68. Hsieh.

69. Interview 154.

70. While the VOA and BBC concentrate on supplying their listeners with international news, RFA specializes in the provision of domestic news to audiences not only in China (including Tibet), but also North Korea, Vietnam, Laos, Cambodia, and Burma. See Holloway; Mann.

71. *Dangdai Zhongguo de Guangbo Dianshi*, vol. 2, p. 237.

72. Roger W. Stump, "Spatial Implications of Religious Broadcasting: Stability and Change in Patterns of Belief," in Brunn and Leinbach, p. 362.

73. *Dangdai Zhongguo de Guangbo Dianshi*, vol. 2, p. 237.

74. Questions about VOA listening are incorporated into general marketing surveys conducted by Hong Kong–based firms such as SRG and Frank Small and Associates. These surveys must be approved by local-level governments, but it is considered likely that officials responsible for giving approval do not read through the questions carefully. At any rate, they have not been reluctant to approve the surveys. However, they do require that a bureaucrat accompany the surveyor on his or her rounds, leading some VOA officials to suggest that the true number of listeners is probably much higher than 19 million. Interviews 101 and 155.

75. See *Broadcasting to China*.

76. Interviews 101 and 155. The VOA has long maintained a mailbox in Hong Kong that regularly receives about 1,000 letters from Chinese citizens

each month. In April 1995 the service finally opened a mailbox in Beijing. Because the cost of sending a letter to Beijing is much lower than that of sending one to Hong Kong—and because it is not necessary to affix a return address on Chinese domestic mail—the number of letters received immediately increased to 4,000.

77. Interviews 101 and 105. At this writing it is too early to evaluate the likely impact of RFA; presently the service broadcasts only two hours a day and it has yet to conduct audience surveys.

78. Many karaoke bars are located physically in joint-venture (JV) and wholly foreign-owned hotels and restaurants. Partly as a result, these bars tend to be especially fashionable and popular—though steep cover charges do keep out the general population. But the JV and foreign-owned karaoke establishments are not necessarily more apt to play foreign music and videos than their Chinese-owned counterparts, although they may be more apt to play original rather than pirated versions. Interviews 133 and 167.

79. Interviews 126, 133, and 167; see also Shao Ling.

80. Gold, p. 919.

81. Interview 133.

82. Audio imports need not be formally vetted.

83. Interview 167; see also Xingzhengyuan Xinwenju; Forney, "Piracy: Now We Get It."

84. Shao Ling.

85. Interview 145.

86. Interview 167; personal observations.

87. Personal observations.

88. One other factor influencing the decision was China's efforts to join the World Trade Organization. Interview 135; see also "State to Drop Limit on Film Imports."

89. Interviews 124 and 135.

90. Interview 124; see also Dou; "AFP Reports on PRC Film Industry." This program was suspended in mid-1996.

91. Interviews 124 and 135. Between 1979 and 1991, Chinese studios coproduced more than 170 films with Hong Kong and Western studios. In 1994, following film reform, the Center tried to limit coproduction to 26 films per year as well as to ban the creation of permanent joint-venture production companies. But the informants in Interviews 124 and 135 were skeptical that the 26-film limit could be defended after the relaxation on imports announced in April 1995. Moreover, as explained above in the case of the "X Network," some Hong Kong/Western film and teleplay producers had already found ways around the ban on permanent joint-venture production companies even before the relaxation on imports. "AFP Reports on PRC Film Industry"; Xingzhengyuan Xinwenju, p. 151.

92. Foreign-language newspapers and news magazines (with the exception of official Chinese publications) can only be purchased at four- and five-star hotels. Foreign-language novels and some academic publications are widely available at the larger, official bookstores. Both pirated and legal translations of these books can also easily be found.

93. Mao, "Talks at a Conference of Secretaries of Provincial, Municipal, and Autonomous Region Party Committees," in *Selected Readings*, pp. 369–70.

94. Data taken from Wang Zhi.

95. Efforts to test this hypothesis proved impossible because of the inability or unwillingness of Xinhua informants to supply sufficiently detailed data.

96. Chang et al.

97. Ching.

98. Interviews 133 and 165; see also Tian Tian; Dong.

99. Only a handful of foreign magazines may be sold on the street in China, most visibly *Elle*, the women's fashion magazine. All sales of news magazines are restricted to the hotels. See Faison, "A Chinese Edition of *Elle* Draws Ads and Readers."

100. "Shenzhen Assaults Smuggled Hong Kong Newspapers." Similarly, Elizabeth Henderson and others have reported in personal conversations being easily able to purchase Taiwan newspapers in Fujian province.

101. "Printing Industry Management Regulations."

102. Interview 151; see also do Rosario. The *Hongkong Standard* reported in November 1995 that the Swiss publication *Cash* had secured permission to publish a joint-venture financial weekly with the *Shenzhen Special Zone Daily*, starting in 1996. More recent information was unavailable. Pun, "Sino-Swiss Venture to Publish Business Weekly."

103. Cf. the case of *Modern Mankind*, an outspokenly liberal Guangdong paper that formed a loose joint venture with Hong Kong's *Ming Pao* in 1993. *Modern Mankind* lost its sponsoring organization (the Guangdong branch of the China Council for the Promotion of International Trade) in July 1994, and was thereupon ordered to cease publication effective December 31. See Chan Wai-fong.

104. Interview 151.

105. Interview 109.

106. Interview 142.

107. These books are also more likely to be translated than are scholarly books. Both types often are pirated, though probably to a much lesser degree by the legal, official publishing houses than before 1995. Interview 140.

CHAPTER 5. THE PLURALIZATION OF THOUGHT WORK

1. See, for example, the speeches made at the 1994 National Propaganda Conference and collected in *Quan Zhongguo*.

2. An anecdote illustrates this problem: When Chen Yun, the second most powerful person in all of China, died on April 10, 1995, the news was printed on the front pages of all the major newspapers and broadcast by all the major television and radio stations. On April 11, CCTV devoted a full 25 minutes of its 30-minute national evening newscast to an elaborate eulogy. But twenty or so informal conversations with Beijing shopkeepers, cab drivers, waiters, and the like over the next few days revealed that not a single one had heard of Chen's death, and many did not even know who he was. On the other hand, all of them had heard about the March suicide of Beijing Deputy Mayor Wang Baosen, despite the fact that Wang's suicide was not announced in any of the mass media until April 28.

3. Yin Yen, "Zhejiang TV Station Officials Penalized."

4. Guojia Tongjiju, *Zhongguo Tongji Nianjian, 1997*, p. 708; *Guangbo Dianshi Jianming Cidian*; Interview 138; "TV Industry Witnesses 'Rapid Development'"; Yu Huang.

5. Guojia Tongjiju, *Zhongguo Tongji Nianjian, 1997*, p. 709. They did, however, rely extensively on trade with other lower-level stations.

6. Cao Guanghui; Guojia Tongjiju, *Zhongguo Tongji Nianjian, 1997*, p. 709.

7. Interview 138.

8. Interviews 117, 123, and 126; see also Ai Zhiseng, "Zai Quanguo Guangbo Yingshi Xuanchuan Gongzuo Huiyishang de Jianghua," in *Quan Zhongguo*, pp. 313–27; Sun Jiazheng, "Chinese Radio, Film, and Television"; Yin Yen, "Over 100 Radio, Television Stations in Shandong to Be Shut Down."

9. See "Regulations on Radio."

10. Interview 117; see also Gu Hongnian.

11. Jinglu Yu, "The Structure and Function of Chinese Television, 1979–1989," in Chin-Chuan Lee, p. 73.

12. Interview 123.

13. Guojia Tongjiju, *Zhongguo Tongji Nianjian, 1997*, p. 709.

14. CCTV has long been responsible for profits and losses and therefore faces a strong incentive to generate income.

15. Ai Zhisheng, "Zai Quanguo Guangbo Yingshi Xuanchuan Gongzuo Huiyishang de Jianghua," in *Quan Zhongguo*, p. 320. Ai's successor, Sun Jiazheng, raised the problem again two years later in a *Renmin Luntan* article. The problem was also singled out for discussion at the Sixth Plenum of the Fourteenth Central Committee in October 1996. See Dai.

16. Interviews 123, 126, and 145.

17. The county stations do carry some CCTV programs, of course, but not consistently, and frequently they block out the CCTV ads to insert their own.

18. This particular component of the crackdown had not yet succeeded by early 1998.

19. Guojia Tongjiju, *Zhongguo Tongji Nianjian, 1997*, p. 321; *Zhongguo Guangbo Dianshi Nianjian, 1991*; *Zhongguo Guangbo Dianshi Nianjian, 1990*.

20. Guojia Tongjiju, *Zhongguo Tongji Nianjian, 1997*, p. 708; Guojia Tongjiju, *Zhongguo Tongji Nianjian, 1988*.

21. "Ministry Predicts Rise in Radio, TV Coverage."

22. Guojia Tongjiju, *Zhongguo Tongji Nianjian, 1997*, p. 709. Of course, many of these programs consisted of recorded music that other units (or foreigners) produced.

23. Ibid.; "Ministry Predicts Rise in Radio, TV Coverage."

24. Interviews 127, 128, 161, and 166.

25. Interview 128.

26. Interview 127.

27. Alan P. L. Liu, p. 119.

28. *Dangdai Zhongguo de Guangbo Dianshi*, vol. 1, pp. 373–74.

29. Ibid., p. 28; Leo Ou-fan Lee and Andrew J. Nathan, "The Beginnings of Mass Culture: Journalism and Fiction in the Late Ch'ing and Beyond," in Johnson et al., p. 377. In the early 1980s, the effort to put a loudspeaker into every peasant home was abandoned as too costly and replaced by a policy to put a loudspeaker in every village. Interview 117.

30. *Guangbo Dianshi Jianming Cidian*, pp. 423–24; "Ministry Predicts Rise in Radio, TV Coverage," p. 6.

31. Interview 117.

32. Ibid. For a good overview of the problems facing wired broadcasting, see Sun and Chen.

33. *Dangdai Zhongguo de Guangbo Dianshi, Volume 1*, p. 400; Interview 117.

34. Interview 117. Of course, this could change as the general level of affluence rises and radio listeners begin to demand an increasingly diverse selection of high-quality music, transmitted by optical fiber into the home. Informants in Interview 128 articulated this vision.

35. *Zhongguo Tongji Nianjian, 1997*, p. 321. From that point on, however, the number began to fall.

36. *Dangdai Zhongguo de Guangbo Dianshi*, vol. 2, p. 399.

37. "Television, Radio Stations Increasing in Number."

38. The reluctance is palpable in Minister of Radio, Film, and Television Ai Zhisheng's speeches at the January 1994 National Propaganda Conference. See, in particular, Ai Zhisheng, "Jianchi Liangshou Zhua, Liangshou Dou Yao Ying de Fangzhen," in *Quan Zhongguo*, pp. 313–27.

39. See Jinglu Yu, "The Structure and Function of Chinese Television, 1979–1989," in Chin-Chuan Lee, p. 80. The term "local stations" meant *tai* at the provincial and municipal level, not the retransmitting *zhan* at even lower levels.

40. Zhang and Hui.

41. Interview 137.

42. Interviews 123 and 125.

43. Ai Zhisheng, "Jianchi Liangshou Zhua, Liangshou Dou Yao Ying de Fangzhen," in *Quan Zhongguo*, p. 318.

44. Sun Jiazheng, "Jianchi Zhengque Daoxiang."

45. Interview 127.

46. One source asserts that, even as early as 1983, over two-thirds of radio news throughout China was local, station-originated news, as opposed to news imported from other sources. *Dangdai Zhongguo de Guangbo Dianshi*, vol. 2, p. 66.

47. Of course, the phonograph had long been present, as had cassette and reel-to-reel tapes and tape players, but only a minuscule proportion of the population ever came into contact with these technologies.

48. Xingzhengyuan Xinwenju, pp. 156–62.

49. Qu and Li.

50. Shen Weixing.

51. Most of the material on reforms in the film industry was provided by the informants in Interviews 124 and 135. See also *Dangdai Zhongguo de Dianying*; Dou.

52. In the mid-1990s the studios produced approximately 150 feature films annually, a figure basically constant since 1987. Prices for documentaries, cartoons, and certain other studio products were not as high as the 900,000 *yuan* price for feature films.

53. After the reform, the monopolistic distribution company was merged with the monopolistic Import-Export Company, and the resulting new conglomerate concentrated almost solely on imports, purchasing only one film from a Chinese studio between 1993 and 1995.

54. See Minister of Radio, Film, and Television (1994–98) Sun Jiazheng's article, "Jianchi Zhengque Daoxiang."

55. For a good overview, see "Ban Transactions in Publication Numbers."

56. Of particular importance to this chapter is the remarkable increase in number of locally published newspapers. On this point, see Zhang Zhongcai.

57. Quoted in Fang Zhen.

58. *Zhongguo Chuban Nianjian, 1990–1991*, pp. 696–97; *Zhongguo Chuban Nianjian, 1992*, p. 512; Yu Youxian, "Kaituo Jinqu, Zhazhashishi Zuohao Xinwen Chuban Gongzuo," in *Quan Zhongguo*, p. 127; Interview 138.

59. Interview 112. Below the provincial level, non-party print media publishers are regulated by either the ministerial system to which they belong, the MoC, or territorial-level government committees.

60. Interview 140.

61. Actually, Wang was named in January 1987, but Du—though identified as the first SPPA director in April 1987—was not officially assigned to the post until May 1988. For details on the SPPA's establishment, see Xingzhengyuan Xinwenju; Yun.

62. Interview 142. For religious publications, the SPPA must defer to the State Council's Bureau of Religious Affairs, acting essentially as its agent.

63. Hao.

64. The informants in Interview 142 asserted that provincial and subprovincial governments "have a great deal of power in determining the direction of the publishing industry" as a result of their authority to issue territory-specific laws and regulations. Thus, while in principle the SPPA system "takes the vertical system as predominant," in reality a situation of "harmonizing the vertical and the territorial" necessarily prevails. This gives rise in particular to serious difficulties controlling religious publications, for which the SPPA acts as an agent for the State Council's Bureau of Religious Affairs. In the early 1990s some minority-area regions were freely publishing religious tracts without first seeking the Bureau's permission. See Tien, "CPC Plan to Gag Press Freedom"; "Xinjiang Confiscates Publications."

65. Why the central government does not respond by strengthening the SPPA—perhaps by upgrading it to ministerial status—is unclear.

66. An internal "Propaganda Bulletin" circulated by the propaganda apparatus also contributed to fulfilling this function, as did the publication *News Front* (*Xinwen Zhanxian*), targeted at journalists.

67. Television stations were of minute importance in the thought-work enterprise until after 1978.

68. A provincial-level paper could originate stories on news within its province, but not on news from any other province; a municipal-level paper was forced to rely on the provincial Xinhua service for news from other cities within its province; and so on. See Frederick T. C. Yu; Alan P. L. Liu.

69. The blossoming of local-level newspapers that emerged during the Great Leap Forward (1958–60) did not survive the subsequent economic depression. Both these newspapers and the many publications that burst onto the scene during the Cultural Revolution were not, at any rate, truly autonomous, but instead examples of "societal totalitarianism."

70. Polumbaum, "The Tribulations of China's Journalists After a Decade of Reform," in Chin-Chuan Lee, pp. 52–53.

71. Interviews 108, 111, and 137. Cadres responsible for interpersonal thought work within media units tend to come from the ranks of journalists, but are not especially well liked, both because they are perceived to have become arrogant upon promotion and because, in general, their average level of education is lower than that of the younger journalists. "There is no need for us to listen to the thought-work cadres because we have our own thoughts" (Interview 108). And, in general, the thought-work cadres do leave the journalists alone because they face little incentive actively to indoctrinate, particularly given the perception that indoctrination would in any case be ineffective.

72. Interview 112.

73. Guoguang Wu.

74. Data extracted from Chin-Chuan Lee, "Mass Media: Of China, About China," in Lee; Yan Shan-ke; Wang Zhi.

75. Yan Shan-ke, p. 4; Liu Shu.

76. The most popular papers in China now are the generally light-hearted and entertaining evening papers, such as Guangzhou's *Yangcheng Wanbao*, which, like several other such papers, now circulates nationally, competing directly and successfully with the Center's more politicized papers. Interviews 108 and 112; see also Chang Yi-cheng.

77. Interview 143.

78. It is important for enterprises to reach the people who actually read *Renmin Ribao* because, even though they are few in number, such people are likely to be politically influential and capable of helping or hindering the enterprises in their myriad efforts to make money.

79. Wang Zhi, p. 23. *Guangming Ribao*'s assigned social function is to link the party with intellectuals, while *Qiushi* is the party's premier "theoretical" journal.

80. Of course, they can still read the papers at public viewing places, but the fact that in January 1994, as part of the general crackdown on heterodox thought work, the Party Center issued an order requiring all party members not only to read at least one central party paper each day, but also to take periodic tests on the contents, suggests that many people were not reading the papers anywhere.

81. For an excellent illustration of this problem, see "Investigation."

82. Xinhua also acts as a foreign and domestic intelligence-gathering agency for the Chinese leadership, publishing at least three important restricted-circulation journals that discuss China's problems with accuracy and objectivity: *Cankao Xiaoxi*, *Da Cankao*, and *Neican*. The three publications increase in frankness the more restricted the readership; *Neican* is the most restricted, followed by *Da Cankao* and then *Cankao Xiaoxi*. *Cankao Xiaoxi* specializes in accurate translations of the foreign press, but foreigners are not permitted to purchase it. Interview 109.

83. The actual terms used were *jia, yi, bing, ding*. Interview 112.

84. Interview 109. According to informants, Xinhua soon became "rather frustrated" by its loss of authority, and the anxiety of editors also increased as they had to exercise extreme caution to avoid making political mistakes. The editors' anxiety had lessened appreciably by the early 1990s, however.

85. For example, some provincial papers have sent reporters to Shanghai to file stories on the Pudong development district and its implications for their readers (Interview 162). All of the major central news outlets—CCTV, *Renmin Ribao*, et al.—have their own foreign news bureaus, and sometimes provincial-level outlets dispatch reporters abroad to write or produce feature stories.

86. In January 1996 Xinhua was granted the right to channel all incoming commercial information previously supplied independently to Chinese subscribers by Reuters, the Associated Press, and other foreign firms. But two years

later, Internet development had rendered this monopoly a mere irritant to the smooth flow of information.

87. Interviews 108, 111, 139, 143, 162, and 172. (Cf. note 2 on lack of knowledge among Beijing citizens about Chen Yun's death.) In addition to the "extremely important" news, media outlets rely on Xinhua for filler stories; the agency distributes some 100,000 characters of copy per day.

88. As of early 1995, "about half" of Xinhua's budget was supplied by the central government, but the absolute amount had been fixed so the proportion was steadily falling each year. The eventual goal was zero subsidization. Interview 113.

89. Ding Guan'gen, "Run Our Party Papers Better."

90. "Circular Calls for Setting Up Newspaper Reading Boards."

91. Interview 102.

92. Interviews 130, 131, and 144. Hu may have adopted this vision from Zhao, known to have been an avid reader of the American "futurologist" Alvin Toffler. On this point, see Hamrin, pp. 75–80.

93. Interviews 102, 103, and 131.

94. Interview 131; see also Fei Chang He.

95. John Ure writes that Hu also suggested a secret "Golden Sea" project to link the Communist Party into an advanced, nationwide telecommunications network, but no one in China would admit to having heard of the project, and Ure himself was frustrated in his efforts to find out more. Ure; Interview 103.

96. Pei, "Electronic Information Network."

97. Interview 141.

98. Ibid.

99. It should be emphasized that personality politics was only one of several factors that contributed to the State Council's decision, and that economic factors may eventually have produced the same outcome regardless of personality characteristics.

100. Interview 102. Jiang Zemin, Li Peng, Zhu Rongji, Zou Jiahua, and other senior officials all provided congratulatory calligraphy to Liantong and Jitong, underlining the companies' high-level support.

101. "China to Build Information Superhighway"; see also Wu Jichuan, "Build a Nationwide Economic Information Network."

102. "Beijing to Establish State Economic Information Network."

103. "Vice Premier Discusses Communications Development."

104. Interviews 102 and 114. Liantong repeatedly threatened to construct a completely separate network if the MPT refused to grant it access at a reasonable cost.

105. Because of its status as a unit directly subordinate to the State Council, Liantong took the lead in negotiating terms of access both for it and for the bureaucratically lower-ranking Jitong.

106. Although innocuous-sounding in English, these terms resonate deep into Chinese history, when officials were sanctified by imperial Confucian ideology as far superior, socially and morally, to "parasitic" merchants and traders.

107. Interview 132.

108. Interview 131.

109. Ibid.; see also Murray.

110. As of 1995, Liantong expected to control 10 percent of the intranational long-distance market by 2000 and to be making inroads into the international long-distance market. It also hoped to secure a 30-percent share of the cellular market, to be actively involved in the rapidly growing VSAT market, and possibly even to be launching satellites. Interview 131; see also Murray; "Local Telephone Network Operation Opens Wider"; "State Monopoly in Telephone Service Ends."

111. Interviews 102, 131, and 132.

112. See "Wu Jichuan Attends Opening of New Information Ministry."

113. See Kornai, pp. 396–408.

114. Interview 131.

115. Of course, the Center will always be able to monitor select individuals by "tapping" their phones, but will not be able to monitor all the calls of the entire telephone-using population.

CHAPTER 6. THE STRUGGLE TO REASSERT CONTROL

1. See, for example, Deng Xiaoping's speech on the eve of the 1983 Campaign Against Spiritual Pollution, "The Party's Urgent Tasks on the Organizational and Ideological Fronts," in Deng, *Fundamental Issues*, pp. 24–40.

2. Originally from volume 3 of Deng's *Selected Works* (p. 305); quoted in *Quan Zhongguo*, p. 10.

3. Ibid., p. 325 and p. 10.

4. The term "omnidirectional crackdown" is used to distinguish this very serious, long-term effort—vast in scope and scale—from the relatively minor, short-term crackdowns that preceded it, as well as from the "sub-crackdowns" that constitute it.

5. Liu Zhongde, "Several Theoretical and Practical Questions."

6. Liu, "Zai Quanguo Wenhua Ting, Juzhang Huiyishang de Jianghua," in *Quan Zhongguo*, pp. 249–66; see also "Minister on Building 'Cultural Market' Management."

7. Liu himself does not explicitly link commercialization with globalization and pluralization, but the logical and empirical connections among these phenomena are straightforward.

8. Fang Yuan, "The First Propaganda Work Meeting."

9. The seven other meetings were: (1) the all-China meeting of heads of

provincial departments of culture; (2) the all-China broadcasting and film propaganda meeting; (3) the meeting of heads of provincial-level press and publications offices; (4) the meeting of the Xinhua News Agency's domestic bureau chiefs; (5) the meeting of *Renmin Ribao*'s domestic bureau chiefs; (6) an external propaganda work meeting; and (7) the all-Army propaganda ministers' meeting. See the *gaikuang* in *Quan Zhongguo*.

10. Quoted in Kwan.

11. Yu Youxian, "Adhering to the Theory"; see also Yu, "Adhere to the Set Direction."

12. Ai Zhisheng, "Jianchi Liangshou Zhua, Liangshou Dou Yao Ying de Fangzhen," in *Quan Zhongguo*, p. 125.

13. "Minister on Improving Television Industry."

14. "Beijing Has Again Checked Up."

15. "Minister on Improving Television Industry."

16. Literally, "fists and pillows" (*quantou jia zhentou*). See Ai Zhisheng, "Zai Quanguo Guangbo Yingshi Xuanchuan Gongzuo Huiyishang de Jianghua," in *Quan Zhongguo*, pp. 319–20.

17. Sun Jiazheng, "Jianchi Zhengque Daoxiang."

18. Hsiao.

19. Several interview informants mentioned having heard of the eight key cities and regions in 1995, but no supporting documentation could be found.

20. Interviews 145, 158, and 159.

21. The order is reprinted in *Zhongguo Guangbo Dianshi Nianjian, 1991*, pp. 71–72.

22. Nan Hsun.

23. "Hong Kong Satellite Service."

24. Exactly what these two personages discussed during their meeting is not clear from the only news report of the event, "Ding Guan'gen Meets STAR-TV Executive." Nor was Richard Li available (or willing) to be interviewed about the matter.

25. See "Television's Final Frontier"; Amdur; Goll and Witcher.

26. Quoted in Karp, "Prime Time Police."

27. "Regulations on Satellite Receiving Equipment."

28. "Rules for the Implementation."

29. Interview 107; see also Karp, "Prime Time Police," p. 73. In December 1994 the MRFT took the additional step of formally banning the importation and sale of decoders for viewing scrambled satellite programs. "Ministry Bans Import."

30. "Vice Minister Discusses Satellite TV Reception."

31. Kuang Tianpu.

32. Kaye.

33. See Karp, "Do It Our Way."

34. Ai Zhisheng, "Jianchi Liangshou Zhua, Liangshou Dou Yao Ying de Fangzhen," in *Quan Zhongguo*, pp. 124–25 (emphasis added).

35. As one foreign analyst suggested, "licenses for satellite dishes only increased opportunities for corruption." Interview 156.

36. Interview 115.

37. Interview 113.

38. Interview 124. This source, a high-ranking government official in the radio and television xitong, acknowledged that "very few" satellite dishes had been taken down after October 1993 and that "no one" was taking them down in the spring of 1995.

39. Interview 145.

40. Interview 155.

41. Interviews 159 and 160.

42. Interview 170. The view from the top of a Kunming hotel revealed a panoramic sea of satellite dishes.

43. Several hotel managers in Kunming said they carry both the southern and northern beams of Asiasat (Interview 164). The BBC News was always available at the author's three-star hotel in the summer of 1995.

44. Perhaps that is why Tibet's radio and television, public security, and state security bureaus announced jointly on March 4, 1994, that all units there—including hotels for foreign guests—would be required immediately to stop receiving and retransmitting externally originated satellite television. Hotels were even ordered explicitly not to retransmit BBC World Television News. See "Tibet Bans Relay of BBC, STAR TV Programs."

45. Jordan.   46. Interviews 145, 149, and 156.

47. Interviews 145, 150, and 156.   48. Interview 123.

49. This history is detailed in *Dangdai Zhongguo de Guangbo Dianshi*, vol. 2, p. 16 and p. 232; Yu-li Liu; see also "China: TV or Not TV?"

50. Yu-li Liu, p. 218.

51. The regulations are reprinted in *Zhongguo Guangbo Dianshi Nianjian, 1991*, pp. 72–73.

52. Yu-li Liu, p. 228.

53. These data were extracted from Manuel, "Consumers Purchase 500,000 Satellite Receivers"; "Urban, Rural"; Xu Yang; Interview 123.

54. Interview 156. Technically it is illegal for these units to supply non-unit members with cable television. Interview 126.

55. Interview 126. Minister of Radio, Film, and Television Ai Zhisheng addressed this topic at the January 1994 National Propaganda Conference. See Ai Zhisheng, "Zai Quanguo Guangbo Yingshi Xuanchuan Gongzuo Huiyishang de Jianghua," in *Quan Zhongguo*, p. 325.

56. Interview 126.

57. Interviews 126, 158, 159, and 171. These networks are to be distin-

guished from the county-level over-the-air retransmission stations discussed in Chapter 5.

58. Wang Feng, "Zai Quanguo Guangbo Yingshi Xuanchuan Gongzuo Huiyishang de Fayan," in *Quan Zhongguo*, pp. 328–38.

59. Interview 126.   60. Yu-li Liu, p. 223.

61. Karp, "Do It Our Way," p. 70.   62. Interviews 146 and 149.

63. Reported in Yu-li Liu, p. 225.

64. See "Propaganda and Management." By all accounts, hundreds or even thousands of work units continue to do precisely what the Heilongjiang factory did without facing any sanctions.

65. Chu Wei-ching argues that one reason the State Council acted was because a jealous CCTV was lobbying for the suspension. CCTV frequently carries American sports programs, but only on tape, several weeks after the event.

66. Some Hong Kong sources also suggested that an ESPN promotional advertisement contained images of the 1989 crackdown in Tiananmen Square, but this could not be confirmed.

67. Goll.

68. Wang Feng, "Zai Quanguo Guangbo Yingshi Xuanchuan Gongzuo Huiyishang de Fayan," in *Quan Zhongguo*, pp. 329–31. Of course, Beijing Cable was granted an exception when the MRFT decided to allow it to carry taped ESPN programs.

69. Sun Jiazheng, "Jianchi Zhengque Daoxiang," p. 4; Xu Yang; Gao Jin; Interview 126.

70. The bulk of the information concerning cable television in Guangzhou was supplied by the informants in Interviews 158 and 159.

71. All central-level informants quietly acknowledged the veracity of this observation.

72. On these early efforts to deal with the new video technology, see Xingzhengyuan Xinwenju, pp. 163–65.

73. "Li Ruihuan Tongzhi zai Quanguo Zhengdun Qingli Shubaokan he Yinxiang Shichang Dianhua Huiyi shang de Jianghua," in *Zhongguo Gaige Quanshu*, pp. 217–21; quotation on p. 219.

74. "Zhonggong Zhongyang Bangongting, Guowuyuan Bangongting Guanyu Zhengdun, Qingli Shubaokan he Yinxiang Shichang Yanli Daji Fanzui Huodong de Tongzhi," in *Zhongguo Gaige Quanshu*, pp. 226–29; see also "Publications Will Be Streamlined."

75. "Zhonggong Zhongyang Bangongting, Guowuyuan Bangongting Guanyu Yasuo Zhengdun Baokan he Chubanshe de Tongzhi," in *Zhongguo Gaige Quanshu*, pp. 231–34.

76. "System to Improve Quality of Periodicals"; see also Li and Ni; Pun, "Tighter Grip on Propaganda System Planned."

77. Interviews 111 and 112.

78. Guojia Tongjiju, *Zhongguo Tongji Nianjian, 1997*, p. 705.
79. Cited in "Special Dispatch."
80. Interview 112.
81. Cited in Zhang Yizhang.
82. Thus, the MoC also announced plans in January 1997 to "basically wipe out the country's influx of pornography and protect intellectual property rights by 2000." Cited in "Ministry to Improve Administration of Cultural Market."
83. Cited in Zhao Lanying.
84. "Regulations Penalizing Pornography Announced"; Lo.
85. "Propaganda Official on Antipornography Efforts."
86. Interview 133.
87. Interview 167.
88. See Liu Zhongde, "Jiaqiang Xuexi, Shenhua Gaige, Guanhao Shichang Fanrong Wenyi," in *Quan Zhongguo*, pp. 111–20.
89. For detailed discussions of some of these difficulties, see Li and Ma; Wen.
90. Interview 133.
91. Perhaps one reason it proved difficult to purchase photographic pornography in Beijing was because the city government had literally just concluded an autumn crackdown campaign, which resulted in the confiscation of 18,134 books and 4,430 calendars, among other items. Ding Yatao.
92. Efforts to secure an interview with the distributor proved fruitless.
93. For example, by the knowledgeable informant in Interview 133.
94. Quoted in Wang Li; see also "Conference Held."
95. Quotation from Dong Fangse. The plan to "resolutely root out" was first announced publicly in October. See "Mingling Jinzhi Maimai Shuhao"; Xu Weicheng.
96. Interview 169; see also "Government Clamps Down on Book Registration Numbers." Any publishing house caught reselling book numbers would henceforth have its allotment of numbers cut by 15 percent.
97. Guojia Tongjiju, *Zhongguo Tongji Nianjian, 1997*, p. 705; Interviews 109, 115, and 142. Throughout China, 69,779 new book titles were published in 1994, but only 59,159 were published in 1995. The number rose back to 63,647 in 1996.
98. The reissued regulations were published by Xinhua on January 29, 1997, and translated in *FBIS Daily China Report*, January 31, 1997.
99. Following the crackdown, only one publishing house nationwide had been punished for selling book numbers as of mid-1995: the relatively obscure Xinjiang University Press (Interview 169; see also Qu, "Publishing House Closed for Rectification"). A Chinese journalism professor told the *Hongkong Standard* in May 1996 that the licenses of more than 1,000 internally circulating newspapers and magazines had been revoked between late 1994 and early 1996—about one-sixth of all periodicals published. But no official Chinese media outlet has reported this dramatic figure. See Pun, "Publication Crackdown."

100. Interview 169.

101. Interview 142; see also "China's Publication Undertaking."

102. SPPA director Yu Youxian announced in late 1995 that "this year has seen a rapid increase in such activities as manufacturing pornography and peddling pornography with the help of computers and other high-tech means." "Stress Focal Points."

103. In addition, all of the major telecommunications providers are planning to get into the cable television business, and the GBRFT system wants permission to provide telephone service. Interviews 131, 132, 134, 141, and 144; see also Xu Yang.

104. Interviews 117, 132, and 160.

105. Thus, the CPD cannot easily influence the content of domestic Internet Web sites, because they are regulated by the MII. Interview 131; "Control of Public Multimedia."

106. In fact, one foreign telecommunications analyst even detected a positive fascination among MPT officials with the profitability of pornographic Internet services in the United States. Interview 157.

107. Interview 131.

108. "PRC Regulations."

109. Interviews 134 and 141.

110. Interview 114.

111. Interview 157.

112. Interview 103.

113. See Faison, "Chinese Cruise Internet, Wary of Watchdogs." A foreign telecommunications businessman reported confidentially that he heard one impetus for this new set of regulations was Prime Minister Li Peng's personal irritation at e-mail debates among Chinese college students concerning the contemporary significance of the December 9, 1935, student movement. The debates took place in conjunction with the movement's sixtieth anniversary.

114. "Text of Interim Internet Management Rules." Two months after the promulgation of these rules, the MPT took the additional step of formally forbidding paging services from providing customers with such value-added content as news and pornography. Interview 102; see also Wang Yanrong, "Minister Discusses Telecommunications Control"; "Paging Services Prohibited."

115. "Public Security Ministry Circular on Internet Use."

116. "Ministry Adopts Internet Measures." The State Council revised and formally promulgated restrictions on direct hook-ups to overseas networks a year later. "Li Peng Promulgates Computer Regulation."

117. Vivien Wong.

118. See Mufson; "Singapore Bans"; Vatikiotis.

119. The regulations are available in translation from the Web page of the U.S. Embassy in Beijing: http://www.redfish.com/USEmbassy-China/sandt/sandt.htm.

120. See Eckholm.

121. Interview 157.

122. Interview 144; see also Lewis.

123. Interviews 102, 103, 114, and 157. Several businesspeople taking part in a July 1997 Hong Kong Internet trade conference reported being approached by representatives of three Chinese central government bureaucracies about purchasing some of the advanced new censoring technologies. But "the degree of filtering they want to achieve is demanding," one businessman said, and it would take at least eighteen months of negotiation and explanation before anything of an advanced nature could be sold, with no guarantees that the new technologies could meet Beijing's needs.

124. Interview 114.

125. Zita, p. 42.

126. Internet accounts are, at present, centrally administered, but this will change as the number of external access nodes continues to increase. Interviews 134, 153, and 157.

127. See Markoff, "Industry Split"; Markoff, "U.S. to Urge a New Policy on Software."

128. Interviews 142, 168, and 169.

129. Quoted by Shu.

130. Qu, "Publishing Industry Adopts a Job Certification System."

131. "Reportage on *Renmin Ribao.*"

132. Reported in Wang Zhi.

133. Cary Huang, "CPC Orders Grassroots Cells to Subscribe to Party-Run Press."

134. "Step Up Journalistic Ethics Building"; "Ding Guan'gen zai Jiaqiang"; Li Zirong.

135. "Enhance Professional Ethics." Paid news was once again strictly banned during the Sixth Plenum of the Fourteenth Central Committee (October 1996). See "Resolution of the CPC." And "Several Regulations on Forbidding Paid News" were "reiterated and formulated" by the CPD and SPPA in January 1997. "Text of Regulations."

136. Quotation from the informant in Interview 108. There are no data on the volume of soft advertising and paid news in the media, but the fact that there is a great deal of it is evident even from the most casual observations. See also Wang Yitang.

137. Quoted in Fang Yuan, "Controls on Media 'Strengthened' since Plenum."

138. "Jiaqiang Baokan Kongzhi." This group obviously resembles the "radio-TV study committees" that monitor the broadcast media in at least some of China's major cities. It is unclear how—or how effectively—the newspaper reading group operates.

139. "Authorities Reportedly 'Tighten' Grip on Cinema." The relationship between this initiative and the removal of restrictions on the number of foreign film imports announced in April 1995 is unclear.

140. "Central Propaganda Department."

141. Forney, "Propaganda Man."

142. "Circular Addresses."

143. Zhang and Feng.

144. For example: "In the future everything will be called a commune. . . . Cities and villages will be called communes, [and] universities and neighborhoods will establish communes. . . . I think in the future a few large cities will be dispersed; residential areas of 20,000 to 30,000 people will have everything; villages will become small cities where the majority of philosophers and scientists will be assigned. Every large commune will have highways constructed . . . with no trees planted [alongside] so that airplanes can land." Quoted in MacFarquhar et al.

145. Deng, "Speech Greeting the Fourth Congress of Chinese Writers and Artists," in *Selected Works*, p. 202.

146. The document appears on pp. 159–60 of the section on "Constructing a Spiritual Civilization" in the encyclopedic volume *Zhongguo Gaige Quanshu*. Apparently, every effort was made to locate all early usages of the term "socialist spiritual civilization," so it seems unlikely that the term was uttered publicly before February 1981—although the term "spiritual civilization" had been used before. The "five talks" of the 1981 campaign, incidentally, were "talk civility, talk courtesy, talk sanitation, talk order, and talk morality"; the "four beautifuls" were "beautiful spirit, beautiful language, beautiful behavior, and a beautiful environment."

147. See Chen Yun, "Liangge Wenming Yao Yiqi Zhua," and "Zhonggong Zhongyang Guanyu Shehuizhuyi Jingshen Wenming Jianshe Zhidao Fangzhen de Jueyi," in *Zhongguo Gaige Quanshu*. One high-ranking propaganda official explained in 1995 that although the definition of the socialist spiritual civilization was admittedly "still evolving" nine years after the programmatic statement was issued, its basic components remain to (1) encourage the people enthusiastically to cultivate both themselves as individuals and the collective, always putting the collective first, and (2) raise the people's level of education, understanding of science, and appreciation of fine art. The concept of a socialist spiritual civilization may seem vague, this official said, but no propaganda cadres in his province have problems understanding it because "I make sure they understand it!" Interview 160.

148. Two party propaganda officials and numerous other sources in the propaganda xitong openly acknowledged these facts in 1995 interviews, even while remaining officially hopeful about the future.

149. Jiang's speech was widely reprinted in all the major media, including in the *Quan Zhongguo*. The quotation here is taken from "Jiang Zemin's Speech." (Emphasis added.)

150. "Resolution of the CPC"; see also "Fan Out."

151. See Eastman.
152. See "Wei Jianxing."
153. See Huang Chien.
154. Lam, "Team to Draft Ideological Program"; Hua.
155. See Forney, "Patriot Games."
156. On the concept of the "selectorate," see Shirk.

CHAPTER 7. THOUGHT WORK AND THE TRANSITION FROM
AUTHORITARIAN RULE

1. O'Donnell et al., p. 6.
2. See, for example, Adam Przeworski, "Some Problems in the Study of the Transition to Democracy," in O'Donnell et al., pp. 47–63; Przeworski, *Democracy and the Market*.
3. Students of democratization do not usually address the even more original transitions of ancient Greece.
4. See, in particular, John W. Meyer's "The World Polity and the Authority of the Nation-State," in Bergesen, *Studies of the Modern World-System*, pp. 109–37; Thomas and Meyer; Robinson.
5. Both Meyer and his students focus their attention on interpersonal transmission of the global culture, such as in international organizations. For an outstanding example of this sort of study, see Finnemore.
6. Good examples of this treatment of the media can be found in Larry Diamond, "Nigeria: Pluralism, Statism, and the Struggle for Democracy," in Diamond et al., *Democracy in Developing Countries*, vol. 2, *Africa*, pp. 70–71; Masipula Sithole, "Zimbabwe: In Search of a Stable Democracy," in ibid., p. 243.
7. Huntington, *The Third Wave*, pp. 100–106.
8. Ibid., p. 105.
9. See Party General Secretary Jiang Zemin's keynote address, summarized on the front page of *Renmin Ribao*, January 25, 1994. See also "Foreign Propaganda Commission."
10. The definition is given in Price, p. 74. Consider also James Curran's discussion of Jurgen Habermas' public sphere: "Within this public sphere, people collectively determine through the processes of rational argument the way in which they want to see society develop, and this shapes in turn the conduct of government policy. The media facilitate this process by providing an arena of public debate, and by reconstituting private citizens as a public body in the form of public opinion." Curran, "Mass Media and Democracy: A Reappraisal," in Curran and Gurevitch, p. 83.
11. See the early pages of Price, as well as Price and Roberts.
12. Su.
13. Sun and Wu.

14. Ibid., p. 35. By "radio station," Sun and Wu mean a cellular telecommunications network, not an over-the-air broadcast station.

15. "Mobile Phones Silenced."

16. See, for example, Strand; Martin K. Whyte, "Urban China: A Civil Society in the Making?" in Rosenbaum; McCormick et al.; White; Tong.

17. McCormick et al., p. 182.

18. See Keane; Habermas.

19. White, p. 67.

20. Ibid., p. 85.

21. Putnam.

22. One problem is that China is indeed sui generis: No other society in history has combined a Leninist government with a rapidly developing market economy in which the significance of the state-owned sector shrinks considerably and foreign investment and trade become essential to continued growth. Even Taiwan's "Leninist" state under the Kuomintang did not penetrate society the way the PRC's state did—and in some spheres of life still does.

23. Superficially, the same might be said of the United States and other industrialized democracies, but with one key distinction: In the industrialized democracies, individuals who wish to participate in the public sphere can easily do so, with little fear of government repression. Islands of autonomous civic consciousness and public participation flourish, and are linked into networks by advanced and multifarious communications systems—even if sometimes the islands are hard to perceive because of the oceans of drivel that surround them.

24. The tendency to view state-society relations in this way persists despite Alfred Stepan's 1985 work designed partially to rebut it, "State Power and the Strength of Civil Society in the Southern Cone of Latin America," in Evans et al., pp. 317–43.

25. See "Spokesman Comments on Jamming of Radio Free Asia."

Frequently cited sources have been identified by the following abbreviations:

AFP	Agence France-Presse
CD	*China Daily*
FBISDCR	*FBIS Daily China Report*
FEER	*Far Eastern Economic Review*
HKS	*Hongkong Standard*
JPRSCR	*JPRS (Joint Publications Research Service) China Report*
JPRSCSTR	*JPRS China Science and Technology Report*
MC	*Modern China*
MP	*Ming Pao*
RR	*Renmin Ribao*
SCMP	*South China Morning Post*
XNA	Xinhua News Agency
ZXS	Zhongguo Xinwenshe

Abler, Ronald F. "Hardware, Software, and Brainware: Mapping and Under-standing Telecommunications Technologies." Pp. 31–48 in Brunn and Lein-bach, eds., cited below.

"Advertising Industry Sees 'Fastest' Development." XNA, Feb. 17, 1993. Trans. in *FBISDCR*, Feb. 18, 1993, p. 37.

"AFP Reports on PRC Film Industry." AFP, Feb. 18, 1994. Trans. in *FBISDCR*, Feb. 18, 1994, p. 17.

"Agencies Set Up in Bid to Beat Ad Cheats." *CD*, Aug. 4, 1993, p. 3. Trans. in *FBISDCR*, Aug. 6, 1993, pp. 32–33.

Ai Zhisheng. "Persist in the Policy of Doing Two Types of Work Simultane-ously." *RR*, Mar. 10, 1994, p. 5. Trans. in *FBISDCR*, Mar. 24, 1994, pp. 26–29.

Alexander, Jeffrey C. *Twenty Lectures: Sociological Theory Since World War II.* New York: Columbia University Press, 1987.

Amdur, Meredith. "Murdoch STAR Deal Transforms Asia." *Broadcasting and Cable*, Aug. 2, 1993, pp. 34–35.

Anderson, Benedict. *Imagined Communities*. New York: Verso, 1983.

Applebaum, Herbert, ed. *Perspectives in Cultural Anthropology*. Albany: State University of New York Press, 1987.

"AsianNet Launches 'Massive' Internet Training Program." ZXS, Oct. 22, 1996. Trans. in *FBISDCR*, Oct. 24, 1996.

"Authorities Reportedly 'Tighten' Grip on Cinema." AFP, Jan. 24, 1994. Rpt. in *FBISDCR*, Jan. 24, 1994, p. 23.

Badie, Bertrand, and Pierre Birnbaum. *The Sociology of the State*. Trans. Arthur Goldhammer. Chicago: University of Chicago Press, 1983.

"Ban Transactions in Publication Numbers, Bring About Audio-Visual Prosperity." *RR*, Dec. 23, 1995, p. 1. Trans. in *FBISDCR*, Jan. 29, 1996.

Bandura, Albert. "Social Cognitive Theory of Mass Communication." Unpublished manuscript, Stanford University, 1988.

———. *Social Learning Theory*. Englewood Cliffs, N.J.: Prentice Hall, 1977.

Bandura, Albert, Dorothea Ross, and Sheila A. Ross. "Imitation of Film-Mediated Aggressive Models." *Journal of Abnormal and Social Psychology* 66(1), 1963, pp. 3–11.

Barnathan, Joyce. "Who'll Rake In China's Telecom Bonanza?" *Business Week*, Nov. 8, 1993, p. 52.

Barzel, Yoram. *Economic Analysis of Property Rights*. Cambridge, U.K.: Cambridge University Press, 1989.

Baum, Richard. *Burying Mao: Chinese Politics in the Age of Deng Xiaoping*. Princeton, N.J.: Princeton University Press, 1994.

"Beijing Buys U.S. Telecommunications Satellite." XNA, Dec. 2, 1992. Trans. in *JPRS Telecommunications Report*, Dec. 17, 1992, p. 5.

"Beijing Has Again Checked Up on News and Cultural Circles and Will Considerably Reduce Television and Radio Programs from Outside the Mainland." *MP*, Aug. 9, 1993, p. 10. Trans. in *FBISDCR*, Aug. 10, 1993, pp. 20–21.

"Beijing Punishes Illegal Publication Activity." ZXS, Apr. 13, 1993. Trans. in *FBISDCR*, May 4, 1993, p. 22.

"Beijing Raids Underground Publishing House, Seizes 3,000 Banned Books." *MP*, Oct. 7, 1994, p. B3. Trans. in *FBISDCR*, Oct. 7, 1994.

"Beijing to Establish State Economic Information Network." XNA, May 10, 1994. Trans. in *FBISDCR*, May 10, 1994, pp. 33–34.

Beniger, James R. *The Control Revolution*. Cambridge, Mass.: Harvard University Press, 1986.

Bergesen, Albert, ed. *Studies of the Modern World-System*. New York: Academic Press, 1980.

Bernhard, Michael. "Civil Society and Democratic Transition in East Central Europe." *Political Science Quarterly* 108(2), 1993, pp. 307–26.

Bi Bo. *Meiguo zhi Yin Toushi*. Qingdao: Qingdao Chubanshe, 1991.

Blatherwick, David E. S. *The International Politics of Telecommunications*. Berkeley: Institute for International Studies, University of California, 1987.

Braman, Sandra, and Annabelle Sreberny-Mohammadi, eds. *Globalization, Communication, and Transnational Civil Society*. Cresskill, N.J.: Hampton, 1996.

Broadcasting to China: Applying the Lessons from European Freedom Radios. Hearing before the Subcommittee on European Affairs and the Subcommittee on East Asian and Pacific Affairs of the Committee on Foreign Relations, United States Senate, Nov. 21, 1991. Washington, D.C.: U.S. Government Printing Office, 1992.

Brunn, Stanley D., and Thomas R. Leinbach, eds. *Collapsing Space and Time: Geographic Aspects of Communication and Information*. London: HarperCollins Academic, 1991.

Buci-Glucksmann, Christine. *Gramsci and the State*. Trans. David Fernbach. London: Lawrence and Wishart, 1980.

"Campaign Launched to Educate Journalists on 'Press Ethics.'" XNA, Apr. 25, 1994. Trans. in *FBISDCR*, Apr. 26, 1994, p. 26.

Cao Guanghui. "Broadcast, TV Industry Makes 'Giant Strides.'" XNA, Oct. 21, 1993. Trans. in *FBISDCR*, Oct. 26, 1993, p. 37.

Carey, James W. *Communication as Culture: Essays on Media and Society*. London: Routledge, 1989.

"Cellular Mobile Phone Calls Available in Qinghai." XNA, Apr. 3, 1994. Trans. in *FBISDCR*, Apr. 5, 1994, pp. 80–81.

"Censors to License Private Bookstands." *SCMP* (Internet edition), Jan. 19, 1998.

"Centering on One Basic Principle, Performing Four Major Tasks Well—Excerpts of Speeches Made by Leaders of Some Provincial, Municipal, and Autonomous Regional Party Committees at Local Conferences on Propaganda and Ideological Work." *RR*, June 14, 1994, p. 3. Trans. in *FBISDCR*, June 30, 1994, pp. 23–24.

"Central Propaganda Department Issues Order Banning Import of Western Films." *MP*, July 5, 1996, p. A10. Trans. in *FBISDCR*, July 9, 1996.

Chaffee, Steven H. "Mass Media and Interpersonal Channels: Competitive, Convergent, or Complementary?" In *Inter/Media: Interpersonal Communication in a Media World*, ed. C. Cumpert and R. Cathcart, 2d ed. New York: Oxford University Press, 1982, pp. 57–77.

Chamberlain, Heath B. "On the Search for Civil Society in China." *MC* 19(2), Apr. 1993, pp. 199–215.

Chan, Joseph Man. "Commercialization Without Independence: Media Development in China." *China Review* 25, 1993, pp. 1–19.

———. "Communication Networks in the Asia-Pacific: An Overview." *Media Asia* 18(1), 1991, pp. 35–43.

———. "Media Internationalization in China: Processes and Tensions." *Journal of Communication* 44(3), 1994, pp. 70–88.

———. "Penetrating China's Cultural Shield: The Impact of Hong Kong Television on Guangzhou Residents." Paper delivered at the Conference on Chinese Communication in the Age of Modern Media, Minneapolis, June 1996.

Chan Wai-fong. "Case of Suspended Guangdong Paper Detailed." *SCMP*, Jan. 26, 1995, p. 15. Rpt. in *FBISDCR*, Jan. 26, 1995.

Chang, Julian. "The Mechanics of State Propaganda: The People's Republic of China and the Soviet Union in the 1950s." Pp. 76–124 in Cheek and Saich, eds., cited below.

Chang Min-yi. "China's Press Reform as Perceived from the Fate of *Shenzhen Qingnian Bao*." *Pai-Hsing* 221, Aug. 1, 1990, pp. 22–23. Trans. in *JPRSCR*, Oct. 25, 1990, pp. 81–83.

Chang, Tsan-kuo, Chin-hsien Chen, and Guo-Qiang Zhang. "Rethinking the Mass Propaganda Model: Evidence from the Chinese Regional Press." *Gazette* 51, 1993, pp. 173–95.

Chang Yi-cheng. "Mainland Slashes Papers, Journals, Electronic Media to Give More 'Space' to Official News Media." *Sing Tao Jih Pao*, Aug. 22, 1997, p. A7. Trans. in *FBISDCR*, Sept. 8, 1997.

Cheek, Timothy, and Tony Saich, eds. *New Perspectives on State Socialism in China*. Armonk, N.Y.: M. E. Sharpe, 1997.

Chen Chongshan. "Shouzhong Diaocha Yanjiu 10 Nian." *Xinwen Yanjiu Ziliao* 58, Sept. 1992, pp. 1–17.

Chen Xi, Yang Long, and Luo Jing. *Zhongguo Tushuye Jingji Fenxi*. Shanghai: Xuelin Chubanshe, 1990.

Chen Yun. "The Media Should Watch Out for Dishonest Ads." XNA, Sept. 18, 1988. Trans. in *FBISDCR*, Sept. 21, 1988, p. 44.

Chen Yunqian. "Driving Forces Behind China's Explosive Telecommunications Growth." *IEEE Communications Magazine*, July 1993, pp. 20–22.

"China: Breaking Up?" *Business China*, May 2, 1994.

"*China Daily* Newspapers Start Global Desktop Delivery Service." *CD*, Mar. 2, 1994, p. 3. Trans. in *FBISDCR*, Mar. 4, 1994, pp. 22–23.

"China to Build Information Superhighway." XNA, May 5, 1994. Trans. in *FBISDCR*, May 9, 1994, p. 28.

"China: TV or Not TV?" *Business China*, Mar. 7, 1994, pp. 1–2.

"China Without Borders." *Economist*, Jan. 30, 1993, pp. 31–32.

"China's Posts and Telecommunications Have Returned to Normal." ZXS, June 19, 1989. Trans. in *JPRS Telecommunications Report*, July 18, 1989, p. 1.

"China's Publication Undertaking Is Nearly Out of Control Because of Serious Political Problems." *MP*, Aug. 26, 1996, p. A6. Trans. in *FBISDCR*, Aug. 29, 1996.

Ching Chi. "More than 100 Mainland Newspapers Increase Pages and Issues from New Year's Day While Facing More Intense Competition." *MP*, Jan. 7, 1994, p. 9. Trans. in *FBISDCR*, Jan. 21, 1994, pp. 28–29.

Chou Wen-chiang. "Guangdong Destroys Pirated Audio, Video Products." *Wen Wei Po*, Apr. 22, 1994, p. 11. Trans. in *FBISDCR*, Apr. 22, 1994, pp. 42–43.

Chu Baoping. "Growth in Telecommunications, Post Industry Discussed." XNA, Jan. 17, 1996. Trans. in *FBISDCR*, Jan. 25, 1996.

———. "Zou Jiahua on Improving Posts, Telecommunications." XNA, May 17, 1994. Trans. in *FBISDCR*, May 24, 1994, pp. 32–33.

Chu, Godwin C., and Francis L. Hsu, eds. *Moving a Mountain: Cultural Change in China*. Honolulu: University Press of Hawaii, 1979.

Chu Wei-ching. "State Suspends Beijing Cable TV Sports Channel." *Lien Ho Pao* (Hong Kong), Feb. 8, 1994, p. 10. Trans. in *FBISDCR*, Feb. 10, 1994, pp. 23–24.

Chung Chih-ming. "Xu Weicheng Is to Leave the Central Propaganda Department and Become Deputy Secretary General of the CPPCC." *MP*, June 9, 1993, p. 7. Trans. in *FBISDCR*, June 10, 1993, pp. 25–26.

"Circular Addresses Non-Official Broadcasts Banned for Many Hotels." XNA, Sept. 25, 1995. Trans. in *FBISDCR*, Sept. 25, 1995.

"Circular Calls for Setting Up Newspaper Reading Boards." Central China Television Channel 1, Aug. 6, 1996. Trans. in *FBISDCR*, Aug. 8, 1996.

"Circular Concerning Cracking Down on Unauthorized Radio Stations and Punishing Personnel Involved." *Anhui Ribao*, June 26, 1995, p. 1. Trans. in *FBISDCR*, June 26, 1995.

"Circular of the Telecommunications Administration Department of the Ministry of Posts and Telecommunications on Further Strengthening of the Telecommunications Business Market." *RR*, June 14, 1995, p. 12. Trans. in *FBISDCR*, June 14, 1995.

Clifford, Mark. "China: A Question of Money." *FEER*, Apr. 7, 1994, pp. 47–48.

———. "Communications: China Calling." *FEER*, Mar. 31, 1994, pp. 56–58.

———. "Crossed Lines: Peking Policy Statement Causes Confusion." *FEER*, Nov. 4, 1993, p. 74.

"Commentary on Radio, Television Responsibilities." Anhui People's Radio Network, Sept. 10, 1991. Trans. in *FBISDCR*, Sept. 16, 1991, p. 43.

"Commercial Satellite Network Takes Shape." Central People's Radio Network, June 20, 1992. Trans. in *FBISDCR*, June 25, 1992, p. 25.

"Communications Sector to Consolidate." XNA, Sept. 18, 1990. Trans. in *JPRSCSTR*, Sept. 28, 1990, pp. 4–5.

"Computer Network to Connect Universities." XNA, Oct. 30, 1994. Trans. in *FBISDCR*, Oct. 30, 1994.

"Conference Held on Pornography Crackdown." XNA, July 24, 1997. Trans. in *FBISDCR*, July 29, 1997.

"Control of Public Multimedia Communication Tightened." XNA, Oct. 7, 1997. Trans. in *FBISDCR*, Oct. 10, 1997.

"Control of Telecommunications Market Strengthened." XNA, Sept. 13, 1993. Trans. in *FBISDCR*, Sept. 14, 1993, p. 43.

"'Convention' Drawn Up to Protect Audio, Video Copyrights." XNA, Apr. 30, 1994. Trans. in *FBISDCR*, May 2, 1994, pp. 41–42.

Cowhey, Peter F. "The International Telecommunications Regime: The Political Roots of Regimes for High Technology." *International Organization* 44(2), Spring 1990, pp. 169–99.

"CPC Issues Circular on Journalistic Ethics." XNA, Apr. 25, 1994. Trans. in *FBIS-DCR*, May 3, 1994, p. 22.

"Crackdown on 'Largest' Case Reported." Zhongguo Tongxun She, Dec. 25, 1991. Trans. in *FBISDCR*, Dec. 26, 1991, p. 28.

Crothall, Geoffrey. "Authorities Cancel Radio 'Phone-In Show.'" *South China Sunday Morning Post*, Aug. 8, 1993, p. 1. Rpt. in *FBISDCR*, Aug. 10, 1993, p. 21.

———. "'Disparity' Between Rules, Reality in Radio, TV." *SCMP*, Feb. 21, 1992, p. 23. Rpt. in *FBISDCR*, Feb. 21, 1992, pp. 21–22.

———. "Second National Public Telephone Network Requested." *SCMP (Business Post)*, Feb. 18, 1993, pp. 1, 3. Rpt. in *FBISDCR*, Feb. 18, 1993, pp. 36–37.

Crothall, Geoffrey, and Owen Hughes. "Mainland Still Bans Hong Kong Satellite TV." *SCMP*, Mar. 3, 1992, p. 6. Rpt. in *FBISDCR*, Mar. 3, 1992, pp. 86–87.

Curran, James, and Michael Gurevitch, eds. *Mass Media and Society*. London: Edward Arnold, 1991.

Dai Zhou. *Shehuizhuyi Jingshen Wenming Jianshe de Jige Zhongyao Wenti*. Beijing: Zhonggong Zhongyang Dangxiao Chubanshe, 1997.

Dangdai Zhongguo de Chuban Shiye. 3 vols. Beijing: Dangdai Zhongguo Chubanshe, 1993.

Dangdai Zhongguo de Dianying. 2 vols. Beijing: Zhongguo Shehui Kexue Chubanshe, 1989.

Dangdai Zhongguo de Dianzi Gongye. Beijing: Zhongguo Shehui Kexue Chubanshe, 1986.

Dangdai Zhongguo de Gong Shang Xingzheng Guanli. Beijing: Dangdai Zhongguo Chubanshe, 1991.

Dangdai Zhongguo de Guangbo Dianshi. 2 vols. Beijing: Zhongguo Shehui Kexue Chubanshe, 1987.

De Fleur, Melvin L., and Sandra Ball-Rokeach. *Theories of Mass Communication*. 4th ed. New York: Longman, 1982.

Deng Xiaoping. *Fundamental Issues in Present-Day China*. Beijing: Foreign Languages Press, 1987.

———. *Selected Works of Deng Xiaoping*. Beijing: Foreign Languages Press, 1984.

"Deng's 1950 Ideas Identical with Press Reform." ZXS, Jan. 15, 1988. Trans. in *FBISDCR*, Jan. 15, 1988, p. 10.

Deutsch, Karl. *The Nerves of Government*. New York: The Free Press, 1963.

Diamond, Larry, Juan J. Linz, and Seymour Martin Lipset, eds. *Democracy in Developing Countries*. 4 vols. Boulder, Colo.: Lynne Rienner, 1988–89.

Ding Guan'gen. "Run Our Party Papers Better." *Guangming Ribao*, Apr. 5, 1995, p. 2. Trans. in *FBISDCR*, Apr. 5, 1995.

———. "Work Hard to Pursue Propaganda and Ideological Work Well Under the New Situation." Excerpts from address given at the Central Party School, Mar. 24, 1993. *Guangming Ribao*, May 8, 1993, pp. 3–7. Trans. in *FBISDCR*, June 3, 1993, pp. 20–27.

"Ding Guan'gen Appointed Director of CPD, and Guo Chaoren Director of Xinhua News Agency." *Ta Kung Pao*, Dec. 3, 1992. Trans. in *FBISDCR*, Dec. 3, 1992, p. 21.

"Ding Guan'gen Meets STAR-TV Executive." XNA, Nov. 17, 1992. Trans. in *FBISDCR*, Nov. 17, 1992, p. 60.

"Ding Guan'gen Speaks on Economy." XNA, Jan. 29, 1994. Trans. in *FBISDCR*, Jan. 31, 1994, p. 22.

"Ding Guan'gen zai Jiaqiang Xinwen Zhiye Daode Jianshe Zuotanhui shang de Jianghua." *Zhongguo Jizhe*, Aug. 15, 1993, pp. 4–5.

Ding, X. L. "Institutional Amphibiousness and the Transition from Communism: The Case of China." *British Journal of Political Science* 24(3), July 1994, pp. 293–318.

Ding Yatao. "Chen Xitong, Secretary of the Beijing Municipal CPC Committee, Urges Further Expanding the Dynamics of Eradicating Pornography and Attacking Unlawful Publications." *Beijing Ribao*, Nov. 18, 1994, p. 1. Trans. in *FBISDCR*, Nov. 18, 1994.

"Directors of Economic Broadcast Stations from Across the Country Get Together in Border City to Discuss Ideas for Reforming, Developing Economic Radio Stations." *Xinjiang Ribao*, Aug. 6, 1994, p. 1. Trans. in *FBISDCR*, Aug. 6, 1994.

do Rosario, Louise. "Self-Control." *FEER*, Mar. 3, 1994, p. 28.

Domes, Jürgen. *The Government and Politics of the PRC: A Time of Transition*. Boulder, Colo.: Westview, 1985.

Dong Fangse. "Zhou Hong Signs First Deal as 'Indentured' Writer; Xinwen Publishing Office to Mop Up Publishing's Strange Births." *Kuang Chiao Ching* 12, Dec. 16, 1993, pp. 50–53. Trans. in *JPRSCR*, Feb. 16, 1994, pp. 30–34.

Dou Shoufang. "Dianying Gaige de Qushi, Yuce, he Qiantu." *Dianying Tongxun* 1, 1995, pp. 21–23.

"Du Daozheng Denies That the Press and Publication Administration 'Makes People the Target of Attack.'" ZXS, Mar. 15, 1988. Trans. in *FBISDCR*, Mar. 16, 1988, pp. 18–19.

Duan Cunzhang. "National Forum of Heads of Propaganda Departments Ends in Beijing." *RR*, Jan. 18, 1993, pp. 1, 4. Trans. in *FBISDCR*, Feb. 8, 1993, pp. 12–14.

Duan Cunzhang and He Ping. "Ding Guan'gen on Propaganda Affairs." XNA, Jan. 17, 1993. Trans. in *FBISDCR*, Jan. 19, 1993, pp. 25–27.

Eastman, Lloyd E. *The Abortive Revolution: China Under Nationalist Rule, 1927–1937*. Cambridge, Mass.: Harvard University Press, 1974.

Eckholm, Erik. "China Cracks Down on Dissent in Cyberspace." *New York Times* (Internet edition), Dec. 31, 1997.

Ellul, Jacques. *Propaganda: The Formation of Men's Attitudes*. New York: Knopf, 1965.

———. *The Technological Society*. Trans. by John Wilkinson. New York: Knopf, 1964.

"Enhance Professional Ethics, Ban 'Paid News.'" *RR*, May 8, 1996, p. 1. Trans. in *FBISDCR*, May 8, 1996.

"Environment for Press Reform Explored." *Ta Kung Pao*, Nov. 25, 1987, p. 1. Trans. in *FBISDCR*, Nov. 25, 1987, pp. 19–20.

Evans, Peter B., Dietrich Rueschemeyer, and Theda Skocpol, eds. *Bringing the State Back In*. Cambridge, U.K.: Cambridge University Press, 1985.

Faison, Seth. "A Chinese Edition of *Elle* Draws Ads and Readers." *New York Times*, Jan. 1, 1996, p. 29.

———. "Chinese Cruise Internet, Wary of Watchdogs." *New York Times*, Feb. 5, 1996, pp. A1, A3.

"Fan Out from Point to Area, Jointly Build Civilization." *RR*, Mar. 25, 1997, p. 4. Trans. in *FBISDCR*, Apr. 11, 1997.

Fang Ching. "Anti-American Sentiment Surfaces in Publishing Circles." *MP*, Aug. 3, 1996, p. A7. Trans. in *FBISDCR*, Aug. 8, 1996.

Fang Yuan. "A Number of Books and Underground Publications Are Banned on the Eve of National Day." *MP*, Oct. 3, 1994, p. B1. Trans. in *FBISDCR*, Oct. 3, 1994.

———. "Controls on Media 'Strengthened' since Plenum." *MP*, Nov. 24, 1993, p. A13. Trans. in *FBISDCR*, Nov. 24, 1993, pp. 21–22.

———. "The First Propaganda Work Meeting in 36 Years Is to Be Held in Beijing." *MP*, Dec. 20, 1993, p. 2. Trans. in *FBISDCR*, Dec. 22, 1993, pp. 11–12.

Fang Zhen. "Is the Chinese Press Experiencing a Silent Revolution?" *Liaowang* 4, Jan. 25, 1993, pp. 22–26. Trans. in *JPRSCR*, Mar. 10, 1993, pp. 1–6.

Fang Zhi. "A Modern *Jin Ping Mei*: Jia Ping'ao's New Work *Ruined Capital* Is Banned." *Kaifang* 9, Sept. 18, 1993, pp. 102–3. Trans. in *JPRSCR*, Dec. 14, 1993, pp. 53–54.

Featherstone, Mike, ed. *Global Culture: Nationalism, Globalization, and Modernity*. London: Sage, 1990.

Finnemore, Martha. *National Interests in International Society*. Ithaca, N.Y.: Cornell University Press, 1996.

"Five Films Banned Last Year for Sexual Content." *Zhongguo Tongxun She*, Mar. 15, 1994. Trans. in *FBISDCR*, Mar. 24, 1994, p. 30.

"Foreign Propaganda Commission Reportedly Set Up." *MP*, Feb. 11, 1998, p. A11. Trans. in *FBISDCR*, Feb. 12, 1998.

"Foreign Satellite TV Returns to Hotels." AFP, Oct. 11, 1989. Trans. in *FBISDCR*, Oct. 11, 1989, p. 26.

Forney, Matt. "Patriot Games." *FEER*, Oct. 3, 1996, pp. 22–28.

——. "Piracy: Now We Get It." *FEER*, Feb. 15, 1996, pp. 40–43.

——. "Propaganda Man: Deng Protégé Wields the Censor's Whip for Jiang." *FEER*, Dec. 5, 1996.

Frank-Keyes, John. "Six Television Stations Launch Interregional Hook-Up." *SCMP (Business Post)*, Sept. 1, 1993, p. 5. Rpt. in *FBISDCR*, Sept. 2, 1993, pp. 33–34.

"Fujian, Taiwan Telecommunications Links Rising." ZXS, Sept. 4, 1996. Trans. in *FBISDCR*, Sept. 5, 1996.

Gao Jin. "Cable TV Off Limits to Overseas Firms." *CD*, Apr. 16, 1994, p. 3. Rpt. in *FBISDCR*, Apr. 18, 1994, pp. 36–37.

Gao Jinan. "State-of-the-Art Satellite's Launch Date Set for 1994." *CD*, Apr. 10, 1993, p. 1. Rpt. in *FBISDCR*, Apr. 13, 1993, pp. 16–17.

Gao Tao. "Information Sector Thrives." *CD* (*Science and Technology* supplement), June 3, 1994, p. 1.

Gao Zhu and Zhang Xiaoyuan. "Sichuan Reaches Agreement with U.S.'s AT&T to Manufacture 1-Million-Line Digital Stored-Program-Controlled Telephone Switch." *Keji Ribao*, Feb. 10, 1993, p. 1. Trans. in *JPRSCSTR*, Mar. 22, 1993, p. 42.

Garnham, Nicholas. "The Media and the Public Sphere." *Communicating Politics: Mass Communications and the Political Process*, ed. Peter Golding, Graham Murdock, and Philip Schlesinger. New York: Holmes and Meier, 1986, pp. 37–53.

Garside, Roger. *Coming Alive: China after Mao*. New York: McGraw-Hill, 1981.

Geertz, Clifford. *The Interpretation of Cultures*. New York: Basic Books, 1973.

Gellner, Ernest. "Civil Society in Historical Context." *International Social Science Journal* 129, Aug. 1991, pp. 495–510.

——. *Nations and Nationalism*. Ithaca, N.Y.: Cornell University Press, 1983.

Giddens, Anthony. *Central Problems in Social Theory: Action, Structure, and Contradiction in Social Analysis*. Berkeley: University of California Press, 1979.

Gilley, Bruce. "Shenzhen Viewers Required to Remove Satellite Dishes." *Eastern Express*, Apr. 20, 1994, p. 8. Rpt. in *FBISDCR*, Apr. 20, 1994, pp. 51–52.

Gold, Thomas B. "Go with Your Feelings: Hong Kong and Taiwan Popular Culture in Greater China." *China Quarterly* 136, Dec. 1993, pp. 907–25.

Goll, Sally D. "Asia Households Receiving ESPN Jumped to Over 10 Million in 1994." *Asian Wall Street Journal*, Mar. 2, 1995, p. 6.

Goll, Sally D., and S. Karene Witcher. "News Corp. Plans to Buy 36.4 Percent

Stake in STAR-TV, Giving It Full Ownership." *Asian Wall Street Journal*, July 24, 1995, p. 6.

Gorham, Sid, and Achmad M. Chadran. "Communicating on the Go." *China Business Review*, Mar.–Apr. 1993, pp. 26–30.

———. "Telecommunications Paces Ahead." *China Business Review*, Mar.–Apr. 1993, pp. 18–25.

"Government Boosts Post, Telecommunications." XNA, Nov. 5, 1992. Trans. in *JPRS Telecommunications Report*, Dec. 17, 1992, pp. 6–7.

"Government Clamps Down on Book Registration Numbers." Zhongguo Tongxun She, June 13, 1994. Trans. in *FBISDCR*, June 22, 1994, p. 21.

"Government, ROK Sign Fiber Optic Cable Pact." XNA, Nov. 24, 1993. Trans. in *FBISDCR*, No. 27, 1993, p. 5.

"Government to Adopt a National Ad Agency System." XNA, Jan. 9, 1993. Trans. in *FBISDCR*, Jan. 12, 1993, p. 33.

Granovetter, Mark. "Economic Action and Social Structure: The Problem of Embeddedness." *American Journal of Sociology* 91(3), Nov. 1985, pp. 481–510.

———. "Threshold Models of Collective Behavior." *American Journal of Sociology* 83(6), May 1978, pp. 1420–43.

"The Great Wall Wired." *Economist* (Internet edition), Jan. 1998.

Groves, Theodore, Yongmiao Hong, John McMillan, and Barry Naughton. "Autonomy and Incentives in Chinese State Enterprises." *Quarterly Journal of Economics* 109(1), Feb. 1994, pp. 183–208.

Gu Hongnian. "Xietiao Fazhan Youshi Hubu—Guanyu Xianji Guangbo Dianshi Shiye Jianshe de Shijian yu Sikao." *Zhongguo Guangbo Yingshi* 1, 1993, pp. 18–19.

Gu Ping. "Asia Is Disgusted with Awful Noise of Cold War." *RR*, Oct. 16, 1996, p. 6. Trans. in *FBISDCR*, Oct. 21, 1996.

Guangbo Dianshi Jianming Cidian. Beijing: Zhongguo Guangbo Dianshi Chubanshe, 1989.

"Guangdong Boasts Telecommunications Service." XNA, May 20, 1992. Trans. in *JPRS Telecommunications Report*, June 10, 1992, pp. 9–10.

"Guangdong Plans Commercial TV Station." ZXS, Dec. 13, 1993. Trans. in *FBISDCR*, Dec. 15, 1993, pp. 47–48.

"Guangdong Program Airs Environmental Concerns." Guangzhou Guangdong People's Radio Network, Dec. 9, 1994. Trans. in *FBISDCR*, Dec. 9, 1994.

"Guangdong Satellite Broadcasting Trial Begins." Guangdong People's Radio Network, May 31, 1996. Trans. in *FBISDCR*, June 6, 1995.

"Guangdong Starts Satellite Television Transmission." XNA, July 15, 1996. Trans. in *FBISDCR*, July 23, 1996.

"Guangzhou's Telecommunications Development Viewed." Zhongguo Tongxun She, Aug. 10, 1992. Trans. in *FBISDCR*, Aug. 28, 1992, pp. 44–45.

"Guide People with Correct Public Opinion." *RR*, Feb. 4, 1994, p. 1. Trans. in *FBISDCR*, Feb. 10, 1994, pp. 16–17.

Guo Zhenzhi. "Shichang Jingji zhong de Guangbo Dianshi." *Xinwen yu Chuanbo Yanjiu* 1(3), 1994, pp. 2–8.

Guojia Gong Shang Xingzheng Guanliju and Guojia Jihua Weiyuanhui. "Guanyu Jiakuai Guanggaoye Fazhan de Guihua Gangyao." *Zhongguo Guanggao* 4, 1993, pp. 3–6.

Guojia Tongjiju, ed. *Zhongguo Tongji Nianjian, 1988.* Beijing: Zhongguo Tongji Chubanshe, 1988.

———. *Zhongguo Tongji Nianjian, 1990.* Beijing: Zhongguo Tongji Chubanshe, 1990.

———. *Zhongguo Tongji Nianjian, 1991.* Beijing: Zhongguo Tongji Chubanshe, 1991.

———. *Zhongguo Tongji Nianjian, 1992.* Beijing: Zhongguo Tongji Chubanshe, 1992.

———. *Zhongguo Tongji Nianjian, 1993.* Beijing: Zhongguo Tongji Chubanshe, 1993.

———. *Zhongguo Tongji Nianjian, 1994.* Beijing: Zhongguo Tongji Chubanshe, 1994.

———. *Zhongguo Tongji Nianjian, 1995.* Beijing: Zhongguo Tongji Chubanshe, 1995.

———. *Zhongguo Tongji Nianjian, 1996.* Beijing: Zhongguo Tongji Chubanshe, 1996.

———. *Zhongguo Tongji Nianjian, 1997.* Beijing: Zhongguo Tongji Chubanshe, 1997.

Guojia Tongjiju Gongye Jiaotong Si, ed. *Zhongguo Yunshu Youdian Shiye de Fazhan.* Beijing: Zhongguo Tongji Chubanshe, 1989.

Gurevitch, Michael, Tony Bennett, James Curran, and Janet Woollacott, eds. *Culture, Society, and the Media.* London: Routledge, 1982.

Habermas, Jürgen. *The Structural Transformation of the Public Sphere.* Trans. Thomas Burger. Cambridge, Mass.: MIT Press, 1989.

Hamrin, Carol Lee. *China and the Challenge of the Future: Changing Political Patterns.* Boulder, Colo.: Westview, 1990.

Hamrin, Carol Lee, and Suisheng Zhao, eds. *Decision-Making in Deng's China: Perspectives from Insiders.* Armonk, N.Y.: M. E. Sharpe, 1995.

Hann, Chris, and Elizabeth Dunn, eds. *Civil Society: Challenging Western Models.* London: Routledge, 1996.

Hao Te-hsien. "Yantai Propaganda Conference Makes Arrangements for Consolidating the Press." *MP*, Aug. 13, 1996, p. A9. Trans. in *FBISDCR*, Aug. 22, 1996.

Harding, Harry. *China's Second Revolution: Reform after Mao.* Washington, D.C.: The Brookings Institution, 1987.

Hayek, Friedrich A. "The Price System as a Mechanism for Using Knowledge." *Comparative Economic Systems*, ed. Morris Bornstein. Homewood, Ill.: Richard D. Irwin, 1974, pp. 22–33.

He, Fei Chang. "Lian Tong: A Quantum Leap in the Reform of China's Telecommunications." *Telecommunications Policy* 18(3), Apr. 1994, pp. 206–10.

He Jun. "Computer Network to Link 1, 000 Universities." *CD*, Dec. 1, 1994, p. 3. Rpt. in *JPRSCSTR*, Feb. 13, 1995, pp. 12–13.

———. "Digital Network to Upgrade Data Links." *CD*, Mar. 24, 1994, p. 1. Rpt. in *FBISDCR*, Mar. 24, 1994, p. 31.

He P'in. "Analysis of Press Suppression Since Tiananmen." *Cheng Ming* 10, Oct. 1989, pp. 18–19. Trans. in *JPRSCR*, Feb. 7, 1990, pp. 71–73.

Hines, Christopher. "Official on Satellite Dish Use, Foreign Programming." *AFP*, Nov. 29, 1993. Rpt. in *FBISDCR*, Dec. 2, 1993, pp. 25–26.

Hoare, Quintin, and Geoffrey Nowell Smith, eds. *Selections from the Prison Notebooks of Antonio Gramsci*. New York: International Publishers, 1971.

Hobsbawm, E. J. *Nations and Nationalism Since 1780: Programme, Myth, Reality*. Cambridge, U.K.: Cambridge University Press, 1990.

Holden, Doug. "BBC Prepares to Beam Television News Bulletins into China." *SCMP*, Aug. 11, 1994, p. 5. Rpt. in *FBISDCR*, Aug. 11, 1994.

Holloway, Nigel. "Troubled Persuader: Hard Knocks Await Radio Free Asia's Soft Line." *FEER*, Aug. 1, 1996, pp. 22–23.

Hong, Junhao. "China's TV Program Imports 1958–1988: Towards the Internationalization of Television?" *Gazette* 52, 1993, pp. 1–23.

Hong, Junhao, and Marlene Cuthbert. "Media Reform in China since 1978: Background Factors, Problems, and Future Trends." *Gazette* 47, 1991, pp. 141–58.

"Hong Kong Reporters' Situation Reported." *Jiushi Niandai* 11, Nov. 1, 1993, pp. 37–39. Trans. in *JPRSCR*, Feb. 16, 1994, pp. 38–41.

"Hong Kong Satellite Service Cut in Beijing Hotels." *AFP*, Jan. 21, 1992. Trans. in *FBISDCR*, Jan. 21, 1992, p. 38.

Hong Wen. "Official Cited on Telecommunications Investment." Zhongguo Tongxun She, Nov. 29, 1993. Trans. in *FBISDCR*, Dec. 9, 1993, pp. 41–43.

Hood, Marlowe. "Effects of Press Law Reform on Media Viewed." *South China Sunday Morning Post* (*Spectrum* section), Apr. 24, 1988, p. 4. Rpt. in *FBISDCR*, Apr. 25, 1988, pp. 25–26.

Hou Bing and Lu Hongde. "Push Press Reform to a New Stage—Interviews with Responsible Persons of Some Press Units in the Capital." *Xinwen Zhanxian* 1, 1988, pp. 8–11. Trans. in *FBISDCR*, Jan. 27, 1988, pp. 10–13.

Hou Chung-wen. "Central Propaganda Department Tightens Control over Press; Guangdong Reorganizes Five Newspapers and Four Magazines." *MP*, Jan. 15, 1994, p. A9. Trans. in *FBISDCR*, Jan. 18, 1994, pp. 16–17.

Hou Guining. "Three Tendencies We Should Avoid in Ideological and Political

Work." *Lilun yu Shijian* 7, Sept. 5, 1989, pp. 18–19. Trans. in *JPRSCR*, Jan. 8, 1990, pp. 14–15.

Houn, Franklin. *To Change a Nation*. New York: The Free Press, 1961.

Hsiao Peng. "Authorities Urge All Localities to Publicize Sixth Plenary Session and Main Trend, to Stop Airing Foreign Television Plays During Prime Time." *Sing Tao Jih Pao*, Nov. 4, 1996, p. A4. Trans. in *FBISDCR*, Nov. 7, 1996.

Hsieh Ying. "Radio and Television of Hong Kong Has Stretched Its Hand Too Far." *Wen Wei Po*, Dec. 26, 1992, p. 7. Trans. in *FBISDCR*, Dec. 28, 1992, pp. 66–67.

"Hu Yaobang on Journalism, 'Spiritual Pollution.'" *RR*, Apr. 14, 1985, pp. 1–3. Trans. in *FBISDCR*, Apr. 15, 1985, pp. K1–K15.

Hua Hsia. "Theme of Sixth Plenary Session Is Fixed." *Hsin Pao*, June 19, 1996, p. 10. Trans. in *FBISDCR*, June 20, 1996.

Huang, Cary. "CPC Orders Grassroots Cells to Subscribe to Party-Run Press." *HKS*, Oct. 3, 1996, p. 6. Rpt. in *FBISDCR*, Oct. 4, 1996.

———. "CPC Resumes Prepublication Censorship." *HKS*, Sept. 20, 1991, p. A8. Rpt. in *FBISDCR*, Sept. 24, 1991, pp. 29–30.

Huang Chien. "Rigorous Control of Ideology Reiterated." *Tangtai* 44, Nov. 15, 1994, pp. 24–25. Trans. in *FBISDCR*, Jan. 9, 1995.

Huang, Philip C. C. "'Public Sphere'/'Civil Society' in China?" *MC* 19(2), Apr. 1993, pp. 216–40.

Huang Shijian. "Present, Future Technology." *Dianzi Shichang*, Feb. 9, 1989, pp. 2–4. Trans. in *JPRSCSTR*, July 3, 1989, pp. 87–91.

Huang, Yu. "Peaceful Evolution: The Case of Television Reform in Post-Mao China." *Media, Culture, and Society* 16, 1994, pp. 217–41.

"Hubei to Use Satellite for Radio, TV Broadcasts." Hubei People's Radio Network, Dec. 17, 1993. Trans. in *FBISDCR*, Dec. 21, 1993, pp. 59–60.

Hughes, Owen. "Up, Up, and Away—But Not All Are Happy with STAR TV." *IPI Report*, Feb. 1992, pp. 19–21.

Huntington, Samuel P. *Political Order in Changing Societies*. New Haven, Conn.: Yale University Press, 1968.

———. *The Third Wave: Democratization in the Late Twentieth Century*. Norman, Okla.: University of Oklahoma Press, 1991.

"Indirect Phone, Postal Links Opened with Mainland." China News Agency, June 7, 1989. Trans. in *JPRS Telecommunications Report*, June 30, 1989, p. 3.

"'Infohighway Space' to Start Operation at Year End." XNA, Oct. 29, 1996. Rpt. in *FBISDCR*, Oct. 30, 1996.

Inkeles, Alex, and David Horton Smith. *Becoming Modern*. Cambridge, Mass.: Harvard University Press, 1974.

"Inspire the People with Outstanding Literary Works." *RR*, Feb. 6, 1994, p. 1. Trans. in *FBISDCR*, Feb. 10, 1994, pp. 18–20.

"International Telecoms Capacity Increasing." XNA, May 2, 1993. Trans. in *FBISDCR*, May 4, 1993, p. 26.

"Internet Becomes Part of Daily Life." XNA, June 27, 1996. Rpt. in *FBISDCR*, July 1, 1996.

"Investigation of Hainan and Shenzhen Senior Cadres' Spiritual Life." *Cheng Ming* 187, May 1, 1993, p. 19. Trans. in *JPRSCR*, June 24, 1993, pp. 6–7.

Jia Chunfeng. "Market Economy and Cultural Development." *RR*, Feb. 9, 1994, p. 5. Trans. in *FBISDCR*, Feb. 22, 1994, pp. 29–32.

Jiang Yaping. "Zou Jiahua on Role of Information." XNA, Apr. 18, 1997. Trans. in *FBISDCR*, Apr. 22, 1997.

"Jiang Zemin's Speech Delivered at the National Working Conference on Propaganda and Ideological Work on 24 January." XNA, Mar. 6, 1994. Trans. in *FBISDCR*, Mar. 7, 1994, pp. 29–36.

"Jiaqiang Baokan Kongzhi, Zhonggong She Dubao Xiaozu." *Shijie Ribao*, Aug. 15, 1996.

Jin Jian and Chen Xiaobo. "Significance of, Measures for Developing Domestic Information Resources." *Zhongguo Keji Luntan* 2, Mar. 1993, pp. 44–45. Trans. in *JPRSCSTR*, June 29, 1993, pp. 4–6.

Jing Hou. "1993-nian Zhongyang Dianshitai Guanggao Jiage Tiaozheng." *Zhongguo Guanggao* 1, 1993, pp. 19–20.

Johnson, David, Andrew J. Nathan, and Evelyn S. Rawski, eds. *Popular Culture in Late Imperial China*. Berkeley: University of California Press, 1985.

Joint Publications Research Service. "Translations on Communist China" 109, June 23, 1970.

Jordan, Andrew. "Satellite Services in Asia: An Update." Paper delivered at the Pacific Telecommunications Conference, Honolulu, Jan. 1994, pp. 662–65.

"Journalists' Code of Profession Ethics Adopted." *Zhongguo Jizhe* 15, May 15, 1991, pp. 4–5. Trans. in *FBISDCR*, July 5, 1991, pp. 31–33.

Judge, Joan. "Public Opinion and the New Politics of Contestation in the Late Qing, 1904–1911." *MC* 20(1), Jan. 1994, pp. 64–91.

Karp, Jonathan. "Cast of Thousands." *FEER*, Jan. 27, 1994, pp. 46–50.

———. "Do It Our Way." *FEER*, Apr. 21, 1994, pp. 68–70.

———. "Don't Adjust Your Set." *FEER*, Apr. 28, 1994, p. 80.

———. "Getting Wired: Wharf Cable Signs On, and May Face Competition." *FEER*, Nov. 11, 1993, p. 74.

———. "Prime Time Police: China Tries to Pull the Plug on Satellite TV." *FEER*, Oct. 21, 1993, pp. 72–73.

———. "Ready for Prime Time?" *FEER*, Nov. 18, 1993, pp. 46–50.

———. "Who Needs News?" *FEER*, Mar. 24, 1994, p. 58.

Kaye, Lincoln. "Shooting Star: Peking May Find Ban Is Unenforceable." *FEER*, Oct. 21, 1993, pp. 73–74.

Keane, John, ed. *Civil Society and the State: New European Perspectives*. London: Verso, 1988.

Keenan, Faith. "Battle of the Titans: Murdoch Cracks Tough Asian Television Markets." *FEER*, Apr. 4, 1996, pp. 56–57.

Kenez, Peter. *The Birth of the Propaganda State: Soviet Methods of Mass Mobilization, 1917–1929.* Cambridge, U.K.: Cambridge University Press, 1985.

Keohane, Robert O., and Joseph S. Nye. *Power and Interdependence: World Politics in Transition.* Boston: Little, Brown, 1977.

Kepplinger, Hans Mathias. "The Changing Functions of the Mass Media: A Historical Perspective." *Gazette* 44, 1989, pp. 177–89.

King, Gary, Robert O. Keohane, and Sidney Verba. *Designing Social Inquiry: Scientific Inference in Qualitative Research.* Princeton, N.J.: Princeton University Press, 1994.

Kishore, Krishna. "The Emerging Marketplace of Communication Satellites in the Asia-Pacific: A Case Study of Asiasat I and STAR TV." Paper delivered at the Pacific Telecommunications Conference, Honolulu, Jan. 1994, pp. 51–56.

Ko, Kenneth. "Government to Buy Two Transponders on AsiaSat-2." *SCMP*, May 6, 1994, p. 5. Rpt. in *FBISDCR*, May 6, 1994, p. 44.

Kohli, Atul, ed. *The State and Development in the Third World.* Princeton, N.J.: Princeton University Press, 1986.

Kornai, Janos. *The Socialist System: The Political Economy of Communism.* Princeton, N.J.: Princeton University Press, 1992.

Krasner, Stephen D. "Global Communications and National Power: Life on the Pareto Frontier." *World Politics* 43, Apr. 1991, pp. 336–66.

Kristof, Nicholas D. "Via Satellite, Information Revolution Stirs China." *New York Times*, Apr. 11, 1993, pp. 1, 6.

Kuang Tianpu. "Abiding by Law to Manage Ground Equipment for Receiving Satellite Television Broadcasts." *RR*, Jan. 16, 1994, p. 3. Trans. in *FBISDCR*, Feb. 2, 1994, pp. 20–22.

Kuang Zong. "Social Management Department of the Ministry of Radio, Film, and Television Holds Meeting to Discuss Ways to Develop Strong Points and Avoid Weak Points in 'Call-In Hotline' Programs." *Guangming Ribao*, May 14, 1994, p. 2. Trans. in *FBISDCR*, June 6, 1994, pp. 37–38.

Kwan, Daniel. "Deng Calls for Maintaining 'Spiritual Purity.'" *SCMP*, Jan. 22, 1994, p. 9. Rpt. in *FBISDCR*, Jan. 24, 1994, p. 24.

Lam, Willy Wo-lap. "Authorities Suppress Journal, Promote *Renmin Ribao*." *SCMP*, May 5, 1994, p. 12. Rpt. in *FBISDCR*, May 6, 1994, p. 25.

———. "Deng Cautious on 'Theoretical' Disputes." *SCMP*, June 4, 1993, p. 9. Rpt. in *FBISDCR*, June 4, 1993, p. 19.

———. "Deng Said to Regain 'Control over Propaganda.'" *SCMP*, Mar. 31, 1992, p. 1. Rpt. in *FBISDCR*, Mar. 31, 1992, pp. 29–30.

———. "Government to Liberalize Control of Some Papers." *SCMP*, Dec. 28, 1992, p. 8. Trans. in *FBISDCR*, Dec. 29, 1992, pp. 27–28.

———. "Leaders Plan 'to Tighten Control over Ideology.'" *SCMP*, June 30, 1993, p. 1. Rpt. in *FBISDCR*, June 30, 1993, pp. 22–23.

———. "Propaganda Chief Relinquishes Post to 'Moderate.'" *SCMP*, Nov. 27, 1992, p. 12. Rpt. in *FBISDCR*, Nov. 27, 1992, p. 15.

———. "Reformers Said Ready to Revamp Propaganda Field." *SCMP*, Nov. 9, 1991, p. 10. Rpt. in *FBISDCR*, Nov. 12, 1991, p. 22.

———. "Team to Draft Ideological Program for Next Century." *SCMP*, May 16, 1996, p. 10. Rpt. in *FBISDCR*, May 20, 1996.

"Largest Cable TV Network Develops in Shanghai." XNA, Dec. 7, 1993. Trans. in *FBISDCR*, Dec. 7, 1993, p. 16.

Laris, Michael. "Power for the Web." *FEER*, Oct. 17, 1996, pp. 45–46.

Lasswell, Harold D. *Propaganda Technique in the World War*. New York: Peter Smith, 1927.

Lasswell, Harold D., Daniel Lerner, and Hans Speier, eds. *Propaganda and Communication in World History, Volume 1: The Symbolic Instrument in Early Times*. Honolulu: The University Press of Hawaii, 1979.

Lau, Angel. "Coastal TV Stations Told to Limit Overseas Programs." *HKS*, Oct. 29, 1993, p. 7. Rpt. in *FBISDCR*, Nov. 2, 1993, p. 42.

Law, S. L. "'Conservatives' Block Propaganda Post Appointment." *HKS*, Nov. 28, 1992, p. 10. Rpt. in *FBISDCR*, Nov. 30, 1992, pp. 32–33.

———. "Former Minister Wang Meng Accepts Party Post." *HKS*, Dec. 3, 1992, p. 12. Trans. in *FBISDCR*, Dec. 3, 1992, pp. 21–22.

"Leaders Vocalize Support for Press Reform." Zhongguo Tongxun She, May 15, 1989. Trans. in *FBISDCR*, May 16, 1989, pp. 52–53.

Lee, Chin-Chuan, ed. *Voices of China: The Interplay of Politics and Journalism*. New York: Guilford, 1990.

Lee, Jae-Kyoung. "Press Freedom and National Development: Toward a Reconceptualization." *Gazette* 48, 1991, pp. 149–63.

Lee, Keun. "Property Rights and the Agency Problem in China's Enterprise Reform." *Cambridge Journal of Economics* 17, 1993, pp. 179–94.

Lerner, Daniel. *The Passing of Traditional Society*. New York: The Free Press, 1959.

Lewis, Peter H. "The Internet's Very Nature Defies Censorship by Government or Individual." *New York Times*, Jan. 15, 1996.

Li Bian. "Near-Term Goals in Press Reform." *Zhongguo Jizhe* 6, June 15, 1988, p. 1. Trans. in *FBISDCR*, July 14, 1988, pp. 26–27.

Li Feng. "CPC Makes Arrangements for 14th Party Congress Propaganda Work." *Ching-chi Jih-pao* (Hong Kong), Aug. 28, 1992, p. 7. Trans. in *FBISDCR*, Sept. 1, 1992, p. 11.

Li Guangru. "Zou Jiahua Addresses Information Leading Group's Inaugural." XNA, May 27, 1996. Trans. in *FBISDCR*, June 20, 1996.

Li Jiaju. "National [Fiber Optics] Statistics Provided." *Dianxin Jishu* 2, Feb. 1990, p. 47. Trans. in *JPRSCSTR*, May 3, 1990, p. 39.

"Li Peng Promulgates Computer Regulation." XNA, May 30, 1997. Rpt. in *FBISDCR*, June 2, 1997.

Li Ping-hua. "Interviewing Fan Jingyi, Editor-in-Chief of *Jingji Ribao*, on Press Reform and Changing Concepts." *Ta Kung Pao*, Oct. 16, 1992, p. 2. Trans. in *FBISDCR*, Oct. 20, 1992, pp. 39–41.

Li Qin and Ma Yuan. "Suppress the Surging Pornography Tide." *Liaowang* 4, June 14, 1993, pp. 12–13. Trans. in *JPRSCR*, Aug. 17, 1993, pp. 34–35.

Li Qiongmu. "China's Satellite Communications in the Ascendant." *Zhongguo Dianzibao*, July 7, 1989, p. 1. Trans. in *JPRSCSTR*, 29 Sept. 1989, p. 12.

Li Ren. "Book *My Father, Deng Xiaoping* Pirated; Author Deng Rong Takes Legal Action." *Fazhi Ribao*, Mar. 2, 1994, p. 1. Trans. in *FBISDCR*, Mar. 22, 1994, p. 48.

Li Tzu-ching. "Deng and Chen Factions Differ on Propaganda Work." *Cheng Ming* 197, Mar. 1, 1994, pp. 10–12. Trans. in *FBISDCR*, Mar. 3, 1994, pp. 26–28.

Li Xiaoping. "The Chinese Television System and Television News." *China Quarterly* 126, June 1991, pp. 340–55.

Li Xingjian and Curtis Smith. "Ad Expansion Sees Problems." *Beijing Review*, May 15–21, 1989, pp. 13–14.

Li Yan. "China to Get Internet via SprintLink." *CD*, Aug. 31, 1994, p. 2. Rpt. in *JPRSCSTR*, Oct. 18, 1994, pp. 26–27.

Li Zhengfu. "Jiushi Niandai Tongxin Chanye Zhanwang." *Keji yu Chuban* 1, 1993, pp. 39–41.

Li Zhongchun. "Wo Guo Dianshi Shiye Fazhan Xunsu." *RR*, Aug. 30, 1993, p. 1.

Li Zhurun and Ni Siyi. "Official: Law, Self-Discipline to 'Eventually' Guide Press." XNA, Feb. 27, 1994. Trans. in *FBISDCR*, Mar. 1, 1994, p. 24.

Li Zirong. "The Uncrowned Kings' Laurels Fall: A View of the Unhealthy State of Mainland Journalism." *Jiushi Niandai* 9, Sept. 1, 1993, pp. 62–64. Trans. in *JPRSCR*, Nov. 30, 1993, pp. 53–55.

Liang Hsiao-tien. "'Instruction' Urges Reducing 'Critical Reports.'" *MP*, June 4, 1993, p. 9. Trans. in *FBISDCR*, June 4, 1993, pp. 18–19.

Liang Ruojie. "Eight Special Features That Have Emerged in Chinese Newspapers During the Decade of Reform." *Zhongguo Jizhe* 3, Mar. 1989, pp. 20–22. Trans. in *JPRSCR*, July 6, 1989, pp. 36–40.

Lieberthal, Kenneth G. *Governing China: From Revolution Through Reform*. New York: Norton, 1995.

Lieberthal, Kenneth G., and Michel Oksenberg. *Policy Making in China: Leaders, Structures, and Processes*. Princeton, N.J.: Princeton University Press, 1988.

Lieberthal, Kenneth G., and David M. Lampton, eds. *Bureaucracy, Politics, and Decision Making in Post-Mao China*. Berkeley: University of California Press, 1992.

Link, Perry. *Mandarin Ducks and Butterflies: Popular Fiction in Early Twentieth-Century Chinese Cities*. Berkeley: University of California Press, 1981.

Lintner, Bertil. "Heavy Static: Washington's Radio Free Asia Runs into Trouble." *FEER*, Mar. 24, 1994, p. 26.

Littlejohn, Stephen W. *Theories of Human Communication.* 2d ed. Belmont, Calif.: Wadsworth, 1983.

Liu, Alan P. L. *Communications and National Integration in Communist China.* Berkeley: University of California Press, 1971.

Liu, Amy. "Government Bans Latest Edition of *Newsweek.*" *HKS*, Mar. 22, 1994, p. 1. Rpt. in *FBISDCR*, Mar. 22, 1994, p. 48.

Liu Baozheng. "Zhongguo de Guanggaoye Zheng Xiang Fazhihua, Zhuanyehua, Gao Jishuhua de Fazhan." *Zhongguo Guanggao* 3, 1993, pp. 3–4.

Liu Cai. "Tasks and Targets of Building China's Information Infrastructure." *RR*, May 18, 1995, p. 9. Trans. in *FBISDCR*, May 18, 1995.

Liu Jui-shao. "Propaganda Departments Instructed to Take Initiative in Conducting Press Reforms." *Wen Wei Po*, May 27, 1988, p. 2. Trans. in *FBISDCR*, June 1, 1988, pp. 28–29.

Liu Manjun. "Posts and Telecommunications Goals for Ninth Five-Year Plan Period Drawn Up." *RR* (overseas edition), Jan. 25, 1996, p. 1. Trans. in *FBISDCR*, Mar. 15, 1996.

Liu Qinglu. "Nation's Information Networks Realize International Connections." *RR* (overseas edition), May 1, 1993, p. 3. Trans. in *JPRSCSTR*, May 13, 1993, p. 15.

Liu Renwei. "On Colonial Culture." *Qiushi*, Mar. 1, 1996, pp. 26–33. Trans. in *FBISDCR*, Sept. 4, 1996.

Liu Shen. "Status of China's Domestic Commercial Satellite Communications." *Dianxin Jishu* 4, Apr. 1990, pp. 6–7. Trans. in *JPRSCSTR*, July 5, 1990, pp. 18–19.

Liu Shu. "Politics Inside the *People's Daily.*" *Minzhu Zhongguo* 11, Aug. 1992, pp. 66–69. Trans. in *JPRSCR*, Jan. 8, 1993, pp. 1–5.

Liu Weiling. "AT&T Inks Two Deals to Supply Equipment." *CD*, May 9, 1994, p. 2. Rpt. in *JPRSCSTR*, May 24, 1994, p. 19.

Liu Wenzhong. "The Characteristics of Socialist Commercial Advertising." *Guangming Ribao*, Feb. 15, 1986, p. 3. Trans. in *FBISDCR*, Feb. 27, 1986, pp. K21–K22.

Liu, Yu-li. "The Growth of Cable Television in China: Tensions Between Local and Central Government." *Telecommunications Policy* 18(3), Apr. 1994, pp. 216–28.

Liu Zhenying and He Ping. "Further on Jiang's Remarks." *XNA*, Jan. 24, 1994. Trans. in *FBISDCR*, Jan. 26, 1994, pp. 16–18.

———. "Jiang Zemin Discusses Propaganda Situation." *XNA*, Jan. 15, 1993. Trans. in *FBISDCR*, Jan. 19, 1993, pp. 23–25.

Liu Zhongde. "Several Theoretical and Practical Questions Concerning Cultural Work Under the New Conditions." *Qiushi* 15, Aug. 1, 1993, pp. 19–25. Trans. in *FBISDCR*, Sept. 22, 1993, pp. 34–40.

———. "Zai Quanguo Wenhua Ting, Juzhang Huiyishang de Jianghua." Pp. 249–66 in *Quan Zhongguo Xuanchuan Sixiang Gongzuo Huiyi Wenjian Huibian*, cited below.

Liu Zuyu. "Society Is Watching Journalistic Circles Closely." *RR*, March 17, 1997; trans. in *FBISDCR*, April 3, 1997.

Lo Dic. "Sentencing Guidelines Established for Pornography." *HKS*, Aug. 9, 1990, p. 10. Rpt. in *JPRSCR*, Aug. 14, 1990, p. 87.

"Local Telephone Network Operation Opens Wider." XNA, May 23, 1997. Rpt. in *FBISDCR*, May 27, 1997.

Lu, Ding. "The Management of China's Telecommunications Industry: Some Institutional Facts." *Telecommunications Policy* 18(3), Apr. 1994, pp. 195–205.

Lu Lin. "1992-nian de Zhongguo Guanggaoye." *Zhongguo Guanggao* 3, 1993, pp. 4–6.

Lu Ren. "Shao Huaze, *Renmin Ribao* Editor-in-Chief." *Ching Pao* 10, Oct. 5, 1992, pp. 34–36. Trans. in *JPRSCR*, Jan. 25, 1993, pp. 1–3.

Lu Ting-yi. *Let Flowers of Many Kinds Blossom, Diverse Schools of Thought Contend!* Peking: Foreign Languages Press, 1957.

———. "Message of Greetings from the Central Committee of the Chinese Communist Party and the State Council." In *The National Conference of Outstanding Groups and Individuals in Socialist Construction in Education, Culture, Health, Physical Culture, and Journalism*. Peking: Foreign Languages Press, 1960.

Lu Wangda. "Shanghai Closes Down Four Illegal Publications." *RR*, May 20, 1994, p. 4. Trans. in *FBISDCR*, May 23, 1994, pp. 60–61.

Lu Yu-sha. "Jiang Zemin Summons 'Huangfu Ping' to Beijing for Help." *Tangtai* 29, Aug. 15, 1993, pp. 9–10. Trans. in *FBISDCR*, Aug. 25, 1993, pp. 11–12.

Ma Chenguang. "War Intensifies on Book Piracy." *CD*, June 21, 1994, p. 3.

Ma Dawei. "Shilun Wo Guo Dianshi Guanggao de Fazhan." *Xinwen Yanjiu Ziliao* 60, 1993, pp. 17–27.

Ma, Josephine. "Approval Needed to Set Up Large Information Networks." *SCMP*, June 22, 1996. Rpt. in *FBISDCR*, July 2, 1996.

Ma Wenrui. "Guard Against Corrosive Influences and Never Be Tainted with Bad Practices." *Qiushi* 5, Mar. 1, 1994, pp. 7–10. Trans. in *FBISDCR*, Mar. 31, 1994, pp. 35–38.

MacFarquhar, Roderick, Timothy Cheek, and Eugene Wu, eds. *The Secret Speeches of Chairman Mao*. Cambridge, Mass.: Harvard University Press, 1989.

Madsen, Richard. "The Public Sphere, Civil Society, and Moral Community." *MC* 19(2), Apr. 1993, pp. 183–98.

"Mainland Tightens Control of External Reporters." *Hsin Pao*, May 9, 1994, p. 2. Trans. in *FBISDCR*, May 26, 1994, pp. 20–21.

Manasco, Britton, and Jonathan Karp. "Flying High?" *FEER*, May 26, 1994, pp. 75–76.

Mann, Jim. "After 5 Years of Political Wrangling, Radio Free Asia Becomes a Reality." *Los Angeles Times*, Sept. 30, 1996, p. A5.

Manuel, Gren. "Consumers Purchase 500, 000 Satellite Receivers." *SCMP (Business Post)*, Apr. 1, 1993, p. 2. Rpt. in *FBISDCR*, Apr. 2, 1993, pp. 48–49.

———. "STAR-TV Renews Attempt to Enter Mainland Market." *SCMP*, Mar. 26, 1996, p. 3. Rpt. in *FBISDCR*, Mar. 27, 1996.

Mao Zedong. "Jieshao Yige Hezuoshe." *Hongqi* 1, June 1, 1958, pp. 3–4.

———. *Selected Readings from the Works of Mao Tse-tung*. Peking: Foreign Languages Press, 1967.

March, James G., and Johan P. Olsen. *Rediscovering Institutions: The Organizational Basis of Politics*. New York: The Free Press, 1989.

Markoff, John. "AT&T May Have Edge in Future on Line." *New York Times*, Aug. 21, 1995, pp. C1, C4.

———. "Industry Split Emerges over Computer Data Secrecy Issue." *New York Times*, Aug. 14, 1995, pp. C1, C6.

———. "U.S. to Urge a New Policy on Software." *New York Times*, Aug. 18, 1995, pp. C1, C6.

Martz, Larry. "Revolution by Information." *Newsweek*, June 19, 1989, pp. 28–29.

McCombs, Maxwell, and Sheldon Gilbert. "News Influence on Our Pictures of the World." *Perspectives on Media Effects*, ed. Jennings Bryant and Dolf Zillmann. Hillsdale, N.J.: Lawrence Erlbaum, 1986, pp. 1–15.

McCormick, Barrett L., Su Shaozhi, and Xiao Xiaoming. "The 1989 Democracy Movement: A Review of the Prospects for Civil Society in China." *Pacific Affairs* 65, Summer 1992, pp. 182–202.

McGinn, Robert E. *Science, Technology, and Society*. Englewood Cliffs, N.J.: Prentice Hall, 1991.

McGregor, James, and John J. Keller. "AT&T, China Set Broad Pact for Phones, Gear." *The Wall Street Journal*, Feb. 24, 1993, p. A3.

McPhail, Thomas L. *Electronic Colonialism: The Future of International Broadcasting and Communication*. Beverly Hills, Calif.: Sage, 1981.

"Media Minister Warns Against 'Decadent Overseas Ideologies.'" Zhongguo Tongxun She, Mar. 11, 1994. Trans. in *FBISDCR*, Mar. 15, 1994, p. 50.

"Media Must Serve People, Socialism—Jiang." *Beijing Review*, Dec. 11–17, 1989, pp. 7–9.

Meisner, Maurice. *Mao's China and After: A History of the People's Republic*. New York: The Free Press, 1986.

Michaels, James W., and Nancy Rotenier. "There Are More Patels Out There than Smiths." *Forbes*, Mar. 14, 1994, pp. 84–88.

Migdal, Joel S. *Strong Societies and Weak States: State-Society Relations and State Capabilities in the Third World*. Princeton, N.J.: Princeton University Press, 1988.

Milor, Vedat, ed. *Changing Political Economies: Privatization in Post-Communist and Reforming Communist States*. Boulder, Colo.: Lynne Rienner, 1994.

Min Dahong. "Gechu Duanbing de Lishi Toushi." *Zhongguo Jizhe* 7, 1993, pp. 8–10.

"Mingling Jinzhi Maimai Shuhao." *RR*, Oct. 29, 1993, p. 1.

"Minister Discusses Telecommunications Plans." XNA, May 12, 1994. Trans. in *FBISDCR*, May 17, 1994, p. 50.

"Minister on Building 'Cultural Market' Management." XNA, Dec. 7, 1994. Trans. in *FBISDCR*, Dec. 7, 1994.

"Minister on Improving Television Industry." *RR*, Oct. 14, 1993, p. 5. Trans. in *FBISDCR*, Oct. 25, 1993, pp. 33–34.

"Minister on Telecommunications Targets." XNA, Apr. 24, 1993. Trans. in *FBISDCR*, Apr. 27, 1993, pp. 42–43.

"Ministry Adopts Internet Measures." ZXS, May 22, 1996. Trans. in *FBISDCR*, May 22, 1996.

"Ministry Bans Import, Sale of Decoders for TV." Hangzhou Zhejiang People's Radio Network, December 6, 1994; trans. in *FBISDCR*, December 6, 1994.

"Ministry Predicts Rise in Radio, TV Coverage." *CD*, June 6, 1991, p. 3. Rpt. in *JPRSCR*, Aug. 1, 1991, p. 6.

"Ministry to Improve Administration of Cultural Market." XNA, Jan. 22, 1997. Rpt. in *FBISDCR*, Jan. 24, 1997.

Mo Ru. "Exploration, Debate, and Progress." *Zhongguo Jizhe* 12, Dec. 15, 1988, p. 1. Trans. in *FBISDCR*, Jan. 13, 1989, pp. 18–19.

"Mobile Phones Silenced in Clampdown on Rebels." *SCMP*, July 3, 1995, p. 12.

"Molding People with Lofty Spirit." *RR*, Feb. 5, 1994, p. 1. Trans. in *FBISDCR*, Feb. 10, 1994, pp. 17–18.

"More Foreign Funding for Telecommunications Sought." XNA, May 13, 1994. Trans. in *FBISDCR*, May 18, 1994, p. 70.

"More on State Council Circular on Advertising." XNA, Nov. 23, 1985. Trans. in *FBISDCR*, Nov. 27, 1985, pp. K18–K19.

Mosco, Vincent. "Toward a Theory of the State and Telecommunications Policy." *Journal of Communication* 38(1), Winter 1988, pp. 107–24.

Mou Weixu. "Cable Television Gains Popularity in China." XNA, Sept. 29, 1990. Trans. in *JPRS Telecommunications Report*, Nov. 2, 1990, p. 4.

Mufson, Steven. "Beijing Tightens Its Control." *Washington Post*, Sept. 17, 1996, p. A9.

Murray, Geoffrey. "Competition Begins in Telecommunications Services." Kyodo News Agency, July 29, 1995. Rpt. in *FBISDCR*, July 29, 1995.

Nan Hsun. "Guangzhou People Install Dish Antennas to Receive Hong Kong Television." *MP*, Oct. 16, 1991, p. 2. Trans. in *FBISDCR*, Nov. 12, 1991, pp. 56–57.

Nan Lin. "Puzzling Book Titles." *Guangming Ribao*, Jan. 2, 1997, p. 2. Trans. in *FBISDCR*, Jan. 24, 1997.

Nathan, Andrew. *Chinese Democracy*. Berkeley: University of California Press, 1985.

"National Hi-Tech Project to Be Implemented in Shenzhen." *Ta Kung Pao*, Feb. 28, 1996, p. A4. Trans. in *FBISDCR*, Mar. 18, 1996.

"National Publications Network Established." XNA, Feb. 24, 1994. Trans. in *FBISDCR*, Feb. 28, 1994, p. 45.

"Nation's Banking System to Invest 1 Billion Yuan for Construction of Satellite Communications Network." *Jisuanji Shijie* 19, May 19, 1993, p. 1. Trans. in *JPRSCSTR*, June 29, 1993, p. 30.

Naughton, Barry. "Chinese Institutional Innovation and Privatization from Below." *American Economic Review* 84(2), May 1994, pp. 266–70.

———. *Growing Out of the Plan: Chinese Economic Reform, 1978–1994*. Cambridge, U.K.: Cambridge University Press, 1995.

Nettl, J. P. "The State as a Conceptual Variable." *World Politics* 20(4), July 1968, pp. 559–92.

"New Communications Satellite Successfully Launched." XNA, Nov. 30, 1994. Trans. in *FBISDCR*, Nov. 30, 1994, pp. 21–22.

"New Propaganda, *Renmin Ribao* Officials Appointed." *Ta Kung Pao*, Apr. 26, 1993, p. 2. Trans. in *FBISDCR*, Apr. 26, 1993, pp. 24–25.

"New Regulations Implemented for Advertising." XNA, Apr. 16, 1993. Trans. in *FBISDCR*, Apr. 20, 1993, p. 31.

"Newspapers Plan More Ad Pages." *Ching-chi Jih-pao* (Hong Kong), Apr. 8, 1993, p. 10. Trans. in *FBISDCR*, Apr. 23, 1993, pp. 17–19.

Ngai, Agatha. "Movie 'Should Not Be Shown' Without Clearance." *SCMP*, May 19, 1994, p. 15. Rpt. in *FBISDCR*, May 20, 1994, pp. 84–85.

North, Douglass C. *Structure and Change in Economic History*. New York: Norton, 1981.

"Number of Radio Pager Customers Soars." XNA, Aug. 7, 1997. Rpt. in *FBISDCR*, Aug. 8, 1997.

O'Donnell, Guillermo, Philippe C. Schmitter, and Laurence Whitehead, eds. *Transitions from Authoritarian Rule: Tentative Conclusions about Uncertain Democracies*. Baltimore: The Johns Hopkins University Press, 1986.

Office of Promotion of Electronic Information System Applications, State Council. "Status of China's Fiber-Optic Communications." *Dianxin Jishu* 1, Jan. 1989, pp. 2–4. Trans. in *JPRSCSTR*, July 3, 1989, pp. 83–87.

"Official Affirms Ban on Private TV Dishes." *CD*, Oct. 9, 1993, p. 3. Rpt. in *FBISDCR*, Oct. 13, 1993, pp. 37–38.

"Official Predicts $4.8 Billion Ad Budget." XNA, Nov. 8, 1993. Trans. in *FBISDCR*, Nov. 9, 1993, p. 37.

"Official Views Ad Boom among Enterprises." XNA, Feb. 24, 1994. Trans. in *FBISDCR*, Feb. 25, 1994, p. 41.

Oi, Jean C. "Fiscal Reform and the Economic Foundations of Local State Corporatism in China." *World Politics* 42, Oct. 1992, pp. 99–126.

Oksenberg, Michel. "Methods of Communication Within the Chinese Bureaucracy." *China Quarterly* 57, Jan./Mar. 1974, pp. 1–39.

"On Inculcation." *Qiushi* 21, Nov. 1, 1990, pp. 2–6. Trans. in *JPRSCR*, Dec. 27, 1990, pp. 1–4.

"Opening of Public Switching Data Network Reported." XNA, Aug. 31, 1993. Trans. in *FBISDCR*, Sept. 1, 1993, p. 24.

"Overseas Firms Cannot Manage Communications." XNA, May 10, 1993. Trans. in *FBISDCR*, May 11, 1993, p. 37.

"Paging Services Prohibited from Distributing News." ZXS, Apr. 7, 1996. Trans. in *FBISDCR*, Apr. 12, 1996.

Pang Wei and Wang Qingxian. "Asia-Europe Fiber Optic Cable Overall Construction Begun." *RR* (overseas edition), Feb. 28, 1994, p. 1. Trans. in *JPRSCSTR*, Apr. 1, 1994, p. 22.

Pei Jianfeng. "Electronic Information Network Is on Horizon." *CD (Business Weekly)*, Mar. 20–26, 1994, p. 8. Rpt. in *FBISDCR*, Mar. 24, 1994, pp. 32–33.

———. "IBM to Invest in Data Network." *CD*, May 4, 1994, p. 2. Rpt. in *JPRSCSTR*, May 24, 1994, pp. 18–19.

Perry, Elizabeth J. "Trends in the Study of Chinese Politics: State-Society Relations." *China Quarterly* 139, Sept. 1994, pp. 704–11.

Peterson, Neville. "Laws Relating to Satellites and Their Implication for Asia-Pacific Development." *Media Asia* 17(4), 1990, pp. 198–203.

Poggi, Gianfranco. *The Development of the Modern State: A Sociological Introduction*. Stanford, Calif.: Stanford University Press, 1978.

Polumbaum, Judy. "The Tribulations of China's Journalists after a Decade of Reform." Pp. 33–68 in Lee, Chin-Chuan, ed., cited above.

Pool, Ithiel de Sola. *Technologies Without Boundaries: On Telecommunications in a Global Age*. Cambridge, Mass.: Harvard University Press, 1990.

"Postal, Telecommunications Services Boom." XNA, Jan. 13, 1993. Trans. in *FBISDCR*, Jan. 14, 1993, p. 33.

"PRC Estimates Post, Telecom Industry Growth in 1998." XNA, Jan. 21, 1998. Rpt. in *FBISDCR*, Jan. 23, 1998.

"PRC Interim Regulations Governing Management of Computer Information International Networks." XNA, Feb. 3, 1996. Trans. in *FBISDCR*, Feb. 7, 1996.

"PRC Regulations on Safeguarding Computer Information Systems." XNA, Feb. 23, 1994. Trans. in *FBISDCR*, Mar. 24, 1994, pp. 34–36.

"Press, Publications Reform to Be Deepened." XNA, Dec. 29, 1992. Trans. in *FBISDCR*, Dec. 29, 1992, p. 28.

"Press Reform Discussed at Mass Media Seminar." XNA, July 1, 1989. Trans. in *FBISDCR*, July 6, 1989, pp. 53–54.

"Press Reform Fails as a Result of All-Around Rectification Following the 4 June Incident." *MP*, June 7, 1990, p. 54. Trans. in *FBISDCR*, June 7, 1990, p. 31.

"Press Reform Subject of Beijing Seminar." XNA, Dec. 2, 1987. Trans. in *FBISDCR*, Dec. 3, 1987, p. 21.

Price, Vincent. *Communication Concepts 4: Public Opinion*. Newbury Park, Calif.: Sage, 1992.

Price, Vincent, and Donald F. Roberts. "Public Opinion Processes." *Handbook of Communication Science*, ed. C. R. Berger and S. H. Chaffee. Beverly Hills, Calif.: Sage, 1987, pp. 781–816.

"Printing Industry Management Regulations." XNA, Mar. 21, 1997. Trans. in *FBISDCR*, Apr. 8, 1997.

Problems Unit, Literature and Art Bureau, CPC Central Committee Propaganda Department. "New Problems in the Literature and Art Field Under the Socialist Market Economy." *Wenyi Bao*, Feb. 13, 1993, pp. 1, 3 and Feb. 20, 1993, pp. 1, 4. Trans. in *JPRSCR*, Apr. 20, 1993, pp. 16–27.

"Propaganda and Management of Cable Television Stations Must Not Be Neglected." Harbin Heilongjiang People's Radio Network, Oct. 28, 1993. Trans. in *FBISDCR*, Nov. 2, 1993, pp. 76–77.

"Propaganda Official on Antipornography Efforts." XNA, Dec. 18, 1991. Trans. in *FBISDCR*, Dec. 26, 1991, pp. 23–27.

Przeworski, Adam. *Democracy and the Market: Political and Economic Reforms in Eastern Europe and Latin America*. Cambridge, U.K.: Cambridge University Press, 1992.

"Public Security Ministry Circular on Internet Use." Zhongguo Tongxun She, Feb. 29, 1996. Trans. in *FBISDCR*, Mar. 7, 1996.

"Publications Will Be Streamlined." *Beijing Review*, Oct. 2, 1989, pp. 8–9.

Pun, Pamela. "Publication Crackdown Designed to 'Purify Media.'" *HKS*, May 9, 1996, p. 6. Rpt. in *FBISDCR*, May 10, 1996.

———. "Sino-Swiss Venture to Publish Business Weekly." *HKS*, Nov. 17, 1995, p. 6. Rpt. in *FBISDCR*, Dec. 11, 1995.

———. "Tighter Grip on Propaganda System Planned." *HKS*, Jan. 10, 1995, p. 6. Rpt. in *FBISDCR*, Jan. 10, 1995.

Putnam, Robert D. *Making Democracy Work: Civic Traditions in Modern Italy*. Princeton, N.J.: Princeton University Press, 1993.

Putterman, Louis. "The Role of Ownership and Property Rights in China's Economic Transition." *China Quarterly* 144, Dec. 1995, pp. 1047–64.

Pye, Lucian W., ed. *Communications and Political Development*. Princeton, N.J.: Princeton University Press, 1963.

Qu Zhihong. "Publishing House Closed for Rectification." XNA, Oct. 20, 1994. Trans. in *FBISDCR*, Oct. 20, 1994.

———. "Publishing Industry Adopts Job Certification System." XNA, Jan. 17, 1996. Trans. in *FBISDCR*, Jan. 25, 1996.

Qu Zhihong and Li Guangru. "Meeting Views Overhaul of Audio, Video Market." XNA, Apr. 23, 1991. Trans. in *FBISDCR*, Apr. 26, 1991, pp. 37–38.

Quan Zhongguo Xuanchuan Sixiang Gongzuo Huiyi Wenjian Huibian. (Neibu faxing.) Beijing: Xuexi Chubanshe, 1994.

Rankin, Mary Backus. "Some Observations on a Chinese Public Sphere." *MC* 19(2), Apr. 1993, pp. 158–82.

Reeves, Byron, and Robert Hawkins. *Effects of Mass Communication*. Chicago: Science Research Associates, 1986.

"Regulations on Radio and Television Management." XNA, Aug. 19, 1997. Trans. in *FBISDCR*, Aug. 26, 1997.

"Regulations on Satellite Receiving Equipment." XNA, Oct. 7, 1993. Trans. in *FBISDCR*, Oct. 13, 1993, pp. 36–37.

"Regulations on the Security and Management of Computer Information Networks and the Internet."

"Regulations Penalizing Pornography Announced." XNA, July 16, 1990. Trans. in *JPRSCR*, July 27, 1990, pp. 91–92.

Ren Jiaji. "Answer to the Riddle 'Small Book, Big Magazine'—Further Discussion of the *Ban Yue Tan* Phenomenon." *Zhongguo Jizhe* 47, Nov. 15, 1990, pp. 41–42. Trans. in *JPRSCR*, Feb. 14, 1991, pp. 7–9.

Ren Xianglin. "Zhongguo Weixing Guangbo Fazhan zhi Lu." *Xinwen yu Chuanbo Yanjiu* 1(4), 1994, pp. 15–20.

"*Renmin Ribao* to Publish Local Editions." XNA, Feb. 25, 1994. Trans. in *FBIS-DCR*, Feb. 25, 1994, p. 28.

"*Renmin Ribao* Urges Enhancing Ideological Work." XNA, Apr. 12, 1993. Trans. in *FBISDCR*, Apr. 12, 1993, p. 18.

"Report on the Survey on 'Social and Cultural Life and Ethics Education in the Middle Schools.'" *Chinese Education and Society* 26(2), Mar.–Apr. 1993, pp. 6–39.

"Report Views Telecommunications Usage Nationwide." XNA, Feb. 5, 1994. Trans. in *FBISDCR*, Feb. 9, 1994, pp. 29–30.

"Reportage on *Renmin Ribao* Circulation, Coverage." *RR*, Aug. 23, 1993, p. 1. Trans. in *FBISDCR*, Sept. 2, 1993, pp. 31–33.

"Resolution of the CPC Central Committee on Certain Important Questions on Strengthening the Building of Socialist Spiritual Civilization." XNA, Oct. 13, 1996. Trans. in *FBISDCR*, Oct. 17, 1996.

"Review of Guangdong Radio 'Hotline' Program." *FBISDCR*, July 14, 1993, pp. 46–50.

"Review of Guangdong Radio 'Hotline' Program." *FBISDCR*, Jan. 5, 1994, pp. 46–47.

"Roaming Beijing by Phone." *CD*, Mar. 1, 1993, p. 3. Rpt. in *FBISDCR*, Mar. 3, 1993, p. 34.

Roberts, Donald F. "Media Effects." Lecture series delivered at Stanford University, Jan.–Mar. 1994.

Robinson, William I. *Promoting Polyarchy: Globalization, US Intervention, and Hegemony*. Cambridge, U.K.: Cambridge University Press, 1996.

Rogers, Everett M. *The Diffusion of Innovations*. 3d ed. New York: The Free Press, 1983.

Rogers, Everett M., and L. Kincaid. *Communication Networks: Toward a New Paradigm for Research*. New York: The Free Press, 1981.

Rosenau, James N. *Turbulence in World Politics: A Theory of Change and Continuity.* Princeton, N.J.: Princeton University Press, 1990.

Rosenbaum, Arthur Lewis, ed., *State and Society in China: The Consequences of Reform.* Boulder, Colo.: Westview, 1992.

Rowe, William T. "The Problem of 'Civil Society' in Late Imperial China." *MC* 19(2), Apr. 1993, pp. 139–57.

———. "The Public Sphere in Modern China." *MC* 16(3), July 1990, pp. 309–29.

"Rules for the Implementation of the 'Provisions on the Management of Ground Receiving Equipment for Satellite TV Broadcasting.'" XNA, Feb. 25, 1994. Trans. in *FBISDCR*, Mar. 3, 1994, pp. 43–46.

Saich, Tony, and Hans van de Ven, eds. *New Perspectives on the Chinese Communist Revolution.* Armonk, N.Y.: M. E. Sharpe, 1995.

Sanbonmatsu, David M., and Russell H. Fazio. "Construct Accessibility: Determinants, Consequences, and Implications for the Media." *Perspectives on Media Effects,* ed. Jennings Bryant and Dolf Zillmann. Hillsdale, N.J.: Lawrence Erlbaum, 1986, pp. 281–301.

"Satellite Technology Brings Economic 'Benefits.'" XNA, Nov. 12, 1993. Trans. in *FBISDCR*, Nov. 15, 1993, p. 51.

Schell, Orville. "Letter from China: To Get Rich is Glorious." *New Yorker*, July 25, 1994, pp. 26–35.

Schramm, Wilbur. *Mass Media and National Development.* Stanford, Calif.: Stanford University Press, 1964.

———. "The Nature of Communication Between Humans." *The Process and Effects of Mass Communication,* ed. Wilbur Schramm and Donald F. Roberts. Rev. ed. Urbana: University of Illinois Press, 1974, pp. 3–53.

Schramm, Wilbur, and Daniel Lerner, eds. *Communication and Change: The Last Ten Years—And the Next.* Honolulu: University Press of Hawaii, 1976.

Scott, James C. *Weapons of the Weak: Everyday Forms of Peasant Resistance.* New Haven, Conn.: Yale University Press, 1985.

Selbin, Eric. "Revolution in the Real World: Bringing Agency Back In." *Theorizing Revolution,* ed. John Foran. London: Routledge, 1997, pp. 123–36.

Seligman, E. R. A., and A. Johnson, eds. *Encyclopedia of the Social Sciences, Volume 12.* New York: Macmillan, 1934.

"Shanghai Eastern Radio Station Goes on Air." XNA, Oct. 28, 1992. Trans. in *JPRS Telecommunications Report*, Dec. 17, 1992, p. 9.

Shao Huaze. "Caiqu Jianjue Cuoshi Jinzhi 'Youchang Xinwen.'" *Zhongguo Jizhe* 8, 1993, pp. 6–7.

Shao Ling. "Official Supports Crackdown of Pirated Audio Tapes, CD's." *Zhongguo Tongxun She*, Mar. 5, 1994. Trans. in *FBISDCR*, Mar. 7, 1994, pp. 45–46.

Shapiro, Michael A., and Annie Lang. "Making Television Reality: Unconscious Processes in the Construction of Social Reality." *Communication Research* 18(5), Oct. 1991, pp. 685–705.

She Qijiong and Yu Renlin. "Telecommunications Services in China." *IEEE Communications Magazine*, July 1993, pp. 30–33.

Shen Peijun. "We Need an Environment in which One Can Speak Freely and Truthfully." *Shijie Jingji Daobao*, May 1, 1989, p. 3. Trans. in *JPRSCR*, June 27, 1989, pp. 64–67.

Shen Weixing. "Due to Excessive Imports of CD Production Lines, the Department Concerned Calls for Import Suspension and Standardized Management." *Guangming Ribao*, Feb. 8, 1994, p. 1. Trans. in *FBISDCR*, Feb. 17, 1994, pp. 48–49.

"Shenzhen Assaults Smuggled Hong Kong Newspapers and Journals in Mopping-Up Operations." *Ping Kuo Jih Pao*, May 5, 1996, p. A4. Trans. in *FBISDCR*, May 9, 1996.

"Shenzhen Restrictions on Satellite TV Reception." Zhongguo Tongxun She, Apr. 18, 1994. Trans. in *FBISDCR*, Apr. 19, 1994, p. 38.

Shi Mang. "Free Discussion on Functions of Literature and Art." *Zhenli de Zhuiqiu* 2, Feb. 11, 1993, pp. 26–29. Trans. in *JPRSCR*, Apr. 28, 1993, pp. 34–36.

"Shichang Jingji yu Xue Lei Feng." *Zhongguo Qingnian Bao*, Feb. 8, 1993, p. 1.

Shih Liu-tzu. "The Beginning of Journalistic Freedom in Mainland China—the Rise of a 'Semi-Official' Press." *Ming Pao Yuekan*, Feb. 1994, pp. 82–86. Trans. in *JPRSCR*, June 28, 1994, pp. 60–64.

Shu Si. "Loss of Control over the Publishing Industry Causes Headache for Higher Echelons of CPC Leadership." *Cheng Ming* 194, Dec. 1, 1993, pp. 32–34. Trans. in *FBISDCR*, Dec. 21, 1993, pp. 17–21.

Shuang Yu. "Ads Lead China into Consumers' Era." *Beijing Review*, Feb. 24–Mar. 1, 1992, p. 11.

Shue, Vivienne. *The Reach of the State: Sketches of the Chinese Body Politic*. Stanford, Calif.: Stanford University Press, 1988.

Siebert, Fred S., Theodore Peterson, and Wilbur Schramm. *Four Theories of the Press*. Freeport, N.Y.: Books for Libraries Press, 1956.

Sinha, Nikhil. "Telecommunications Capabilities and Development: Towards an Integrated Framework for Development Communication." Paper delivered at the Pacific Telecommunications Council conference, Honolulu, Jan. 1994, pp. 57–68.

Skinner, G. William, and Edwin O. Winckler. "Compliance Succession in Rural Communist China: A Cyclical Theory?" In *A Sociological Reader on Complex Organizations*, ed. Amitai Etzioni. 2d ed. New York: Holt, Rinehart, and Winston, 1969, pp. 410–38.

Smith, Anthony. *The Geopolitics of Information: How Western Culture Dominates the World*. New York: Oxford University Press, 1980.

"Socialist Spiritual Civilization Must Be Stressed in Advertisements." XNA, July 5, 1985. Trans. in *FBISDCR*, July 8, 1985, p. K18.

Song Muwen. "Nuli Tigao Chubanwu de Wenhua Pinwei." *RR*, May 29, 1993, p. 3.

Song Xiren. "On 'Changing Empty to Solid, Changing Soft to Hard.'" *RR*, May 3, 1993, p. 5. Trans. in *JPRSCR*, July 9, 1993, pp. 7–8.

Soroos, Marvin S. "The Commons in the Sky: The Radio Spectrum and the Geosynchronous Orbital Belt as Issues in Global Policy." *International Organization* 36(3), Summer 1982, pp. 665–78.

Sparks, Colin, and Anna Reading. "Understanding Media Change in East Central Europe." *Media, Culture, and Society* 16, 1994, pp. 243–70.

"Special Dispatch: Large-Scale Rectification of Media." *MP*, Apr. 5, 1997, p. A8. Trans. in *FBISDCR*, Apr. 14, 1997.

"Spokesman Comments on Jamming of Radio Free Asia." AFP, Aug. 20, 1997. Rpt. in *FBISDCR*, Aug. 21, 1997.

"Spokesman Gives Update on Satellite Communications." XNA, Oct. 20, 1993. Trans. in *FBISDCR*, Oct. 21, 1993, p. 27.

"State Issues Regulations on Publishing Industry." XNA, Jan. 14, 1997. Trans. in *FBISDCR*, Jan. 17, 1997.

"State Makes Provisions for Satellite Reception Equipment Sales." XNA, Jan. 14, 1994. Trans. in *FBISDCR*, Jan. 27, 1994, p. 35.

"State Monopoly in Telephone Service Ends." XNA, Sept. 14, 1997. Rpt. in *FBISDCR*, Sept. 16, 1997.

State Science and Technology Commission, People's Republic of China. *A Guide to China's Science and Technology Policy: White Paper on Science and Technology No. 5*. Trans. in *JPRSCSTR*, Apr. 8, 1994, pp. 1, 50–53.

"State to Decentralize Movie Distribution System." Kyodo News Agency, Nov. 16, 1992. Trans. in *FBISDCR*, Nov. 16, 1992, pp. 27–28.

"State to Drop Limit on Film Imports." *CD*, Apr. 20, 1995, p. 2.

"State to Join with Overseas Chinese Companies to Develop Internet." XNA, Oct. 25, 1996. Trans. in *FBISDCR*, Oct. 28, 1996.

Steinfeld, Edward S. "Reforming China's State-Owned Enterprises: A Property Rights Perspective." Ph.D. diss., Harvard University, 1996.

"Step Up Journalistic Ethics Building." *RR*, Aug. 5, 1993, p. 1. Trans. in *FBISDCR*, Aug. 10, 1993, pp. 18–19.

Stepan, Alfred. *The State and Society: Peru in Comparative Perspective*. Princeton, N.J.: Princeton University Press, 1977.

Stinchcombe, Arthur L. "Social Structure and Politics." *Handbook of Political Science, Volume 3: Macropolitical Theory*, ed. Fred I. Greenstein and Nelson W. Polsby. Reading, Mass.: Addison-Wesley, 1975, pp. 557–622.

Strand, David. "Protest in Beijing: Civil Society and Public Sphere in China." *Problems of Communism* 39, May–June 1990, pp. 1–19.

"Strengthening Propaganda and Ideological Work, Promoting All-Round Progress of Society—Interviews of Wei Jianxing, Xie Fei, and Huang Ju." *Liaowang* 22, May 27, 1996, pp. 4–7. Trans. in *FBISDCR*, June 27, 1996.

"Stress Focal Points, Persistently Wipe Out Pornography, Boost Publishing Industry." *RR*, Dec. 25, 1995, p. 5. Trans. in *FBISDCR*, Feb. 7, 1996.

"Strictly Ban Illegal Publications." *Guangming Ribao*, Apr. 19, 1987, p. 1. Trans. in *FBISDCR*, Apr. 29, 1987, pp. K33–K34.

"Stronger Management over Publications Urged." XNA, May 6, 1993. Trans. in *FBISDCR*, May 12, 1993, pp. 15–16.

Stross, Randall. "The Return of Advertising to China: A Survey of the Ideological Reversal." *China Quarterly* 123, Sept. 1990, pp. 485–502.

Su Xiaokang. "Bandiaozi de Shimin Shehui." *Minzhu Zhongguo* 11, Aug. 1992, pp. 1–3.

Sun Hui and Wu Mengshuan. "Underground Criminal Societies Rapidly Expand Their Influence." *Shehui* 105, Oct. 1993, pp. 47–48. Trans. in *JPRSCR*, Mar. 22, 1994, pp. 34–36.

Sun Jiazheng. "Chinese Radio, Film, and Television Must Enter the World's Top Rank." *Renmin Luntan*, Jan. 8, 1996, pp. 23–25. Trans. in *FBISDCR*, Apr. 17, 1996.

———. "Jianchi Zhengque Daoxiang, Tigao Jiemu Zhiliang, Nuli ba Guangbo Dianying Dianshi Gongzuo Tigao dao Xin Shuiping." *Dianying Tongxun* 1, 1995, pp. 3–9.

Sun, Lin. "Funding Telecommunications Expansion." *China Business Review*, Mar.–Apr. 1993, pp. 31–33.

———. "Mobile Communications Takes Off in China." *Telecom Asia*, Apr. 1993, pp. 86–88.

———. "Telecommunications Development in China." *Global Telecommunications Policies*, ed. Meheroo Jussawalla. Westport, Conn.: Greenwood, 1993, pp. 171–92.

Sun Wude and Chen Chongshan. "Fazhan Nongcun Guangbo Bu Bi Qiangqiu Yilu." *Xinwen Yanjiu Ziliao* 59, Dec. 1992, pp. 53–59.

Sun Xupei. "Chuyi Shehuizhuyi Shichang Jingji Tiaojian xia de Xinwenye." *Xinwen Yanjiu Ziliao* 61, June 1993, pp. 40–57.

"System to Improve Quality of Periodicals." *RR*, Apr. 13, 1994, p. 3. Trans. in *FBISDCR*, May 6, 1994, pp. 26–28.

Tacey, Elisabeth. "Threat to Limit Internet Access." *SCMP*, May 25, 1995, p. 10.

Tan, Zixiang. "Challenges to the MPT's Monopoly." *Telecommunications Policy* 18(3), Apr. 1994, pp. 174–81.

Tang Xujun. "Press Freedom Must Be Protected by Law." *Xinwen Chubanbao*, Jan. 28, 1989, p. 4. Trans. in *JPRSCR*, May 25, 1989, pp. 51–52.

Teiwes, Frederick C. *Politics and Purges in China*. 2d ed. Armonk, N.Y.: M. E. Sharpe, 1993.

"Telecommunications Industry Grows 30 Percent in 1997." XNA, Jan. 15, 1998. Rpt. in *FBISDCR*, Jan. 17, 1998.

"Telecommunications Minister on Improvements." XNA, Jan. 12, 1994. Trans. in *FBISDCR*, Jan. 13, 1994, p. 55.

"Telecommunications Sector on Major Investment Program." ZXS, May 8, 1996. Trans. in *FBISDCR*, May 8, 1996.

"Television Financed by Advertising Revenue." XNA, Apr. 8, 1989. Trans. in *FBISDCR*, Apr. 12, 1989, pp. 31–32.

"Television Industry Witnesses 'Rapid Development.'" China Central Television Program One Network, Jan. 29, 1994. Trans. in *FBISDCR*, Feb. 4, 1994, p. 15.

"Television, Radio Stations Increasing in Number." XNA, Oct. 20, 1993. Trans. in *FBISDCR*, Oct. 21, 1993, p. 26.

"Television's Final Frontier." *Economist*, July 31, 1993, pp. 57–58.

"Text of Interim Internet Management Rules." XNA, Feb. 4, 1996. Trans. in *FBISDCR*, Feb. 10, 1996.

"Text of Regulations Forbidding Paid News, Other Abuses." XNA, Jan. 23, 1997. Trans. in *FBISDCR*, Jan. 28, 1997.

Thomas, George M., and John W. Meyer. "The Expansion of the State." *Annual Review of Sociology* 10, 1984, pp. 461–82.

Thomas, George M., John W. Meyer, Francisco O. Ramirez, and John Boli, eds. *Institutional Structure: Constituting State, Society, and the Individual*. Newbury Park, Calif.: Sage, 1987.

Thomson, Oliver. *Mass Persuasion in History*. Edinburgh, U.K.: Paul Harris, 1977.

Tian Congming. "Dangqian Zhongguo Dianying de Xingshi he Women de Zhuyao Duice." *Dianying Tongxun* 1, 1995 , pp. 10–13.

Tian Tian. "280 Publishing Houses Banned." *Cheng Ming* 197, Mar. 1, 1994, p. 19. Trans. in *FBISDCR*, Mar. 15, 1994, p. 47.

"Tibet Bans Relay of BBC, STAR TV Programs." Lhasa Tibet Television Network, Mar. 4, 1994. Trans. in *FBISDCR*, Mar. 9, 1994, pp. 89–90.

Tien Chen. "CPC Plan to Gag Press Freedom." *Cheng Ming* 184, Feb. 1, 1993, pp. 42–44. Trans. in *FBISDCR*, Feb. 1, 1993, pp. 21–24.

———. "New Ban on Literature and Art Creation." *Cheng Ming* 190, Aug. 1, 1993, pp. 32–33. Trans. in *FBISDCR*, Aug. 10, 1993, pp. 16–18.

Ting, Lee-hsia Hsu. *Government Control of the Press in Modern China, 1900–1949*. Cambridge, Mass.: East Asia Research Center, Harvard University, 1974.

Tong, Yanqi. "State, Society, and Political Change in China and Hungary." *Comparative Politics* 26(3), Apr. 1994, pp. 333–53.

Tsuruoka, Doug. "Let It Beam." *FEER*, Nov. 4, 1993, p. 75.

"Unhealthy Ads to Be Corrected." China Central People's Radio Network, Feb. 22, 1986. Trans. in *FBISDCR*, Feb. 24, 1986, p. K23.

"Urban Residents Increasingly Installing Private Telephones." XNA, Dec. 8, 1991. Trans. in *JPRS Telecommunications Report*, Dec. 26, 1991, p. 14.

"Urban, Rural Areas Receive Access to Cable TV." FBISDCR, Jan. 3, 1997.

Ure, John. "Telecommunications, with Chinese Characteristics." *Telecommunications Policy* 18(3), Apr. 1994, pp. 182–94.

Vatikiotis, Michael. "Net Police: Asean Seeks to Control Cyberspace." *FEER*, Mar. 28, 1996, p. 22.

"Vice Premier Discusses Communications Development." XNA, May 17, 1994. Trans. in *FBISDCR*, May 19, 1994, pp. 31–32.

Wakeman, Frederic, Jr. "The Civil Society and Public Sphere Debate." *MC* 19(2), Apr. 1993, pp. 108–38.

Walder, Andrew G. "Local Governments as Industrial Firms: An Organizational Analysis of China's Transitional Economy." *American Journal of Sociology* 101(2), Sept. 1995, pp. 263–301.

Wan Siding. "An Overview of Telecommunications Planning in China." *IEEE Communications Magazine*, July 1993, pp. 18–19.

Wang Chuanzhen. "Guangdong Begins First 'Specialized' TV Station." XNA, Dec. 16, 1993. Trans. in *FBISDCR*, Dec. 29, 1993, p. 70.

Wang Feng. "Vice Minister Discusses Satellite TV Reception." XNA, Oct. 15, 1993. Trans. in *FBISDCR*, Oct. 20, 1993, pp. 28–29.

Wang, Georgette. "Satellite Television and the Future of Broadcasting Television in the Asia-Pacific." *Media Asia* 20(3), 1993, pp. 140–48.

Wang Jing. "Government to Tighten Internet Security Control." XNA, Dec. 30, 1997. Rpt. in *FBISDCR*, Jan. 1, 1998.

Wang Jue. "The Principle of Party Spirit in Journalism Is Unshakeable—Commenting on the Theory 'The People's Spirit Is Above Party Spirit.'" *Qiushi* 17, Sept. 1, 1989, pp. 13–17. Trans. in *JPRSCR*, Oct. 24, 1989, pp. 4–8.

Wang Li. "Audio, Visual Products Management Conference Opens." XNA, May 15, 1996. Trans. in *FBISDCR*, May 15, 1996.

Wang Liwen. "Hu Qiaomu, Deng Liqun Hold Forum on Party History and Party-Building Theory for Propaganda Department." *Sixiang Zhengzhi Gongzuo Yanjiu* 2, Feb. 8, 1992, p. 48. Trans. in *JPRSCR*, May 22, 1992, p. 1.

Wang Rong. "Advertisers Approve 'Code of Self-Discipline.'" *CD*, Jan. 24, 1991, p. 3. Trans. in *FBISDCR*, Jan. 24, 1991, p. 37.

———. "Advertisers Told to 'Get onto Right Track.'" *CD*, Apr. 23, 1990, p. 3. Trans. in *FBISDCR*, Apr. 24, 1990, pp. 28–29.

Wang Ruiming. "Xinwen Fagui, Zhiye Daode yu 'Youchang Xinwen.'" *Zhongguo Jizhe* 7, 1993, pp. 5–7.

Wang Xiangdong. "Lun Gaige Kaifang zhong de Youdian Tongxinye he Xinxi Chanye." *Jingji Gaige*, Apr. 1992, pp. 22–25.

Wang Xiaohui. "Interview with Du Daozheng, Director of Journalism and Publishing Bureau." ZXS, Apr. 26, 1987. Trans. in *FBISDCR*, Apr. 29, 1987, pp. K35–K36.

Wang Xiyu. "Beijing Files." *Jiushi Niandai* 242, Mar. 1, 1990, pp. 56–57. Trans. in *JPRSCR*, Apr. 30, 1990, pp. 24–26.

Wang Yanrong. "Minister Discusses Telecommunications Control." XNA, Nov. 5, 1993. Trans. in *FBISDCR*, Nov. 16, 1993, pp. 41–42.

————. "Radio Stations to Be Surveyed, Registered." XNA, May 28, 1993. Trans. in *FBISDCR*, June 7, 1993, p. 29.

Wang Yitang. "There Should Be No Quota for News Reporting." *RR*, Dec. 1, 1997, p. 4. Trans. in *FBISDCR*, Dec. 15, 1997.

Wang Yong. "Motorola Homing In on Beeper Market." *CD*, May 5, 1994, p. 2. Rpt. in *JPRSCSTR*, May 24, 1994, p. 18.

————. "Projects to Help Ease Telecommunications Bottleneck." *CD (Business Weekly)*, May 24, 1993, p. 1. Rpt. in *JPRSCSTR*, June 14, 1993, p. 28.

Wang Zhi. "CPC Newspapers, Journals Lose More than 100 Million Yuan." *Cheng Ming* 3, Mar. 1, 1994, pp. 22–23. Trans. in *JPRSCR*, May 26, 1994, pp. 23–24.

Warwick, William. "A Review of AT&T's Business History in China: The Memorandum of Understanding in Context." *Telecommunications Policy* 18(3), Apr. 1994, pp. 265–74.

"Wei Jianxing on Promoting Spiritual Civilization in Beijing." XNA, Jan. 30, 1997. Trans. in *FBISDCR*, Feb. 5, 1997.

Weigle, Marcia A., and Jim Butterfield. "Civil Society in Reforming Communist Regimes: The Logic of Emergence." *Comparative Politics* 25(1), Oct. 1992, pp. 1–24.

Weinstock, Jordan, Greg Apostolou, and Chen Yunqian. "Fiber Optic Networks in China's Drive for Economic Development." Paper delivered at the Pacific Telecommunications Council conference, Honolulu, Jan. 1994, pp. 735–38.

Wellman, Barry, and S. D. Berkowitz, eds. *Social Structures: A Network Approach.* Cambridge, U.K.: Cambridge University Press, 1988.

Wen Jinhai. "The Evil Waves of Mad, Illegal Publications." *Wenyi Bao*, Oct. 17, 1992, p. 7. Trans. in *JPRSCR*, Mar. 9, 1993, pp. 30–36.

Westlake, Michael. "China: Long Spoon Shortens." *FEER*, Apr. 8, 1993, pp. 46–48.

————. "Joint Venture: Millions Calling." *FEER*, Apr. 8, 1993, pp. 48–51.

————. "Reach for the Stars." *FEER*, May 30, 1991, pp. 60–61.

White, Gordon. "Prospects for Civil Society in China: A Case Study of Xiaoshan City." *Australian Journal of Chinese Affairs* 29, Jan. 1993, pp. 63–87.

Whiting, Susan. "The Micro-Foundations of Institutional Change in Reform China: Property Rights and Revenue Extraction in the Rural Industrial Sector." Ph.D. diss., University of Michigan, 1995.

"The Whole Party Must Attach Importance to Propaganda and Ideological Work." *RR*, Feb. 2, 1994, p. 1. Trans. in *FBISDCR*, Feb. 2, 1994, pp. 7–9.

Whyte, Martin King. "Small Groups and Communication in China: Ideal Forms and Imperfect Realities." *Moving a Mountain: Cultural Change in China.* Honolulu: University Press of Hawaii, 1979, pp. 113–124.

————. *Small Groups and Political Rituals in China.* Berkeley: University of California Press, 1974.

Wilkie, A. R. "Former CPC Official: Leftists 'Biding Their Time.'" *Eastern Express*, May 3, 1994, p. 9. Rpt. in *FBISDCR*, May 4, 1994, pp. 20–21.

Wong, Michael. "Dissident Movement Taps into Internet." *HKS*, Mar. 19, 1995, p. 1. Rpt. in *FBISDCR*, Mar. 19, 1995.

Wong, Vivien. "Ideology Chief Visits Singapore for Tips on Internet." *HKS*, July 13, 1996, p. 6. Rpt. in *FBISDCR*, July 19, 1996.

Worth, Sol, and Larry Gross. "Symbolic Strategies." *Journal of Communication* 24, 1974, pp. 27–39.

Wright, Mary Clabaugh, ed. *China in Revolution: The First Phase, 1900–1913*. New Haven, Conn.: Yale University Press, 1968.

Wu, Guoguang. "Command Communication: The Politics of Editorial Formulation in the *People's Daily*." *China Quarterly* 137, Mar. 1994, pp. 194–211.

Wu Jichuan. "Build a Nationwide Economic Information Network, Improve Information Services for the National Economy." *RR*, Apr. 13, 1994, p. 5. Trans. in *FBISDCR*, May 9, 1994, pp. 26–28.

———. "Telecom Sector Expands International Cooperation." *Beijing Review*, June 26–July 2, 1995, pp. 8–11.

"Wu Jichuan Attends Opening of New Information Ministry." XNA, Apr. 1, 1998. Rpt. in *FBISDCR*, Apr. 3, 1998.

Wu Zhong and Fong Tak-ho. "Regulation Prevents Foreign Investment in PRC Media." *HKS*, Jan. 7, 1998. Rpt. in *FBISDCR*, Jan. 10, 1998.

Xie Guomin and Zhu Changze, eds. *Xinwen Lilun Baiti Huida*. Beijing: Zhongguo Xinwen Chubanshe, 1988.

Xie Liangjun. "Canadian Telecommunications Giant Flexes Muscles." *CD (Business Weekly)*, Oct. 18, 1993, p. 2. Rpt. in *JPRSCSTR*, Nov. 16, 1993, pp. 25–26.

———. "China Links Up with the World." *CD*, Oct. 8, 1993, p. 5. Rpt. in *FBISDCR*, Oct. 8, 1993, pp. 17–18.

———. "Post Offers Incentives for Foreign Investment." *CD*, Feb. 22, 1993, p. 1. Rpt. in *FBISDCR*, Feb. 23, 1993, p. 39.

———. "Ringing Success: Cellular Phones Catching On." *CD (Business Weekly)*, Feb. 13–19, 1994, p. 4. Rpt. in *FBISDCR*, Feb. 14, 1994, p. 63.

———. "Telecommunications Expansion Unabated." *CD (Business Weekly)*, Feb. 21, 1993, p. 8. Rpt. in *FBISDCR*, Feb. 23, 1993, pp. 38–39.

Xie Xiao'an. "Support the Telephone Industry to Satisfy Communications Needs." *Zhongguo Dianzibao*, July 20, 1992, pp. 1–2. Trans. in *JPRS Telecommunications Report*, Oct. 20, 1992, pp. 8–10.

Xingzhengyuan Xinwenju, ed. *Dalu Diqu Dazhong Chuanbo Meiti ji Qi Guanli Jigou Gaikuang*. Taipei: Xingzhengyuan Xinwenju, 1991.

"XINHUA Features Role of TV in Chinese Society." XNA, Dec. 25, 1996. Rpt. in *FBISDCR*, Dec. 27, 1996.

"Xinjiang Confiscates Publications Which Undermine Unity." *Xinjiang Ribao*, Mar. 13, 1998, p. 1. Trans. in *FBISDCR*, Apr. 7, 1998.

"*Xinwen Zhanxian* Carries Commentator's Article on Press Reform." *RR*, May 6, 1993, p. 4. Trans. in *FBISDCR*, May 12, 1993, pp. 14–15.

Xinwenxue Lunji. Beijing: Zhongguo Renmin Daxue Chubanshe, 1992.

Xu, Ante. "Telecommunications Network Development in China." Paper delivered at the Pacific Telecommunications Council conference, Honolulu, Jan. 1994, pp. 248–55.

Xu Binglan. "Telephone Boom Has Nice Ring." *CD (Business Weekly)*, Mar. 25, 1996, p. 8.

Xu Dechang and Zhang Jianyu. "Chengdushi Dianshi Shouzhong Diaocha Baogao." *Zhongguo Guanggao* 4, 1993, pp. 9–10.

Xu Guangchun. "What Is Wrong with News Media Guidance for the Public?" *Zhongguo Jizhe* 33, Sept. 15, 1989, pp. 16–17. Trans. in *JPRSCR*, Dec. 22, 1989, pp. 72–74.

Xu Guoping. "New Style in Broadcasting: Telephone Hotline." *Zhongguo Jizhe* 6, June 15, 1993, pp. 20–22. Trans. in *FBISDCR*, July 22, 1993, pp. 17–20.

Xu Renzhong. "Xinwen Gaige yu Shichang Jingji." *Zhongguo Jizhe*, June 15, 1993, pp. 13–16.

Xu Weicheng. "Zai Fanrong Chuban Shiye, Jinzhi 'Maimai Shuhao' Zuotanhui shang de Jianghua." *Guangming Ribao*, Oct. 29, 1993, pp. 1–2.

Xu Yang. "Fresh Bid to Switch Viewers on to Cable TV." *CD*, Mar. 22, 1994, p. 3. Rpt. in *FBISDCR*, Mar. 24, 1994, pp. 36–37.

Yan Shan-ke. "The Party's Mouthpiece and the People's Flesh." *Cheng Ming* 184, Feb. 1, 1993, pp. 28–31. Trans. in *JPRSCR*, May 12, 1993, pp. 1–5.

Yan Yitao. "On Lessons Learned from Erroneous Guidance of Public Opinion." *Jiefang Ribao*, Oct. 12, 1989, p. 1. Trans. in *JPRSCR*, Dec. 13, 1989, pp. 53–59.

Yang Hsiao-yang. "China's First People-Run Radio Station to Start Broadcasting in Fuzhou Next Month." *Ta Kung Pao*, Oct. 28, 1991. Trans. in *FBISDCR*, Nov. 8, 1991, p. 36.

Yang Xueming. "Current State of Development in Satellite Communications in China." *Dianxin Jishu* 1, Jan. 1989, pp. 9–10. Trans. in *JPRSCSTR*, July 3, 1989, pp. 92–96.

"Yao Chongfen Yunyong Youxiu Yingshi Pian Mudui Zhong, Xiao Xuesheng Jinxing Aiguo Jiaoyu." *RR*, Oct. 9, 1993, p. 1.

Yao Yan, Cao Zhigang, and Yu Renlin. "R & D Activities on Wireless Systems in China." *IEEE Communications*, July 1993, pp. 42–45.

Ye Rong. "First High-Tech Fiber-Optic Cable TV Network Operational in Jiading County." *Keji Ribao*, Sept. 29, 1992, p. 1. Trans. in *JPRS Telecommunications Report*, Dec. 17, 1992, p. 9.

Yin Yen. "China to Merge Ministries." *Sing Tao Jih Pao*, Feb. 5, 1998, p. A6. Trans. in *FBISDCR*, Feb. 6, 1998.

———. "Over 100 Radio, Television Stations in Shandong to Be Shut Down." *Sing Tao Jih Pao*, Oct. 14, 1997, p. A7. Trans. in *FBISDCR*, Oct. 16, 1997.

————. "Zhejiang TV Station Officials Penalized for Major 'Political Accidents.'" *Sing Tao Jih Pao*, June 2, 1997. Trans. in *FBISDCR*, June 3, 1997.

Yu, Frederick T. C. *Mass Persuasion in Communist China*. New York: Praeger, 1964.

Yu Guoming. "High-Level People in Beijing Discuss Press Reform." *Liaowang Overseas* 16, Apr. 18, 1988, pp. 18–19. Trans. in *FBISDCR*, Apr. 25, 1988, pp. 22–25.

Yu Han. "Press Reform on the Mainland Brooks No Delay." Zhongguo Tongxun She, May 17, 1989. Trans. in *FBISDCR*, May 19, 1989, pp. 42–43.

Yu, Lulu. "State-run Telecommunications Industry to Be Commercialized." *Eastern Express*, Apr. 1, 1994, p. 24. Rpt. in *FBISDCR*, Apr. 1, 1994, p. 52.

Yu, Xuejun. "Government Policies Toward Advertising in China (1979–1989)." *Gazette* 48, 1991, pp. 17–30.

Yu Youxian. "Adhere to the Set Direction and Deepen Reforms to Achieve a Phased Change in Press and Publication Work." *RR*, Apr. 7, 1994, p. 5. Trans. in *FBISDCR*, May 5, 1994, pp. 32–36.

————. "Adhering to the Theory of 'Grasping with Both Hands' to Promote the Healthy Development of the Press and Publication Sector." *RR*, Feb. 3, 1994, p. 5. Trans. in *FBISDCR*, Feb. 17, 1994, pp. 19–22.

————. "Jianchi Fangxiang, Shenhua Gaige, Shixian Xinwen Chuban Gongzuo de Jieduanxing Zhuanyi." Pp. 347–64 in *Quan Zhongguo Xuanchuan Sixiang Gongzuo Huiyi Wenjian Huibian*, cited above.

Yuan Yang. "Cross-Strait Mail Exchange Makes Slow Progress." *Liaowang* 51, Dec. 18, 1995, pp. 28–29. Trans. in *FBISDCR*, Feb. 6, 1996.

Yun Yang. "Major Current Tides in China's News Media." *Tang Tai* 33, Dec. 15, 1993, pp. 92–94. Trans. in *JPRSCR*, Feb. 16, 1994, pp. 37–39.

Zeng Xiancheng. "Fujian Radio Station Officially Begins Broadcasting." ZXS, May 1, 1994. Trans. in *FBISDCR*, May 26, 1994, p. 52.

Zhang Chuanxi. "'Vagabond Reporters' Swarm into Guangzhou." Zhongguo Tongxun She, Apr. 12, 1994. Trans. in *FBISDCR*, Apr. 15, 1994, p. 41.

Zhang Dazhen. "Shixian Guanggao Dailizhi hai Xuyao Zuo Xie Shenmo?" *Zhongguo Guanggao* 3, 1993, pp. 7–9.

Zhang Jianmin and Hui Jinyi. "Television Station Cooperation Group Achieves Good Results." XNA, Sept. 8, 1990. Trans. in *JPRS Telecommunications Report*, Sept. 11, 1990, p. 6.

Zhang Shengyou and Li Guangru. "Beijing Media Leaders Discuss Press Reform." XNA, Dec. 1, 1987. Trans. in *FBISDCR*, Dec. 8, 1987, pp. 18–19.

Zhang Sutang and Feng Yingbing. "Amplify the Main Theme of the Time." XNA, Jan. 25, 1996. Trans. in *FBISDCR*, Jan. 30, 1996.

Zhang Weiguo. "All About Hu Jiwei—Affinity to the People and New Breakthroughs in Journalistic Freedom." *Lien-ho Pao* (Taipei), June 27–28, 1993, pp. 10–11. Trans. in *JPRSCR*, Aug. 17, 1993, pp. 31–33.

————. "Discussing Democracy and Journalistic Freedom with Hu Jiwei." *Cheng Ming* 8, Aug. 1, 1993, pp. 62–65. Trans. in *JPRSCR*, Sept. 3, 1993, pp. 36–40.

————. "Reporters and Editors on the Mainland Fight for a Larger Margin of Journalistic Freedom." *Pai Hsing* 283, Mar. 1, 1993, pp. 44–45. Trans. in *JPRSCR*, June 29, 1993, pp. 23–24.

Zhang Xiaogang. "The Market Versus the State: The Chinese Press since Tiananmen." *Journal of International Affairs* 47, Summer 1993, pp. 195–221.

Zhang Xiaohu. "On the Need to Bring the Advantages of Party Newspapers into Full Play for Better Guidance of Public Opinion." *Zhongguo Jizhe*, Apr. 15, 1995, pp. 12–14. Trans. in *FBISDCR*, Nov. 14, 1995.

Zhang Ximing. "China's Press-Related Lawsuits." *China Exchange News* 22(3), Fall 1994, pp. 13–16.

Zhang Yizhang. "Central Party School Takes Over China Market Newspaper." *Sing Tao Jih Pao*, June 7, 1997, p. A7. Trans. in *FBISDCR*, June 10, 1997.

Zhang Yongjing. "Wo zhi Tongsu Dianshiju Guan." *Xuexi yu Yanjiu*, Dec. 1993, pp. 34–36.

Zhang Zhongcai, ed. *Quanguo Dibao Hao Xinwen, 1979–1986*. Beijing: Zhongguo Xinwen Chubanshe, 1988.

Zhao Baochen. "What Businesses Are at the Top of Culture Markets?" *Jingji Ribao*, Aug. 17, 1993, p. 5. Trans. in *JPRSCR*, Oct. 12, 1993, p. 33.

Zhao, Di Ang, and Liu Junjia. "Telecommunications Development and Economic Growth in China." *Telecommunications Policy* 18(3), Apr. 1994, pp. 211–15.

Zhao Lanying. "In the Midst of Improvement and Rectification, Shanghai News Publishing Enterprises Focus on Development." *Liaowang* 10, Mar. 5, 1990, pp. 25–26. Trans. in *JPRSCR*, June 19, 1990, pp. 82–84.

Zhao Shijie. "Nongcun Renkou de Bianqian yu Dazhong Chuanbo." *Xinwen Yanjiu Ziliao* 58, Sept. 1992, pp. 42–47.

Zheng, Cindy. "Opening the Digital Door: Computer Networking in China." *Telecommunications Policy* 18(3), Apr. 1994, pp. 236–42.

"Zhi Wo Zhonghua, Ai Wo Zhonghua, Xing Wo Zhonghua." *RR*, Nov. 28, 1993, p. 1.

Zhong Cheng. "CPC Gives Vigorous Publicity to Jiang Zemin." *Cheng Ming* 192, Oct. 1, 1993, p. 19. Trans. in *FBISDCR*, Oct. 5, 1993, pp. 21–22.

Zhong Chengxiang. "Dianshiju Zenyang Zouxiang Shichang." *Guangming Ribao*, June 3, 1993, p. 6.

Zhong Mingyi. "Dual-Beam Satellite TV Receiving System Unveiled." *Zhongguo Jidianbao*, Sept. 19, 1989, p. 1. Trans. in *JPRSCSTR*, Jan. 17, 1990, p. 35.

Zhonggong Zhongyang Xuanchuanbu and Xinwen Chubanshe. "Guanyu Jinzhi 'Youchang Xinwen' de Tongzhi." *Zhongguo Jizhe* 8, 1993, p. 5.

Zhonggong Zhongyang Xuanchuanbu Xinwenju, ed. *Zhongguo Gongchandang Xinwen Gongzuo Wenxian Xuanbian, 1938–1989*. Beijing: Renmin Chubanshe, 1990.

Zhongguo Chuban Kexue Yanjiusuo, ed. *Chuban Keyan Lunwen Xuancui*. Zhejiang: Zhejiang Jiaoyu Chubanshe, 1992.

Zhongguo Chuban Nianjian, 1990–1991. Beijing: Zhongguo Shuji Chubanshe, 1993.

Zhongguo Chuban Nianjian, 1992. Beijing: Zhongguo Chuban Nianjian She, 1993.

Zhongguo Gaige Quanshu, 1978–1991, Volume 3: Jingshen Wenming Jianshe Juan. Dalian: Dalian Chubanshe, 1992.

Zhongguo Guangbo Dianshi Nianjian, 1990. Beijing: Beijing Guangbo Xueyuan Chubanshe, 1990.

Zhongguo Guangbo Dianshi Nianjian, 1991. Beijing: Beijing Guangbo Xueyuan Chubanshe, 1992.

Zhongguo Guangbo Dianshi Nianjian, 1992. Beijing: Beijing Guangbo Xueyuan Chubanshe, 1993.

Zhongguo Guoji Nianjian, 1993. Beijing: Zhongguo Tongji Chubanshe, 1993.

Zhongguo Jiaotong Nianjian, 1992. Beijing: Zhongguo Jiaotong Nianjian She, 1992.

Zhongguo Jiaotong Nianjian, 1993. Beijing: Zhongguo Jiaotong Nianjian She, 1993.

Zhongguo Xinwen Nianjian, 1990. Beijing: Zhongguo Shehui Kexueyuan Xinwen Yanjiusuo, 1991.

Zhongguo Xinwen Nianjian, 1991. Beijing: Zhongguo Shehui Kexueyuan Xinwen Yanjiusuo, 1992.

Zhongguo Xinwen Nianjian, 1992. Beijing: Zhongguo Shehui Kexueyuan Xinwen Yanjiusuo, 1993.

Zhongguo Xinwen Nianjian, 1993. Beijing: Zhongguo Shehui Kexueyuan Xinwen Yanjiusuo, 1994.

Zhou Yanwen. *Dui Fengkuang de Yindao: Zhongguo Chubanye de Jingji Guanzhao*. Beijing: Zhongguo Jingji Chubanshe, 1991.

Zhu Dai'an and Wu Mingjian. "County in Tibet Last to Receive Communications Lines." ZXS, July 17, 1992. Trans. in *JPRS Telecommunications Report*, Dec. 17, 1992, p. 8.

Zhu Mingzuo. "Baoye Jingzheng yu Shichang Jingji." *Xinwen Zhanxian*, Sept. 1993, pp. 17–19.

"Zhu Rongji Addresses Reform Issue." XNA, Jan. 28, 1994. Trans. in *FBISDCR*, Jan. 31, 1994, pp. 21–22.

Zhu Xiachu and Wang Fushun, eds. *Zhongguo Guangbo Dianshi Xue*. Beijing: Zhongguo Guangbo Dianshi Chubanshe, 1990.

Zhu Xiangxia. "Dianshi dui Beijing Xiaoxuesheng Zeye he Ouxiang Chongbai de Yingxiang." *Xinwen Yanjiu Ziliao* 58, Sept. 1992, pp. 91–108.

Zita, Ken. *Modernizing China's Telecommunications*. London: The Economist Intelligence Unit / Hong Kong: Business International Corporation, 1987.

Zou Qingli. "State Regulates Satellite TV Equipment Production." XNA, June 21, 1994. Trans. in *FBISDCR*, June 23, 1994, pp. 25–26.

Zuo Feng. "Chinese Masses Go On-Line." *Window*, July 7, 1995, p. 3. Rpt. in *FBISDCR*, July 7, 1995.

In this index an "f" after a number indicates a separate reference on the next page, and an "ff" indicates separate references on the next two pages. A continuous discussion over two or more pages is indicated by a span of page numbers, e.g., "57–59." *Passim* is used for a cluster of references in close but not consecutive sequence.

Library of Congress Cataloging-in-Publication Data

Lynch, Daniel C.
After the propaganda state : media, politics, and "thought work"
in reformed China / Daniel C. Lynch.
      p.   cm.
   Includes bibliographical references.
   ISBN 0-8047-3461-5 (cloth ; alk. paper)
      1. Mass media—Social aspects—China.   2. Communication—
Social aspects—China.   3. Social change—China.   4. Political
participation—China.   I. Title.
HN740.Z9M35   1999
302.2—dc21   99-11807

⊗   This book is printed on acid-free, recycled paper.

Original printing 1999
Last figure below indicates year of this printing:
08   07   06   05   04   03   02   01   00   99

Designed by Janet Wood
Typeset by James P. Brommer in 10/14 Palatino
and Palatino display